DEVELOPMENT CENTRE SEMINARS
SÉMINAIRES DU CENTRE DE DÉVELOPPEMENT

ENVIRONMENTAL MANAGEMENT IN DEVELOPING COUNTRIES

GESTION DE L'ENVIRONNEMENT DANS LES PAYS EN DÉVELOPPEMENT

EDITED BY
SOUS LA DIRECTION DE
DENIZHAN ERÖCAL

DEVELOPMENT CENTRE
OF THE ORGANISATION FOR ECONOMIC CO-OPERATION AND DEVELOPMENT

CENTRE DE DÉVELOPPEMENT
DE L'ORGANISATION DE COOPÉRATION ET DE DÉVELOPPEMENT ÉCONOMIQUES

Pursuant to Article 1 of the Convention signed in Paris on 14th December 1960, and which came into force on 30th September 1961, the Organisation for Economic Co-operation and Development (OECD) shall promote policies designed:

— to achieve the highest sustainable economic growth and employment and a rising standard of living in Member countries, while maintaining financial stability, and thus to contribute to the development of the world economy;
— to contribute to sound economic expansion in Member as well as non-member countries in the process of economic development; and
— to contribute to the expansion of world trade on a multilateral, non-discriminatory basis in accordance with international obligations.

The original Member countries of the OECD are Austria, Belgium, Canada, Denmark, France, Germany, Greece, Iceland, Ireland, Italy, Luxembourg, the Netherlands, Norway, Portugal, Spain, Sweden, Switzerland, Turkey, the United Kingdom and the United States. The following countries became Members subsequently through accession at the dates indicated hereafter: Japan (28th April 1964), Finland (28th January 1969), Australia (7th June 1971) and New Zealand (29th May 1973). The Commission of the European Communities takes part in the work of the OECD (Article 13 of the OECD Convention). Yugoslavia takes part in some of the work of the OECD (agreement of 28th October 1961).

The Development Centre of the Organisation for Economic Co-operation and Development was established by decision of the OECD Council on 23rd October 1962.

The purpose of the Centre is to bring together the knowledge and experience available in Member countries of both economic development and the formulation and execution of general economic policies; to adapt such knowledge and experience to the actual needs of countries or regions in the process of development and to put the results at the disposal of the countries by appropriate means.

The Centre has a special and autonomous position within the OECD which enables it to enjoy scientific independence in the execution of its task. Nevertheless, the Centre can draw upon the experience and knowledge available in the OECD in the development field.

Les textes réunis dans cet ouvrage ont été présentés lors d'une conférence tenue du 3 au 5 octobre 1990 dans le contexte du programme 1990/1992 du Centre de Développement intitulé "Faire face aux menaces qui pèsent sur l'environnement". Ils sont publiés ici dans leur langue d'origine uniquement, accompagnés d'un résumé dans l'autre langue officielle de l'Organisation.

The papers included in this volume were presented to a conference held from 3rd to 5th October 1990 in the context of the Development Centre's 1990/1991 programme on "Coping with Environmental Threats". They are published here in their original language only, with a summary in the other official language of the Organisation.

TABLE OF CONTENTS

Acknowledgements 7

Preface
by Louis Emmerij 8-9

Keynote addresses

A DEVELOPMENT PLANNER LOOKS AT ENVIRONMENTAL MANAGEMENT
by Nitin Desai 11

ENVIRONMENTAL MANAGEMENT OR MANAGEMENT FOR SUSTAINABLE DEVELOPMENT
by David Runnalls 23
Notes and References 45

NEW ENVIRONMENTAL POLICIES: THE RECENT EXPERIENCE OF OECD COUNTRIES AND ITS RELEVANCE TO THE DEVELOPING WORLD
by David Pearce 47
Notes and References 78

ECONOMIC INCENTIVES IN ENVIRONMENTAL MANAGEMENT AND THEIR RELEVANCE TO DEVELOPING COUNTRIES
by Theodore Panayotou 83
Bibliographical References 127

INCENTIVES FOR CONSERVATION: THE EXAMPLE OF KAFUE FLATS, ZAMBIA
by C.A. Drijver and A.B. Zuiderwijk 133
Bibliographical References 155

ENVIRONMENTAL MANAGEMENT IN INDONESIAN AGRICULTURAL DEVELOPMENT
by Faisal Kasryno, Ning Pribadi, Achmad Suryana and Jamil Musanif 157
Bibliographical References 173

AN ECONOMIC PERSPECTIVE ON MANAGEMENT IN THE PUBLIC SECTOR
by Dennis Anderson 175
Notes 194
Bibliographical References 197

RECENT EVOLUTION OF ENVIRONMENTAL MANAGEMENT IN THE BRAZILIAN PUBLIC SECTOR: ISSUES AND RECOMMENDATIONS
by Ronaldo Serôa da Motta 201
Notes 220
Bibliographical References 221

TOWARD MORE EFFECTIVE ENVIRONMENTAL REGULATION IN DEVELOPING COUNTRIES
by Faith Halter 223

EFFECTIVE ENVIRONMENTAL REGULATION: THE CASE OF THE PHILIPPINES
by Delfin J. Ganapin, Jr. 255

COUNTRY ENVIRONMENTAL STUDIES: A FRAMEWORK FOR ACTION
by Walter Arensberg 275
Bibliographical References 295

THAILAND'S EXPERIENCE WITH ENVIRONMENTAL PLANNING
by Dhira Phantumvanit and Juliet Lamont 297
Bibliography 309

COUNTRY ENVIRONMENTAL PROFILES: THE CASE OF COLOMBIA
by Diana Pombo Holguin 311

STRENGHTHENING GOVERNMENT CAPACITY FOR ENVIRONMENTAL MANAGEMENT IN LATIN AMERICA
by Kirk P. Rodgers 323
Bibliography 337

L'EXPÉRIENCE DU RWANDA EN MATIÈRE D'ENVIRONNEMENT
par Augustin Ngirabatware 341

ENVIRONMENTAL MANAGEMENT IN POLAND
by Piotr Wilczyński 353

NEW CO-OPERATION MODELS FOR STRENGHTHENING ENVIRON-MENTAL MANAGEMENT CAPACITIES IN DEVELOPING COUNTRIES: A CASE STUDY OF BRAZIL
by Hans-Jürgen Karpe and Hans-Peter Winkelmann 367

NON-GOVERNMENTAL ORGANISATIONS AND ENVIRONMENTAL MANAGEMENT: LESSONS FROM THE COSTA RICAN EXPERIENCE
by Alvaro Umaña 379

INTERNATIONAL NGO EXPERIENCE
by Richard Sandbrook 393

THE ROLE OF ENVIRONMENTAL EDUCATION IN DEVELOPING COUNTRIES: ISSUES FOR RESEARCH
by Hartmut Schneider 401

Annex 1
List of conference participants and their addresses 411

Annex 2
Conference Agenda 415

AVERTISSEMENT

Les opinions contenues dans les articles qui suivent n'engagent que leurs auteurs. Elles ne relèvent ni de leurs organismes de rattachement ni du Centre de Développement.

REMERCIEMENTS

Nous exprimons notre gratitude à l'Overseas Development Agency du Royaume-Uni qui a pris en charge les frais de mission de certains des participants venus des pays en développement.

Micheline Dabos a assumé la responsabilité de l'équipe d'assistance de la Conférence avec le concours de Laurence Berretti et de Christine Johnson, toutes du Centre de Développement.

GENERAL DISCLAIMER

The views expressed in the following papers should be considered as the authors' own and not those of the organisations they are associated with or of the Development Centre.

ACKNOWLEDGEMENTS

We would like to express our gratitude to the Overseas Development Agency of the United Kingdom which financed the attendance at the Conference of a number of participants from developing countries.

The support staff team for the Conference and the preparation of its documents was led by Micheline Dabos and included Laurence Berretti and Christine Johnson, all of the Development Centre.

PRÉFACE

Le besoin d'avoir de meilleurs systèmes de gestion de l'environnement dans les pays en développement croît avec l'urgence toujours plus pressante des problèmes écologiques de ces pays, et avec la progressivité des menaces que ces problèmes font peser sur un développement durable. Le Centre, par son nouveau programme de recherche sur l'environnement, s'efforce d'aider à découvrir et à définir des moyens plus efficaces pour assurer l'application, le développement et la viabilité de systèmes de gestion de l'environnement dans les conditions et les difficultés propres aux pays en développement.

Le premier résultat de ce nouveau programme a été d'organiser une conférence qui a réuni des hommes de terrain et des chercheurs travaillant sur les problèmes de gestion de l'environnement. La Conférence, à laquelle participaient une vingtaine de spécialistes de pays en développement, plus vingt autres faisant partie d'organisations internationales, d'ONG, de sociétés de conseil etc., servait à plusieurs fins : elle donnait l'occasion de faire le point des connaissances actuelles sur les problèmes et les pratiques de gestion de l'environnement dans les pays en développement ; c'était un lieu de rencontre permettant de mettre en commun l'expérience acquise et d'exposer quelques nouvelles idées qui, espérons-le, seront mises en application par les autorités nationales, avec le concours éventuel d'une aide financière et technique ; enfin, elle nous aidait à définir notre propre programme d'études à entreprendre, en coopération avec d'autres acteurs, dans les deux prochaines années.

Ce volume doit servir avant tout à faire connaître plus largement les nombreux et intéressants exposés qui ont été présentés à la Conférence. Ces exposés ont été sommairement révisés et mis en forme pour publication après la réunion, mais la rapidité de la parution a pris le pas sur le polissage des textes, vu l'intérêt généralement porté à ce sujet et l'évolution rapide de l'état des connaissances. Nous envisageons de publier un autre volume, plus tard, en 1991, qui résumera les parties appropriées des contributions écrites et les débats de la réunion.

Louis Emmerij
Président du Centre de Développement de l'OCDE
mars 1991

PREFACE

The need for better environmental management systems in developing countries grows with the increasing urgency of their environmental problems and the progressive nature of the threats to sustainable development that these problems pose. Through the Centre's new research programme on environment we are seeking to contribute to the process of finding and defining better ways for environmental management systems to be introduced, developed and sustained in the circumstances of -- and special difficulties of -- the developing countries.

Our first product from this new programme was a Conference of practitioners and researchers working on environmental management issues. With the participation of about 20 specialists from developing countries plus another 20 from international agencies, NGOs, consultant firms etc., the Conference served several purposes: it was an opportunity to take stock of the present status of understanding of the issues and the practice regarding environment management systems in the developing countries; it served as a forum to exchange experience and to put some new thinking on the table, hopefully, for follow up action by country authorities, perhaps supported by aid and technical assistance; and it helped to define our own agenda of studies that we will be undertaking, in association with others, in the next couple of years.

This volume from the Conference is being made available primarily as a way of bringing the many useful papers that were discussed there to a wider audience. The papers have been lightly revised and edited following the meeting, but refinements have been subordinated to quick release, in view of the widespread interest in this subject and the rapidly developing state of the art. We plan a further volume for publication later in 1991, which will summarise both the relevant parts of the written submissions and the discussions at the meeting.

Louis Emmerij
President of the OECD Development Centre
March 1991

KEYNOTE ADDRESS *

A Development Planner Looks at Environmental Management

by

Nitin Desai **

---

* Transcription of speech.

** Formerly, Special Secretary, Planning Commission, and Secretary and Chief Economic Adviser, Ministry of Finance, Government of India. Now, Deputy Secretary-General of United Nations Conference on Environment and Development (UNCED).

RÉSUMÉ

Bien que la croissance soit une priorité très pressante, nombre de pays en développement, dont l'Inde, ont reconnu depuis bien des années l'importance de l'environnement et de la viabilité. Pourtant, en dépit des efforts déployés, la situation ne cesse d'empirer. L'incapacité de contrôler les effets de l'inégalité est un facteur déterminant. Qu'il s'agisse des individus ou des nations, les riches contrôlent les ressources mais supportent rarement toutes les conséquences de la pollution ou de la surexploitation. Les pauvres souffrent, mais ils ne peuvent pas faire changer le comportement des riches et, comme ils n'ont que de maigres ressources, ils se trouvent souvent contraints de surexploiter le peu dont ils disposent. De l'avis de l'auteur, tous les éléments suivants sont importants : la décentralisation de l'autorité (car les problèmes sont souvent des problèmes locaux qui doivent recevoir une solution locale) ; l'"habilitation" , en sorte que tous les intéressés devront être associés à la prise de décision ; une plus claire définition des droits de propriété, y compris la reconnaissance des droits traditionnels, l'obligation effective d'indemniser le dommage causé lorsque la responsabilité est engagée ; l'utilisation plus fréquente d'instruments touchant la fiscalité et la tarification et une meilleure planification du développement afin de fournir les ressources nécessaires pour atteindre les objectifs en veillant à l'application des mesures susdites.

SUMMARY

While growth is a very compelling priority, many developing countries, including India, recognised the importance of environment and sustainability many years ago. Yet despite the efforts that have been made, matters continue to get worse. A key factor is the inability to control the effects of inequality. With parallels between individuals and nations, the rich control the resources but rarely suffer the full consequences of pollution or over-exploitation. The poor suffer, but cannot change the behaviour of the rich and since they have so few resources, often find themselves forced to over-exploit what little they have. The author suggests that decentralisation of authority (since many problems are local and need local solutions), "empowerment", so that all who are affected should participate in decision-taking, clearer definitions of property rights, including recognition of traditional rights, enforcement of the liability to pay for damage caused, more use of fiscal and pricing instruments and better development planning so as to support the objectives by giving attention to such measures, are all important.

I was asked to participate in this seminar essentially as a country representative but between the invitation and the seminar I have changed my hat. I am working in an international organisation, but I intend to focus essentially on the perspective on environmental management as it would look to a country practitioner. I would also like to clarify that my perspective is not that of an environmentalist but of a development planner, which is what I have been for most of my working life. Later in the discussion, if you wish, I could certainly take up some of the issues which are relevant for the international conference, but I would leave this mainly to David Runnalls.

My starting point for the discussion is the acceptance of the urge for development, the urge for growth. I do accept however, unlike perhaps some development planners, that the way in which some of this growth and development has been secured has led to an unacceptable degree of environmental degradation, unacceptable in the sense that had we known that this is what would have happened we would perhaps have made our choices a little differently.

I think the issue of growth and development has to be the starting point for any discussion on environmental issues in developing countries. I know growthmanship is a little disreputable in the West and the origins of this, certainly amongst environmentalists, possibly lie in the old limits to growth type of theses. But I assure you the limit to growth type of theses is not very convincing in most developing countries most of whom, in fact, are more concerned about declining commodity prices than about exhaustion of commodity supplies. In fact, the environmental consequences of that loss of earnings may possibly have been far more difficult than what was perhaps projected in the old limits to growth theses.

I would also point out that it is true that growth does depend on more intensive exploitation of resources: land resources, mineral resources, energy resources, etc. And to a certain extent the environmental deterioration that we see today is a result of this more intensive resource exploitation. But I think we should not forget that the greater part of post-war growth is due to an increase in the productivity of resource use, not necessarily a more intensive exploitation of resources. Material and energy productivity has gone up significantly in the post-war period. Land productivity has risen sharply in the developed world and in many developing countries. In India in particular the greater part of the increase in agricultural production has come not from an extension of cultivation into new lands, but from the increase in yields.

You may, of course, question the way in which this yield increase was obtained. The run-offs from fertilizers, pesticides residues, the depletion of ground water, and so on. But whether these consequences are worse for people than the consequences of food scarcity or the extension of cultivation into marginal lands is surely open to question.

I am saying these things because I think it is important to recognise that it is very difficult to reject everything that has been done in the name of growth and development as totally unsound and something which needs to be comprehensively modified and changed. It is true that because the gains from development were so tangible, so immediate, so real, many Third World countries did argue at one time that environmental management was a luxury that they could not afford, that the first priority was development and that environmental management would come later.

But this argument was not accepted by all. India, for instance, showed an awareness of environmental concerns well before they were taken up at the international level. The Fourth Five-Year Plan of India, formulated in 1968 and 1969, long before the Stockholm Conference, deals explicitly with the issues of environmental management. The National Committee on Environmental Planning and Co-ordination was set up under Pitamber Pant, the great perspective planner of India -- in fact, before Stockholm. Partly this was because of Mrs. Gandhi's deep concern for this issue. The first special programmes for ecologically disadvantaged areas were put in place around the late 1960s/early 1970s. I am referring to area programmes for drought-prone areas and for hill areas.

Later, in the 1980s, Indian planners started talking in terms of sustainable development, once again before the phrase was canonised in the international pantheon of ideas. If you take the other themes which today dominate the environmental discussion, the theme of non-governmental and grass-roots organisations, there is again a long tradition of voluntary work which has always combined environmental and developmental compulsions at the grass-roots levels. More explicit environmental movements like the Chipko movement are decades old now in India. The judicial system has also shown a remarkable degree of creativity and constructiveness in dealing with issues of environmental liability.

I am drawing attention to these things not for the purposes of establishing any question of priority, because what matters is not priority in words, but priority in action. But I am drawing attention to this to emphasize that the politicians, the people, the planners of the Third World do not need to be prompted from outside to take environmental considerations into account. They have been doing so and if they have not been able to realise their programmes fully, it is for reasons other than lack of concern.

Concern for the environment has gone through some clear stages. It started off initially as what we call a "Maharajah movement" focusing more on tigers and pretty trees. A lot of countries went through this in the early phases, but most of them did get out of it. By the early 1970s certainly in India, the focus had shifted onto what I would call "pollution-related" issues as pollution control legislation, environmental impact assessment, and maybe even a certain amount of cost-benefit analysis.

During this period the concern for rural problems such as shifting cultivation, degradation of land, particularly in dryland areas, deforestation, figured prominently in development planning. These issues were brought into the development agenda essentially by development planners, by economists, not by environmentalists. Examples are the special programmes for drought-prone areas, the issues about forest management, the concern for shifting cultivation in North-eastern India, and so on. The focus came from the concern about poverty and the erosion of the livelihood base of the poor due to the loss of productive potential in what today we would describe as ecologically disadvantaged areas. I stress this because in many ways those early attempts were doing environmental management without even knowing they were doing environmental management. The focus came not from environment but from people and the concern about poverty.

If you take environmental action proper, there is a further shift which takes place in the 1980s, into what I would describe as great set-piece environmental projects like the cleaning up of the river Ganges or the big national programme on wasteland development.

Today I sense a further shift in concerns about environment and development in India. A major example of this is what is being contemplated now on agricultural planning. Up till now, the focus of agricultural planning at the national level, in India at least, was largely on targets for specific crops and inputs. The agricultural planner was happiest when he had assured water supply, flat alluvial land, a local topography which was easily manageable. Whenever he confronted conditions where this did not hold, his instinct was to correct that. If it is an arid area, bring in water, if the topography is too undulatory, level the land. Basically he tried to fight the climate rather than work with the climate, and particularly in areas outside the alluvial plains and the delta areas this is a strategy which does not deliver results.

Because of this, today a major effort is being made in India to shift the focus of agricultural planning away from crop and input targeting to area-specific agriculture plans that focus on working *with* the climate, rather than fighting the local climate. It is an approach which is also trying to expand the possibilities of sustainable development at a local level by covering not just a few, two or three or four, major crops but a large of subsidiary crops, a large number of subsidiary activities. It is focusing attention explicitly on the quality of the resource base, the land, the water, the forests, and so on as distinct from the output and the production you get from it. It is focusing attention on the need for insuring a sustainable livelihood. Anyway, these are early days, this approach is still being worked out and is expected to be implemented essentially in the Eighth Plan which began in 1990.

I have spoken of this long-standing concern for the environment and for environmental degradation. But nevertheless we do know that in terms of what is happening on the ground to land and water resources, we have not seen a major improvement. The pace of deterioration of land and water resources in India continues, despite two decades of concern for environmental matters at the national level-- the highest national level, as the phrase is used in UN circles. I believe a major reason for this is the fact that the economic and social structures of our market economy are not able to ensure equity between and within generations. I do not think that the argument is theoretical. A forest contractor cuts down some upland forests and the benefit accrues to him and, perhaps, to the owner of the forests. The impact of this deforestation on the watershed is borne by all who live in that watershed. Even here, the poor, who can least afford protective measures suffer the most. Within cities the most congested and most vulnerable areas are generally inhabited by the poor who bear a disproportionate part of the cost of urban pollution and industrial accidents. As was shown in Bhopal virtually every single person who was affected by that accident was essentially a person who was poor. Hardly anybody who was above the poverty line was affected by that accident in Bhopal.

In market economies the poor are seldom powerful but those who hold out the promise for prosperity with schemes for forest exploitation or water resource development or mineral production, are able to dominate decision making structures which control not just the resources that they pay for but also other common property resources. The legal framework for pollution control and enforcement of liability is too weak to contain the damage that large producers inflict on these resources and indirectly on the productive assets and general well-being of the local population. The gap between the power to use and the responsibility to conserve prevails also in the use or abuse of other types of resources, for example, resources shared between nations.

At the heart of most environmental problems there is some major injustice. The injustice in the use of common resources is not the only problem. Inequities in the access to privatisable resources is also relevant. Essentially when we talk of poverty what we are really talking about is inequities in the access to resources. It is these inequalities which force people to extend cultivation to marginal lands and hill areas, over-stock grazing areas, clear forests, etc.

A further problem that arises is that poverty reinforces the pressure of short-term compulsions. Drought can lead farmers to slaughter cattle, cut down their trees, deplete productive assets, to meet the compulsions of survival. Poor households lack the reserves to cope with short-term stress, and one could argue that the same holds at an international level where poor countries lack the reserves, the options to cope with short-term stress.

I believe that the essence therefore lies in widening options for poor households and for poor countries. It also lies to a certain extent in the integration of economics and ecology in development planning. I think the development planner has to build a bridge between economics and ecology. I believe the problem lies in the inadequate treatment of the interactions of environment and production processes in most planning models and in the production and cost functions which underlie our policy analysis. There is a tendency to ignore the stock of natural resources when we specify production functions or input/output relations. There certainly is a tendency to neglect this in the whole system of national income accounting which underlies much of our planning.

Another difficulty is the tendency to ignore irreversibilities in microeconomic analysis. The productivity of land today depends not just on the decisions that you are taking today but on the whole history of decisions that you took. This type of production function is not something which is often used in analyses. There are other problems like threshold effects which are not adequately captured in the types of analysis that we use for planning and policy formulation. The analyses of technological risks, not just external risks which shift the production function up and down, but risks which arise from the decisions that you are taking within the production function are also not very adequately reflected.

I believe that there are many deficiencies in the intellectual baggage that we have inherited which need to be corrected. I would accept that this is possibly not the most important problem but it is certainly a problem which an institution like the Development Centre could contribute greatly to addressing, because of its orientation.

I would also accept that the argument that developing countries cannot bear the cost of environmental management is not valid. It is quite misleading. Environmental degradation always involves real costs. When we say that we cannot afford the cost what we really mean is that we can pass on the cost to somebody else. When a factory spews out muck and you say you cannot afford to clean that up, it is not that the costs are not being borne: the costs are being borne by the people who breathe in that muck or use that water. They are borne in the form of ill-health. The issue therefore is not whether a country can bear the costs of environmental management -- the costs will be borne by somebody or the other and the real issue is how they can be minimised and fairly shared.

Within this broad rubric of integration of environment and economics, I would say that if I had to look at what one would expect in an environmentally sound development plan, the first thing that I would focus on is the need for a greater emphasis on regional planning and anti-poverty planning at the local level. The developmental focus of major sectors like agricultural, rural development, etc. must be (a) highly location specific and regionalised, and (b) focus strongly on the notion of sustainable livelihood.

I do not believe that it is ever going to be possible to protect or conserve a resource unless the problem of sustainable livelihood for the people who depend on that resource is solved. In area after area we see biosphere reserves where you try to drive people out and protect the tiger or the lion or something. It just does not work because you cannot expect people to give up a source of livelihood and starve in order to protect some plant or some animal. Equally, the reverse. If you think that you can provide livelihood to people in a manner which does not conserve the land and the water and the forests on which they depend for their livelihood, it is not going to work for very long also. I would say, therefore, that a focus on sustainable livelihood almost inevitably leads to a very sensible and valid focus on conserving the resource base on which the poor depend for their livelihood.

There is of course much more which needs to be done. Population policies to reduce fertility rates are important, not necessarily because the poor are eating into resources of the rich but because the poor are reducing their own options by their larger family size. Second, I believe that investments in urban infrastructure to stem the deterioration in living conditions and to reduce hazards are important. Emission regulations and measures to control the impact of industrial production and energy use, controls on hazardous technologies -- all of these are important factors to take into account in integrating environmental considerations into the development process.

Well, how is this plan to be realised? I think one of the great dangers of development planning is that it creates the illusion that the planner can control the projections -- that if I project that food output is going to be this, I actually control what food output is going to be. In fact, our instruments of control are all indirect in most developing countries. We do not have direct controls of any substantial sort, particularly in rural areas. Hence, if we are to look for an environmentally sensitive plan, we would also have to look into the policy structures underlying this plan, and ask ourselves "what is it in these policy structures that has failed to protect the environment".

I believe environmental problems generally arise out of ignorance, injustice or irresponsibility. The answer therefore lies in measures that remove ignorance through education and research, that correct injustice by empowering those who depend on the resource for survival, and that enforces responsibility for all the consequences of production and consumption decisions.

This distinction between injustice and irresponsibility may seem a little tenuous but I believe it is a useful distinction. Correcting injustice really involves restructuring, often of property relations or of property rights. Correcting for irresponsibility may also involve such radical restructuring; but it is more likely to involve enforcement of liability through pollution or rehabilitation charges or through other legal arrangements.

With regard to methods, as a general rule, the reach of fiscal policy in developing countries is limited. Very few people pay direct taxes; there are a large number of exemptions even for indirect taxes. Therefore if you try and use the fiscal system essentially to encourage ecologically sound development you must accept that the reach of your policy is likely to be very, very limited. It covers a very small fraction of the population. The reach of the administered pricing system, however, is broader, particularly concerning forestry products, agricultural prices, or energy prices. At the same time, direct regulation of a large number of producers is also difficult, if nothing else because the reach of the bureaucracy is only marginally different from the reach of the fiscal system. More than that, the implementation of direct regulations, e.g., of land use, through the bureaucracy will tend to be subverted. So I would not, because of the lack of reach of fiscal policy jump to the other conclusion that therefore let us put in a large measure of direct regulation.

Concluding Remarks

What do we do then? I would focus on six points here.

First, decentralisation. Integration of environment and development is essentially a location-specific measure. It needs local adaptation, a great deal of local knowledge of plant varieties, local conditions, of water bodies etc. and one way of doing this is to decentralise effective responsibility and control over whatever regulations you have on land use, water use, etc.

Second, empowerment. All those who depend on the water body, of forests or of common grazing land should have a say in the decisions affecting the resource through the political process or through specialised local bodies, or what we call "panipanchayats" which are a sort of water co-operatives, or through land boards etc.

Third, a clearer definition of property rights. The individual's right to do what he likes with property is already constrained in certain ways by municipal regulations. We need to examine whether the way in which we constrain these rights is adequate for enforcing the common good and common interests. This concept of zoning, of municipal regulation, may have to be extended to cover certain other aspects of property rights. The redefinition of property rights will also, I believe, help to reinstate some valuable traditional rights which provided a livelihood base for the poor.

Fourth, enforcement of liability for damage. I would say that in most developing countries many industries get away quite literally with murder. A legislative framework for liability exists but it is not at all effective. Also liability arises after the event. There are some things which one needs to do before the event by way of prior clearance procedures. Hence a series of measures -- such as public hearings on matters involving hazardous activities, creating monitoring mechanisms for of hazardous substances, strict liability, etc. -- are necessary. The OECD in particular has some experience in this area which could be of some interest and value if it could be elaborated for developing countries.

Fifth, we must ensure that full costs are included in environmental management costs in administered prices for energy, agricultural products, mineral royalties, etc.

Finally, as a more speculative remark, a sustainability analysis of fiscal and monetary policies, particularly those elements which involve explicit and implicit subsidies could be institutionalised.

Let me end where I began -- development planning. Much of what we need to do to correct development policies and planning for environmental management is not very different from what we need to do to bring in a stronger emphasis on equity and longer term growth in development policies. Hence, the critical issue is how to change the agenda of the development planner.

KEYNOTE ADDRESS

Environmental Management or Management for Sustainable Development?

by

David Runnalls *

---

* David Runnalls is Director, Environment and Sustainable Development Program, Institute for Research on Public Policy (IRPP), Ottawa, Canada.

RÉSUMÉ

L'évolution des préoccupations relatives à l'environnement dans l'aide extérieure a connu trois phases : une première phase, dans les années 70, à laquelle correspondait la naissance d'un mouvement des ONG de portée internationale, la prise de conscience des problèmes d'environnement et l'inclusion, par les organismes d'aide, de normes de protection de l'environnement dans leurs projets ; une deuxième phase, dans les années 80, pendant laquelle on a élargi l'éventail des activités de protection de l'environnement, notamment l'aide directe aux activités de défense de l'environnement, et étoffé les effectifs des agences. Pour l'essentiel, il s'agissait encore de ce que le rapport Brundtland appelait "la méthode standard", en grande partie consacrée à atténuer les effets secondaires de la croissance, et non d'un nouveau programme de développement. L'apparition de problèmes planétaires comme l'appauvrissement de la couche d'ozone et le changement climatique, peuvent annoncer une nouvelle ère dans laquelle l'environnement, sous la forme d'un développement durable, va émerger comme l'un des problèmes dominant la politique comme l'économie.

Deux thèmes seront probablement au centre de l'effort pour parvenir à un développement planétaire et national durable, à savoir que ce qui compte réellement, ce sont les politiques (c'est-à-dire la macro-économie) et non les projets et, deuxièmement, la capacité des populations locales à se prendre de plus en plus en charge. Maintenant seulement, on commence à prendre conscience de l'énorme pouvoir d'incitation et, en même temps, de l'effet pervers de bien des mesures en faveur d'un développement durable. Mais, dans le cadre d'une réflexion nouvelle sur l'ajustement structurel, une nouvelle conditionnalité axée sur un développement durable renferme bien des nouveaux germes de discorde. Toutefois, la nature globale des problèmes peut donner aux pays en developpement un impact réel sur les nouveaux flux d'aide. La montée en puissance d'un immense élan afin de forcer la croissance -- problème ô combien ardu -- à revêtir des formes plus économes en ressources et en énergie permet d'accomplir des progrès qui auraient semblé irréalisables voici quelques mois seulement. Les organismes d'aide auront fort à faire en ces temps qui sont à l'évidence extraordinairement intéressants mais en même temps affolants.

SUMMARY

The development of environmental concerns in foreign assistance divides into three phases: a first phase, in the 1970s, saw the beginnings of an NGO movement of international significance plus recognition of environmental issues and the introduction of environmental standards by aid agencies for their projects; a second phase, in the 1980s, expanded the range of environmental activities, including direct assistance for environmental activities, and agency staffing was greatly strengthened. However, this was still largely an exploration of what Brundtland called "the old agenda", largely focused on mitigating the side-effects of growth, not a new development agenda. The emergence of global issues such as ozone depletion and climate change, may usher in a new age in which environment in the guise of sustainable development emerges as a dominant political as well as economic issue.

Two central themes in the drive to achieve global and national sustainable development are likely to be that policies (ie macroeconomics) not projects is what really matters and secondly, the empowerment of local people to take more and more into their own hands. The enormous power of incentive and, currently, the perversity of much incentive for sustainable development is only now being realised. But as part of a rethinking of structural adjustment, there is much new potential for discord from a new conditionality focused on sustainable development. However, the global nature of the issues may provide the developing world with real leverage in new flows of assistance. A huge momentum building up to tackle the immensely hard problems of pushing growth into less resource and energy intensive forms is causing progress to be made that seemed impossible just months ago. There will be plenty for the aid agencies to do in what is evidently both an extraordinarily interesting and a bewildering time.

INTRODUCTION

The last eight or ten years have seen a flurry of interest in the environmental policies and activities of the international aid agencies. Hearings before various committees of the US Congress, television programmes about the environmental bankruptcy of Brazilian forestry and settlement programmes and frequent articles in the press have raised serious questions about the effects of large scale interventions on the natural resource base of the Third World. All of this interest and pressure has brought about very rapid changes in at least the cosmetics of how the large agencies evaluate the environmental consequences of their lending and grants programmes.

In response, many of the agencies have pointed out that these concerns are not new. Indeed, many have had procedures and practices for environmental impact analysis in place for a number of years. They also point out that they are not their own masters; it is the governments of developing countries who make the final decisions on location, design and implementation of projects. Lastly, the multilateral financial institutions in particular, emphasize that they are also the prisoners of their own system of finance and governance. They largely depend for their revenues on the private bond markets. These markets place a high premium on the maintenance of creditworthiness, soundness of economic appraisal, and speed and efficiency of disbursement. Their Boards of Directors are composed not of environmentalists or natural scientists, but of Ministers of Finance and their representatives, the latter sharing a good many of the concerns of the financial markets.

The bilateral agencies are elements of national foreign policy, usually at least responsive, if not subordinate, to foreign ministries. Policies are determined by their concerns as well as the influence of a number of domestic pressures, both public and private. These range from the desire to promote domestic industries and encourage exports, building up the small business sector, urban industrialisation, all the way through to safeguarding human rights, enhancing the role of women in society and preserving the environment. Because of the greening of the electorates in all OECD countries, the latter has become a matter of considerable political importance.

The development of environmental concern in the foreign assistance agencies can be divided into three parts: first, the end of the age of innocence; second the beginning of the age of environmental enlightenment; and third, the transition to sustainable development

The first phase lasted throughout most of the 1970s, the second throughout the 1980s and is still continuing. The third phase is now under way in a few agencies.

1. The End of the Age of Innocence

A number of developments which occurred throughout the 1970s formed and shaped the relationship between the agencies and the environment.

In 1968 the US Conservation Foundation and Washington University of St. Louis convened a conference at Airlie House, near Washington, D.C. The conference and the subsequent publication of its proceedings as *The Careless Technology*[1] marked the first systematic attempt to document the relationship between development assistance projects and environmental deterioration. The Conference had a positive effect on the World Bank. According to the late William Clark, the results of the Conference, augmented by a lively meeting between the eminent British environmentalist E.M. Nicholson and Robert McNamara, helped to convince the latter of the need for a systematic incorporation of environmental factors into the Bank's procedures and policies.

Accordingly, in 1970, the World Bank established the Office of Environmental Advisor. In his address to the Stockholm Conference in 1972, McNamara described the reason for the change:

> The question is not whether there should be continued economic growth. There must be. Nor is the question whether the impact on the environment must be respected. It has to be. Nor, least of all, is it a question of whether these two questions are interlocked. They are. The solution of the dilemma revolves clearly not about whether, but about how.

The United Nations Conference on the Human Environment had been proposed in the General Assembly by Sweden, backed by most of the other members of the OECD. Almost from the outset, it became clear that the developing countries were at best lukewarm, at worst hostile, toward the exercise. Many viewed environmental problems such as air and water pollution and contamination by toxic substances, as problems resulting primarily from affluence. They feared that environmental rules and regulations would slow down their development, that stringent health regulations aimed at carcinogens or toxic substances would be used to block their exports and that their attempts to exploit their forest and mineral wealth would be curtailed in the name of conservation. Finally, many of them feared that these new found environmental concerns of the North would add substantially to the costs of their development projects, and prolong the already tortuous project execution process without making additional financial resources available to cover these costs. Additionality was one of the issues which confronted the development assistance community.

This scepticism on the part of the Third World was one of the reasons for the appointment of Maurice Strong as Secretary-General of the Conference. Strong, then President of the Canadian International Development Agency (CIDA), was held in high regard by many developing country officials. He determined to change the political dynamic so that the upcoming Conference would devote a substantial portion of its time to the environmental problems facing the Third World. As a results of Strong's efforts, the developing world, led by Mrs. Gandhi, attended the Conference in force and played a major role in its deliberations.

Stockholm made environmental planning and management a respectable, if relatively minor part of the 1970s debate about development, basic needs and the New International Economic Order by exploring the relationships between environmental decay and poverty and demonstrating that development would better achieve its goals only if environmental factors are fully taken into account. It also led to a stream of literature, both popular and scientific, and a wealth of studies on the relationship between development and environmental deterioration, and to the beginnings of formal environmental procedures and practices by the foreign assistance agencies.

In 1975, the US Agency for International Development (USAID) was sued by four American environmental groups for its failure to prepare an environmental impact statement on the use of pesticides in some of its projects. The suit also related to the Agency's failure to establish procedures under the National Environmental Policy Act (NEPA) to review its projects. This led to the preparation of new regulations for implementing the intent of NEPA in the foreign assistance programme, and new pesticide regulations. By 1977-78, these regulations had been incorporated by Congress into the Foreign Assistance Act. This made USAID the only development assistance agency with regular, legally enforceable procedures for assessing the environmental impacts of development projects.

In 1977, the International Institute for Environment and Development (IIED), anxious to determine the operational importance of the new found rhetoric on environment and development, undertook a study of the environmental procedures and practices of nine multilateral development finance agencies. Published as *Banking on the Biosphere*[2], the study pointed out that only the World Bank had "shown ... a unique practical concern over the environmental impact of its lending" in addition to "intellectual leadership in environmental matters in the international development community". The report also stressed that the Bank's procedures and practices were far from ideal -- they looked better than they should, largely by comparison with the other agencies -- who had done very little. The report concluded that most of the institutions lacked:

-- clear procedures for the environmental assessment of their projects;

-- criteria for assessing environmental impacts;

-- alternative forms of analysis and accountancy which include long term social and environmental effects of development projects; and

-- personnel with training appropriate to the task of ensuring proper consideration of the environmental dimensions of development projects.

Banking on the Biosphere contained 11 recommendations which led to the "Declaration of Environmental Policies and Procedures Relating to Economic Development"[3]. The Declaration, prepared under the auspices of UNEP, was signed by the nine agencies in 1980. The Declaration commits the agencies to five broad lines of policy: institution of procedures for the systematic examination of development activities to ensure that appropriate measures are prepared to minimise environmental problems; co-operation to ensure that appropriate environmental measures are incorporated in project design; provision of technical assistance to developing countries to develop their indigenous capabilities; development of project proposals that are especially designed to protect, rehabilitate, manage or otherwise enhance the human environment and quality of life; training of their operational staff; and conducting studies leading to the improvement of project appraisal methodologies and disseminating information about what they are doing in this area.

The signatories also agreed to the establishment by UNEP of a Committee of International Development Institutions on the Environment (CIDIE). Originally set up with eight members, the committee now numbers fifteen (soon to become 16) and has met annually since the Declaration was signed.

This affirmation of the need to incorporate environmental considerations in the policies of the multilateral donor agencies was accompanied by the publication of a major statement by the environmental non-governmental (NGO) community. The *World Conservation Strategy*[4], produced by the International Union for the Conservation of Nature and Natural Resources (IUCN), highlighted a major shift in the attitudes of the conservation groups away from what many had seen as an excessive concentration on the preservation of individual species toward the preservation of ecosystems through land use planning and more sustainable forms of development. It recognises that this can only be accomplished by the integration of these concepts into national development strategies.

The third event of significance in this area in 1980 was the publication by the IIED of the results of its two-year study of the environmental policies of six of the bilateral development assistance agencies: those of Canada, the Federal Republic of Germany, Netherlands, Sweden, United Kingdom and United States. *The Environment and Bilateral Aid*[5] concluded that, largely because of the litigation mentioned earlier, USAID was much further advanced than the other agencies. Although modest progress had been made in the other agencies, they had an urgent need for almost the entire repertoire of environmental tools: high level policy statements, better data, enforceable assessment procedures, guidelines and checklists and project evaluation techniques.

The motivating factors for the modest changes which did take place during this period are quite clear. Stockholm represented the first great wave of international concern for the environment and as such it generated immense publicity and enthusiasm. (It was said that more journalists attended the Conference than were present at the Munich Olympics later that year.) More than 120 governments created environmental ministries or agencies equipped with the usual panoply of laws, regulations, environmental impact assessment procedures and the like. Although most of these agencies were domestic in their concerns, many began to ask questions about the environmental aspects of foreign policy. The Conference created a UN agency concerned with the environment which continued to ask questions of the rest of the system. The continued questioning by two international NGOs (the IIED and IUCN) helped to keep the questions on the table. Finally, the AID case represented the beginnings of a trend that would drive and dominate the next phase of the transition -- the involvement of the environmental NGOs, led by the large, well financed US environmental groups.

2. The Beginning of the Age of Environmental Enlightenment

The decade following the Stockholm Conference saw a flurry of activity on the environmental front.

Yet the picture presented by the report which opened the decade of the 1980s was sombre indeed. *The Global 2000 Report to the President*[5], published in the dying days of the Carter Administration, painted a picture of a world whose natural systems were in desperate trouble. The so-called renewable resource bases of many Third World countries were beginning to look as if they were not only non-renewable but they were disappearing at alarming rates. The Conference in Nairobi organised by the United Nations Environment Programme (UNEP) to celebrate the ten years since Stockholm, was dominated by similar considerations.

The United States environmental community, hitherto very parochial in its outlook, now began to turn its attention to international environmental issues. The establishment of the World Resources Institute, the emergence of Worldwatch as a public information force, the development of strong international programmes by many of the domestic environmental groups, and the unlikely collaboration of the Reagan administration helped initially to focus this concern on the multilateral banks and the USAID.

In 1983, a series of Congressional hearings began on the policies of the multilateral development banks. The initial reaction by the Treasury Department on behalf of the Administration tended to brush aside the criticism and to defend the status quo. The environmental community countered by "attacking" with what has by now become a familiar list of projects. Polonoroeste in Brazil -- a huge road building and forest colonisation project; the Narmada River scheme in India which would, upon completion, displace up to a million people; the Indonesian transmigration scheme -- a plan to resettle thousands of Javanese peasants to the outer islands; and the Botswana livestock project -- a plan to fence thousands of acres of open savannah for cattle raising.

The response of the Congress and the Treasury (which was in its early ideological phase and did not like the multilateral agencies on principle) was to send a detailed questionnaire to the Banks inquiring about their environmental procedures and practices. The responses to this questionnaire provided the first detailed view of the agencies' performance available to outsiders. They appeared defensive, overly secretive, and unprepared to admit to their mistakes.

This led to more Congressional hearings, more fact-finding tours by the environmental groups and a proliferation of both money and staff resources available to the environmental community. The Reagan Treasury, seeing a way to appease an environmental community which was constantly taking it to task for its domestic performance, assigned a full time staff person to the issue. Conservative Senators who disliked the Banks and AID on principle and yet were under attack by some of their constituents for their own environmental performance, became unlikely bedfellows of the Sierra Club. The publication of a hard-hitting pamphlet "Bankrolling Disasters"[6] by the Club and its distribution to many of its 250 000 members helped to raise the political temperature still further.

At the same time the realisation that the so-called African drought was in fact the breakdown of the environmental infrastructure of an entire continent led European Governments and NGOs to question many of the large scale development schemes of the continent. Several analyses by both the World Bank staff and some of the other agencies raised similar questions about the long-term viability of many of these projects.

The appointment of Barber Conable as President of the World Bank, the debate over the replenishment of IDA (which required a vote in Congress) and the reorganisation of the Bank served to bring these issues to a head. In a speech to the World Resources Institute (WRI) before his appointment, Conable sought to reassure the critics by promising the creation of an environmental department within the Bank, greatly increased staffing, more open relations with the NGO community and increased funding for projects targeted at the environment and natural resource sector.

Since that speech, undoubted progress has been made. The World Bank now has an environmental department with more staff, although the department has been criticised for being too far removed from the day to day operations of the Bank. The operational units have more staff to assess the impacts of Bank projects. An environmental assessment process is finally being defined and implemented. And the Bank appears to have greatly expanded its portfolio of "environmental" projects. Heavy criticism remains, however, of the environmental impacts of many of the Bank's larger projects, particularly its forestry projects.

Many of the other multilateral agencies have also moved to increase both staff and the resources available to deal with environmental problems. The advent of another veteran of the Stockholm process, Enrique Iglesias, at the Inter-American Development Bank (IDB) has led to major changes. The IDB, which had resisted the establishment of a specific environmental division for many years, now has such a group with a staff of fifteen. It has developed a sophisticated environmental screening and assessment process and has launched a number of initiatives to build up the capacities of national environmental agencies. It has pledged to integrate environmental considerations at each level of the Bank's decision-making process. In another precedent setting move, the IDB, long regarded as the least open to NGOs, has pledged itself to involve local NGOs and peoples' organisations in the planning and execution of its own projects. And Iglesias appears to be open to high level policy rethinking. The IDB, along with UNDP, has appointed a high level commission, composed of a number of senior figures from the continent, including the former Presidents of Colombia and Ecuador and Mexico, to report on environment and development in Latin America and the Caribbean[7].

The Asian Development Bank (ADB) is instituting procedures for the systematic environmental examination of all of its development activities; co-operating with member countries and international organisations to ensure appropriate environmental protection measures are incorporated in the design and implementation of projects; supporting environmental and natural resource programmes and projects; training and informing Bank staff of the environmental aspects of economic development; conducting studies and disseminating documentation to provide guidance on the environmental implications of economic development; and developing or strengthening environmental institutions in member countries.

Beginning in 1989, a number of new activities were initiated to strengthen environmental and natural resources planning and management, including processing and administering the Division's technical assistance projects, integrating environmental considerations into programme lending and enhancing the environmental dimension of traditional sectoral projects, including piggy-backed technical assistance projects.

Other initiatives include strengthening and formalising the integration of environmental considerations into country programming exercises and supporting global issues. The ADB is also taking the tentative first steps toward a sustainable development policy through a regional study on "Economic Policies for Sustainable Development: Implementing the Brundtland Commission Recommendations in Selected Developing Member Countries".

The bilateral agencies have also made great strides in developing policies and programmes to deal with environmental problems. A recent report by the newly established DAC (the OECD's Development Assistance Committee) Working Party on Development Assistance and Environment[8] details many of these changes. The report examines the changes under three broad headings: Environmental assessment policies and procedures; programmes to upgrade the environment in developing countries and to strengthen their capability to deal with environmental issues; and aid responses to global environmental problems.

It is obvious that much has changed since the publication of the IIED Report in 1980. Most, if not all of the DAC members now have formal environmental policies and personnel within their agencies to implement them. Perhaps the most notable of the latter is USAID's recent announcement that it plans to add 60 environmental experts to its staff within the next three years and to train a minimum of 100 existing staff in environmental matters.

The agencies are also beefing up the quantity and quality of the environmental tools at their disposal. Eleven of them have formal procedures for assessing the environmental aspects of their development assistance policies; most of the others have made a commitment to the establishment of such procedures in the near future. Country environmental studies -- profiles, conservation strategies and the like -- are now common. Many of the agencies have made commitments to help countries to improve the quality of their natural resource and environmental data bases. And many of the agencies are just now beginning to experiment with such economic techniques as resource accounting, improved cost/benefit analysis and the like.

Human resource development and training, largely aimed at strengthening environmental agencies in the developing world have become part of every agency's portfolio, along with measures to improve the quality of environmental education. Some of the agencies are also providing increased funding both to their own environmental NGOs with overseas projects and to indigenous groups.

Finally, as in the case of the multilateral agencies, every bilateral agency now has a portfolio of projects which are principally environmental in their intent. Although this surely involves an element of "creative bookkeeping" whereby projects with a natural resource component automatically become environmental projects, it is undeniable that progress is being made. And these projects, taken together, represent a sizeable pool of financial resources.

So there has been rapid change in a short period of time. Yet, not all the problems of incorporating environmental considerations into development projects have been solved, by any means. Recent documents produced by both the Canadian and other environmental groups are eloquent testimony to that conclusion. The current furore over the Tropical Forestry Action Plan (TFAP) is but one example. And the World Bank in particular seems to be destined for heavy criticism for a number of its existing and proposed mega-projects.

And in the multilateral agencies an additional political problem has arisen. Many of the Third World members of the Boards of these agencies still feel that these issues are being imposed upon them by the developed countries in general and the United States and US environmental groups in particular. They already feel that the conditionality increasingly attached to multilateral lending is an affront to their sovereignty. Attempts to introduce environmental conditionality are therefore not welcome.

In conclusion, therefore, the donor community has moved a very long distance since the beginning of the 1980s. Although the new environmental measures are far from perfect, they should noticeably reduce the number of poorly planned, sited and executed development projects in the future. They should help developing countries to perfect their own skills at project analysis and siting and to develop their own environmental regulations within significantly strengthened environmental agencies. They should help the NGO community to increase the number and quality of their own projects and to better train their own staffs in environmental procedures.

But these adjustments have been relatively painful for many of the donor agencies. They have been achieved at a cost both in money and, in some cases, in morale and to their relations with many of their recipient countries who still feel that much of this concern is marginal to the real business of development.

There is also a feeling that these efforts, while valuable, will not in themselves succeed. With some distinguished exceptions, they have been directed at what the Brundtland Commission called the "old agenda" of environmental assessment, pollution control, national parks and protected areas and the like. They have largely focused on dealing with the physical side-effects of growth (or poverty) instead of anticipating and preventing problems before they happen. This is partly a reflection of the experience in the developed world with environmental protection policies throughout the 1970s and 1980s. Both the governmental and non-governmental communities in the North are still largely committed to this approach to environmental protection in their own countries. The immediate pre and post Stockholm periods may have seen the rise of the environment as an issue, but it is still seen in many quarters as a marginal issue, one which should not be permitted to interfere with the real economic issues of development and economic growth. President Bush's remarks after the Houston economic summit that the United States would not trade jobs for progress on climate change is perhaps the latest indication of this approach.

Again, with some distinguished exceptions, the tools used to execute these policies are also marginal to the real political processes of resource allocation within the agencies and recipient governments. While environmental profiles and conservation strategies improve the quality of environmental data bases, there is little evidence that they have influenced the traditional economic analyses that the multilateral agencies use to formulate their overall policies toward recipient countries. Even the inspired idea of environmental issues papers prepared within the World Bank, largely by Bank economists, appears to have had mixed success in influencing country economic strategies. Environmental impact assessments, while valuable in designing and siting projects, have little impact on the earlier policy decisions on the types and number of projects to be funded, and upon the sectors to be stressed. While it is too early to judge the eventual fate of Environmental Action Plans, it seems likely that they in their turn will have little influence on the overall direction of country allocations. Finally, the emphasis by some agencies on refining some of the economic tools seems to be misplaced -- especially in the case of cost/benefit analysis. There are some environmental values that will simply never be adequately captured in the analysis and will therefore always be undervalued. The real benefits from reforming economic tools such as natural resource accounting, eliminating ecological perverse subsidies and tax incentives, and exploring ways to counteract market failure have been barely explored, let alone realised. On the few occasions when they have been explored by competent analysts within the agencies, they have seldom formed the basis for major policy change.

The mechanisms used to express these new policies have often been marginal to the real political processes in the agencies and in the recipient governments. The environmental units in the agencies are often small, staffed by highly competent technical specialists, and well removed from the main economic decisions affecting the allocation of massive financial resources and the determination of tax, pricing, and fiscal policies. Their counterparts in the Third World are often more marginalised -- small, understaffed, underfunded bands of dedicated professionals who have little influence over the macroeconomic decisions of Prime Minister's Offices, national planning agencies and the other central spending departments of government. Efforts to build up the human resources of these departments are essential to their success in environmental management in the traditional sense. But will they make them more effective in their dealings with the major economic decision-makers?

3. The Transition to Sustainable Development

The publication of the Brundtland Report and the rise of ozone depletion and climate change to the top of the political agenda signal a new era in environmental policy. For the first time, it is becoming apparent to a whole range of decision makers that the earth's environment and its natural resource base are so totally interlocked that the natural environment has become one of the principal constraints on development. And if the political decision-makers in the donor countries do not see it now, an aroused public opinion will soon see that they do. Stockholm saw the emergence of the environment as an issue. The 1992 Conference may see it emerge as one of the dominant economic and political issues for the remainder of the century.

The adoption of Sustainable Development as a major policy goal for aid agencies does not negate the progress made so far. Indeed, it requires that the new measures for environmental assessment, lending for natural resources projects and the like be continued and strengthened. It requires more effective measures to preserve and protect prized ecological assets such as coastal resources, national parks and protected areas, watershed management areas and the like.

More importantly, however, it requires that the environment become a mainstream economic issue, central to the national planning and decision-making process and not something to be handed to a politically weak, underfunded and understaffed department of the environment and natural resources. It requires pride of place in the planning documents and country strategies of the foreign assistance agencies. It can even be argued that the locus of environmental decision-making in an agency not be in the environment division, but in the line departments and those responsible for economic analysis.

If sustainable development were to become the guiding principle behind a foreign assistance agency, what would it look like in policy terms? To answer that question, the Canadian International Development Agency asked the Institute for Research on Public Policy to suggest some specific ways by which Canada's aid policies could more effectively support sustainable development in the Third World. Further, it agreed that the Institute's work should reflect an open process of consultation with a broad cross-section of informed Canadians, many of them with wide experience in the Third World. In response, the Institute commissioned a number of papers and organised a series of five public consultations involving more than 500 people across the country. These consultations told us that the non-governmental community writ large (private companies, academics, NGOs) had moved much farther than either their political or bureaucratic counterparts in government.

The report, *CIDA and Sustainable Development* [9] contains more than seventy recommendations and suggestions for action. Collectively, these represent a formidable challenge to promote change on all fronts -- macro-policy, sectoral policy, resource and economic accounting, assessments, education, research, public participation, standards and the like.

Underlying the report are two central themes. The first is that unlike most development agendas which are principally project driven, this one is largely policy driven. Secondly, it is a combination of top down and bottom up. That is to say that much of the emphasis is on macroeconomic reform at the level of the Cabinet and much of it relates to empowering local people to deal with the natural resource issues that will affect their own destiny.

The report begins by examining the role of central agencies of government. Governments have invariably failed to make these powerful central economic and sectoral agencies in any way responsible for the implications of their policies and expenditures on the environment. Yet these are the agencies with the policy power and the budgets to determine the form and content of growth, and whether it is sustainable or not. Sustainable development requires the reform of a whole series of ecologically perverse policies which are often the source of degradation and depletion of a country's stock of ecological capital. These policies are much more powerful than any conceivable counter strategies aimed at prevention, preservation and rehabilitation. Recent research has indicated that certain kinds of economic policies, often designed for perfectly logical political or economic reasons, but with no thought of the environment at all -- are of overwhelming importance in creating and driving patterns of development which are unsustainable. Two recent examples come to mind with great clarity. One is the increasing conversion of good cropland devoted to food production for domestic consumption to cash crops for export in order to generate foreign exchange. This can lead to small food farmers being forced on to more and more marginal lands with all the potential that implies for deforestation and soil erosion and degradation. The second comes from a series of studies[10] prepared for the World Bank which illustrate that much of the deforestation in Latin America is driven by companies and individuals seeking to develop pasture for cattle raising or to make a hefty profit in the timber industry. The studies conclude that few of these investments has ever shown a profit or are likely to show a profit. These investments are often made to take advantage of favourable income tax treatment or of subsidies.

Our report recommended that human resource development policies and institutional strengthening programmes be directed principally at strengthening the sustainable development capacity of central agencies. It also suggested that the analytical capacity of these agencies be bolstered to enable them to undertake their own examinations of subsidies, incentives and tax credits both to identify those which indirectly promote deforestation, desertification and species loss and to redeploy them to encourage a more sustainable utilisation of the natural resource base. Given that these analyses can be politically rather delicate in a number of countries (including our own), we also recommended support for independent Third World policy research institutes where appropriate. Our Institute has enjoyed a long and fruitful relationship with one of the institutions represented at this meeting, the Thailand Development Research Institute and we have first hand experience of the abilities of such a group to bring authoritative, non-partisan advice to bear on public policy. We also felt that it was essential to move from the library and the conference room to experiment with a number of the new economic techniques to be presented later in this Conference. We therefore called for the development of a series of pilot projects designed to explore the potential for new kinds of resource and environmental accounting. We also felt that opportunities should be provided for the development of new kinds of environmental profiles and state of the environment reports that fully incorporate both economic and environmental data.

The debate over conditionality is perhaps the most controversial subject before the development community today. And opinion is sharply divided even within the donor community on how much an agency should insist upon in its dialogue with its partners. Nevertheless, we felt it important that an agency make its support for a whole series of projects in the agricultural/irrigation, forestry, and energy sectors contingent upon an examination of prices, subsidies, tax and other incentives which encourage inefficient energy use, overuse of agricultural chemicals and other inputs and deforestation and species loss. We made this recommendation in full awareness that such an examination of Canadian domestic policies in these areas would result in nothing short of a major scandal.

The report also turns to the second aspect of conditionality: the whole process of structural adjustment. It called for a re-examination of the policy shift that led to the emphasis on structural adjustment in the first place. But as long as the policy remains in place, there may be ways to modify it so that it promotes the kinds of restructuring necessary for the transition to sustainable development. Much of the literature on sustainable development contains references to the fact that pressure to generate foreign exchange is leading to a substitution of export crops for food crops and to an over-exploitation of the natural resource bases of a number of countries in an effort to generate increased export earnings. To my knowledge, no one has yet done a proper case study in any country, let alone a series of countries to determine to what extent this is true.

Meanwhile, it seems that there are a number of common sense things that both agencies and governments can do. Most, if not all, of the structural adjustment packages have to do with reducing government expenditures, the size of the civil service, streamlining decision-making and the like. Many of them also, as in the case of Central America, are aimed at restoring the physical infrastructure of the region which has fallen into disrepair after many years of war and general neglect. Yet, few if any plans, Central America's again being a prime example, have paid any attention to the restoration of the natural infrastructure -- the region's soils, its water supplies, its forests -- which are the keys to the 80 per cent of its exports that come from agriculture, forestry and fishing. Few have paid any attention to the restructuring of many of the natural resource industries such as forestry, to ensure that its pricing regimes, its subsidy and tax structures, its export policies, its stumpage rates and its silvicultural policies and the like are designed to ensure the sustainable management of the resource. Without this sort of examination, individual forestry or agricultural projects are doomed to failure.

The report also felt that agencies had a responsibility to help governments to develop programmes to protect, preserve and enhance their natural resource bases. This is the area that is perhaps the closest to the current policies of many of the agencies. Here we emphasized the need for more sustainable energy development policies, placing a heavier reliance on efficiency and conservation than in the past; and upon the continued need for some renewable energy equivalent of the CGIAR (Consultative Group on International Agricultural Research). The report also contained a number of recommendations to make agricultural practices more sustainable, both through reorienting some of the work of the CGIAR centres, reorienting local agricultural research and extension programmes to concentrate more on marginal farmers on marginal lands; and building local capacity to control and regulate agricultural chemicals. Finally, the report strongly recommends the modification of existing government and aid agency policies which promote deforestation.

I said at the outset that this was both a top down and a bottom up process. We feel that the involvement of people themselves in the planning and management of their own natural resource base is one of the main keys to sustainable development. This means involving those in the Third World who are affected by the development process. It also involves, as many agencies have found to their cost, the involvement of concerned citizens and NGOs in the donor countries themselves. Perhaps the overriding requirement of any people oriented development process is that it be as transparent as possible, i.e. information about projects and actions are made readily available. A second key requirement is that the disadvantaged, such as women and indigenous peoples, are able to play their full part in the development process.

To this end, we felt that the environmental assessment process urgently needs extensive reform in almost all agencies. First, it must be modified so that assessments examine the sustainability of prospective projects from an economic and social point of view as well as from the environmental perspective. Second, the process should be modified to take account of traditional political and cultural values; the current systems are culture bound and they are bound to a western cultural point of view. The assessments must be made public. Finally, it is obvious that these sorts of assessments are more effective the earlier they occur in the process. Perhaps the most effective of all could be assessments performed as a prerequisite for major policy decisions. This idea is being actively discussed in Canada and elsewhere for domestic policy decisions; it could equally apply to the policy decisions of foreign assistance agencies. Although these changes in the assessment process will generate much opposition, they may be the only way to remove the suspicion with which many of the poor in the Third World and many of the NGOs in the North currently regard the development process.

Since the Stockholm process, NGOs have played a unique role in the formulation of international environmental policy. In no other area of public policy have they been more active, or some would argue, more effective. The active participation and co-operation of the NGO community is a critical ingredient in the achievement of sustainable development at a number of levels. The work of such policy oriented groups as IIED and WRI has helped to shape the direction of international policy. The lobbying efforts of many of the membership organisations have been largely responsible for many of the changes in donor agency policy over the past ten years. And the NGO community in the South is becoming increasingly active and increasingly vocal in the area of environment and natural resource management. They have forged close links with their counterparts in the North and increasingly with the newly emerging groups in Eastern Europe. Although this kind of rambunctious grouping may make things uncomfortable for the agency staff and the politicians who direct them at times, they have become an indispensable part of the policy process. As such, they deserve increased financial support from the agencies themselves.

At the operational level, the strengths and weaknesses of NGOs are well known. What is perhaps less well understood is the changing relationship between the NGOs based in the developed world and the Southern NGOs. Over the past few years the relationship between the two has evolved from one where most of the NGO projects in regions such as Africa were run by Northern NGOs or by local branches of Northern NGOs to one where local groups are increasingly taking over all aspects of the projects themselves. This poses a number of politically risky problems for some of the bilateral agencies. We felt, that at least in CIDA's case, it should take the risk and fund local NGOs directly to design and execute projects that could be part of a sustainable development strategy.

Finally, the report makes a series of recommendations on how an agency should prepare itself for the new realities of sustainable development. We suggested a new structure for country programme plans which involved the integration of environmental and economic information. We suggested the need to involve local experts in the preparation of these plans both to make them more relevant and to build up local capability, much as the Danish International Development Authority (DANIDA) has begun to do in some African countries. We also suggested a more environmentally conscious procurement policy for the agency and a range of internal changes necessary to familiarise agency staff and consultants with the challenges of sustainable development.

I should stress that this report was written for CIDA, within the context of the political debate in Canada. As such, it has much that is uniquely Canadian (and unique to CIDA) within it. Nevertheless, I feel that much of it would apply to any development assistance agency that adopts the idea of sustainable development as one of its two or three major priorities.

4. The International Context

Sustainable development is a very tall order both for the governments of the developing world and the development assistance agencies in the North. It involves fundamental changes in the economic systems of the developed world to make them far less resource and energy intensive. It involves reorienting many of the strategies for foreign assistance and for development with which we have become comfortable over the past two or three decades. It involves greatly increased financial transfers against the backdrop of budget austerity which is now sweeping the developed world. It involves finally getting to grips with the debt crisis now paralysing much of Latin America and Africa. What leads us to believe that it might happen?

The answer, in a word, is global change, particularly climate change, linked to a new definition of national and international security. These factors are at or near the top of the international agenda. And for the first time this agenda is being driven by environmental concerns rather than the other way round. Much of this agenda is expressing itself in the preparations for the 1992 United Nations Conference on Environment and Development (UNCED) to be held in Brazil.

One factor that donors will need to bear in mind is that the Third World, perhaps for the first time, perceives that it has an issue that gives it real leverage with the North. And all indications are that the developing world intends to use that leverage. The Preparatory process for the Brazil Conference has provided ample evidence of the degree of that determination.

Environmentalists are fond of describing all sorts of problems as global, often with shaky justification. But the problems of climate change and ozone depletion are genuinely global, requiring genuinely global solutions and very real concessions by the developed world. This was perhaps best illustrated by the progress of the ozone negotiations. After the negotiations which led to the Montreal protocol were completed, some observers wondered if the protocol with its provision for reducing CFC production by 50 per cent by the year 2000, would ever be ratified by the requisite number of countries to bring it into force. Following revelations that the ozone hole was much worse than expected and the rather unexpected greening of Mrs. Thatcher, the protocol was not only ratified but significantly strengthened, with provisions for a full phase out in the developed world by the turn of the century. In addition, two additional chemicals were added to the phase out list -- methyl chloroform and carbon tetrachloride. But this solution required the participation of the developing countries to be effective. India and China, for example, were unwilling to bear the additional burden of cost of the substitutes for CFCs in light of the fact that the problem had been almost exclusively caused by CFC use in the North. Within a matter of months, what appeared to be root and branch objections from some countries to the creation of a fund to help finance the transition away from CFCs had been overcome and a facility with an initial sum of $300 million over three years had been created. India and China have now pledged themselves to ratify the protocol. Seldom has an issue moved across the international agenda with such speed.

The ozone question is merely a warm-up to the main event, the negotiations over global warming and the reduction of greenhouse gas emissions. The recent report of the Intergovernmental Panel on Climate Change predicts significant increases in global average temperatures over the next few years with corresponding (and unpredictable) effects on rainfall and wind patterns and increases in sea levels. Their findings by and large support the conclusions of the Toronto Conference on the Changing Atmosphere in 1988 that reductions in CO_2 emissions of up to 70 per cent are needed to stabilize the situation and that reductions of 20 per cent should be achieved by the year 2005. Although infinitely more complex than the ozone question, this issue could also "take off" in an unpredictably rapid fashion.

When the 20 per cent goal was originally proposed, many energy analysts and private industries wrung their hands in despair. Reductions of this sort were not possible without massive disruptions of the domestic economies of the developed world and might not even be possible under any circumstances. Dire predictions were issued of cities without cars and homes without adequate light. Yet, two years later the Federal Republic of Germany, already one of the world's more efficient energy users, has set a national goal of reducing CO_2 emissions by 25 per cent over the same period, without significant changes in life styles. Scandinavia and the Netherlands have also agreed to reductions. Japan, the world's most efficient user appears to have agreed to a virtual freeze. Even my own country, Canada, the world's champion energy glutton, has committed itself to a freeze by the year 2000. When this was first proposed less than a year ago, it was pronounced impossible to achieve.

But none of this will work over the medium to long term without the co-operation of the developing world. China alone has plans to build up to 200 more coal fired generating stations. And most other countries have substantial plans for the expansion of their electricity generating systems on the drawing board. It is this sort of realisation that gives developing countries a good deal of leverage in the formulation of the so-called global bargain, or as Jim MacNeill more accurately points out, a series of small bargains leading up to a larger bargain[11]. And as the preparations for the 1992 Conference have shown, the Third World intends to use that leverage to bring attention to its priority issues of trade, debt and the need for economic growth in exchange for action on climate change.

It is not yet clear what form such a bargain would take or under whose auspices it would be constructed. But the general lines seem to be as follows. Standards would be set for emissions of greenhouse gases (including CFCs). These standards would call for drastic reductions for the industrialised countries and some expansion for those in the Third World. Some allowance would also be made for the role of forests as possible "carbon sinks". Major changes in the terms of technology transfer would be necessary in order to give developing countries access to the latest non-pollutive energy technologies as soon as they become available.

Any bargain must also include the creation of the kind of fund which the Bush Administration feared when it agreed to the CFC fund. This fund, versions of which have already been proposed by Rajiv Gandhi, Mrs. Brundtland, and the Toronto Conference, would need to be quite large by traditional international standards -- the Dutch estimate its requirements at $20-40 billion annually[12] -- but small when compared with world arms expenditure. It appears that a start had been made on a $2.5 billion fund at Houston, but Chancellor Kohl, its main advocate, was unable to persuade his host to go along. It is also likely that the question of Third World debt will appear on the agenda. Some have suggested that the principle of "debt for nature" swaps which have been tried on a modest basis in a few countries, be greatly expanded to provide some sort of debt relief or debt reduction in exchange for major reforestation efforts to create the kind of carbon sinks necessary to make a difference.

It is tempting to think that all of these various arrangements will come to a head in some grand poker game with all the countries of the world sitting down to hammer out a "grand bargain". This is highly unlikely. As my colleague Jim MacNeill has pointed out, these arrangements are likely to be much more haphazard, perhaps following the pattern that seems to be evolving for CFC reduction -- a series of bilateral and some multilateral deals between selected countries[13]. If the process appears to be gathering momentum, the international community might begin to move to some grander schemes.

There are plenty of fora to accommodate this process. This fall sees the convening of the World Climate Conference. It is hoped that a "framework convention" on climate change will be discussed at that time. The argument here is between those who favour a convention with specific commitments for the limitation of greenhouse gases, arrangements for technology transfers and the like and those who are arguing for an "empty shell" containing a general commitment to deal with the issue with the details to be worked out later. The latter group seems to be led by the United States, but there is a suspicion that some other countries may also hold this view, content to let the Americans take the blame.

The denouement of this issue may well come at the 1992 Conference when the optimists hope to have a convention opened for signature. This will partly depend upon whether or not Houston signalled the long awaited change in the economic power relationships away from exclusive US leadership. It would be interesting to see what would happen if the other six members of the summit decided to establish the initial $2.5 billion fund on their own.

Another issue driving the debate is tropical deforestation and species extinction. Although linked to the climate change discussions through their potential as "carbon sinks", many feel that forests also need to be discussed on their own, especially in the light of the recent conclusions by the Food and Agriculture Organization (FAO) that the rate of deforestation has jumped to 18 million hectares per annum. This argument holds that forests perform a range of functions, providing employment to forest dwellers and loggers alike, acting as carbon sinks, providing the most diverse ecosystems known to mankind, and providing a whole range of valuable services from climate moderation to water management. Of all the issues on the agenda, nothing has affected public opinion as much as the realisation that the world's main repositories of genetic diversity and untold natural wealth are disappearing at a frightening rate. This led the G-7 Summit in Houston to propose a world agreement or convention on forestry, to be prepared in time for the 1992 Conference in Brazil. The announcement of this convention and its pursuit at the recent Preparatory Committee Meeting of the 1992 Conference has left a number of questions. Is this primarily designed to avoid specific protocols with teeth being attached to the climate change convention? And how will it relate to the proposed convention on biological diversity? If successful, will it lead to calls for a specific World Forestry Organization, removing that function from FAO which currently devotes only a small fraction of its total budget to forestry questions?

As any casual viewer of television over the past few years must know, the world's tropical forests are the greatest reservoirs of biological diversity. Alarmed by the disappearance of several million species and threats to many more, WRI, UNEP, IUCN and the FAO have been developing a possible convention on biological diversity. It is also hoped to have this convention ready for signature at the time of the 1992 meeting.

A further complication to this already twisted tale lies in the fate of the Tropical Forestry Action Plan (TFAP). This plan emerged in 1985 from an effort by the World Resources Institute and a number of international agencies to attract increased interest and funding to forestry in developing countries. TFAP was based on the concept of the preparation of action plans for each country, followed by substantial investments by the aid agencies. Over the first five years of its existence, the plan involved 75 countries and several billion dollars in new commitments. But it has been dogged by controversy since the inception. The plan has recently been reviewed by an expert panel directed by Ulla Olsten, the former Prime Minister of Sweden. The review is not at all favourable, and the panel has recommended major changes in the execution of the plan and in its administration by the FAO. The FAO is reviewing the plan and preparing its own response, but it is fair to say that many in the forestry community are pessimistic about the future of TFAP unless and until the programme is more clearly oriented toward the conservation and sustainable development of forest lands and less toward exploitation, the participation of the people to be affected by TFAP and its projects is ensured, and a fund is created to finance both the full participation of developing countries and some sort of independent secretariat at the international level. Interestingly, the evaluation panel sees the proposed forestry convention as providing a new level of legitimacy to the TFAP process.

It is not at all clear how these issues will resolve themselves, but it seems reasonable to assume that we will not have a protocol to the climate convention, a world forestry convention and a convention on biological diversity by 1992, as well as a clear course for the TFAP. Indeed, it is beginning to look as if none of the conventions will be ready for opening in Brazil.

There are a number of other emerging issues which space prevents us from exploring in more detail. The environmental content of trade, the question of population growth and others are perhaps of equal relevance to the debate as those mentioned above.

Suffice it to say that it will be an interesting and somewhat bewildering time for the foreign assistance agencies. These agencies are still new to the idea of environmental management. They have just begun to come to grips with all the traditional issues of environmental assessment, emissions standards, pollution control strategies, standards and the like. They are just starting to retrain their staffs in these rather unfamiliar arts and to recruit new specialists to complement them. In the case of the International Monetary Fund (IMF), perhaps the most powerful and influential of them all, the new environmental unit promised to the US Congress has yet to be even set up.

And, rather suddenly, the Brundtland Commission, new scientific evidence of global change and an aroused public opinion have combined to thrust this new sectoral issue with which they are just becoming comfortable, into the driving force behind many international discussions. And these discussions are being conducted at the highest level with very high stakes. The sums of money being discussed are indeed large and the maneuvering for control and administration of them is already intense. Will they be "programmed" in the conventional fashion by the existing conventional agencies? Will they be drawn in large part from the existing resources available for development assistance? Will the flows be exclusively public or a combination of public and private? What will be the allocation principle? Will the sums be as large as some have speculated?

Finally, and perhaps most significant for those concerned with the poorest of the poor, the potential targeting of resources on those countries who have the most effect on global change, could leave many of the poorest countries out in the cold. Eight large developing countries produce over 75 per cent of the Third World's emissions of Greenhouse Gases. Funds devoted to that problem will be targeted at them. Relatively few countries account for the vast majority of the earth's remaining tropical forests. Debt swaps, reforestation schemes and the like will clearly be targeted at them. And there are relatively few countries with substantial biological diversity. These so-called "megadiversity" countries will benefit from any attention devoted to that issue.

The importance now accorded environmental issues can perhaps best be judged against the recent decision of the 1992 Preparatory Committee that the first part of the Brazil Conference be reserved for Heads of State and Heads of Governments -- an event truly without precedent.

The process of preparing for the 1992 Conference is now stimulating a good deal of debate about the kind of international institutional arrangements needed to cope with global change. There is a feeling among many that none of the existing United Nations agencies has a sufficiently broad mandate to encompass all of the issues. The calls for institutional change range from strengthening the Secretary General's Office to enable it to genuinely co-ordinate UN system activities in sustainable development or to provide a new and broader mandate for the United Nations Environment Programme, to Maurice Strong's proposal to revise the UN Charter to enable the now moribund Trusteeship Council to be reinvigorated with a mandate to be the Trustees of the Earth. Other suggestions have involved redefining the word "security" to encompass environmental security, thus expanding the role of the Security Council.

At the functional level, there is intense speculation about the institutional arrangements which may emerge from 1992. The TFAP evaluation and the calls for an international forestry convention have kindled discussion about the possibility of a World Forestry Organization which could also encompass the International Tropical Timber Organization. What will happen to UNEP? Will it be greatly expanded or strengthened as a monitoring agency only? Who will deal with climate change and the new energy arrangements required by efforts to cut Greenhouse Gas emissions? Will the Bretton Woods institutions handle the money or will new funds be needed?

The feeling of urgency led the French, Norwegian and Dutch Governments in the preparation for last year's summit in The Hague to seriously propose the creation of a supranational agency to preserve the earth's atmosphere. This agency would be able to act on majority vote in some cases (i.e. no automatic veto), and would have the power to impose mandatory economic sanctions recommended by the International Court of Justice on "... goods produced under conditions with negative impact on the atmosphere"[14]. The authority would also have the power to raise money to compensate those countries for whom compliance would be an unfair burden. Although this proposal was not fully accepted, the fact that it was even submitted by three sovereign governments -- one of whom was the host of last year's G-7 summit where a version of it again appeared on the agenda -- is indicative of the very real possibility of movement which many now sense.

NOTES AND REFERENCES

1. FARVAR and MILTON, eds., *The Careless Technology*, Garden City, Natural History Press, 1972.

2. Robert E. STEIN and Brian JOHNSON, *Banking on the Biosphere*, Lexington, Lexington Books, 1979.

3. Quoted in STEIN and JOHNSON, 1979.

4. INTERNATIONAL UNION FOR THE CONSERVATION OF NATURE AND NATURAL RESOURCES (IUCN) *et al.*, *World Conservation Strategy*, Gland: IUCN-UNEP-WWF, 1980.

5. INTERNATIONAL INSTITUTE FOR ENVIRONMENT AND DEVELOPMENT (IIED), *The Environment and Bilateral Aid*, London and Washington, D.C., IIED, 1980.

6. SIERRA CLUB, "Bankrolling Disasters", Washington, D.C., Sierra Club, 1986.

7. LATIN AMERICAN AND CARIBBEAN COMMISSION ON DEVELOPMENT AND ENVIRONMENT, *Our Own Agenda*, New York, IDB and UNDP, 1990.

8. The essence of this report is included in Part 2 of ORGANISATION FOR ECONOMIC CO-OPERATION AND DEVELOPMENT (OECD), *Development Co-operation. Efforts and Policies of the Members of the Development Assistance Committee, 1990 Report*, Paris, OECD, December 1990 (editor's note).

9. Jim W. MacNEILL, John COX and David RUNNALLS, *CIDA and Sustainable Development*, Ottawa, Institute for Research on Public Policy, 1989.

10. D.J. MAHER, *Government Policies and Deforestation in Brazil's Amazon Region*, Washington, D.C., World Bank, 1989, and Ernest LUTZ and Herman DALY, *Incentives, Regulations and Sustainable Land Use in Costa Rica*, Washington, D.C., World Bank, Environment Working Paper No. 34, July 1990.

11. Jim W. MacNEILL, Pieter WINSEMIUS, Taizo YAUSHIJI, *Beyond Interdependence*, forthcoming.

12. *Protecting the Global Atmosphere: Funding Mechanisms -- Second Interim Report to Steering Committee for Ministerial Conference on Atmospheric Pollution and Climate Change*, Noordwijk, The Netherlands, McKinsey and Co., November 1989.

13. MacNEILL *et al.*, supra No. 12.

14. Draft circulated by the organisers of The Hague Summit, 1989.

NEW ENVIRONMENTAL POLICIES: THE RECENT EXPERIENCE OF OECD COUNTRIES AND ITS RELEVANCE TO THE DEVELOPING WORLD

by

David Pearce *

* London Environmental Economics Centre, and Department of Economics, University College London.

RÉSUMÉ

L'auteur fait valoir que, pour la gestion de l'environnement, les instruments du marché qui prennent en compte le coût en ressources des activités économiques sont généralement, mais non universellement, plus efficaces que les méthodes de réglementation directe. Dans le passé pourtant, il est arrivé souvent que certains instruments du marché, les taxes par exemple, n'aient pas été bien utilisés, c'est-à-dire n'aient pas été assez étroitement liés aux dommages causés ou aux niveaux de rejets polluants. Les instruments du marché réduisent au minimum les coûts de mise en conformité et permettent de produire des recettes, même si ce n'est pas leur principal objectif.

Ayant passé en revue l'expérience récente acquise en matière d'instruments du marché dans 14 pays de l'OCDE, l'auteur démontre la pertinence de cette approche pour les pays en développement. L'application doit toutefois être placée dans son contexte. Il existe une liste d'options en matière de réformes et poursuivre une option à l'exclusion des autres pourrait aller à l'encontre du but visé. Par exemple, fixer les prix à leur juste niveau ne sera probablement efficace que si les droits sur les ressources sont, eux aussi, déterminés comme il convient. Les domaines d'action prioritaires sont définis dans différentes perspectives chronologiques. A court terme, ils concernent la politique de calcul des coûts pour le secteur privé et la réforme de la politique fiscale ; à moyen terme, les droits sur les ressources et le régime foncier ; à long terme, le domaine prioritaire est le calcul des coûts supportés par la collectivité.

SUMMARY

This paper argues that market-based instruments (MBIs) for environmental management which take into account the resource cost of economic activities are generally, though not universally, more efficient than "command-and-control" (CAC) approaches. In the past, however, MBIs such as taxes have often not been implemented properly, ie were not closely enough related to damage done or to levels of noxious emissions. MBIs minimise compliance costs and have the potential to raise revenues, even though this is not their main purpose.

After a review of recent experience with MBIs in 14 OECD countries the paper establishes the relevance of this approach to developing countries. However, its application has to be placed in context. There is a menu of reform options and pursuing one option to the exclusion of others could be counterproductive. For example, "getting prices right" is likely to be effective only if resource rights are also right. Priority areas for action are defined for different time horizons. For the short term, they concern private cost pricing policy and tax policy reform; in the medium-long term they lie with resource rights and land tenure; the long-term priority area is social cost pricing.

1. *New Environmental Policies*

Although economists have long advocated the use of economic instruments to direct environmental policy, it is only in the last few years that their ideas have been seriously entertained at the political level[1]. The essence of the economic approach may be simply stated in a set of propositions:

i) Environmental degradation has an economic cost which shows up as both forgone measured GNP and as unmeasured GNP. Unmeasured GNP losses include depreciation of natural capital stock (e.g. natural forests), morbidity and mortality from pollution, aesthetic damage, and so on.

ii) The dominant factors giving rise to environmental degradation are population growth; undefined, ill-defined or insecure resource rights; bad central planning; the failure of markets to price resources and outputs to reflect true social costs; the failure of governments to price resources and outputs to reflect true social costs.

iii) All of the causal factors cited are subject to redress through wise management policy, and all are subject to the use of economic instruments. Essentially, it is economic activity and human numbers that degrade natural and built environments, and both can be influenced by economic incentives.

iv) Economic instruments include the adjustment of subsidies which hold prices below private costs of production; the use of input or output taxes to correct the divergence between private and social costs of production; the creation of markets in resource use permits ("tradeable permits"); and returnable tax schemes ("deposit-refund" schemes). Legal-cum-economic instruments include requirements for compensation for damage done, and strict liability regulations.

v) The use of economic instruments contrasts with traditional forms of environmental regulation based on "command-and-control" approaches. Economic instruments are generally, though not universally, more *efficient* than command-and-control (CAC) approaches since they make use of markets, allocating control costs between polluters so as to minimise overall compliance costs[2].

At its simplest, economic instruments drive a "wedge" between economic activity and the impact of that activity on the environment. That it is possible to "decouple" economies from an excess burden on the environment is illustrated by the decline in sulphur oxide emissions in OECD countries per unit of GNP. The decoupling concept is of paramount importance since it implies at least the *possibility* of combining economic growth and environmental quality[3]. The alternatives are *either* to allow growth to damage environments, in which case welfare losses can be very large indeed (see below), *or* to constrain growth to protect the environment. The incentives approach is therefore very much "middle ground" between wholesale free market approaches which are insensitive to environmental concerns, and "anti-growth" views which appear insensitive to the wishes of ordinary people and the needs of the underprivileged.

2. *Attractions of Economic Approaches*

The benefits of economic approaches to environmental control have been widely discussed[4]. Briefly, they are:

i) By allocating control costs to those who can most easily bear them, *market-based instruments* (MBIs) such as pollution taxes and tradeable permits, minimise compliance costs. Contrary to popular impression, therefore, the MBI approach should be more appealing, not less, to industry and to consumers;

ii) The minimum cost argument is of considerable significance at a time when "new" environmental threats are likely to require stricter controls and hence higher levels of investment in protective policy. The new threats include ozone layer depletion, global warming, coastal zone clean-ups and the need to assist the developing world to protect international biodiversity. Likely cost increases can be illustrated by the average expenditure in OECD countries on environmental protection of around 1.5 per cent of GNP compared to the anticipated 3 per cent of GNP under the Dutch Environmental Programme;

iii) The minimum cost argument is potentially even more relevant to the developing world where public funds for environmental protection are scarce;

iv) Some MBIs, in the form of taxes and user charges, have the potential to raise revenues, even though this is not their main purpose, which is the creation of incentives to avoid payment by adopting abatement processes. Two uses of revenues might be envisaged. In the developed world, and perhaps in the developing world, revenues can be used to offset other distorting taxes in the economy. In this way, fiscally neutral pollution taxes, for example, can achieve two welfare gains -- reductions in pollution damage and reductions in deadweight losses from distortionary taxes on effort or enterprise. In the developing world, it is more likely that such revenues would offer the prospect of net gains to the public revenue, but, as in developed economies, such revenues might also be used to offset tax-incidence on low income groups[5];

v) By acting as *continuous* charges on pollution or excess resource use, MBIs encourage the search for better and better environmentally-friendly technology. While CAC approaches can induce technological change by setting standards slightly ahead of what is the "best available technology" (BAT), technology-based standards are typically static in concept. Moreover, BAT standards are subject to "capture" by polluters who can, and do, influence the nature of the standard and, frequently, the rigour with which it is enforced;

vi) MBIs economise on information gathering costs. With CAC approaches, the authorities have to find out about individual polluters' control costs, which means acquiring information from the polluters. Under the MBI approach the authorities do not have to acquire this information.

If MBIs are so attractive, why have they not been used more widely? An OECD survey of the economic instruments in place found that few if any of the charging and taxing procedures used reflected the economic approach[6]. Rather, they were designed to "recycle" monies back to polluters to encourage the adoption of abatement technology, cover administrative charges, and so on. The essence of the economic approach is that charges must be related, however loosely, to damage done, or to emission levels if the objective is the efficient achievement of a standard.

Past hostility to MBIs has various explanations. The whole history of environmental regulation derives from public health legislation in which standard-setting to protect human health is the dominant paradigm. Any departure from long-entrenched traditions is difficult. Industry itself has tended to favour standard setting for two reasons: (a) "legislative capture" as described earlier, and (b) certainty. Indeed, business is often happier with a stricter regulation of which they are certain than a less strict regulation about which they feel uncertain. This risk aversion derives from many different concerns but they include the fear that a tax measure might be "misused" to become something more than an incentive tax and akin to a pure revenue-raising tax. This puts industry further at the mercy of the vagaries of the trade cycle as government fiscal policy adapts (if, indeed, fiscal policy is used for this purpose). Politicians are suspicious of MBIs partly because they are not always easy to understand -- witness the public discussion of environmental taxes but the almost complete absence of public discussion of tradeable permits. Other doubts, often deeply ingrained, relate to the effect of taxes on prices and international competitiveness[7].

In the context of developing countries, and in light of OECD experience, the issue that arises is: what scope, if any, is there for the introduction of environmental taxes and tradeable permits?

To gain some insight into the answer we first outline new policy measures in the OECD, then look at the problem of resource degradation in the developing world and then at the possible role of MBIs in the developing country environmental policy.

3. *Recent OECD Country Initiatives with Market-based Instruments*

The OECD Environment Directorate reviewed experience with the use of economic instruments up to 1988[8]. But the policy change since 1988 has been very rapid indeed. Accordingly, there is a need to gain some evidence of events since 1988. What follows is a country-by-country review of that experience[9]. For readers concerned to use the following descriptions for reference only, the following broad implications of changing policy can be inferred from the case studies:

i) There has been a distinct shift in political thinking on the appropriate way to pursue environmental policy. This shift is towards the "economic" approach, based on the use of economic instruments, and offsets, to some extent, the traditional reliance on "command and control" approaches;

ii) As far as economic instruments relating to *pollution* are concerned, there is a preference for the use of environmental taxes and user charges. As yet, the United States' experience with tradeable emission permits has not been imitated in the rest of OECD, Nonetheless, some countries have intimated that tradeable emission permits are being studied seriously (e.g. the United Kingdom for some air pollution problems);

iii) Tradeable resource-use permits are in place in several countries for *fisheries*. The evidence is not reviewed here, but tradeable permits appear highly suited for the solution to overfishing problems (the New Zealand experience has been well studied);

iv) Policy-makers' concerns with economic instruments are focused on their impact on prices and hence on the social incidence, inflation and competitiveness effects. There is limited appreciation at the political level of the fact that taxes can be used in a fiscally-neutral way to dampen these impacts, and that, in any event, *any* regulation imposes costs on polluters, part of which will be passed on to consumers;

v) OECD's own advocacy of economic instruments has borne fruit. In December 1990 the European Commission announced its own guidelines for EC members on the use of economic instruments;

vi) While not surveyed here, there is serious consideration of the use of carbon taxes and internationally tradeable permits for the achievement of global CO_2 reduction targets under a convention on climate change which, it is hoped, will be drawn up for 1992.

In what follows, the information is thought to be correct at the time of writing -- December 1990.

3.1 Austria

Under the provisions of the Contaminated Sites Clean-up Act (July 1989) two different charges are intended to finance the clean-up of contaminated sites. Their respective rates are:

-- $15 (about 200 shillings) per ton of hazardous waste;
-- $ 3 (about 40 shillings) per ton of household waste.

These rates are thought by many to be too low and a five-fold increase has been under consideration.

A deposit on beverage containers, other packaging and batteries was scheduled for approval by Parliament on 1st January 1990 (Ordinances to the Waste Management Act) but it has been dropped. Ordinances are not now planned until 1991. Meanwhile the Federal Government has invited industries to undertake measures to reduce the volume of packaging.

A water pollution charge is presently under discussion.

A proposal for a primary energy tax is under discussion within the framework of the second tax reform programme of the Coalition Cabinet.

Environmental taxes exist on fertilizers and pesticides. Despite a low charge rate and an expected low price elasticity, the reduction in use was about 10 per cent in the 1st year (1986-87) and another 20 per cent in the 2nd year (1987-88) of implementation. Income raised per year was about 1 billion shillings ($75 million).

Austria has a differential tax rate on leaded/unleaded petrol.

3.2 Belgium

Within the framework of the "MINA" plan, the Flemish Regional Government has carried out a study which will assist calculation of the means of achieving an "ecological quality" of surface water before 1995. Charges on individuals and firms for water use are expected to be increased significantly. BF 200 billion are to be raised by 1995. The Vallon Region and Brussels are both considering economic instruments in preparing similar plans.

Belgium also has differential taxation of vehicles according to their environmental impacts.

3.3 Canada

Economic instruments are under examination as part of the Canadian Environment Action Plan. Canada is expected to launch a national energy policy plan in 1990 that will attempt specific target reductions for CO_2 reductions. A 20 per cent cut on 1988/1990 $C0_2$ emission levels is being considered and a carbon tax is being discussed as the means of achieving the reduction.

3.4 Denmark

Denmark already has a set of environmental taxes. In 1990 these have been the subject of a review as follows:

Taxes on	Charges:
-- CFCs	30 Krone per kg (unchanged)
-- beverage containers (refundable)	0.5 to 2.25 Krone (unchanged)
-- solid waste	125 Krone per ton (proposed tripling)
-- disposal of waste table-wares	33 per cent of retail price (unchanged)
-- pesticides in small containers	20 per cent of price to producer/importer
-- raw materials	5 Krone per m3 (previously 0.5 Krone)
-- tax reduction on unleaded petrol	0.5 Krone
-- tax increases on petrol	

These charge rates are due to be introduced in 1991. New charges are being considered as follows:

-- deposit-refund on cadmium and mercury batteries 10 to 50 Krone.

Denmark also subsidises waste reduction investments by industry and offers once-off subsidies for converting agricultural land to organic farming[10].

3.5 Ireland

Dublin has a severe smog problem, with 80 per cent of smoke emissions arising from the burning of bituminous coal by domestic households. Major reductions are required to honour EC air quality directives on smoke by 1993. Smoke control zones have been designated but progress has been slow due to the limited availability of Exchequer grants for conversion to smokeless fuels.

In 1989 the junior minister for the environment openly contemplated a bituminous coal tax. Such a tax had been proposed in 1988 by the Bord Gais (Irish Gas Board). The aim was to tax coal suppliers at some £11-13.50 per tonne on imported coal for domestic use, to yield some £8-10 million per annum in revenues. The revenues would be used for convert households to use smokeless fuel and to subsidise the smokeless fuel itself. The proposal included a price constraint to prevent the tax being passed on to coal consuming households who, typically, are in the lower income groups. The proposal did not find political acceptance. In October 1990 the sale of soft coal in Dublin is being banned.

3.6 Finland

The Ad Hoc Committee on Environmental Economics presented its report in May 1989. It contains about 40 proposals for the application of economic instruments for environmental protection. The Committee anticipates both the Environment and Finance Ministry starting a study on the feasibility of a tax on carbon emissions proportionate to the relative carbon content of fuels. The State Budget Proposal for 1990 included several environmental tax measures:

1) A tax on phosphate fertilizers effective from June 1990, but with offsets for farmers through the farm price setting mechanism so that farm incomes do not decline;

2) A carbon tax of $6.1 per tonne (FIM 24.5) CO_2 for natural gas, coal, fuel oil and peat. The CO_2-tax is intended to bring about the amendment of the existing Fuels Tax Law. In 1986 tax on fuels other than gasoline and diesel was abolished. In 1990 an excise tax was reintroduced on the most important fossil fuels and the tax on vehicle fuels was increased;

3) Abolition of the 17 per cent general sales tax for industrial investments that are environmentally friendly.

The overall tax changes are broadly neutral: the extra 1 per cent of revenue is offset by the reduced sales tax and much of the remainder is earmarked for environmental protection. Further tax measures may be considered in 1992[11].

Also under discussion are the possible use of effluent charges and the question of the "earmarking" of charges and taxes.

Other taxes proposed by the Committee concern fertilizers, noise and hazardous chemicals. The Committee also calls for a more extended use of deposit-refund schemes for all types of bottles, cadmium and mercury batteries, car batteries, hulks and tyres.

3.7 France

The *Plan Vert* [12], published in June 1990, espouses economic instruments as a means of providing incentives for pollution control and to raise revenues to meet anticipated increases in public environmental expenditures of some $5-6 billion by 1995. The main proposals are:

-- Water charges administered by the Agences de Bassin would be raised by 100 per cent and the charging system would be extended to other sectors, including agriculture;

-- Taxes on sulphur oxides, nitrogen oxides, hydrocarbons and solvents;

-- A charge on waste disposal sites, the revenues being earmarked for waste reduction measures;

-- Unspecified products charges to finance waste reduction schemes and recycling schemes;

-- Replacement of existing noise taxes by airport landing charges, the revenues being used to finance noise insulation.

The *Plan Vert* also embraces environmental tax harmonization within the European Community.

3.8 Germany

The four major political parties in Germany all have proposals for the use of economic incentives for environmental control. Table 1 summarises the proposals as far as they are known.

Current government proposals include a new scheme for car taxation which is expected to come into force in 1993 whereby vehicle taxes will be based on environmental indicators, especially noise and CO_2 emissions. A carbon tax designed to achieve 20 per cent CO_2 emission reductions on 1990 levels by 2005. Cars fitted with three-way catalysts are already exempt from tax until 1992, and gasoline prices have been raised for environmental reasons. Reverse vending machines exist for re-usable glass bottles. A draft regulation of August 1990 proposes a deposit of 0.5 DM per beverage package (bottles, cartons, cans etc) that cannot be refilled. All refillable beverage packaging would, however, be subject to a mandatory return system. There is a waste oil tax, the revenues from which are used to help finance re-refining.

3.9 Italy

Italy has proposed a set of "ecological taxes". They were approved in principle by the Italian Cabinet in October 1989 as part of the 1990 budgetary proposals. They have been opposed by the Ministries of Industry and Agriculture. The exact proposals are unclear in some cases. They are:

a) An SO_2 tax of 50 000-150 000 lire ($50-150) per tonne emitted;

b) A particulate matter tax of 100 000-500 000 lire ($100-500) per tonne emitted;

c) A "plastics" tax on plastics products equal to 5 per cent of the sales price;

d) A herbicides tax of 30 per cent of the sale price;

e) A livestock tax on pigs, of 10 000 lire ($5-10) per pig on farms with over 200 pigs and without waste treatment plants;

f) Increases in airport landing charges of 6-30 per cent to reflect noise nuisance from take-off and landing. 40 per cent of the proceeds will be used for noise amelioration and airport safety measures. This proposal is already law;

g) A tax on industrial non-biodegradable waste, the proceeds of which will go to municipalities for treating the waste;

h) Charges for water withdrawal will be increased, and charges on municipal and industrial effluent disposal will be used to treat waste;

i) A tax on plastic bags has already gone into effect (May 1989). A 100 lire charge has been levied, making 50 lire bags retail at 150 lire. The effect has been dramatic. Plastic bag purchases have fallen by 40 per cent and paper bag sales have increased but by a smaller amount. The difference is made up of plastic bag re-use by shoppers.

Table 1

ENVIRONMENTAL TAX PROPOSALS IN GERMANY
(DM million as tax yield)

		Proposals			
	Existing taxes	SPD	CDU	FDP	GREENS
Waste oil tax	13	-	-	-	-
Effluent tax	495	+350	-	-	4 500[1]
Nature protection	2[2]	-	X	-	-
Water rate	170[3]	-			
Contaminated sites	50[4]				
Petroleum products tax	X	31 600[5]		X[6]	25 000[8]
Natural gas tax	-				
Air pollution tax	-	X			3 000
Deposit-refund systems:					
Plastic bottles (50pf)	X				
Glass bottles (50pf)	-	4 000			
Aluminium cans (20pf)	-				
Block packs	-				
Tax on cattle stocks	-	X			
Car exhaust taxes	-	X		X[7]	
CO_2 tax	-	X		-	-
Packaging tax	-	-		-	3 000
Chemicals tax	-				4 000[9]
Heavy vehicles tax	-				4 000

Notes to Table 1

1. Includes a charge for groundwater use
2. Baden-Wurtemberg
3. Baden-Wurtemberg
4. Licence charge for rehabilitation in N. Rhine-Westphalia
5. Offset by reductions in other taxes
6. A tax on energy in general and applied Europe-wide
7. Europe-wide
8. On gasoline, 50pf/litre
9. Includes SO_X tax.

3.10 The Netherlands

In 1989, the Dutch Government produced its National Environmental Policy Plan (NEPP), which is a strategic plan directed at the long term implementation of "sustainable development": 1990-2010[13]. Although the NEPP notes that there are a very broad set of instruments available to the government -- legislation and regulations, fiscal measures (charges and taxes), setting environmental standards for products and influencing the development of technology -- the use of MBIs is likely to be fairly limited. The NEPP was modified in April 1990 with the "NEPP+".

Three scenarios have been analysed to provide insight into the costs of environmental policy (see Table 2). Current environmental policy is continued in Scenario I. The real annual costs in this Scenario increase from Dfl. 8.3 billion in 1985 to Dfl. 16 billion in 2010 -- about 2 per cent of GNP. Scenario II is based on the maximum introduction of emission-orientated measures, incurring annual costs of Dfl. 26.3 billion in 2010, and amounting to about 3 per cent of GNP. Scenario III reflects an environmental policy that goes beyond emission-orientated measures to fundamental structural economic changes. By 2010 this would involve annual gross costs of Dfl. 55.8 billion, but because of savings on energy and raw materials, *net* costs would be Dfl. 36.8 billion annually, or 4 per cent of GNP.

The NEPP calls for "the use of financial instruments with a regulatory character". Implementation will be largely through the improvement of existing regulatory instruments, primarily through the further integration of legislation in the existing General Environmental Provision Act (GEPA). The type of complementary financial instruments under consideration include:

-- An increase in the excise tax on diesel oil;

-- The termination of the standard tax deduction for commuting costs;

-- Financial compensation for the use of public transport in commuting;

-- A levy on farm animal waste;

-- A pesticides levy.

In November 1989, a tax on carbon dioxide emissions was formally proposed by the Dutch Cabinet. Although details of the rate and distribution of taxation are still being formulated, the tax is aimed at achieving a carbon dioxide reduction target of 2 per cent per year. The tax is estimated to raise Dfl. 150 million ($75 million) per year. NEPP's CO_2 reduction target (stabilisation at 1990 levels by 2000) was tightened by NEPP+ to be stabilisation by 1995 and reductions thereafter.

The NEPP also considers road pricing as a means of reducing congestion, noise and vehicle pollution. Tax rebates for the adoption of three-way catalytic converters and tax increases on gasoline have already been implemented. A deposit-refund system for plastic beverage containers has been contemplated.

Table 2

EFFECT OF NEPP SCENARIOS ON EMISSIONS IN 2010
(Percentage change in 1985 emissions)

	Scenario I	Scenario II	Scenario III
CO_2	+35	+35	-20 to -30
SO_2	-50	-75	-80 to -90
NO_X	-10	-60	-70 to -80
NH_3	-33	-70	-80
Hydrocarbons	-20	-50	-70 to -80
CFCs	-100	-100	-100
Discharges (Rhine & N. Sea)	-50	-75	-75
Waste dumping	0	-50	-70 to -80
Noise[a]	+50	0	-15
Odour[a]	+10	-50	-60

a. For noise and odour the changes refer to percentage of people experiencing nuisance.

Source: NEPP, Table 5.1.1.

3.11 Norway

The Norwegian Parliament has indicated the desirability of a more stringent use of economic instruments for environmental protection. Recent developments in environmental charges are listed below, but it is unclear how far the recent change of government affects these proposals[14]:

1. A carbon tax of 30 ore/litre oil has been discussed. The basic tax rate on oil would also be raised by 1 ore/litre and a sulphur-graded surtax of 2 o/l would be added, making the total additional tax 33 o/l. Heavier oils would rise by 39-49 o/l. The overall effect would be an 85 per cent increase in taxes and a 15 per cent increase in real prices of oil.

2. A carbon tax of 60 o/l has been suggested for gasoline, along with a 10 o/l increase in the leaded/unleaded differential. The overall effect would be a 65 o/l tax increase for unleaded gasoline and 75 o/l for leaded. This amounts to a nominal tax increase of 25 per cent for both types of gasoline and real price rises of about 11 per cent.

3. A deposit-refund scheme for used oil and batteries commenced in 1990.

4. Vehicles:

a. The tax structure will be modified to promote lighter and fuel-efficient cars;

b. The Minister of Finance has signalled a tax on diesel consumption;

c. Implementation of toll stations on roads surrounding Oslo.

5. A tax on CFCs was scheduled for 1990, but industry succeeded in making voluntary changes which led to the tax being shelved until July 1991 when it might be introduced at the rate of 40 krone per kg of CFCs. If industry demonstrates successful reductions in the consumption of CFCs and halons, the tax would again be postponed.

6. Taxes on the nitrogen and phosphorus content of fertilizers already exist and will be doubled in 1991. The resulting revenues will be used for environmentally friendly measures in agriculture.

7. The tax on pesticides will also be increased in 1991 and revenues will be used for agricultural measures.

8. Noise taxes will be introduced at Fornebu and Bodo airports.

3.12 Sweden

Sweden has a Commission on Economic Instruments in Environmental Policy (The Environmental Charge Commission). It has produced two reports:

a) Interim Report SOU 1989:21 which proposed a *sulphur tax* on oil and a tax on *chlororganic discharges* to water;

b) Interim Report SOU 1989:83 which has proposed *energy* and *transport taxes*.

<u>Fuel Taxes</u>

The *sulphur tax* is 30 SKr (£3) per kilo of sulphur emitted for *oil* (the first sulphur tax proposal) and the same for *coal*.

The *NO_X tax* is 40 SKr (£4) per kilo and is applicable to 150-200 large combustion plants. The charge is recyclable, i.e. it would be revenue from the NO_X returned to the same plants in proportion to energy output. The extent to which this reduces the incentive effect is unclear.

The *CO_2 tax* would be 0.25 SKr per kilo of CO_2 and would be levied on oil, coal, natural gas and LPG. *Existing* energy taxes would be reduced by 50 per cent. Energy-intensive industries and electricity production would secure some allowance against the CO_2 charge until such time as there is an international agreement on greenhouse gases.

Fuel Subsidies

Environmentally "friendly" electricity production would be promoted by:

a) A specific subsidy of 4 öre per kwh to CHP (combined heat and power) plant;

b) A subsidy of 10 öre per kwh to any plant not producing net additions to CO_2 concentrations. The total subsidy to CHP would thus be 14 öre;

c) A subsidy of 14 öre per kwh to other "friendly" technologies such as wind power and solar power.

d) Hydropower and nuclear power do *not* attract the subsidies.

Transport Taxes

All new vehicles should be classified as:

a) Category 1: severe restrictions on exhaust gases;

b) Category 2: light vehicles -- restrictions equivalent to Californian regulations; heavy vehicles -- restrictions equivalent to 1991 US new vehicle standards;

c) Category 3: minimum restrictions.

Category 1 would attract a *subsidy*. Category 3 would attract a *tax* which would be added to the existing sales tax. Category 2 would be treated as neutral with respect to tax/subsidy. *Tax revenues* on 3 would be used to finance the Category 1 subsidy. The system would commence 1992/3.

Catalytic Converters

The existing grant for conversion of cars made 1985+ would be raised to 4000 SKr (£400) for 1991 and 1992.

Carbon Tax on Motor Fuels

A tax of 25 öre (2.5 pence) per kilo of CO_2 would be imposed on gasoline. The existing energy tax would be lowered. Taxes on diesel should be differentiated according to quality.

Leaded/Unleaded Gasoline

The tax differential will be widened to favour unleaded gasoline more (see Table 3).

Carbon Tax on Air Travel

A 25 öre tax (2.5 pence) per kilo of CO_2 should be imposed on domestic air travel.

Company Cars

The assessment of income tax benefit from using company cars should be raised to 35 per cent of the price of the car if it is less than three years old i.e. 35 per cent of the price is treated as income for tax purposes.

Diesel Mileage Tax

The existing NO_X tax on diesel-powered vehicles should be raised from 15 SKr per kilo of NO_X to 25 SKr (£2.50) per kilo.

Table 3 summarises the proposed energy taxes.

Table 3

SWEDISH POLLUTION CHARGE PROPOSALS
(Swedish Crowns [SKr])

	Existing tax	New tax structure				
		Tax	CO_2	SO_X (approx)	VAT (approx)	Total
Fuel oil						
No. 2 per m^3	1 078	540	720	30	700	1 990
No. 5 per m^3	1 078	540	720	210	-	1 470
Coal (per ton)	460	230	620	225	-	1 075
Natural gas (per 1 000m^3)	350	175	535	-	-	710
LPG (per ton)	210	105	750	-	-	855
Petrol (per litre)						
Unleaded	2.64	2.40	0.58		1.17	4.15
Leaded	2.84	2.64	0.58		1.18	4.40

Environmental Impacts of the Tax Reforms: Sweden

The following impacts are predicted by end 1990s:

SO_X reduction p.a.15 000 tonnes
NO_X reduction p.a.25 000 tonnes
CO_2 reduction p.a.5-10 million tonnes

Greater reductions still would ensue if investment in public transport was improved.

Cost Impacts and Fiscal Offsets: Sweden

Industrial costs are expected to rise by SKr 1 billion (£100 million) because of the changes, with only marginal effects on costs generally.

Household costs are anticipated to rise by SKr 100-200 per month (£10-20 per month). Average cost of running a car will rise by SKr 100-150 per month (£10-15 per month). Sweden is planning major tax reforms and the environmental taxes will be offset by reductions in other taxes especially the planned income tax reduction. The CO_2 tax is seen as a "permanent" tax due to the absence of abatement technology. The SO_x and chlorine taxes will be temporary revenue-raisers since abatement and substitution will reduce their use.

Government Revenue Impacts: Sweden

Table 4 summarises the revenue impacts:

Table 4

PROJECTED ENVIRONMENTAL TAX REVENUES: SWEDEN (billion SKr)

	As at July 1989	As proposed by Charges Commission
Non-petrol fuels:		
Energy tax + CO_2	9.5	12.0
VAT	-	3.5
SO_x in coal	-	0.4
Electricity:		
Energy tax	9.2	6.9
VAT	-	3.6
Petrol:		
Petrol tax + CO_2	14.8	16.8
VAT	-	6.9
Grants to electricity	-	-0.5
Transport		
Vehicle tax	2.5	2.5
Company car tax	-	1.3
Kilometre tax	3.2	3.5
Environmental categories	-	0
Catalytic converters	0	-0.5
Air traffic tax	0.1	0.4
Total	39.3	56.8

3.13 United Kingdom

The use of environmental charges, pollution taxes and tradeable permits was recommended in a report commissioned by the Department of the Environment in Summer 1989[15]. In September 1990 the UK Government published a White Paper on environmental policy[16]. The policy statement gave some limited approval of MBIs. contemplating the use of a deposit-refund scheme for used tyres, and requesting the beverage containers industry to produce a workable voluntary scheme to encourage recycling. The document anticipates possible future use of effluent discharge charges through the National Rivers Authority; possible allowance of tradeable permits in some areas of air pollution control; and it contemplates eventually raising the relative price of energy (through taxes or tradeable permits, though this is not explicitly stated) if a conditional target of stabilising CO_2 emissions at 1990 levels by 2005 is not achieved by other means.

Other political parties in the UK are also known to favour MBIs. One party, the Liberal Democrats, produced a manifesto for environmental policy which includes a "pollution added tax" on all polluting products -- levied either directly as an environmental tax or through changes in VAT and excise taxes, subsidies to measures which reduce pollution, a 15 per cent VAT tax on electricity and gas, abolition of the flat-rate vehicle excise duty and its replacement with a graduated tax according to engine size or with a higher petrol tax, phasing out of company car allowances, and road pricing for congested areas[17]. Similar measures are proposed by the Labour Party, but a carbon tax is rejected on the grounds of its social incidence and its effect on the coal industry (union membership of which is traditionally allied to the Labour Party).

3.14 United States

Legislation for re-authorising and amending the Clean Air Act is likely to focus on three areas:

i) Acid rain legislation that requires polluting electric utilities to fund the purchase of technology that will result in a 10-million-tonne per year cut in SO_2 emissions by the year 2000. The basic recommendation is the establishment of an "emissions compliance fund" based on "user fees" charged on SO_2 emissions, with electric utilities and industrial boiler owners contributing to a fund at a level based on their SO_2 emissions. Tradeable pollution permits may be another approach taken for control of CO_2 emissions.

ii) The role of "clean-fuelled" vehicles running on low-polluting "alternative fuels" that are intended to cut motor vehicle emissions (especially ozone precursors) versus stricter tail-pipe emissions standards. The Bush Administration would like to see the production of 1 million clean-fuel automobiles beginning in the late 1990s, although there is likely to be insufficient support for this in Congress. The most promising legislation on reducing greenhouse gases would be to raise fuel efficiency standards for automobiles (currently 27.5 miles per US gallon on average) to 34 mpg by 1995 and 45 mpg by 2000, and for light trucks to 25.5 mpg by 1995 and 34 mpg by 2000. This would save 15 million gallons of fuel by 1995, while new cars after 1995 would reduce CO_2 emissions by 150 million tonnes.

iii) Control of the more than 100 toxic industrial air pollutants. The US Environmental Protection Agency (EPA) is expecting tougher amendments reinforcing existing Clean Air Act regulations on toxic air pollutants. The EPA's Office of Toxic Substances (OTS) is planning on using regulations under the Clean Air Act and the Toxic Substances Control Act to force the pace and comprehensiveness of voluntary testing by industry of chlorofluorocarbon (CFC) substitutes.

MBIs appear to have only a limited role in the debates over the re-authorisation of the Clean Air Act and other legislation. 1988 amendments to the Federal Insecticide, Fungicide and Rodenticide Act (FIFRA) require manufacturers of the 600 pesticide active ingredients will have to re-register their products and pay maintenance fees. The fee was $425 per product in 1989, but is expected to go up substantially in 1990 as many products were cancelled and fees not paid. The FIFRA amendment allows EPA to increase the fee to whatever amount is necessary to collect total revenue amounting to $15 million. One of the proposed amendments of the 15-year-old Hazardous Materials Transportation Act proposes that emergency response training for hazardous waste spills and clean-ups be funded from a trust fund financed from the federal motor fuel tax.

The predominantly regulatory approach of most US legislation contrasts sharply with the emphasis on MBIs placed by most recent influential US studies -- including those conducted by the EPA. For example, virtually all of the recommendations of Project 88, *Harnessing Market Forces to Protect Our Environment -- Initiatives for the New President* on the use of MBIs have not been pursued in Congress. Similarly, an EPA study indicated that a market-based approach to acid rain reduction could save companies $3 billion per year when compared to the cost of the standard "dictated technological solution" of most current legislative proposals. In addition there is the EPA's Emissions Trading Program and state-level experiments in the use of tradeable permits in pollution control to draw upon.

The Bush Administration's proposed national energy strategy is not expected to offer any startling initiatives, particularly with regard to MBIs for the environment. The objective is to ensure adequate energy supplies at "reasonable prices", protect US energy security (in the wake of increasing reliance on imported petroleum) and restore the nation's confidence in energy production, including nuclear power. It is anticipated that any change in energy pricing or tax policies, e.g. such as the use of a "carbon tax", will await the outcome of the recommendations of the Intergovernmental Panel on Climatic Change (IPCC).

The 1990 Farm Bill is also not anticipated to make any significant changes in legislation of the 1985 Farm Bill. But areas of debate that have environmental consequences include:

-- Reducing target prices for commodities to shift production toward economic incentives, freeing farmers to respond to market forces rather than growing crops most heavily supported by the US Department of Agriculture's commodity programmes.

-- Revisions to the Conservation Reserve Program (CRP), which was designed to take erodible cropland out of production by paying farmers to plant the land with grasses and trees for ten years. The target set in 1985 was to have 40-45 million acres enroled in CRP by 1990, but so far only 33.9 million acres have been enroled.

-- Reducing contamination of groundwater quality and farmers' use of pesticides by encouraging low-input farming that uses fewer agro-chemicals and possibly fertilizers. Any changes will most likely occur through changes in regulations.

-- Reappraisal of federally supported farm loans and emergency drought relief.

4. Other International Action on Economic Instruments

The extensive list of initiatives in Section 3 indicates clearly that, even if economic instruments are being introduced hesitantly in many cases, the climate of policy opinion has changed dramatically in the last few years. Moreover, a country-by-country analysis still does not portray the full extent of the measures under consideration. At least two other levels of activity deserve to be mentioned.

4.1 The European Community

The European Commission has shown a renewed interest in economic instruments. At a meeting of Ministers of Environment in April 1990 it was concluded that:

> "Ministers acknowledged the value of supplementing existing regulatory instruments ... by the use of economic and fiscal instruments".

At the wider ECE level, the Bergen Conference of May 1990 also agreed:

> "in support of sustainable development ... to make more extensive use of economic instruments in conjunction with ... regulatory approaches".

The European Council of June 1990 also declared that:

> "the traditional 'command and control' approaches should now be supplemented, where appropriate, by economic and fiscal measures if environmental considerations are to be fully integrated into other policy areas, if pollution is to be prevented at source, and if the polluter is to pay".

Under the Italian Presidency of the EC in particular (July-December 1990) efforts are being made to persuade member countries to adopt environmental taxes, deposit-refund systems and, to a lesser extent, tradeable permits. The impetus to the initiative has been accelerated because of fiscal harmonization in 1992. How far harmonization of environmental taxes is economically efficient is, as noted above, open to question. But the EC efforts can only serve to increase the pressure on individual countries to consider MBIs as part of their environmental policy[18]. The EC issued guidelines on the use of economic instruments in December 1990 (not issued at the time of writing).

4.2 The OECD

Since the inception of the OECD Environment Directorate in 1971, OECD has long argued for the use of economic instruments. By and large, its guidance to member governments has been unchanging and may be summarised as one of recommending a judicious mix of regulation and incentive systems. In 1989 a new impetus was given to prepare a set of "guidelines" for the application of economic instruments in environmental policy. Currently, the nature of the guidelines is not public but it is known that they are comprehensive and extend beyond the design of instruments in general to ways in which they might be applied to critical economic sectors such as energy, transport, agriculture and industry. They also consider the use of taxes and tradeable permits at the international level for the control of global warming and CFC release.

What is the relevance of the OECD, EC and individual country initiatives for the developing world? To answer this question we need first to establish that *environment matters* in the developing world.

5. The Costs of Natural Resource Degradation in the Developing World

One of the most important tasks faced by environmental economists in the developing world is to *demonstrate* that environment matters in economic planning. The World Bank has perhaps been the leader in this activity and has sponsored a number of attempts to estimate the costs of soil erosion, deforestation, industrial pollution and so on. In the first instance, what is relevant here is not the costs of controlling these "externalities" -- although clearly that is of critical importance -- but the *economic damage* done by resource degradation and pollution. Major efforts exist in the developed world to calculate such damages, usually for specific instances -- e.g. loss of scenic view, health impairment from air pollution, crop losses etc. -- and less frequently at the national level[19]. The estimates are subject to wide margins of error but "ballpark" figures suggest that pollution damage alone is causing damage equal to around 1 per cent of GNP in the Netherlands and as much as 5 per cent of GNP in Germany. An alternative approach, looking at the benefits of environmental policy, suggests that the United States gained 1.25 per cent of GNP (in terms of measured and unmeasured GNP) from environmental policy controls up to 1978[20].

Efforts to calculate damage costs in the developing world are far more recent. Table 5 brings together some estimates for the developing world and compares them to figures for the developed world. Compared to the developed world, the expectation would be that damage in the developing world would be higher given the absence of environmental protection legislation and institutions. The estimates that exist tend to bear this out. Soil erosion in Indonesia and Mali may cost some 0.4 per cent of GNP. Deforestation in Ethiopia would appear to cause at least 6 per cent GNP losses, while, on a different basis, the cost is 3.6 per cent of GNP in Indonesia. Pollution damage in Poland runs at least 5 per cent of GNP and may be very much higher. Finally, total biomass loss imposes a cost of the Burkina-Faso economy of just under 9 per cent of GNP. Estimates for other countries, not reported here, tend to support the notion that environmental damage costs developing countries some 5 per cent of their GNP. Moreover, this cost is in the form of lost productive potential, i.e. there are real resource flows associated with these losses. In the developed economy cases, probably the major part of the loss shows up in "non-GNP" flows, i.e. changes in human welfare that are not captured by the conventional methods of national accounting. In itself this is telling of the need to adjust the national accounts.

Even if the data are subject to significant degrees of uncertainty -- as seems likely -- they underline a point of major significance: environmental deterioration does damage the economies of both the rich and poor world, and it imposes large costs in particular on the developing world's development capability.

Table 5

SUMMARY OF THE SOCIAL COSTS OF RESOURCE DEGRADATION IN THE DEVELOPED AND DEVELOPING WORLD

Country	Nature of damage	Year	% of GNP
Netherlands	Some pollution damage	1986	0.5-0.8
Germany	Most pollution damage	1983/5	4.6-4.9
United States	*Avoided* damage due to environmental legislation	1978	1.2
Mali	Soil erosion	1988	0.4
Burkina-Faso	Biomass loss	1988	8.8
Ethiopia	Deforestation	1983	6.0-9.0
Indonesia	Deforestation	1984	3.6
Indonesia	Soil erosion	1984	0.4
Poland	Pollution damage	1987	4.4-7.7

Source: D.W.Pearce and J.Warford, *Environment and Development: Managing Natural Resources in the Developing World*, forthcoming, 1991, Chapter 2.

6. *Incentives for Sustainable Development*

The extent to which MBIs can be used in the developing world is the subject of an emerging debate[21]. This section offers a very brief overview of the kinds of disincentives to sustainable resource management that prevail in the developing world. It is against this background that we can judge the extent to which MBIs will correct the distortions that generate environmental degradation.

The clue to achieving sustainable development lies in *incentives* and *information*. Two sets of incentives and information systems are critically important:

-- Those which reduce *uncertainty* about the future, and

-- Those which send out the correct *price and quantity signals* in the market place.

Two further information systems are important:

-- Modifying the presentation of *environmental and economic statistics* so that environmental impacts of economic change can be discerned, and the "services" of the environment highlighted;

-- Revising systems of *appraisal* for investments and policies so that they adequately reflect and integrate environmental impacts.

6.1 Incentive Systems to Reduce Uncertainty

Most economic decisions are made in the context of uncertainty. Yet uncertainty can be both beneficial and adverse for environmental quality. By choosing crops, crop mixes or rotations that minimise the risk of failure in the event of drought, for example, the farmer is likely to adopt weather- and pest-resistant strains. Many problems with agricultural output arise from choosing the wrong technology or output mix in the face of uncertainty, often because of false beliefs about the potential to correct problems once they have occurred, or because the future is "discounted" heavily. The technology and production choice can be seen as one of trading-off *productivity, stability, equitability* and *sustainability*[22]. Highly productive systems may not be sustainable -- as with the Mayan tropical forest agriculture systems in Central America. Equitable and sustainable systems may not be as productive -- as with the Manorial system of agriculture in medieval Europe. Modern examples include large-scale irrigation systems: high productivity appears incompatible with equitability and sustainability. Biological pest control is likely to be more sustainable but will produce more fluctuating yields (instability) and lower productivity. Uncertainty about the future tends to bias the trade-off towards productive but unsustainable systems.

Ensuring sustainability therefore requires efforts to reduce uncertainty. Some of the most important sources of uncertainty lie in "resource rights", i.e. the lack of security of tenure over land and/or the resources on the land. While the evidence is not conclusive, available studies do suggest that secure tenure over land improves long-run productivity and this shows in the capitalization of such gains in land values[23]. Granting tenure of itself may also be insufficient to improve natural resource management. The *way* in which tenure is granted also matters. Thus, in many parts of the developing world tenure is recognised *de facto*, and often *de jure*, only if land is cleared of vegetation. One study in Ecuador shows quite clearly that deforestation is related not only to population pressure but also to the desire to establish land rights through land clearance[24]. The influence of uncertainty shows up clearly in this example. Since there are uncertain rights to forested land, but certain (or near-certain) rights to cleared land, the land is cleared.

Insecurity of tenure may also account for resource destruction by major corporations and government agencies. It is well known from the theory of natural resource economics that uncertainty can accelerate the rate of depletion of an exhaustible resource[25]. An example arises in the context of the logging of tropical forests. The "stumpage value" (the value of the standing stock of timber) of tropical forests is very large. Governments, however, frequently fail to capture the rents because of policies which effectively enable the exploiter of the forest stock to secure the rent. Economics suggests that taxation policies can be designed to appropriate rents, return them to the public revenues as opposed to private logging companies, and yet not deter investment in the country in question[26]. If rents accumulate in the hands of those responsible for exploiting the resource there are two likely environmental effects. First, the concessionaire is likely to deplete the resource rapidly to capture more of the rent earlier rather than later. This tendency will be reinforced if there is uncertainty about policy towards the concession, e.g. doubts about whether it will be renegotiated. Environmental degradation will be made even worse if the concession has a time horizon less than that needed to regenerate the resource, i.e. the rotation period. No new planting is likely to occur under these conditions. Second, the existence of exploitable rents leads to "rent seeking" whereby other economic agents seek to acquire rights to the resource, again accelerating depletion[27].

6.2 Prices as Incentives

Prices are powerful incentives. If resource prices are set too low, excessive use will be made of the resource. The extreme example is zero-priced resources which have no established market -- the carbon-fixing functions of the oceans or forests, for example. But the same argument holds for other resources -- energy, irrigation water, fertilizers, and pesticides for example. If their prices are set too low they will tend to be over-used and such over-use can readily contribute to environmental degradation. To secure an efficient use of resources, outputs should be priced at their marginal social cost which comprises the marginal costs of production and the "external costs" of pollution or resource degradation caused by producing the good. If markets functioned near-perfectly there could be some assurance that prices in the market place would reflect their marginal private costs of production. But there are at least two forms of "market failure".

First, many marketed goods may have prices reflecting private costs of production, but not the social cost. The means of intervening to ensure that social prices are charged are several: regulation by standard-setting, pollution taxes and tradeable permits. Second, many goods have no markets at all and hence prices have to be established for them. Assigning property rights to the "free resource" is one way in which this can be achieved, although it may or may not be associated with full social cost pricing.

In the developing world there is ample evidence that a considerable amount of environmental degradation arises from a failure to price resources and goods at their marginal *private* cost, let alone their marginal social cost. Table 6 shows the level of pesticide subsidies in nine countries. Subsidies range from 19-90 per cent of the full cost of the pesticides, thus maintaining artificially low prices. Damage from excess use of pesticides shows up in several ways. There may, for example, be some 2 million cases of pesticide poisonings per year in the Asia and Pacific region, 40 000 of them probably giving rise to fatality[28]. Exposure is highest among men and death rates among men have risen significantly in communities where insecticides have been introduced on an intensive scale. There is also evidence of health risks from fish caught in pesticide contaminated ponds, paddies and irrigation channels. New pest biotypes have emerged in response to large applications of some pesticides, increasing crop production instability. Clearly, subsidies to pesticides are not the only factor causing excess use -- ignorance of the risks and the use of pesticides that are not permitted in the developed world also contribute. But the subsidies must play a significant role.

What is true of pesticides is also true of irrigation water, energy, fertilizers, lease values for land for mechanised agriculture and other resources[29]. Thus, irrigation charges tend to be a small proportion of the benefits of irrigation water to farmers: 8-21 per cent in Indonesia, 11-26 per cent in Mexico and only 10 per cent in the Philippines, 9 per cent in Thailand and 5 per cent in Nepal. Excess use of irrigation water contributes to waterlogging and salinisation of soils, let alone wasting the water resource itself. Pricing reform thus has a major role to play in securing sustainable development, with the first priority being to relate prices charged to costs of production (and border prices where the resource is tradeable). Later in the process of development, price will need to be related more to the full social costs of production.

But "getting prices right" is not a simple matter in terms of securing the right balance of environmental quality and shorter-term gains in output. This is readily illustrated in the context of agricultural output prices. It is tempting to think that higher farmgate prices will stimulate an aggregate supply increase, making farmers better off and thus more able to invest in longer-term investments needed for sustainability, e.g. soil conservation, tree windbreaks, water conservation, etc. There is certainly evidence to suggest that "price discrimination" against producers (i.e. keeping farmgate prices low relative to border prices) is associated with lower agricultural growth rates. One study for Africa suggested that countries with low or no discrimination had growth rates of 2.9 per cent p.a. (1970-1981); medium price discrimination was associated with growth rates of 1.8 per cent p.a., and high price discrimination produced growth rates of only 0.8 per cent p.a.[30]. Yet, the impacts of reducing discrimination are not clear. First, price changes must be perceived to be permanent for investment decisions to favour conservation practices. Second, the nature of the response will depend on security of tenure, resource rights generally, and access to credit. Third, if open access resources are available -- e.g. virgin forest land -- the supply response may consist of extensification rather than intensification, i.e. "new" lands may be cleared rather than existing lands being subject to conservation investments. Fourth, and offsetting the incentive to extensify, higher farm incomes may lower personal discount rates and improve credit "ratings", even with informal credit markets. These effects should assist conservation. Finally, while there is evidence of supply responses for single crops, price increases may often result in switches between crops rather than an overall increase in output. The nature of the crops matters from the environmental standpoint. Tree crops and perennials, for example, are more likely to be good for soil conditions, whereas many root and grain crops (peanuts, cassava, sorghum, millet) are erosive. Since there is nothing to link price increases with the ecological status of the crop, it is as likely that supply responses will bring increases in erosive crops as not.

As yet, then, the linkages between output price changes and environmental quality in the long run remain to be established. Remarkably, hardly any agricultural supply response studies mention the "sustainability" of the responses.

6.3 Fiscal Policies

Since price is instrumental in changing behaviour it follows that taxation policy will also be an important influence on behaviour which affects the environment. The scope for pollution taxes in developing countries is likely to grow in the future, although taxes in the sense of damage-related charges are still a rarity in the developed world[31]. But other taxation policies are capable of adjustment and existing policies frequently discriminate against the environment. As noted previously, governments frequently fail to capture rents from existing valuable resources such as forests. Table 7 shows data for four countries and reveals that, for the years shown, government rent capture was very low in Indonesia, Ghana and the Philippines. The scale of the rents is worth noting: in Indonesia, for example, actual rents for the four year period were $4.4 *billion*, or some $1.1 billion p.a, and of this the government took only $400 million p.a. There is scope then for the revision of existing fiscal policies even before attention is paid to the potential for introducing pollution and other resource degradation taxes. In much the same way, user charges -- e.g. for water connections -- have high potential for reducing water wastage which, in turn, has pollution impacts.

Table 6

PESTICIDE SUBSIDIES IN EIGHT COUNTRIES

Country	Subsidy as percentage of full cost	Total value of subsidy ($ million)
Senegal	89	4
Egypt	83	207
Ghana	67	20
Honduras	29	12
Colombia	44	69
Ecuador	41	14
Indonesia	82	128
China	19	285

Source: World Resources Institute, *Paying the Price: Pesticide Subsidies in Developing Countries*, Washington D.C., World Resources Institute, 1985.

Table 7

RENT CAPTURE IN TROPICAL FORESTRY

Country and period	Actual rent ($ billion)	Government rent ($ billion)	Gov't share/ Actual rent (%)
Indonesia 1979-82	4.4	1.6	37.5
Sabah 1979-82	2.0	1.7	82.5
Ghana 1971-74	0.08	0.03	38.0
Philippines 1979-82	1.0	0.14	14.0

Source: R. Repetto, "Overview", in R. Repetto and M. Gillis (eds), *Public Policies and the Misuse of Forest Resources*, Cambridge, Cambridge University Press, 1988.

6.4 Information Systems

Information is a major input to sustainable development. At the most "micro" level individual households need to be informed of the consequences of particular input and output decisions. Looked at from the outsider's standpoint there is also a need to utilise local knowledge and to observe and counteract the constraints that prevent sustainable practices from being employed. Extension systems are clearly important in both these respects. Governments also need to be informed. The most important aspect of this information need is to establish that economic policy impacts on the environment and that the environment impacts on economic welfare. Valuation studies are therefore valuable in the latter respect, and these may be sufficiently formalised as to warrant modified presentations of national accounts, as discussed previously. Showing that economic decisions impact on the environment is less easy, but analysis of incentive systems is a useful starting point. Since price policy tends to be fairly easily modified, subject to concerns about the social incidence of price changes and political implications, pricing presents itself as a high priority candidate for action on sustainable development. As noted above, resource rights and land tenure offer another vital dimension of sustainable development policy.

Other information systems deserve far more emphasis too. Geographical Information Systems (GISs) have the capability to mix satellite imagery with more standard ground-based information ("ground truthing") which can be used not just for the traditional purposes of mapping and assessing land capability, but also as a database for interpreting environmental change over time. The systematic interaction of socio-economic databases and satellite imagery is still under-developed[32].

6.5 The Lessons Learned

What can be learned from this brief overview of issues in the environment-economy connection?

First, environmental damage matters not just in the sense of "psychic" or "non-economic" welfare, but also in the sense of costs that show up as lost production possibilities. These costs can be large and examples have been given of damage costs that amount to 5 per cent and more of GNP.

Second, given the scale of environmental damage and its nature, there is sufficient evidence to support the view of advocates of sustainable development that a greater priority to environmental policy needs to be given if policies are to be sustainable.

Third, in so far as past development policy has been influenced by the theory of "optimal growth" -- and it clearly has -- there is a critical need to analyse the conditions under which optimal growth is also sustainable growth.

Fourth, since raising real incomes per capita must remain a major objective, though not the only objective, of development policy, the only way in which growth with environmental quality can be achieved is by decoupling growth from its environmental impacts. Where decoupling cannot be achieved, it is essential to understand the nature of the trade-offs between orthodox development goals and environmental deterioration. That can only be achieved through better and more sophisticated attempts to value environmental functions.

Do priority areas emerge from the analysis? Because of the paucity of studies and their uncertainty hard and fast recommendations are difficult to make. But the evidence does suggest that, for developing countries still at an early stage of development, *deforestation* is likely to be imposing heavy losses on the economy. Even for rapidly industrialising countries there is evidence that forest resources are being mismanaged and that the costs of deforestation are significant. *Soil erosion* is important but perhaps less important than might at first be thought. *Pollution impacts* are important and the experience of the Eastern Bloc and the industrialised countries shows just how important pollution is in terms of economic costs. In the developing world it is likely that *water pollution* is the biggest hazard, primarily because of its health impacts. But costing those impacts still seems very uncertain[33].

7. The Role of Economic Instruments in Developing Countries

The preceding section suggests strongly that a discussion of the role of economic instruments in environmental policy in the developing world has to be placed in context. Clearly, there is a menu of reform options and pursuing one option to the exclusion of others could well be counterproductive. As an obvious example, "getting prices right" is likely to be effective only if resource rights are also right. As far as MBIs as a sub-category of economic instruments are concerned, priority areas for action appear to lie in the following areas:

Short-term:	Private cost pricing policy. Reform of existing tax policy
Medium-long term:	Resources rights and land tenure
Long-term:	Social cost pricing

whilst a continuous theme has to be information for households, productive units and government.

On this analysis, pollution taxes, and user charges reflecting *social* costs follow on from higher priority action to get prices reflecting *private* costs. But the role of social cost pricing should not be overlooked. As previously discussed, some environmental taxes are easily implemented and can serve the dual role of externality correction and revenue raising. Certainly for cities suffering excess vehicle pollution, e.g. Mexico City, gasoline duty must be a priority focus.

What of the other MBIs? In the developed world most attention is being given to deposit-refund schemes and tradeable permits. In some developing economies deposit-refund schemes have an undoubted role to play -- witness the attitudes to litter in a number of the Caribbean islands. Deposit-refund systems do nothing for the bulk of litter (paper, household waste) but can induce environmental consciousness while at the same time reclaiming valuable bottles[34]. Tradeable permits are almost certainly more distant still for the developing world. Opinions differ as to the extent to which they function efficiently in the developed world in their two main applications -- emissions trading under the US Clean Air Acts and over-fishing in New Zealand and other countries. Pollution permit trading is perhaps yet to be validated through more experience in the developed world, and that will come. Resource permit trading on the other hand is more feasible and may have direct relevance to fisheries in some developed countries where monitoring is feasible.

Overall, then, the judgement of this paper is that MBIs have to be seen as part of a broad front in the change to a new environmental policy for the developing world. Resource rights and information systems are likely to be more important than social cost pricing. But if we construe the adoption of economic instruments to include the removal of subsidies then, provided each case is examined on its merits, full private cost recovery is a major weapon in the battle to save third world environments.

NOTES AND REFERENCES

1. Classic treatments of the economic approach, which dates mainly from Pigou in the 1920s, are W. BAUMOL and W. OATES, *The Theory of Environmental Policy*, 2nd edition, Cambridge, Cambridge University Press, 1988; A.V. KNEESE, *Economics and the Environment*, London, Penguin, 1977; and P. DASGUPTA and G. HEAL, *Economic Theory and Exhaustible Resources*, Cambridge University Press, 1979. On the history of environmental economics, see D.W. PEARCE, "Environmental Economics: A Theoretical Survey", in D. GREENAWAY, M. BLEANEY and I. STEWART, *Economics in Perspective*, London, Routledge, forthcoming. For an introductory text see D.W. PEARCE and R.K. TURNER, *Economics of Natural Resources and the Environment*, London, Harvester-Wheatsheaf, 1989.

2. This is the familiar "cost minimisation" property of environmental taxes and tradeable permits. See W. BAUMOL and W. OATES, "The Use of Standards and Prices for Protection of the Environment", *Swedish Journal of Economics*, March 1971, pp. 42-54, and Chapter 11 of BAUMOL and OATES, *op. cit.*

3. We put it no stronger than this since the incentives approach has yet to be "proved" in practice. Assertions that growth and environmental quality simply *are* compatible are dangerous. Some people have wrongly interpreted the Brundtland Commission in this way (World Commission on Environment and Development, *Our Common Future*, Oxford, Oxford University Press, 1987).

4. For accessible discussions see D.W. PEARCE, A. MARKANDYA and E. BARBIER, *Blueprint for a Green Economy*, London, Earthscan, 1989, and R. STAVINS *et al.*, *Project 88: Harnessing Market Forces to Protect Our Environment*, Washington D.C., 1988. In both cases these documents are being extended, the first as D.W. PEARCE *et al.*, *Blueprint II: Greening the World Economy*, London, Earthscan, forthcoming 1991; and R. STAVINS *et al.*, *Project 88 II*, Washington, D.C., forthcoming 1991.

5. This is the argument in D. ANDERSON, *Environmental Policy and the Public Revenue in Developing Countries*, Environment Department Working Paper No. 36, Washington, D.C., World Bank, July 1990. See also D. ANDERSON, this conference. On the distributional incidence of environmental taxation for one developed economy, the UK, see P. JOHNSON, S. McKAY and S. SMITH, *The Distributional Consequences of Environmental Taxes*, London, Institute for Fiscal Studies, Commentary No. 23, July 1990.

6. J. OPSCHOOR and H. VOS, *Economic Instruments for Environmental Protection*, Paris, OECD, 1989.

7. Precisely these fears in the European Community context have led to calls for the harmonization of new environmental taxes. But just when a tax of any kind should be harmonized and when not is far from straightforward. See H. SIEBERT, *Europe '92: Environmental Policy in an Integrated Market*, Working Paper 365, Kiel Institute of World Economics, Kiel, 1989; and E. MOHR, "EC Fiscal Harmonization, Environmental Taxes and Charges: Theory and Policy", Paper presented to the Italian Ministry of Environment Conference *Economic Instruments for Environmental Protection*, Rome, January 1990.

8. OPSCHOOR and VOS, *op. cit.*

9. The review is not comprehensive since it is based on the author's own efforts to collect data whilst travelling through a number of OECD countries. Comments and updated material would be very welcome. But, however imperfect it is, the survey shows that MBIs have been the subject of a remarkable set of policy initiatives in the last 2-3 years.

10. See A. DUBGAARD, *Danish Policy Measures to Control Agricultural Impacts on the Environment*, Institute of Agricultural Economics, Copenhagen, Report 52, 1990.

11. See, "Green Taxes: Where There's Muck There's Brass", *The Economist*, 17th March 1990.

12. See special supplement to *Environnement Actualité*, on the "Plan National pour l'Environnement", No. 122, September 1990.

13. Ministry of Housing, Physical Planning and the Environment, (The Netherlands), *National Environmental Policy Plan: To Choose or to Lose*, The Hague, The Netherlands, 1989.

14. The information here is taken from Norwegian Ministry of Finance, *The Use of Economic Instruments in Environmental Policies*, Oslo, October 1990. This is a translation of sections 6.1 and 6.2 of the Budget Proposal for 1991.

15. D.W. PEARCE, A. MARKANDYA, E. BARBIER, *Blueprint for a Green Economy*, London, Earthscan, 1989.

16. UK Government, *This Common Heritage*, London, HMSO, 1990.

17. Liberal Democratic Party, *What Price Our Planet*, London, 1990.

18. The relevant document is Commission of the European Communities, *Draft Report of the Working Group of Experts from the Member States on the Use of Economic and Fiscal Instruments in EC Environmental Policy*, DG XI/185/90, Brussels, 1990.

19. For a survey and discussion see D.W. PEARCE and A. MARKANDYA, *Environmental Policy Benefits: Monetary Valuation*, Paris, OECD, 1989.

20. PEARCE and MARKANDYA, *op. cit.*, pp. 10-12.

21. See, for example, ANDERSON, *op. cit.*; J. BERNSTEIN, *Alternative Approaches to Pollution Control and Waste Management: Regulatory and Economic Instruments*, Draft, Infrastructure and Urban Development Department, World Bank, May 1990; PEARCE and WARFORD, *op. cit.*

22. See G. CONWAY and E. BARBIER, *After the Green Revolution*, London, Earthscan, 1990 for a discussion of agricultural systems in terms of these concepts.

23. See, for example, G. FEDER, "Land Ownership Security and Farm Productivity in Rural Thailand", *Journal of Development Studies*, 1987; Y. CHALAMWONG and G. FEDER, *Land Ownership Security and Land Values in Rural Thailand*, World Bank Staff Working

Paper No. 790, 1986, Washington, D.C. The picture is less clear for Africa -- see G. FEDER and R. NORONHA, "Land Rights Systems and Agricultural Development in Sub-Saharan Africa", *World Bank Research Observer*, Vol. 2, No. 2, July 1987.

24. D. SOUTHGATE, R. SIERRA and L. BROWN, *The Causes of Tropical Deforestation in Ecuador: A Statistical Analysis*, London, London Environmental Economics Centre, Paper 89-09, 1989.

25. See, for example, P. DASGUPTA and G. HEAL, *Economic Theory and Exhaustible Resources*, Cambridge, Cambridge University Press, 1979, Chapter 13.

26. This is the theory of resource-rent taxation. See R. GARNAUT and A. CLUNIES-ROSS, "Uncertainty, Risk Aversion and the Taxing of Natural Resource Projects", *Economic Journal*, June 1975.

27. See R. REPETTO and M. GILLIS (eds), *Public Policies and the Misuse of Forest Resources*, Cambridge, Cambridge University Press, 1988.

28. See R. REPETTO, *Economic Policy Reform for Natural Resource Conservation*, Environment Department Working Paper No. 4, Washington, D.C., World Bank, May 1988.

29. For surveys see R. REPETTO, *Economic Policy Reform for Natural Resource Conservation*, Environment Department Working Paper No. 4, Washington, D.C., World Bank, May 1988; and D.W. PEARCE and J. WARFORD, *Environment and Development: Managing Natural Resources in the Developing World*, forthcoming.

30. See M. FONES-SUNDELL, *Role of Price Policy in Stimulating Agricultural Production in Africa*, Uppsala, Swedish University of Agricultural Sciences, International Rural Development Centre, Issue paper No. 2, May 1987.

31. See D. ANDERSON, *Environmental Policy and the Public Revenue in Developing Countries*, Department of Economics, University College London, April, 1990; J. BERNSTEIN, *Alternative Approaches to Pollution Control and Waste Management: Regulatory and Economic Instruments*, Infrastructure and Urban Development Department, Washington, D.C., World Bank, May 1990; D.W. PEARCE, *Public Policy and Environment in Mexico*, Latin America and Caribbean Regional Office, Washington, D.C., World Bank, May 1990.

32. For interesting experiments in this respect, looking at the interactions of poverty and environmental degradation, see V. JAGGERNATHAN, *Poverty, Public Policies and the Environment*, Environment Department Working Paper No. 24, Washington, D.C., World Bank, December 1989.

33. Some idea of the magnitude may be gauged, however. It is estimated that in 1979 something like 360-400 billion working days were lost in Africa, Asia and Latin America because of water-related diseases that prevented work. At 50 US cents per day, this means that these continents lost some US 180-200 billion in that year. GNP in 1979 for these continents was around $370 billion, so that output was below productive potential by perhaps 35 per cent [200/(200+370)]. On working days lost see J. WALSH

potential by perhaps 35 per cent [200/(200+370)]. On working days lost see J. WALSH and K. WARREN, "Selective Primary Health Care: An Interim Strategy for Disease Control in Developing Countries", *New England Journal of Medicine*, 301, 18, 1979.

34. Recycling of aluminium and steel cans is receiving increasing attention in the developed world. For many developing countries there are no plants capable of recycling the metal so that the prospect of beverage can recycling is perhaps some way into the future.

ECONOMIC INCENTIVES IN ENVIRONMENTAL MANAGEMENT AND THEIR RELEVANCE TO DEVELOPING COUNTRIES

by

Theodore Panayotou *

* Harvard Institute for International Development (HIID) and Thailand Development Research Institute (TDRI).

OUTLINE

Introduction

1. The Analytical Foundations of Economic Incentives

2. Policy Instruments for Implementing Economic Incentives
2.1 -- Natural Resource Management
2.2 -- Environmental Protection

3. Why Regulations Don't Work in Developing Countries

4. Why Regulations are Popular with Governments

5. Regulations Versus Incentives on Environmental Management: The Case of Urban Congestion and Industrial Pollution
5.1 -- A Regulatory and Pseudo-Incentive Approach
5.2 -- The Economic Incentives Approach

Case 1: Fighting Urban Congestion with Marginal Cost Pricing in Singapore

6. Economic Incentives in Natural Resource Management: Water Subsidies Versus Full-Cost Pricing

Case 2: Policy Success: Water Pricing in China

7. Economic Incentives and Agricultural Policy

Case 3: Policy Success: Removal of Pesticide Subsidies in Indonesia

Case 4: Policy Failure: Ranching for Subsidies in Brazil

8. Economic Incentives for Sustainable Forestry

Case 5: Turning a Market Failure into a Policy Success: The Dumoga-Bone Irrigation System *Cum* National Park in Indonesia

Case 6: Communal Forest Tenure in Papua New Guinea

9. Expanding the Use of Economic Incentives in Developing Countries

Case 7: Economic Incentives to Avert "Natural" Disasters: A Proposed Land Use and Slope Tax

10. A Postscript

Figures 1-4

Bibliographical References

RÉSUMÉ

Une dissociation des avantages (dont bénéficient ceux qui pèchent contre l'environnement) et des coûts (qui pèsent sur ceux contre qui l'on a péché) est l'élément que l'on trouve au coeur des situations de dégradation durable de l'environnement. Cette dissociation traduit soit une défaillance de l'action des pouvoirs publics (résultant généralement d'une intervention mal orientée qui fausse le marché), soit un dysfonctionnement du marché (reflet d'une situation particulière dans laquelle les droits de propriété ne sont pas attribués ou ne sont pas respectés). On sera souvent bien inspiré de s'occuper d'abord des défaillances de l'action des pouvoirs publics car il est parfois plus simple d'interrompre une intervention que de concevoir une mesure en partant de zéro. A cet effet, il faudra réduire ou supprimer des taxes, des aides, des quotas, etc. ; les cas décrits sont la suppression des aides relatives aux insecticides en Indonésie et des aides au pâturage maigre (*ranching*) au Brésil. L'auteur examine la rectification ou l'atténuation des dysfonctionnements du marché en prenant pour exemples la tarification routière à Singapour et l'adoption de la tarification de l'eau en Chine. Un troisième type d'activité suppose la prise en compte des effets écologiques, sociaux et autres effets secondaires des projets du secteur public, des politiques sectorielles et macro-économiques. A titre d'exemple, l'auteur cite le projet d'irrigation et de parc national de Dumoga, en Indonésie, et l'inclusion de dispositions de protection de l'environnement dans les programmes nationaux d'ajustement structurel (Maroc, Tunisie, Pakistan, Philippines, Népal et Thaïlande, par exemple).

Alors qu'une certaine tendance à utiliser davantage les instruments économiques se dessine dans les pays développés comme dans les pays en développement, le mouvement reste hésitant et nulle part encore les instruments économiques ne sont en train de se substituer à la réglementation directe. Or, en termes d'efficacité, des instruments économiques bien conçus doivent être préférés à la réglementation et, pour de nombreuses raisons, la réglementation reste généralement lettre morte dans les pays en développement. L'approche économique devrait donc être poursuivie avec beaucoup plus de détermination qu'elle ne l'est à présent.

SUMMARY

A disassociation between benefits (enjoyed by the environmental sinner) and the costs (borne by those sinned against) is the essential element in situations of sustained environmental damage. The disassociation reflects either a policy failure (typically brought about by a misguided intervention causing a market distortion) or a market failure (reflecting particular conditions where property rights are unassigned or not enforced). Dealing with policy failures first often makes sense because the removal of an intervention may be simpler than devising a measure *de novo*. This involves the reduction or elimination of taxes, subsidies, quotas, etc; the cases described are the elimination of pesticide subsidies in Indonesia and of ranching subsidies in Brazil. The correction or mitigation of market failures is discussed using as examples road pricing in Singapore and the introduction of water pricing in China. A third type of activity involves the consideration of environmental, social and other side effects of public projects, sectoral and macroeconomic polices. Examples include the Dumoga irrigation *cum* national park project in Indonesia and the inclusion of environmental provisions in national programmes of structural adjustment e.g. Morocco, Tunisia, Pakistan, Philippines, Nepal and Thailand.

While there is some tendency towards a greater use of economic instruments in developed as well as in developing countries the movement is hesitant and nowhere yet are economic instruments displacing the regulatory approach. But well designed economic instruments should be preferred on grounds of efficiency to regulations and in developing countries there are many reasons why regulations typically do not work. Thus, the economic approach should be much more aggressively pursued than hitherto.

INTRODUCTION

The controversy over economic or market-based incentives and regulatory commands and controls has a long history in areas as diverse as economic planning, international trade and environmental management. The command and control approach has dominated the scene in environmental management worldwide while a mixture of both systems prevailed in most other areas except in the command economies of Eastern Europe and Asia, and some developing countries. The economic approach to environmental management found only experimental use in OECD countries with some notable exceptions of wider use (see OECD 1989a, b).

The non-spectacular performance of the regulatory approach and the promising potential of the economic approach have encouraged many countries, including a few in the developing world, to explore more seriously the market-based incentives. The massive collapse of the command economies of Eastern Europe, which, incidentally revealed the failure of the command systems not only in economic but also in environmental management, gave added impetus to the search for workable market-based incentives. Thus, without much ado about the cost-ineffectiveness of regulatory systems, several countries have introduced economic incentives in parallel with regulations. The fact that there is no instance of economic incentives replacing regulations is indicative of how tentative and precarious the consideration of economic instruments is. Related to this tentativeness is the failure to set taxes and charges at economically meaningful levels that can actually induce a change in behaviour.

The OECD Progress Report concludes "Economic incentives have proved useful in raising revenues but in most cases have not been successful in changing behaviour or stimulating innovation". This is a disturbing finding since the *raison d'être* of economic incentives is not to raise revenues but to change behaviour, to induce polluters to minimise the costs to the environment with the same fervour they minimise the costs to themselves. The OECD report does recognise that its finding is probably due to the low level at which the charges have been set for political considerations. However, investment decisions and innovations are not based on current charges but on expectations about future charges. The initial charges must be set low to provide time for adjustment and to elicit wide acceptance by the industry but, at the same time, a predictable schedule of escalation to meaningful levels must be provided to shape expectations, influence investment decisions, and stimulate innovations. The reluctance and tentativeness with which economic incentives are being introduced does not create sufficient confidence in their durability to warrant behaviourial changes and long-term investments. Moreover, economic incentives take time to work simply because it takes time to change behaviour. But, by the time incentives begin to work, they lose their force (face value) due to inflation or political manipulation. It is only a slight exaggeration to say that regulations have been given too much time to fail; economic incentives too little time to succeed.

The impatience with economic incentives is particularly disturbing to developing countries who are watching to see if they offer a viable alternative (or complement) to the quagmire of unenforceable regulations they have eagerly imported from developed countries in the past. Over the years regulations have gone through many iterations and trials and errors. Economic incentives would need nothing less.

The objective of this paper is five-fold: (a) to review the analytical foundations of economic incentives as management instruments of natural resources and the environment in a developing country context; (b) to briefly outline the available tool kit of economic incentives for natural resource and environmental management and assess its applicability to developing countries; (c) to explain why the regulatory approach works even less in developing countries than in developed countries and why, contrary to conventional wisdom, the economic incentives approach might work better, if given a chance; (d) to review the experience of a few developing countries that have used economic incentives; such experience is likely to be more relevant and convincing than that of developed countries; and, (e) to explore how governments might go about introducing economic incentives that improve environmental management without slowing down the growth process.

1. The Analytical Foundations of Economic Incentives

While it is the physical manifestations of environmental degradation -- denuded hillsides, scarred landscapes, foul air and polluted waters -- that prompt us to action, they are poor guides as to what is the appropriate course of action to take. By "appropriate" I mean the most cost-effective means for attaining the desired level of environmental quality. We all agree, I hope, that we should not expend more resources per unit of environmental improvement than we have to. Those who disagree have to explain why they prefer less environmental quality than more for the same amount of money.

If we do agree on the cost minimisation principle we should resist the temptation to draw direct -- and I am afraid very naive -- policy conclusions from the physical manifestations of environmental degradation such as: if logging results in deforestation, ban logging; if industry pollutes, force it to treat its waste before dumping it; if burning fossil fuels generates CO_2 that might lead to climatic change, freeze the consumption of fossil fuels. While we all agree this approach is too simplistic to be taken seriously we should not underestimate its tremendous public appeal manifested in all shapes and forms in conventional wisdom. Resisting this temptation is half the battle. The other half is constructing a solid foundation for environmental policy and designing policy instruments that are cost-effective in specific cases yet flexible enough to adjust to changing circumstances. This requires understanding of the causes of environmental degradation; treatment of symptoms is rarely a cure, much less a cost-effective one.

The first step for understanding the root cause of environmental degradation is to look for its economic manifestations, which can help define the true dimension of the problem and suggest the scope and opportunity for cost-effective intervention. Here is a sample of such economic manifestations or puzzles:

a) Wasteful and inefficient use of resource (water, energy) persists despite a growing resource scarcity and shortages;

b) An increasingly scarce resource (land, water, forests) is put to inferior use when superior high-return uses exist;

c) Renewable resources capable of sustainable management (forest, land, fisheries, groundwater) are exploited (mined) as extractive resources;

d) A larger amount of effort is incurred when a smaller amount of effort and cost would have generated a higher level of output, more profit and less damage to the resource (e.g. fisheries);

e) Investments in the protection and enhancement of the resource base are not undertaken even though they would generate a positive net present value by increasing productivity and enhancing sustainability (e.g. tropical forest);

f) Public projects of marginal economic value and considerable environmental impact (e.g. certain roads and many dams) are undertaken while projects of high economic and environmental value (e.g. rehabilitation of watersheds, urban mass transit systems, urban sewage systems are rejected;

g) Resources and byproducts (e.g. palm oil residues, car batteries, paper and cans) which if recycled can generate economic and environmental benefits far in excess of their recycling costs are simply dumped;

h) Hazardous wastes treatable at a negligible cost to the industry, are dumped into public spaces and water bodies causing huge damages to health, groundwater and environment in general;

i) Finally, unique sites and habitats are lost and animal and plant species go extinct without compelling economic reasons to even mitigate the irreversible loss of uniqueness, diversity and future options.

The answers to these puzzles are to be found in the disassociation between scarcity and price, benefits and costs, rights and responsibilities, actions and consequences. This disassociation exists because of a combination of market and policy failures. The prevailing configuration of markets and policies leaves many resources outside the domain of markets, unowned, unpriced and unaccounted for and more often than not, it subsidises their excessive use and destruction, despite their growing scarcity and rising social cost. This results in an incentive structure that induces people to maximise their profits not by being efficient and innovative but by appropriating other peoples' resources and shifting their own costs onto others. Common and public property resources (e.g., forests, fisheries) are being appropriated without compensation; the cost of growing scarcity is diluted through subsidies paid by the general taxpayer and the cost of ultimate depletion is borne by the poor who lack alternatives and by future generations whose interests are sacrificed to short-term political expediency. Preventing prices from rising in line with growing scarcities and rising social costs distorts the signals that in a well-functioning market would have brought about increased efficiency, substitution, conservation and innovation to restore the balance between supply and demand (see Figure 1).

While policy and market failures are often intertwined and mutually reinforcing, for both analytical and policy reform purposes it is important to distinguish between them as clearly as possible. Policy failures or market distortions are cases of misguided intervention in a fairly well-functioning market or unsuccessful attempts to mitigate market failures that result in worse outcomes. Market failures are institutional failures partially attributable to the nature of certain resources and partially to a failure of the government to (a) establish the fundamental conditions (secure property rights, enforcement of contracts, etc.) for markets to function efficiently; and to (b) use instruments at its disposal (e.g., taxation, regulation, public investment and macropolicy) to bring into the domain of markets inputs and outputs (costs and benefits) that the institutional framework fails to internalise.

Market failures outline a *potential* role for government policy against which current policies can be viewed to identify areas of policy failure and policy success. Policy failure, as used here, is defined as a government intervention that distorts a well-functioning market, exacerbates an existing market failure, or fails to establish the foundations for the market to function efficiently. Policy success on the other hand is the successful mitigation of market failures; success is defined in terms of improvement in the allocation of resources among sectors and over time.

Market failures have often led to misunderstanding and advocacy of market replacement by government institutions. First of all, only a part of environmental degradation in developing countries is due to genuine market failure; much of it is due to misguided government interventions (such as tax distortions, subsidies, quotas, interest rate ceilings, inefficient public enterprises, etc.), which distort an otherwise well-functioning market. Second, a good deal of genuine market failure, such as failure arising from open access, insecure tenure, unpriced resources, and to some extent uncertainty and high transaction costs comes about because of government failure to establish the legal foundations of markets, such as secure property rights and enforcement of contracts.

Third, the mere existence of a market failure does not justify government intervention much less abandonment of the market as a mechanism for allocating resources; government intervention must lead to improved allocation outcomes over those of the free market and the ensuing benefits should exceed the costs of such intervention including those of enforcement and side effects (distortions). Fourth, experience suggests that the most cost effective intervention for mitigating market failures is the improvement of the functioning of the market through elimination of policy-induced distortions, the establishment of secure property rights over resources, the internalisation of externalities through pricing and fiscal instruments, the encouragement of competition, the free flow of information and the reduction of uncertainty through more stable and predictable policies and politics.

Therefore, it is a misconception that the presence of market failures justifies the reduction in the role of the market in resource allocation and an increase in the role of government. To the contrary, mitigation of market failures through secure property rights, internalisation of externalities, increased competition and reduced uncertainty will enhance the role of markets in allocating resources such as water, land, fisheries, forests and environmental services and would make unnecessary the establishment of cumbersome and often inefficient public institutions for resource management and conservation. The government need only provide the initial institutional and policy reform necessary to allow the markets to function efficiently.

The first priority under the prevailing circumstances in developing countries is to eliminate policies that have significant environmental cost or which create perverse incentives that encourage the depletion of resources and environmental degradation beyond the free-market level. Reforming policies that distort incentives for efficient resource use is a priority because unless perverse incentives are removed, project investments aiming at improved utilisation and conservation of resources are unlikely to succeed and when they do, their impact would be unsustainable, lasting only as long as the project lasts.

Reforming policies that are detrimental to both the economy and the environment is an easier point at which to start because no difficult development-environment trade-offs or budget outlays are involved. If anything, eliminating policy distortions usually reduces government expenditures and may even generate additional budget revenues. The distributional implications are also in the right direction since many of these distortions (e.g., interest rate ceilings, capital subsidies, untaxed resource rents, monopolies, input subsidies, price supports, etc.) are not only sources of inefficiency but also of inequity and perpetuation of poverty. Finally, eliminating policy distortions can be done by adjusting prices, taxes, subsidies, interest rates, and exchange rates which is easier than introducing new instruments or developing new institutions to deal with market failures.

This is not to say that market failures need not be mitigated, but that both the priority and the acid test of successful policy interventions is the elimination of policy-induced market distortions. Only then can market failures be seen in the right perspective and cost-effective interventions for improving the functioning of the market be formulated and effectively implemented. For example, there is little rationale for trying to internalise the benefits from conserving biological diversity when the wholesale conversion of tropical forests into cattle ranches or pine plantations is heavily subsidised. Yet, eliminating policy distortions is only the place to start but not the place to finish because without correction or at least mitigation of market failures, efficient use and conservation of resources cannot be secured.

The overall objective of policy reform is to re-establish the link between resource scarcity and resource prices that has been severed by a constellation of subsidies, perverse incentives, and unmitigated market and institutional failures such as insecure land tenure, open access fisheries and forests, and unaccounted environmental externalities. Re-establishing the link between resource scarcity and resource prices is critical to improving resource management and sustainable development. Population growth, economic growth and improvement in the quality of life, are all putting additional pressures on a dwindling supply of natural resources and environmental amenities. This pressure, if not allowed to be reflected in higher resource prices or if cushioned through subsidies, will result in accelerated resource depletion and environmental degradation, culminating in unsustainable development, as shown in Figure 1.

If, on the other hand, the growing resource scarcity were allowed to be reflected in increasing resource prices, it would stimulate (a) efforts to reduce the growth of demand through resource conservation, improved efficiency and substitution, (b) efforts to expand supply through recycling, exploration, imports and development of substitutes, and (c) structural change that restructures the use of natural resources from sources of materials and dumpsites for waste disposal to sources of environmental amenities and improved quality of life, consistent with growing incomes and expanding material wealth. This very response to growing resource prices results in both economic growth and environmental conservation through increased efficiency in resource use, increased substitution of lower-cost, more-abundant sources of supply, increased investment in human capital and technological development.

The economic incentives approach to environmental management could be summed up into three sets of policy reforms:

a) Reduction and eventual elimination of policies (taxes, subsidies, quotas, public projects) that distort well-functioning markets or exacerbate market failures. Cases in point are the elimination of the pesticide subsidies in Indonesia and of the ranching subsidies in Brazil (see Cases 3 and 4).

b) Correction or mitigation of market failures such as insecure or absent property rights, unpriced resources, externalities through interventions that improve the functioning of the market or result in outcomes superior to those of the free market. Examples include road pricing in Singapore and the introduction of water pricing in China (see Cases 1 and 2).

c) Consideration and internalisation of environmental, social and other side effects of public projects and sectoral and macroeconomic policies. Examples include the Dumoga irrigation *cum* national park project in Indonesia (see Case 5) and the inclusion of environmental provisions in several structural adjustment programmes (e.g. Morocco, Tunisia, Pakistan, Philippines, Nepal and Thailand).

2. Policy Instruments for Implementing Economic Incentives

There is a panoply of policy instruments that governments can use to implement an economic incentives approach to environmental management. Some are more applicable to natural resource management, others to environmental protection. Yet, others are applicable to both (product and input pricing, taxes performance bends, etc). They are based on the same principles of "getting the prices right" and the property right clear, secure, and tradeable. Some operating through existing markets (e.g. product pricing), while other imitate the market or seek to create new markets (e.g. tradable pollution permits). In many cases such as forest policy and hazardous waste management it is necessary to employ both sets of instruments to obtain cost-effective and efficient outcomes. An economic incentives package for forest policy would include at the minimum concession bidding, resource pricing, resource taxation (royalties) and perhaps performance bonds, and investment incentives for replanting. An economic incentives package for hazardous waste treatment may involve presumptive charges, environment bond and environmental auditing. Following is an indicative list of economic incentive instruments for resources management and environmental protection.

2.1 Natural Resource Management

-- property rights (e.g. land titles, water rights)

-- tradable resource shares (e.g. water capacity shares)

-- use rights (e.g. communal land rights and territorial use rights in fisheries or TURFs)

-- development rights (transferable development right for heritage assets, rural amenities, greenbelts, and coastal resources)

-- concession bidding (e.g. logging concessions, national park concessions)

-- licensing fees (e.g. fishing licenses)

-- tradable quotas (e.g. individual transferable quotas in fisheries)

-- resource pricing (e.g. water pricing, pricing of tropical timber)

-- product pricing (e.g. energy pricing)

-- resource taxation (e.g. forest and mineral royalties)

-- tax concessions (e.g. for reforestation)

-- subsidies (e.g. for tree planting)

-- land use taxes (e.g. to discourage erodible crops on steep slopes)

-- betterment fees (e.g. for infrastructure)

-- user charges/access fees (e.g. for roads/parks)

-- performance bonds (e.g. for forest management)

2.2 Environmental Management

-- tradeable pollution rights/permits (e.g. for air pollution, greenhouse gasses)

-- effluent and emission charges (e.g. for water, air and noise pollution)

-- presumptive charges (e.g. for hazardous waste)

-- product charges (e.g. batteries, lubricants, fertilizers, pesticides)

-- pollution taxes (e.g. carbon tax)

-- input taxes (e.g. on PCBs, CFCs)

-- resource input pricing (e.g. water pricing, energy pricing)

-- tax concessions (e.g. duty free import of pollution abatement equipment)

-- tax differentiation (e.g. for cars based on size and year of purchase, for leaded/lead-free gasoline)

-- subsidies (e.g. for "clean" technologies, for waste products to create a market)

-- location incentives (e.g. for industrial polluters)

-- access fees (e.g. to city centres)

-- performance bonds (e.g. for oil spills)

-- environmental auditing (e.g. for hazardous waste)

-- deposit-refund systems (e.g. for car batteries, beverage can etc.)

-- enforcement incentives (e.g. for hazardous waste)

-- liability insurance.

It is beyond the scope of this paper to discuss in detail the workings and applications of these instruments. A detailed description of most of these instruments and of the experience of OECD countries with their application is found in two excellent OECD documents (OECD, 1989a, b).

The experience of developing countries with economic instruments has been significantly more limited than the OECD experience. This is due partly to the fact that many of these instruments are new and experimental and partly due to a misconception that market-based incentives are less applicable to developing countries. In the next section we argue that in developing countries market-based incentives have a better chance of success than command and control regulations, and in subsequent sections we provide evidence of successful applications of economic incentives in developing countries, to water, urban and industrial pollution, forestry and land use.

3. Why Regulations Don't Work in Developing Countries

Existing regulations, in developing countries are usually replicas of past regulations in developed countries. They have little grounding in local realities and cultures and therefore are largely unenforceable. That the agencies responsible for their enforcement are rarely given the authority and the means for enforcement is symptomatic of this problem. Developing country regulations, following the example of developed countries 10-20 years ago, are based on command-and-control instruments. They set inflexible effluent and emissions standards, or mandate waste treatment facilities coupled with sanctions for non-compliance, rather than flexible market-based mechanisms and fiscal incentives (such as proper pricing, pollution charges, environmental bonds, etc.) which are now increasingly used by the developed countries. This is not just a matter of lagging behind. It draws on a conviction, or rather fallacy, prevalent also in the developed countries, that market-based mechanisms, whatever their record in the developed countries, are not as suitable for developing countries as are command and control systems. This view may have some foundation in countries with undeveloped markets and authoritarian governments. But even there, command-and-control mechanisms do not seem to work if Eastern Europe is an indication.

I will contend here that there are good reasons why command-and-control regulations do not work in the majority of developing countries and that market-based incentives have a better chance. First, following the developed country model, environmental regulations in developing countries stipulate terms of imprisonment and/or fines for non-compliance or violations. However, for cultural reasons, many developing societies, most notably in Asia, are not given to litigation. Courts are used as a last resort, which means they are rarely used. Since this is a common knowledge, regulations rarely become anything more than "paper tigers". Non-enforcement makes it both necessary and easy to introduce additional regulations; rarely people object to regulations which they know are not likely to be enforced. Often industrial polluters readily agree to a new regulation to improve their image and keep the regulators busy and content with paper work. This accounts for the fact that many developing countries have amassed more regulations than developed countries, some inconsistent with each other and most of them unenforceable.

A second reason why regulations do not work in developing countries is because it is virtually impossible to monitor hundreds of thousands of scattered small-scale operations, which individually generate little pollution but taken together account for the bulk of pollution in the country. Even if this was technically possible, economically it makes no sense. Massive non-compliance by small- and medium-scale operations strips environmental regulations of any moral force.

A third reason for the unsuitability of command-and-control regulations for developing countries is the mismatch between their high regulation, monitoring and enforcement cost and the budgetary, manpower and administrative constraints of developing countries. Environmental regulations in developed countries presume a degree of devolution of authority and taxation to representative local government, which increases the ability and reduces the cost of regulation, monitoring and enforcement. Most developing countries are overly centralised with the control of central government diminishing in proportion to the distance from the centre.

A fourth reason is that the fines are set at levels that are too low to deter violators. Since the probability of apprehension of violators in developing countries is very low, the fines need to be very high so that the certainty-equivalent fine exceeds the benefits from the violation. This is rarely the case. Not only are fines set too low to start with they remain unchanged in nominal terms for years and become eroded by inflation.

A fifth reason is that the government's ability to influence attitudes, develop public awareness through education and to elicit voluntary actions that would reinforce regulations and attach a moral stigma to violations, is much weaker in developing countries, partly because of the limited development of the environmental movement and institutions.

The final and perhaps the most damaging flaw of command-and-control regulations in a developing country context is the *rent-seeking behaviour* (not entirely unknown in developed countries) which they elicit. Violators find it to their interest to pay a fraction of the stipulated fine as a bribe to the enforcement official who, being grossly underpaid, is often all too willing to accept it. Increased fines or stepped up enforcement of regulations leads predictably to more bribes rather than less environmental degradation. As a visible example consider the gross violations of the town and country law: 30-storey buildings with perfectly legal papers dominate in areas where 3 storeys is the legal maximum. This is as true in Mexico City and Cairo as it is in Bangkok and Manila. In the face of such obvious violations by the wealthy with immunity, regulations lose whatever moral and legal weight they had to start with.

4. Why Regulations are Popular with Governments

If regulations are so ineffective why do governments have such a strong preference for them. Rent-seeking behaviour is only part of the answer. Even more important is the need to feel in control. Command-and-control regulations satisfy this need, if only on paper. Interestingly, *one OECD study found no case of economic incentives replacing regulations altogether; they are always added on.* At least in some cases the psychological need to feel in control may have played a role. Regulations, unlike market-based incentives, are written in tough and rigid language that carries with it the threat of punishment which gives a sense of power and authority. Regulations carry a big stick, even if it is rarely used, while economic incentives provide for a daily diet of small carrots. Everybody learns of the one big violator who is caught and prosecuted once every few years but no one notices the modified daily behaviour of economic actors who face a new set of relative prices brought about by market-based incentives. Of course, in a political-economy-neutral world the criterion for judging the performance of environmental-improvement instruments is the reduction of pollution damage (or risk) per dollar expended rather than the (false) sense of control.

Another advantage that governments see in regulations over economic incentives is that the price tag (cost) of regulations is usually hidden from the public eye. The costs of regulations, include in addition to direct regulation costs, the cost of compliance by the regulated, loss of output and distortions. Though substantially higher than those of more effective market-based incentives, regulatory costs are less obvious to the taxpayer and the consumer. Producers also tend to prefer regulations to proper pricing and other market-based mechanisms because they can bribe their way out of regulations without modifying behaviour, which they cannot do with the market.

5. Regulations versus Incentives in Environmental Management: the Case of Urban Congestion and Industrial Pollution

Environmental resources (air, water, landscape, atmosphere) are common property, unpriced resources outside the domain of markets. While the use of other resources such as capital and labour is subject to prices and other constraints, the use of environmental resources is not. Urban consumers and industrial producers dump raw wastes into the air and water without regard to the high costs they impose on others and the society at large, precisely because it is economically advantageous for them to do so: waste disposal is free; waste reduction or treatment is costly.

5.1 A Regulatory and Pseudo-Incentive Approach

Under the direct regulatory approach to *industrial pollution*, the government sets maximum permissible levels of discharge of each pollutant from each source (effluent or emission standards) and relies on administrative agencies and the judicial system to enforce them. An alternative (or supplementary) type of standard is the ambient standard which sets the minimum acceptable level of environmental quality for a receiving water-source or airshed. In many developing countries (e.g. Thailand, Malaysia) both standards are used in water pollution in combination with subsidies for construction of waste treatment facilities.

Other common instruments, such as tax write-offs, accelerated depreciation, low-interest loans or outright subsidies for the adoption of "clean" production technologies or the construction of waste treatment facilities are similarly inefficient and ineffective even though they can pass as economic incentives; it is the wrong kind of incentives. They do not make waste reduction or waste treatment any more profitable; they simply subsidise the producers and consumers of the products of these industries. Waste treatment is not always the most efficient means of reducing wastes; in many cases changing production processes, the type and quality of raw materials or the rate of output is more efficient. In some instances, rearrangement of the production process results in both reduction of waste and recovery of valuable by-products such as fertilizer from palm oil extraction and syrup from fruit canning.

Tax breaks, credits, depreciation allowances, and subsidies are a drain on the government budget and a disincentive to industries which might have otherwise developed more efficient methods for reducing emissions.

This direct regulation and subsidisation suffers from many weaknesses: (a) it relies on centralised setting and enforcement of standards which is both costly and ineffective; (b) it promotes inefficiency since it requires similar reduction of pollution of all sources regardless of costs; (c) it emphasizes subsidised end-of-the pipe, capital-intensive solutions (such as waste treatment plants); (d) it results in large bureaucracies and costly subsidies; (e) it requires that the environmental agency masters the technologies of both production and pollution control for hundreds of different types of industries and all their technological alternatives, a monumental task that detracts from the agency's principal monitoring functions; (g) compliance is very limited because the certainty-equivalent amount of the fine (fine times the probability of detection times the probability of conviction) for non-compliance is only a fraction of the cost of compliance in terms of expensive abatement equipment and loss of competitive position; (h) the environmental agency is engaged in endless negotiations with the polluters over the type of equipment to be installed resulting in long delays and compromise of the agency's standards; (i) the moral hazards of "regulatory capture" (the regulators are co-opted by the regulated) and bribing of enforcement officials is higher than in any other pollution control system because of the protracted negotiations and ambiguity of compliance to the set standards; and (j) direct regulation provides ample opportunity for rent-seeking behaviour.

Urban congestion and pollution increasingly dominates the life of large urban centres. Bangkok's commuters spent daily an average of 2.5 hours in crowded buses and congested roads, while school children in Mexico City start school late to avoid the morning smog (*The Economist*, 18th February 1989). Policy responses to congestion problems range from supply management (build more roads, introduce one way traffic, etc.) to rationing the use of scarce roads by doing nothing. Supply management works only temporarily: to the extent that congestion and traffic jams are relaxed by new roads, the benefits from driving increase, inducing car-owners to drive more and non-owners tend to purchase cars. As long as open access to city roads prevails, any rents from using them will be driven to zero. And, this is the basis of rationing by doing nothing; delays are left to become long enough to discourage any further increase in driving. However, this a very inefficient solution. Costs include: (a) loss of productive time, (b) increased use of fossil fuels, (c) increased air pollution (with all the associated health problems, medical bills, and cleaning costs), and (c) increased noise pollution, not to mention the frustration and psychic costs. Ultimately, those who are left using the roads are those who value their time least (low opportunity cost).

A rough calculation of the lost time and increased use of gasoline for Bangkok produced an estimated loss of $1 billion a year. Medical bills and lost days of work due to pollution-related ailments, cleaning costs, damage to infrastructure and buildings from increased pollution and the extra cost that consumers incur for noise insulation, air conditioning of cars and houses that would not have taken place otherwise may double this figure. If we conservatively put the total annual costs of congestion at $1.5 billion and capitalised this figures at a 10 per cent interest rate, we obtain a present value of congestion *cum* added pollution cost of $15 billion. Only a fraction of this amount would suffice to provide Bangkok with a clean and efficient public transport. Charges for the use of city centre roads and surcharges on gasoline can be set high enough to hold traffic down to levels that permit it to move freely, and the proceeds can be used to improve public transportation.

5.2 The Economic Incentives Approach

The environment being left out of the market receives worse treatment than the market can offer: economic assets in the market domain grow and multiply (often at the expense of the environment) while the environmental assets are left unattended and uncared for to depreciate without a price or a record to register their depreciation. The economic incentives approach brings environmental resources into the market and "prices" them at a level that reflects their true scarcity and the opportunity costs of their use. Users would have to pay to use environmental resources and such payments would force them to economise on their use. The entire spectrum of industrial decisions would be affected: the design of industrial processes and technologies, the types and quantities of raw materials used and the nature of products. The ideal solution would be to establish a market for environmental resources by defining property rights by governmental action, since transaction costs prevent the spontaneous emergence of such a market. *Pollution permits* (or pollution rights) could be issued and allocated to current industrial producers in a "grandfather system." Pollution permits should be marketable and transferable so that (a) they will gravitate to the most efficient producers, and (b) their prices will reflect the true scarcity of environmental resources being used.

Despite its many merits, the system of pollution permits has not yet been extensively used and its details have not been fully worked out. The concept of marketable pollution permits is a relatively recent idea which is currently being experimentally tried in the United States. What we propose here is research into the feasibility of such a system in developing countries. In some sense, it might be easier to introduce such a system in a country which is not yet fully industrialised. In industrialised countries, vested interests, sunk investments and damage already done militate against pollution permits.

However, there are alternatives that approximate the working of a market for environmental resources, which have been tried successfully elsewhere. Instead of relying on the market to set prices for environmental resources, the government may set charges for the use of these resources through legislation or executive decision. If these charges are properly set, the external costs will be internalised and environmental resources will be optimally used.

Ideally, *charges for destructive uses* of the environment such as disposal of wastes should be set equal to the damage or external cost that these activities generate. In practice, it is very difficult to estimate the full extent of environmental damage because they are widespread, often not easily quantifiable and take a long time to accumulate. A more workable system of setting charges is one based on ambient standards. This is done in two stages. First, technical experts describe the consequences of different levels of ambient quality: for example, fish survival at different levels of dissolved oxygen or human health at different levels of carbon monoxide. Then, a target level of ambient quality (e.g. a target level of dissolved oxygen or a maximum acceptable level of carbon monoxide) is politically or administratively chosen, and a charge for emissions is set at the level necessary to attain this target. The level of the charge for each area that would accomplish the target level of air or water quality is obtained by estimating the relationship between different charge levels and the emissions from different sources based on the average marginal costs of these sources. The effect of different levels of emission on ambient quality can be determined through mathematical models of river basins or air pollution regions. These two relationships (between charges and emissions and between emissions and ambient quality) provide the link between charges and ambient quality and determine the level of the charges that will bring about the desired (target) ambient quality.

CASE 1

FIGHTING URBAN CONGESTION WITH MARGINAL PRICING IN SINGAPORE

Like many cities, Singapore has suffered from the environmental effects of an increasingly car-driving population: congestion resulting in longer travel times for cars and public transport alike, air pollution, wear and tear on roads, and a lower quality of life for those living and working in heavily congested areas. Because car drivers do not naturally bear the substantial costs they impose on society, charging for urban road use is theoretically appealing. The success of Singapore's Area Licensing scheme demonstrates its practical appeal as well.

In 1975, cars represented half of Singapore's 280 000 registered vehicles and were owned at a rate of one per 16 people. In an attempt to reduce central city traffic by 25-30 per cent during peak hours, the city implemented a scheme which charged drivers for using roads in the city centre during these hours. Specifically, the city aimed to 1) reduce car use within certain areas during particular times, 2) leave economic activity unaffected, 3) enact a scheme which was easy to implement and enforce, and 4) provide those no longer driving into the inner city with attractive travel alternatives. The area pricing scheme required vehicles travelling through the centre city at peak hours to purchase a daily or monthly license, raised daytime parking fees within this area, and instituted a park and ride service to facilitate easy non-car commuting. Cars with more than four passengers, buses and cycles were exempted from the licensing requirements (references are to Watson and Holland, 1978).

The scheme had the following effects. Above all, it achieved a traffic reduction of 73 per cent in the zone during peak hours. In addition, business seemed largely unaffected and, although the park and ride option was not heavily utilised, the city found the overall scheme easy to enforce and implement. Car-pools increased from 10 per cent to 40 per cent of all traffic, while 13 per cent of car-owning commuters into the zone switched to public transit and about the same number changed their commuting time to pre-peak hours. For those who did not change their habits to avoid the zone during peak hours, the monthly average commuting cost rose from $64 to $95. More significantly, all but one-tenth of "through zone" commuters changed their route or departure time to avoid licensing fees. Travel speeds decreased by 10 per cent on incoming roads and by 20 per cent on zone roads. Speeds on substitute "ring" roads increased by 20 per cent. The only group experiencing an increase in travel time were converts to public transit, whose average travel time went up by only 9 minutes on a previously 29-minute trip.

The scheme had additional environmental benefits. Although other pollutants were difficult to measure, the level of carbon monoxide declined significantly during the hours the scheme was in effect. Central city residents and shoppers reported greater ease and safety in getting around, less fumes, and generally happier living and shopping conditions. Overall, all affected groups concurred that the impact on Singapore was positive, with motorists being the only ones to perceive themselves as worse off, although not badly so. Their perceptions were accurate since they were, in fact, shouldering more of the social costs of their car use. With an initial return on investment of 77 per cent, which, with an increase in license fees, rose to 95 per cent, the scheme achieved its goals without undue budgetary costs. Less quantifiable but more significant may be the long-run benefits, specifically, the road construction or future congestion which may be avoided due to changed habits and attitudes towards public transit and car use.

Conclusions:

-- By making drivers bear some of the costs their driving imposes on others, charging for road use can reduce traffic to a more efficient and environmentally sound level.

-- Schemes which charge for road use can be cost-effective and easy to implement and enforce.

A system of charges, thus designed, will not result in polluters paying a price equal to the external costs or damages created by their activities, unless the charges vary according to the location of the source of pollution. Such fine tuning may prove to be prohibitively costly. However, even in its crudest form, a system of pollution charges has advantages over the current system of direct regulation through effluent or ambient standards.

Emission charges are efficient means for achieving the desired level of environmental quality because they minimise the costs of pollution control by leaving the level of individual pollution control and the choice of technology to the polluter. Depending on his own control costs, a polluter faced with a charge on emissions may choose to reduce his output, change his input mix or production process, treat the waste or simply pay the charge. Industries with high control costs would control less and pay more in charges, while industries with low control costs will control more and pay less in charges. Overall, the desired reduction in pollution will be attained at the minimum cost, and the industry will be under constant pressure to develop more cost-efficient ways of reducing or abating pollution in order to reduce its control costs or payment of charges. Enforcement is easier and simpler because charges require no knowledge of the production and abatement technologies of different industries and no bargaining; the incentive structure facing the polluter is such that it promotes self-enforcement; the onus of finding or developing the most efficient approach to reduction of emissions is on the polluters themselves, not on the regulatory agency.

The system of pollution charges has been used with considerable success in several countries. Japan has instituted a system of air and water charges to compensate the victims of pollution-related ailments. The Japanese compensation programme uses statistics and epidemiology to allocate social responsibility for ailments to specific toxic substances. For example, sulphur oxides have been linked to respiratory diseases and the compensation cost was allocated 20 per cent to automobiles (to be paid out of an automobile tax), and 80 per cent to all other sources of airborne sulphur oxides. The automobile tax varies according to car weight and the charge on industry varies according to location in relation to the pollution zone. If an industry is identified as the only source of a particular toxic substance in the area, it is held responsible for all the compensation costs related to that substance regardless of the level of emissions. It is important to note that the national industrial association participated in the structuring of the programme and its implementation, thus minimising monitoring and collection costs.

Variants of emission and effluent charges have been implemented with varying success in several countries. In the United States, towns receiving Federal grants for construction of sewer systems are required by the Water Pollution Control Act to recover their operating costs and part of the capital costs from their users, through municipal sewage treatment user charges. In Germany, the private association of dischargers into the Ruhr Valley has levied charges on its members in proportion to their discharge levels and toxicity in order to finance collective control measures; again, the process works smoothly because the charges are levied and collected by the representatives of the dischargers not by the government. There is no reason why a similar system to the Japanese and the German ones cannot work in developing countries with appropriate industry leadership and some government encouragement.

A comprehensive review of the application of pollution charges is beyond our scope, but a few more examples of potential applicability to developing countries might be useful. These include a lead additive tax; a beverage container deposit; a recycling incentive tax; and product disposal, congestion, and noise charges. The US government taxes leaded gasoline to reduce its price advantage over unleaded gasoline in order to induce a shift to the latter which is less polluting. Many states in the US have instituted refundable deposits on beverage and beer containers to discourage their free disposal and encourage their collection and recycling. Singapore has introduced a *road pricing system* whereby drivers purchase a permit to enter the city centre during rush hours; buses and car pools are excluded, making the system not only efficient but also equitable (see Case 1). London and Los Angeles use congestion charges during rush hours to reduce congestion and air pollution in the city centre (see Case 1), while Japan and the Netherlands have been toying with noise charges for traffic and airport noise control.

It might be worthwhile for developing countries to study the experience of countries with pollution charges and develop their own variants based on their special circumstances and enforcement difficulties. For example, beverage container deposits are likely to be effective in developing countries; even if they do not fully stem free disposal of wastes, they would stimulate the establishment of a new labour-intensive activity: the collection of containers and beer bottles which fits low-cost labour-abundant conditions in many developing countries.

6. Economic Incentives in Natural Resource Management: Water Subsidies versus Full-cost Pricing

Virtually all countries, regardless of the degree of scarcity of water, subsidise water for irrigation (and other uses) and, in many cases, they supply it free of charge. Take the example of Thailand. Both seasonally and spatially, Thailand experiences droughts and floods. Northeast Thailand suffers from perennial water shortages. The Central Region is inundated in the rainy season and imports water from the Northern Region in the dry season. Only 30 percent of the irrigable area covered by the Greater Chao Phraya Project has adequate irrigation in the dry season. Yet this profound and growing water scarcity does not register. According to the *National Resources Profile* (TDRI, 1987), "many farmers continue to think of water as a free, virtually unlimited resource whereas the facts increasingly suggest otherwise." Irrigation water is provided free of charge without any attempt to recover cost or to charge a price reflecting the scarcity value or opportunity cost of water. The result is over-irrigation with consequent salinisation and waterlogging in some areas and inadequate water in others. This gross waste of water limits the efficiency of irrigation systems to about 15 per cent of a potential of 60 to 70 per cent (ADB, 1986), while the failure to achieve any degree of cost recovery deprives the system of operation and maintenance funds.

CASE 2

POLICY SUCCESS: WATER PRICING IN CHINA

For centuries irrigation has played a crucial role in Chinese agriculture. Since the Communist Revolution in 1949, the area of irrigated land has tripled, and 75 per cent of national food production is on irrigated land, contributing to China's food self-sufficiency (ADB, 1986).

In July 1985, the People's Republic of China took an important first step toward promoting greater efficiency in irrigation water usage. The Chinese government instituted agricultural policy reforms which invested a greater degree of financial and managerial autonomy in provincial water management agencies. The policy emphasized "water as a commodity rather than a gift of nature and clearly attributed wasteful consumption and the imbalance between supply and demand to irrationally low water charges" (Ross, 1988). As a result, irrigation water is priced more closely to what it actually costs and problems associated with overuse and inefficient distribution have diminished.

Agency budgets now rely on irrigation service fees paid by water users and income generated by secondary irrigation agency projects such as fishing and livestock production. Irrigation service fees are charged at levels to cover operation, maintenance and amortization of capital costs. Beginning in 1980, the government switched from financing systems with grants to providing loans. The move provided an extra incentive for water management agencies to collect higher water fees. In general, water charges are determined by what the water actually costs for different uses. For example, charges may vary according to season, and in very dry areas progressive water pricing schemes have been adopted to reflect scarcity. Likewise, irrigation for grain crops is priced according to supply costs without profit, while cash crops may be irrigated for slightly higher than cost. The reforms also serve to decentralise authority, making water management agencies more closely tied to both the operation and distribution of irrigation water. As a result, water is often distributed more efficiently. In Hungxian County, for example, farmers reported more reliable water supply and were willing to pay more for the guaranteed supply (ADB, 1986). Management is often further decentralised when a local agency purchases water wholesale and sells in bulk to smaller water user associations responsible for distribution to farmers. These smaller groups strengthen the bond between the water user and the supplier who must recover costs.

Because of these policy reforms, revenues collected by the water management agencies have increased significantly. Farmers have begun to irrigate their crops more efficiently while water use per hectare has declined (ADB, 1986). Decentralised management has led to more efficient distribution through practices such as distributing water according to land area, levying water charges on a volumetric basis rather than a flat rate and preparing distribution plans in advance. Crop production has improved, with China producing twice as much as similarly irrigated crops in India (Rogers, 1985).

Similar problems of growing water scarcity are also found in Indonesia which ranks second in Asia in terms of freshwater endowment. Densely populated Java faces increasing water shortages that are being addressed through supply rather than demand management. But the area that is facing the most critical water scarcity is the Middle East. According to Elias Saleh, a hydrologist with Jordan University, "In the mid 1990s farmers in the high plains and in the swelter of the Jordan Valley will face a crisis because the growing population will lay claim to water for drinking, and irrigation will be curtailed... Water is the future of the whole area... It is very critical" (*The New York Times* (NYT), 16th April 1989, p. 1). Virtually all Middle East countries but particularly Egypt, Yemen, Jordan and Tunisia face severe water shortages, yet water continues to be subsidised throughout the region, and water efficiency is unacceptably low. In Egypt, where 30 per cent of the irrigated lands suffer from salinisation and waterlogging due to over-irrigation (FAO, 1980), "efficiency ratings will have to increase by 60 per cent over the next 11 years to meet the needs of the population, projected to reach 70 million in the year 2000" *(NYT, ibid.)*. According to the same source, "Jordan is expecting a water crisis within a decade and dearth of new water resources by the year 2005."

Irrigation policy throughout the developing world is in need of overhauling to provide incentives for efficient water use, to increase cost recovery and to generate funds for rehabilitation, maintenance, and improvement of existing irrigation systems. The first step in such reform should be to strengthen water-user associations and to make structural modifications to existing irrigation systems such as intermediate storage at the head of distribution and installation of meters in secondary channels. Such modifications would make possible "bulk water sales through contract with water-user associations and co-operatives as irrigation agencies do in Mexico, India, China and other countries" (Repetto, 1986, p. 34). A second step would be to develop cost recovery mechanisms such as user charges indexed to the value of crops, land taxes, water rights, provisions for water trading, etc. which would encourage farmers to value water at its marginal opportunity cost.

Bulk water sales to water user associations could help reduce the metering and collection costs by leaving water distribution to local organisations which can best monitor water use and prevent meter manipulation or damage through peer group pressure. Repetto (1986, p. 33) reports that "in Gujarat State in India, the irrigation agency sells water volumetrically in bulk to co-operatives, which distribute water and collect fees from their members." A similar system operates in Sri Lanka. Ross (1986) reports that the introduction of volumetric irrigation fees in areas of China has induced farmers to use water more efficiently and has generated revenues for maintenance of the irrigation systems (see Case 2).

When volumetric (marginal cost) pricing is not feasible or prohibitively costly, low-cost approximations such as area-based irrigation charges and land taxes could be introduced. The sacrifice of efficiency in this case may be justified by the savings in metering and collection costs. The evidence worldwide suggests that farmers are prepared to pay for reliable irrigation services. Availability and reliability of supply is far more important than cost in this case.

The same principles that apply to irrigation water should apply to all other uses of water, including industry, energy and household use. Water consumers in all sectors in most developing (and many developed countries) pay a flat charge for water, which is well below the real cost of delivery, let alone its opportunity cost or scarcity value. Thus consumers are encouraged, and in many cases explicitly subsidised, to overuse and waste water, often on account of "equity": water is too essential to deprive the poor of its use through pricing. Yet both equity and efficiency objectives could be served by progressive water charges that reflect long-run supply costs. It is the current system which is inequitable because it taxes the general public including the poor (who often bear a disproportionate tax burden because of inability to evade it, e.g. wage earners) to subsidise wasteful water uses by the wealthy (e.g. large lawns and gardens, golf courses, luxury hotels, etc.)

Water is also demanded for use as a receptacle for waste by industry, municipalities and households. In many countries, this use of water for waste disposal is free, and, as expected, water resources near industries, urban centres and tourist towns become over-polluted and degraded. In other countries, especially those at a higher level of development, waste disposal in water resources is regulated by permit, by requirements for water treatment before disposal, or by effluent standards. However, compliance is poorly monitored, the penalties are too low and are not strictly enforced. Such standards and regulations often work better as incentives for rent-seeking behaviour than as regulators of waste disposal. Again, water pricing for waste disposal is a more effective instrument because it manages demand and suggests lower-cost alternatives other than bribing enforcement officials, for example, switching to less polluting inputs and technologies, installing treatment facilities, changing location, etc.

In conclusion, the water user should pay fully for the costs of supply, delivery, depletion and pollution (treatment costs) attributable to his/her use. The payment should be linked to the quantity and quality of use and the link should be transparent enough to channel the user's efforts towards efficient use, conservation and minimisation of waste generation and disposal. As long as there is a divergence between those who use (agriculture, industry, households) and those who pay (taxpayers), there is no built-in conservation mechanism. If there is such a mechanism, it is a perverse one because it encourages internalisation of the benefits from water use and externalisation of the costs. The government, in its attempt to correct one market failure (public goods), has generated another (externalities).

7. Economic Incentives and Agricultural Policy

Applied to agricultural policy the economic incentives approach to environmental management calls for (a) changes in relative prices by reducing price support for certain crops (e.g. sugar cane in Morocco) or reducing taxes for others (rice and rubber in Thailand); and (b) reduction in agricultural input subsidies to reduce the drain on the budget, save foreign exchange (where inputs are imported) and improve the efficiency of resource use (e.g. Philippines, Nepal and Morocco). The environmental impact of such reforms depends on the crops and inputs that are promoted or discouraged by these policies, and the institutional context in which they are implemented. If land is securely owned and forests are effectively protected and managed, better prices for agricultural crops in general would lead to increased investment in land improvement, soil conservation and agricultural intensification. Otherwise, the very same policies may lead to increased forest land clearing, cultivation of marginal lands and agricultural extensification. On the other hand, changes in relative crop prices could benefit or damage the environment depending on the affected crops and the environmental conditions in which they are grown.

For example, the reduction of the *price support* for sugar cane in Morocco has a positive environmental impact because sugar cane is a soil-damaging and water-intensive crop in a water-scarce country. Thus, less price support for sugar cane results not only in less drain on the budget, but also in less drain on soil and water resources. The market is, thus, more free to respond to market signals and shift resources (land and water) to more profitable crops, making a better use of limited natural resources with less damage to the environment.

Reduction of *export taxes* on certain crops such as tree crops help diversify the economy away from soil-eroding crops such as maize, wheat or cassava and towards high value perennial export crops with positive environmental side effects. The irony in the case of Thailand is that high rubber prices and free forest land have encouraged overexpansion of rubber onto steep and fragile slopes contributing to the catastrophic landslides and floods of 1988 that claimed 350 lives and caused nearly half a billion US dollars in short and long-term damages. This case clearly demonstrates that economic incentives that have positive environmental effects under certain conditions, may be environmentally destructive under a different set of circumstances. Increased incentives for perennial crops (coffee, cocoa, rubber) *vis-à-vis* annual field crops such as cotton, ground nuts, or row crops such as maize and sorghum can help protect the soil on gentle slopes but are not a substitute for natural forest cover on steep or fragile slopes.

Reduction of agricultural *input subsidies*, generally has a positive impact on the environment. The Philippines, Nepal, Pakistan, Morocco and Tunisia have all agreed, as part of their structural adjustment programmes to substantially reduce pesticide and fertilizer subsidies. Judicial use of both pesticides and chemical fertilizers has helped countries increase their crop yield on existing land substantially (Pakistan, Indonesia, Philippines), thereby limiting encroachment of forest lands. However, the excessive and indiscriminate use of pesticides encouraged by generous subsidies has proved counter-productive by eliminating the pests' natural predators or promoting the emergence of pesticide-resistant strains of pests (see Case 3). Similarly, over-application of chemical fertilizers over a prolonged period of time, to the total exclusion of organic fertilizers (manure), damages the structure of the soil. Heavy use of pesticides and chemical fertilizers also leads to water pollution and poisoning of aquatic life through runoff into the water systems. It does not matter that chemical subsidies have been cut to reduce the drain on the budget; their reduction also reduces the drain on the environment. Ideally, however, environmentally destructive inputs (pesticides, chemical fertilizers) should be taxed in proportion to their negative externalities, and environmentally beneficial inputs (IPM, organic fertilizers, soil conservation) should be subsidised in proportion to their positive externalities.

Water pricing improves efficiency in resource allocation alleviates budget deficits, converses water resources and reduces environmental costs. Not only is salinisation and waterlogging contained but more importantly the solution of water shortages through demand management averts the environmental problems of constructing new irrigation systems (supply management).

Reductions in subsidies (or import duty exemptions) for farm equipment and land clearing machinery has several positive effects on resource use and the state of the environment because subsidised land clearing machinery: (a) encourages deforestation and the clearing of marginal lands for agriculture or ranching as demonstrated in Case 4 below; (b) compacts and damaged the structure of fragile tropical soils; (c) increases the use of fossil fuels; and (d) distorts the farmer's labour-capital choice in favour of capital and against labour in countries with abundant labour. Aside from the economic inefficiency and misallocation of scarce capital that the latter entails, it also reduces agricultural employment thereby promoting encroachment of forest lands or undue urban migration.

CASE 3

POLICY SUCCESS: REMOVAL OF PESTICIDE SUBSIDIES IN INDONESIA

In 1985, the Indonesian government was subsidising pesticides at 82 per cent of retail price at a total cost of $128 million (Repetto, 1988a). These heavy subsidies encouraged intensive pesticide use by Indonesian farmers. Indeed, pesticide use witnessed a 76 per cent increase between 1976 and 1985. The widespread use of the pesticide Sevin wiped out the natural predators of the rice brown planthopper, leading to significant losses in the annual rice crop. Millions of tons of rice were lost to the pest which five years earlier was not considered a threat (Panayotou, July 1989). In 1976 alone, 364 500 tons of rice valued at $100 million was lost (Conway *et al.*, 1984).

Overuse of pesticides often leads to the evolution of resistant strains of some pests, while natural predators that help control pests are wiped out. Excessive pesticide use has in fact been linked to a reduction in productivity. In Northern Sumatra, brown planthopper population density rose directly with the number of pesticide applications (Barbier, 1989). Meanwhile, research has shown that untreated fields had 75 per cent lower planthopper populations and higher yields (Panayotou, July 1989).

As with other market failures, subsidies obstruct important market signals which would otherwise prevent farmers from overusing pesticides. By paying artificially low prices for pesticides, farmers tend to use more than the economic optimum, the point at which the true cost of pesticide use begins to exceed the benefit of using more pesticide. As a result, farmers continue to use pesticides, perhaps as a substitute for other inputs such as weeding, despite increasing damage to crops and the environment. In Indonesia, insecticides were generously applied 4-5 times per season over millions of hectares of rice fields regardless of the need of individual fields (Panayotou, July 1989).

By late 1985, 70 per cent of Java's rice crop was threatened and numerous economic studies showed negative returns to heavy insecticide use. A policy which aimed to promote rice self-sufficiency had jeopardised the crop yields it had intended to bolster. Supposedly resistant varieties of rice were being attacked by the brown planthopper with increasingly intensive damage. Describing the damage the FAO reported, "Even extremely high dosages of insecticides could not stop these outbreaks. To the contrary, they seemed to make things worse" (FAO, 1988). In November 1986, President Suharto issued a decree banning 57 brands of pesticides, 20 of which were heavily subsidised by the government. The same decree declared integrated pest management (IPM) as the national pest control strategy for rice. Three planting seasons after the decree, FAO reported a 90 per cent reduction of pesticide use. Also, average yields rose from 6.1 tons per hectare to 7.4 tons.

In October 1988, the Indonesian government cut pesticide subsidies from 55 per cent to 40 per cent of retail prices. Shortly after, in December, the government opted to eliminate pesticide subsidies altogether. While fiscal concerns played an important role, policy makers also hoped the cuts would increase farmers' efficiency with pesticide use (*The Jakarta Post*, 1988). The government also issued provisions for raising the floor prices of unhusked rice, yellow corn, soybeans and mung beans increasing farmers' incomes so they could better cope with the policy change.

Table 1

ECONOMIC AND FINANCIAL ANALYSIS OF GOVERNMENT-ASSISTED CATTLE RANCHES IN THE BRAZILIAN AMAZON

$ million

	Net present value (NPV) investment outlay	Total investment outlay (TIO)	NPV / TIO (%)
Economic Analysis			
A. Base case	-2 824 000	5 143 700	-.55
B. Sensitivity analysis			
-- Cattle prices assumed doubled	511 380	5 143 700	+.10
-- Land prices assumed rising 5 per cent/year more than general inflation rate	-2 300 370	5 143 700	-.45
Financial Analysis			
A. Reflecting all investor incentives: tax credits, deductions and subsidised loans	1 875 400	753 650	+2.49
B. Sensitivity analysis			
-- Interest rate subsidies eliminated	849 000	753 650	1.13
-- Deductibility of losses against other taxable income eliminated	-658 500	753 650	-0.87

Source: Robert Repetto, 1988a, p. 42.

CASE 4

POLICY FAILURE: RANCHING FOR SUBSIDIES IN BRAZIL

In the 1960s, the Brazilian government introduced extensive legislation aimed at developing the Amazon region. Over the next two decades, a combination of fiscal and financial incentives emerged which encouraged the conversion of forest to pasture land. During the 1970s, some 8 000-10 000 square kilometres of forest were cleared for pasture each year. The proportion of land used for pasture in the Amazonian state of Rondonia increased from 2.5 per cent in 1970 to 25.6 per cent in 1985 (Mahar, 1989). Without tree cover, the fragile Amazonian soil often loses its fertility and at least 20 per cent of the pastures may be at some stage of deterioration (Repetto, 1988a). Indeed, cattle ranching is considered one of the foremost proximate causes of deforestation.

Furthermore, ranching provides few long-term employment opportunities. Livestock projects offer work only during the initial slash-and-burn-phase. Negative employment effects have been observed when income-generating tree crops such as Brazil nuts are eradicated for pasture (Mahar, 1989).

Operation Amazonia (1966-67) established the Superintendency for the Development of the Amazon (SUDAM) which administered the numerous fiscal incentives designed to attract ranching. Fiscal incentives include tax holidays of 10-15 years, investment tax credits (ITC) and export tax or import duty exemptions. ITCs allowed corporations to exempt 50 per cent of tax liabilities by investing their savings in SUDAM approved projects. (After 1974, ITC is limited to 25 per cent credit.) Projects were prioritised, and those with favourable ratings could be financed 75 per cent by tax credit funds.

Starting in 1974, subsidised credit also played a crucial role in encouraging numerous ranching projects. The Program of Agricultural, Livestock and Mineral Poles in Amazonia (POLAMAZONIA) offered ranchers loans at 12 per cent interest, while elsewhere interest rates were 45 per cent. Subsidised loans of 49 per cent to 76 per cent of face value were typical through the early 1980s (Repetto, 1988b). The programme discriminated against poor tenant farmers who lacked the necessary collateral. Also, tax breaks and cheap money were capitalised into the land making property more expensive and even less accessible to the poor. (Subsidised credit was eliminated completely by mid-1987.)

The subsidies and tax breaks encouraged ranchers to undertake projects which would not otherwise have been profitable. Many projects were pursued solely for their fiscal benefits. A survey of SUDAM projects reveals five projects receiving tax credit funds without ever being implemented. Investments were often made in projects which would normally generate negative returns. A World Resources Institute study showed that the typical subsidised investment yield an economic loss equal to 55 per cent of the initial investment. However when including subsidies received by the private investor, the investment yielded a positive financial return equal to 250 per cent of initial outlay. The fiscal and financial incentives masked what were intrinsically poor investments, and served to subsidise the conversion of a superior asset (tropical forest) into an inferior use (cattle ranching). (For the detailed calculation of financial and economic returns from government-assisted ranches in the Brazilian Amazon, see Table 1).

8. Economic Incentives for Sustainable Forestry

The impact of reduction of agricultural *credit subsidies* (Philippines, Tunisia) is somewhat ambiguous. If credit subsidies are benefiting large farmers and ranchers engaged in large-scale land clearing (as is more the case in Latin America than in Asia or Africa) reduction of these subsidies clearly reduces environmental degradation (see Case 4). If, on the other hand, credit subsidies are benefiting small farmers who have inadequate funds for intensification on existing lands, and investment in land improvement and soil conservation, any reduction of these subsidies will induce more soil "mining" and forest land encroachment than is currently the case. However, even in the case of the small farmer, there are superior policies to outright credit subsidies which are, in any case, fungible and can be used for other purposes. Removal of interest rate ceilings, issue of secure land titles that can be used as collateral, and increased credit availability at competitive rates are better for the farmer, the budget and the environment than credit subsidies, because they optimise the use of both capital and land. Credit subsidies are an incentive to borrow but not an incentive to invest in soil conservation or tree planting if the farmer has no security of land ownership.

Forest policy is an excellent example of a resource-specific policy that needs to be overhauled if the link between scarcity and prices is to be re-established. If indeed we are facing a growing scarcity of forests, forest product prices should be rising to slow down deforestation and accelerate reforestation. At present, not only are most forest products and services not priced, but even timber which is an internationally tradeable commodity is priced below its true scarcity value due to implicit and explicit subsidies and institutional failures. Uncollected resource rents, subsidised logging on marginal and fragile forest lands, and volume-based taxes on timber removal encourage high grading and destructive logging. Forest concessions are typically too short to provide incentives for conservation and replanting. Failure to value non-timber goods and services results in excessive deforestation, in conflicts with local communities, in loss of economic value and in environmental damage. Promotion of local processing of timber often leads to inefficient plywood mills, excess capacity, waste of valuable tropical timber and loss of government revenues. Replanting subsidies often end up subsidising the conversion of a valuable natural forests to inferior mono-species plantations, with the associated loss of the value of both tropical hardwoods and biological diversity, as the experience of Indonesia demonstrates.

Concerns over rapid rates of deforestation and slow rates of replanting have given rise to export bans on unprocessed timber by tropical timber producers such as Thailand, the Philippines and Indonesia. The primary motivation in Thailand has been the conservation of forest resources and, in Indonesia, an increase in value-added through domestic processing and, by implication, forest conservation. The log export bans have largely failed to slow deforestation in all three countries. In Thailand and the Philippines, illegal logging and clearing of land for permanent and shifting cultivation continued unabated. In Indonesia, the inefficient and excessive processing capacity stimulated by the log export ban has led to logging rates above the pre-ban levels.

Following the catastrophic landslides and floods of November 1958 that have been attributed to deforestation, the Thai government introduced an indefinite logging ban. This is a well-meant and popular action. However, unless it is supplemented with effective enforcement and forest management, it is unlikely to succeed in stemming the rate of deforestation. Illegal logging, encroachment and shifting cultivation are likely to continue and even intensify in the absence of the logging concessions, because population pressures, poverty, and incentives for opening land for agriculture have not changed.

Log export bans and logging bans are well-intentioned responses to increase value added from a wasting asset (Indonesia), to the growing scarcity of forest resources (Philippines) and to ecological disasters (Thailand) but they often accomplish the reverse of the intended result. The reason is a fundamental one. These policies depress rather than increase the value of the resource, thereby inducing more waste and less conservation. Making a resource less valuable is usually not an effective way of saving it. What is needed is a reform of current forest policies to encourage efficient harvesting and processing and to promote investments in forest regeneration and conservation. A forest policy reform might include the following elements, most of which can be done by the countries themselves without outside interference and with minimal external support:

1) Reclassify forest lands into (a) land disposable to individuals, (b) land disposable to groups of individuals or communities, and (c) non-disposable land over which the state retains ownership and control. The criterion for this classification should be the extent of externalities in terms of both intensity and spatial distribution: (a) forest lands with no significant externalities can be safely distributed and securely titled to the dispossessed; e.g. landless farmers, chronically idle labourers, shifting cultivators; (b) forest lands with localised externalities, such as local watersheds, can be made communal property provided that a community small and cohesive enough to manage them effectively can be defined; and (c) forest lands with regional or national externalities such as major watersheds or nature reserves should stay under state ownership which would be more likely to be effective over a limited area with reduced outside pressure.

2) Change the procedure for awarding concessions, from negotiations with the concessionaires and licensing with nominal fees, to competitive bidding in order to maximise the government's share of the resource rents, to keep logging out of marginal lands and to reduce the perceived risk of renegotiation of concession agreements; concessionaires should be provided with financial instruments for accumulating equity through forest investments which are transferable and marketable to encourage them to invest in conservation and reforestation.

3) Increase the duration and scope of the exploitation leases sufficiently to internalise non-timber forest products and services and to encourage forest regeneration for subsequent felling cycles. Concession leases are usually 5-20 years in Cameroon and Indonesia, while tropical forests take at a minimum 30-50 years to mature. Venezuela and Ghana grant 50-year-long concessions.

4) Reform the taxation system to eliminate incentives for destructive logging: e.g. change the tax base from the volume of timber removed (e.g. Indonesia) to the volume of merchantable timber on the site to eliminate the incentive for high grading and forest "mining."

5) Determine whether any harvesting of timber, fuelwood, and non-timber goods should be allowed in protective forests, and if so specify the areas, set the conditions and restrictions, define who should be allowed to harvest, and devise an enforceable cost-effective system of incentives and penalties that would regulate access and use without

unacceptable trade-offs between the primary "protective" function and the secondary "productive" function. This would require research and experimentation in assessing trade-offs between competing uses, predicting behaviour in response to penalties and incentives, and evaluating the cost-effectiveness of alternative policy instruments.

6) Promote private forest investments through an appropriate incentive structure and financial mechanisms, such as co-financing of long-term loans: longer grace, disbursement, and repayment periods; establishment of guarantee funds to reduce risk; and insurance against pest outbreaks and forest fires.

7) With regard to public benefits generated by private forest investments, such as downstream irrigation benefits, provide commensurate incentives such as tax exceptions and subsidies linked to these benefits to bring forest investments to a level consistent with long-term economic and social profitability. For instance, the tax structure should favour natural forest management over plantations, mixed-species plantations over single-species plantations, and single-species plantations over erosive crops such as corn and cassava (see Case 7, and Figure 4). Eucalyptus and pine plantations should be taxed or promoted in proportion to their net social and environmental impact on water table, soil erosion, nutrient depletion, etc. Logging companies could be provided with incentives to set aside part of their concessions as nature reserves (for conservation purposes) and extractive reserves (for social purposes) and to manage the rest on a sustainable basis. Farmers and other water users who benefit from irrigation systems downstream could be charged water fees, with a part going towards the protection of the upstream watershed (see Case 5).

8) Recognise and accommodate the customary rights of access and land use of forests by local communities; their physical presence in the forest and their intimate knowledge of the local ecology can be of immense value in the protection and regeneration of the forest and the harvesting and use of non-timber products. Papua New Guinea recognises and protects communal customary tenure over land and forest resources. Logging companies seeking logging rights must negotiate with the communities (see Case 6).

These reforms should be strongly supported by both commercial forestry (producers and consumers) and developing country government because they will ensure sustainable supplies of tropical hardwoods and will transform tropical commercial forestry from an extractive industry into a sustainable economic activity with considerable private and social net benefits. While higher hardwood prices may be perceived as running against the short-term interests of commercial forestry (especially by the importers and consumers), the long-term benefits appropriately discounted exceed any short-term costs. Unless higher prices are paid for tropical hardwoods, there can be no conservation and without conservation there can be no sustainable supplies. Currently, the waste, inefficiency, and damage to regenerations are so great that it is possible, by instituting these reforms, to make every party involved better off. Alternatives such as export bans, logging bans, import bans or other similar prohibitions or trade restrictions are misguided and counter-productive, as the experience of countries such as Thailand, Indonesia and the Philippines demonstrates.

CASE 5

TURNING A MARKET FAILURE INTO A POLICY SUCCESS: THE DUMOGA-BONE IRRIGATION SYSTEM *CUM* NATIONAL PARK – INDONESIA

In 1980, the Indonesian Government with assistance from the World Bank established the Dumoga-Bone National Park in Sulawesi, Indonesia. (At a cost of $1.2 million, the project constituted nearly 2 per cent of a $60 million irrigation project.) The park serves the dual purpose of protecting a major irrigation area as well as conserving valuable wildlands. After construction of the Dumoga Valley highway, the once pristine area fell prey to rapid encroachment, especially via a government-sponsored transmigration scheme. Increasingly, forest in the catchment area was cleared, threatening the water flow from feeder rivers and increasing the likelihood of siltation. Given this steady deterioration, the Indonesian government and the World Bank agreed the watershed area of the Dumoga basin needed more effective management.

Their agreement led to the establishment of the 278 700 ha park which has allowed scientists to make important advances in conservation biology. For example, 160 researchers from 17 countries participated in Project Wallace which was implemented to catalogue the insects of the area.

At the same time the park promotes the conservation of indigenous plant and animal species, it also insures the investment in the irrigation project by guaranteeing a well-protected watershed. Two alternative uses -- an effective watershed for irrigation and conservation land -- complement each other, resulting in a positive externality generating benefits for both uses and society at large. The project's provisions for wildland management also serve to enhance the irrigation system by reducing sedimentation (and related maintenance costs) and helping to ensure a steady and predictable flow of water. Water fees are collected to fund both services: provision of irrigation water and wildlife preservation. For the first time, the Indonesian government explicitly recognised and assigned a value to conservation efforts as part of development (McNeely, 1987).

Both economic and ecological benefits are gained. The free market would not have brought about this result because of prohibitive transaction costs of bringing together thousands of farmers to reach an agreement and enforce it. Government intervention has produced two public goods: watershed protection and biological conservation, neither of which could have been produced by a free market because of the inability to exclude free riders.

Dumoga Park illustrates how an irrigation project can be planned to include provisions for watershed protection which simultaneously fulfil the requirements for conservation land. Both uses complement one another while generating both economic and environmental benefits. The conversion of the watershed area into park land establishes an important linkage between biological conservation and watershed management. The project can serve as a model for other irrigation projects where costs for protecting watersheds are automatically included and justified not only as a means to insure the irrigation investment but also for the inherent conservation value.

CASE 6

COMMUNAL FOREST TENURE IN PAPUA NEW GUINEA

Unlike most of the developing world, Papua New Guinea has maintained its communal tenure customs while adapting to the requirements of an increasingly market-oriented economy. While the latter requires clear land ownership, Papua New Guinea's experience has shown that converting land from communal to freehold may confuse rather than clarify the rights of ownership. On the other hand, absent has been the widespread land degradation encouraged by the insecure tenure, loss of entitlements, and open access characteristic of state-owned land elsewhere.

Most countries have responded to market pressures for clear ownership by imposing a new system of private or state ownership. In contrast, Papua New Guinea's land law builds upon the customs governing its communally held land. The country's Land Ordinance Act calls for local mediators and land courts to base settlements on existing principles of communal ownership. Consequently, 97 per cent of the land remains communal, has been neither surveyed nor registered, and is governed by local custom (Cooter).

This communal tenure seems to provide clearer ownership rights, with all their environmental and market implications, than private ownership. Settlements which convert communal land to freehold are often later disputed with reversion back to customary ownership a frequent outcome. Yet, unlike the reality of state-owned land in other developing countries, communal land in Papua New Guinea is neither unowned nor public. Rather, the bundle of rights deemed "ownership" in the West does not reside in one part. For example, individual families hold the right to farm plots of land indefinitely, but the right to trade them resides in the clan (Cooter).

The island's communal systems have long resulted in the sustainable use of its more densely populated highlands. With a 9 000 year agricultural history, an overly wet climate, and a population growth of at least 2.3 per cent, the highlands remain fertile. The population, which is primarily agricultural, enjoy a per capita income over twice that of El Salvador, Western Samoa or Nigeria (Cooter). In marked contrast to much of the developing world, only 6 million of its 46 million hectares of forest land have been converted to other uses (Australian UNESCO Committee, 1976).

The lack of deforestation comes as no surprise since those who control the land have an interest in the sustainable, productive use of its forest. Rather than dealing with a distant government in need of quick revenues and foreign exchange, companies seeking logging rights must negotiate directly with those who have secure tenure and who use the land not only to farm, but to gather fruit, hunt and collect materials for clothing, buildings, and weapons (HIID, 1988; Australian UNESCO Committee, 1976). Because the communal tenure patterns provide an entitlement to all clan members, individuals have little incentive to sacrifice future value for current use.

-- Basing land law upon customary communal tenure patterns can be a viable adaptation to the requirements of a market economy.

-- Communal tenure may prevent deforestation more effectively than either state or private ownership if it provides an entitlement and secure tenure to a group who benefits from a forest's sustainable use.

9. Expanding the Use of Economic Incentives in Developing Countries

Economic incentives as instruments of environmental management in developing countries have many advantages over command-and-control regulations. First, they can achieve the desired effect at the least possible cost which is vital to developing countries with limited resources and a dire need to maintain their competitiveness in world markets. Second, economic incentives are easier to enforce which is important for countries with limited enforcement capability. Third, economic incentives present fewer opportunities for rent-seeking behaviour than regulations and therefore they are likely to be both more effective and more equitable. Finally, unlike regulations that require bloated bureaucracies and large budgets, economic incentives generate revenues which should be welcome by countries facing tight budgets and budgetary deficits.

Whatever the merits of economic incentives and the experience of other countries with their use, considerable obstacles prevent their wider adoption. First, there is a lack of understanding of how these systems work and their impact on growth and income distribution. Often, they are dismissed as ways to appropriate poor people's resources or to reward polluters with a legal right to pollute. Then, there are those who fear that economic incentives will raise the costs of production and make local industries uncompetitive in world markets. Governments are concerned that, because these systems raise the cost to the public, they would be unpopular and may endanger government stability. Command-and-control regulations appear safer, even if they are not as cost-effective.

Environmental concerns are fairly new in developing countries. Whereas 5-10 years ago, governments could argue that a clean environment is a luxury that only developed countries can afford, today they must be seen by a more environmentally conscious public to be doing something about resource conservation and environmental quality. Logging bans, land zoning, pollution standards backed by legal sanctions are far more visible and easily understood actions than resource pricing, water rights and pollution charges and permits. Since actual compliance, verifiable environmental improvement, and cost-effectiveness are not yet part of the political debate, the argument for economic incentives is not as compelling.

The widely prevailing perception that natural resources are gifts of nature and environment is a free good predisposes people to accept constraints on use but to reject pricing. It is not easy to get people to agree to pay for what has been traditionally free. This applies as much to water pricing for farmers as to pollution charges for industry. "Payment" in terms of water shortages, occupational accidents or lost time in traffic jams is often more palatable than smaller payments in the form of charges. Finally, there is a misconception among the general public that the government should and somehow can finance environmental improvement, without additional taxation; that ultimately it is the taxpayer himself or herself that bears the cost at levels higher than need be and in rates that are regressive is not widely recognised.

These circumstances reinforced by the vested interests created by existing regulations and by their selective enforcement, do not bode well for the wider adoption of economic incentives in developing countries. However, there are also some "favourable" factors emerging: (a) budgetary constraints and deficits impose a rationality of their own that will make full-cost pricing, cost recovery, and cost-effectiveness inevitable; (b) environmental disasters and crises (such as the 1988 landslides and floods in Thailand) present political windows of opportunity when new constituencies emerge (Paterson, 1989) that make more rational choices possible; (c) growing environmental awareness and pluralism in developing countries will gradually put environmental and fiscal accountability on the political agenda; and (d) developing countries increasingly realise the wealth of their own traditional institutions for managing resources such as customary rights of use and access.

Yet, even if the rationality of economic systems prevail their adoption is not guaranteed, for what is rational is not necessarily practical. Consider, for example the problems with introducing pollution charges. First, the industry fearing loss of profitability and competitiveness is likely to resist attempts to introduce charges for the use of infrastructure and the environment; and, they would have a point since the profitability of investments made under the old policy might be adversely affected. Second, the government for political reasons would not want to be perceived as raising the cost to the public or to the industry by introducing environmental or congestion charges. Third, there is always the difficult problem of monitoring and enforcement.

The most critical first step is to make the principles of eventual full-cost pricing and internalisation of external cost acceptable to the industry and the public *in exchange* for recognition of their legitimate concerns and the need for gradual introduction and adjustment assistance. Once the principles have been agreed upon, the next step is a gradual phase-in over a ten year period, which is roughly the time it takes for old investments to depreciate. In this manner we gradually direct the future investments towards a more desirable mix (e.g. less energy intensive, less polluting) without penalising past and current investments. It is preferable for a country to begin today with nominal charges, based on solid principles that earn wide acceptance and support and work its way to full implementation by the end of the century, than to go for a gamut of regulations today that give the illusion of command and control but would leave the situation no further ahead at the end of the decade than it is today.

To preserve the cost-effectiveness advantage of economic incentives and at the same time make their introduction more acceptable to the industry and politically more palatable to the government the following five principles need to be agreed upon at the very start (using again industrial pollution control as an example):

The Ambient Quality Target:

The aim should be the achievement of a desired environmental quality (ambient standard), not a uniform effluent or emission standard or level of waste treatment. This is because ambient quality is the ultimate objective, and it can be achieved through various means; uniform effluent standards is only one, and rarely the most efficient, instrument. The target ambient quality standard should be specific, monitorable and verifiable.

The Minimum Cost Principle:

The desired ambient quality standard must be attained through the most cost-effective means, that is, at the lowest possible cost to the economy -- including cost to the regulatory agency, such as monitoring and enforcement cost; and cost to the industry, such as a reduction in output and an increase in the pollution control cost. This implies that the chosen policy instrument must be enforceable in the local context, at a relatively low cost, and with a minimal leakage.

The Polluter Pays Principle:

The chosen policy instrument must be self-financed, and perceived to be equitable. The polluter pays principle is now widely accepted around the world. While the payment is collected from the industrial producer, the ultimate burden (incidence of the pollution charge) is shared between the producer and the consumer in a proportion determined by the elasticity of demand for the product in question. In the case of an exported commodity sold in competitive world markets (and therefore facing infinitely elastic demand), the full burden is assumed by the producer; therefore, his competitive position might be affected. Hence, the following two principles should be considered:

The Competitiveness Imperative:

The policy instrument chosen should not significantly reduce the *overall* competitiveness of industry, although it would unavoidably change the industrial mix in the medium to long run, if it is effective at all. Maintaining competitiveness while controlling pollution implies the existence of inefficiencies that the chosen instrument should seek to reduce.

Policy Transition:

Changing the industrial mix from high- to low-polluting industries is one of the desirable outcomes of an effective pollution control instrument. However, structural change takes time, since investments have already been made under "pollution haven" conditions that will take time to depreciate. Therefore, for both fairness and efficiency, allowance for adjustment during the transition period must be made. The new policy is also likely to be more acceptable to the industry if it is gradually phased in over an appropriate period. The stability and predictability of the policy is critical if industrial investment is to be gradually shifted from high- to low-polluting industries.

Once an economic incentive system (such as marginal cost pricing or charges) is introduced it should not be allowed to lose its value over time, either through inflation or political manipulation. For example, in Thailand, water and energy prices have been frozen in nominal terms in recent years despite a 6 per cent rate of inflation. A groundwater charge of 1 baht per cubic meter, introduced in 1977 to internalise the environmental cost of land subsidence resulting from groundwater pumping, remains at 1 baht today; in real terms it has lost more than half its value. When the pressure of economic incentives falls rather than rises over time little change in behaviour is accomplished and little investment in new technologies is induced. It is preferable to begin by setting low rates and escalate over time based on a predetermined and preannounced formula. A gradualised scheme has several advantages:

(a) it is easier to get accepted and introduced; (b) it allows time for adjustment, thus minimising resistance and cost; and, (c) it gives the correct signal to investors and innovators.

Another principle that needs to be observed is the minimisation of enforcement and monitoring requirements of the system and of the latitude for discretion by regulators. Compliance should be made in the interest of the resource user or the polluter. The regulators should be indifferent as to whether the polluter pollutes or pays, wastes or conserves water, cuts or plants trees. If the regulator is not indifferent then the price or charge is too low. The need to minimise regulatory, enforcement, and monitoring cost arises from the low enforcement capability in developing countries, and the rent-seeking behaviour that high charges and low salaries bring about. The ideal economic incentive is the one which is incorporated into the price of a resource or product; it can be avoided only by avoiding the use of the resource or product. Other instruments that meet this condition are refundable deposits, performance bonds, presumptive charges at clean-up-cost levels, transferable development rights, property and land use taxes and transaction quotas. Hazardous waste management is an example where an imaginative combination of presumptive charges, performance bonds and environmental auditing can be at least as effective as strong preventive measures and a lot more efficient.

Hybrid systems of economic incentives and regulations do exist but they should not be confused with a mixture of the two, arising from unwillingness of regulators to depart their command and control posts. In the hybrid systems the government sets a long-term target (e.g. ambient standard, rate of reforestation, water conservation) and market-based instruments are used to achieve the target at minimum costs.

To sum up, the causes of natural resource mismanagement and environmental degradation in the developing countries as in the developed countries are policy and market failures. Regulations do not correct these failures; they create new ones. Economic incentives' very purpose is to correct policy and market failures. In terms of cost-effectiveness the superiority of economic incentives to command-and-control regulations cannot be denied at least in the context of developing countries. Yet, the resistance to market incentives should not be underestimated. The fear of market-based incentives is like the fear of flying. Even if one is assured with hard facts that flying is far safer than driving on the road, one always feels more secure at the steering wheel. Yet the fear of flying does not prevent millions from doing so. Hopefully, the false security of regulations and the distrust of the market would not prevent economic incentives from being used more extensively in developing countries for resource management and environmental protection. It is the safest and fastest way to get there.

CASE 7

ECONOMIC INCENTIVES FOR ENVIRONMENTAL MANAGEMENT: AN EXAMPLE USING A LAND USE AND SLOPE TAX

The Problem

The catastrophic landslides and floods of November 1988 in Southern Thailand have been described as the worst natural disaster in Thailand's recorded history. Over 350 people were killed, 2 000 were injured, and 30 000 were displaced. Estimates of damages to crops, property and infrastructure range from $200-300 millions. The cause of the disaster was the combination of the high rainfall, the low natural resilience of steep-sloped granitic mountains, which has been further reduced by human economic activity, particularly the replacement of natural forests on steep slopes by young rubber plantations without land conservation measures.

Through a combination of a more productive variety of rubber, higher rubber prices, and lower costs through implicit subsidies for land clearing and replanting, the profitability of rubber has increased enormously leading to rapid expansion of rubber plantations on high slopes, the only area where land "suitable" for rubber is still available.

While steep-slope rubber is profitable to the farmer, it may not be as profitable to the society that bears the consequences of forest loss, of disturbance of mountain stability (resulting in landslides), of soil erosion and of downstream flooding. The owner of the upland rubber plantation often does not even have to pay the price of the land or even the full cost of clearing and planting. The society as a whole, however, bears all these costs plus any environmental costs resulting from the deforestation and planting of rubber on steep slopes. Obviously, there is considerable discrepancy between private and social benefits and costs as shown in Figure 2. Upland farmers are in effect engaged in an activity that converts social costs into private benefits. The landslides and flood damage of November 1988 can be thought of as the accumulation of unpaid social costs.

A Proposed Solution

If a major cause of the disaster is unsustainable land uses in the uplands, driven by a wedge between private and social costs, a way to deal with the problem is to bridge this gap through an appropriately structured incentive system. One possibility is to increase the export tax on rubber, since overexpansion of rubber is part of the problem. This would help reduce rubber planting on high slopes but will also affect lowland rubber production.

A more targeted land tax that varies with slope and land use (see Figures 3 and 4) would be more efficient. Such a tax should be progressive with: (1) slope, i.e. the higher the slope the higher the tax; (2) size of ownership, i.e. the more land one owns the higher should be the tax; and (3) land use, i.e. the more unsustainable or environment-degrading the land use the higher the tax.

(continued...)

A tax should be combined with rebates (and perhaps subsidies) for land conservation practices and socially beneficial land uses such as forestry (see Figure 4). It may be claimed that such a tax is difficult to introduce and implement. This might be true, but farmers are already familiar with land taxes which they faithfully pay to ensure continued "ownership" of their lands. If such a land tax is combined with degazettment of encroached forest lands and issuance of a secure title, two additional benefits would be generated: (1) the land tax will be more palatable since the value of farmers' land will increase (probably double); and (2) farmers will have more incentive and access to credit for making land improvements and practising soil conservation.

Ideally, an optimal land tax should bridge the entire gap between the private and social cost of cultivating lands of varying slope and fragility, as shown in Figure 3. For example, a slope-specific land tax should vary in such a way that lowlands are lightly taxed because they have minimal externalities while increasing gradually as slope rises, to become prohibitively high above a certain slope, say 35 per cent, where cultivation poses a threat to the slope's structural stability. However, depending on the availability of sustainable agricultural technologies such as mixed farm plantations and agroforestry systems, for higher slopes, the land tax law should provide for tax rebates for those who adopt sustainable land uses and environmentally sound farming practices.

The government may even consider the possibility of rebates exceeding the paid land tax for those who keep their land under permanent forestry. This would discourage farmers who occupy or claim land still covered with forest from clearing it for agriculture, since such clearing would involve, in addition to the clearing cost, loss of the subsidy and substantial tax burden. While it is possible to have a tax that varies both with slope and land use, for both simplicity and enforcement it might be preferable to have a tax that varies with slope, and rebates that vary with land use. In this way, the burden of proof of sustainable land use falls on the land owners. (This economic incentive scheme was recently proposed by the author to the government of Thailand for containing the conversion of steep slopes into rubber plantations and other unsustainable uses. For details see T. Panayotou "The Economics of Man-Made Natural Disasters" in AID, May 1989.)

10. A Postscript

As expected, questions were raised during the conference as to the applicability and effectiveness of market-based incentives as instruments of environmental management in developing countries. Concerns include:

a) The limited reach of fiscal policy, the large underground economy and the competence of the taxman as environmental manager;

b) The "high" informational costs of market-based incentives; and

c) The need for regulations to back-up economic incentives.

In the opinion of the author, these concerns arise from inadequate understanding of narrow interpretation of economic instruments. Environmental taxes or other fiscal instruments are only one type of economic incentive and rarely the most efficient and practicable. Proper pricing of resources and products (to cover the full scarcity rent and environmental impact) has nothing to do with fiscal policy or the taxman. The underground economy can avoid environmental regulations but it cannot avoid paying the full market price (inclusive of environmental charges). Refundable deposits, or transferable development rights again are not subject to the limitations of fiscal authorities or the constraints of the underground economy. There is a rich tool kit of economic instruments to choose from to suit the particular circumstances of the country and environmental problem in question. Combinations, variations, as well as entirely new instruments can be developed to address specific problems and difficulties.

The informational requirements of market-based instruments are far lower than those of control-and-command regulations in the same way and for the same reasons that the information needs of market economies are smaller than those of planned economies. That much is clear. Informational parsimony is a major advantage of market based incentives; if properly designed, they are nearly self-enforced.

Do economic incentives need regulations to back them up? They do, but of a different kind. They need enabling legislation, legitimisation or legal framework; they do not require detailed legislation. Environmental funds need to be instituted, subsidies need to be removed, performance bonds and transferable development rights legislated. But once they are set up they would be more or less self-enforced; otherwise, the economic incentives have not been properly set up. Regulations are needed to set the rules of the game not to specify or arbitrate every move of the game. Economic incentives, unlike regulations are parsimonious in both informational and regulatory requirements.

Two other concerns raised deal with the (a) competitiveness imperative as a quality of economic incentives for environmental management, and (b) the exceptionalism of the Thai case, as a model for other countries. The competitiveness imperative has two aspects. The first is that the desired level of environmental improvement should be attained at the minimum possible cost. This clearly supports economic incentives over regulations. The second aspect is that past investments made under different game rules should not be unduly penalised, i.e. the economic incentives/disincentives should be phased in as to affect the direction and mix of future investments. Assuming past investments take ten years to fully depreciate economic instruments can be introduced at 10 per cent of their full value and be escalated annually to reach their full value in ten years. This attenuation of policy provides time to the industry for adjustment to the new rules of the game. It is both efficient and equitable. It is easier to attenuate economic instruments than rigid regulations.

To be sure, Thailand is unique in certain aspects, and so is every other country. The culture and historical experience are different; the level and rate of development are also different. The instruments of environmental management need to be tailored to accommodate these differences. Economic incentives are inherently easier to tailor to the specific circumstances of each country than command and control regulation that set rigid standards and sanctions for non-compliance.

By necessity regulations and economic incentives are complementary instruments in the sense that a minimum amount of regulation (legal framework) is necessary for economic incentives to become operational. Similarly, without economic incentives regulations either remain on paper or generate *de facto* financial flows through side payments. An efficient system is one that sets a broad regulatory framework which is implemented through a well thought out and structured set of economic instruments.

Figure 1

POLICY AND MARKET SUCCESSES AND FAILURES IN RESPONDING TO INCREASING RESOURCE SCARCITY AND ENVIRONMENTAL DEGRADATION

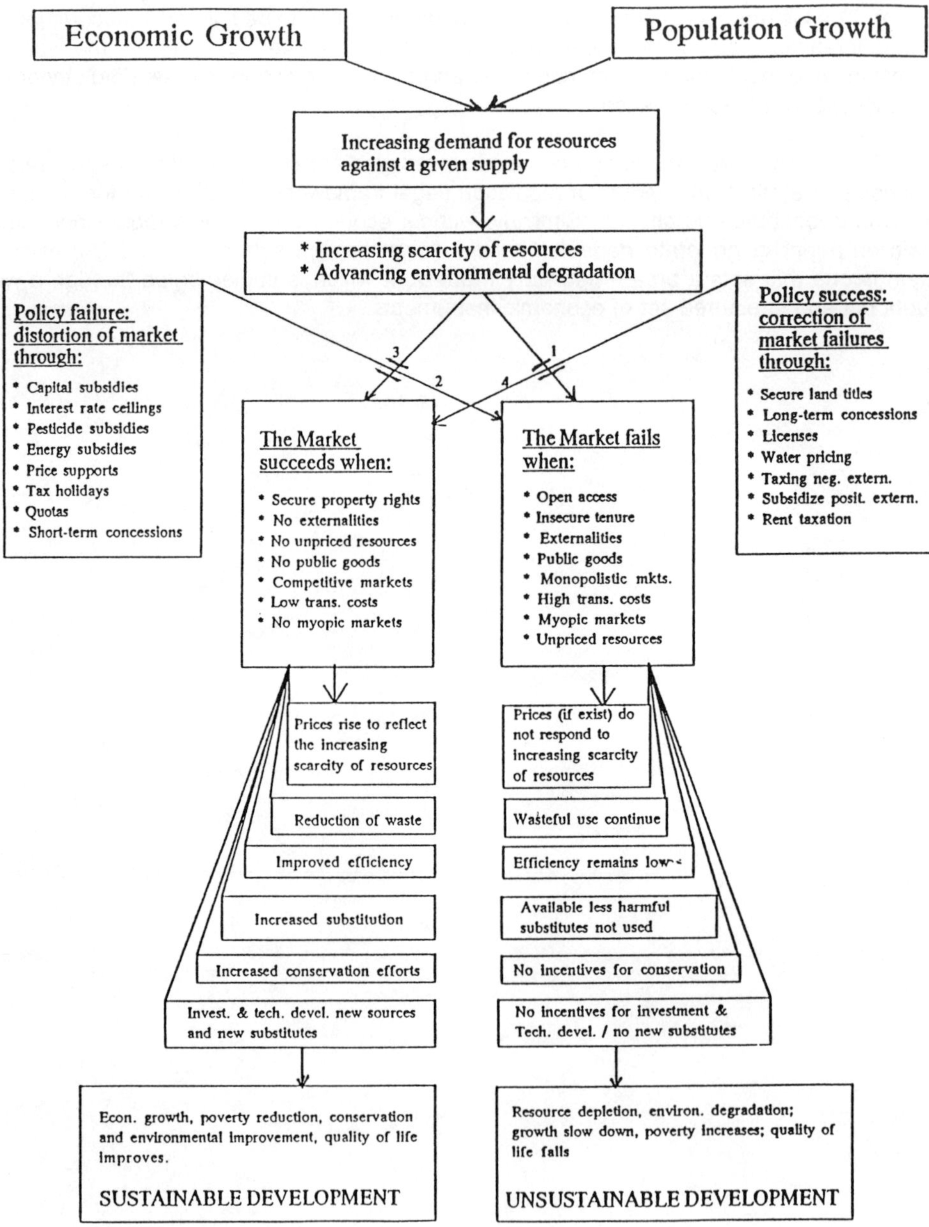

Figure 2

PRIVATE PROFIT AND SOCIAL COSTS OF GROWING RUBBER ON HIGHER SLOPES

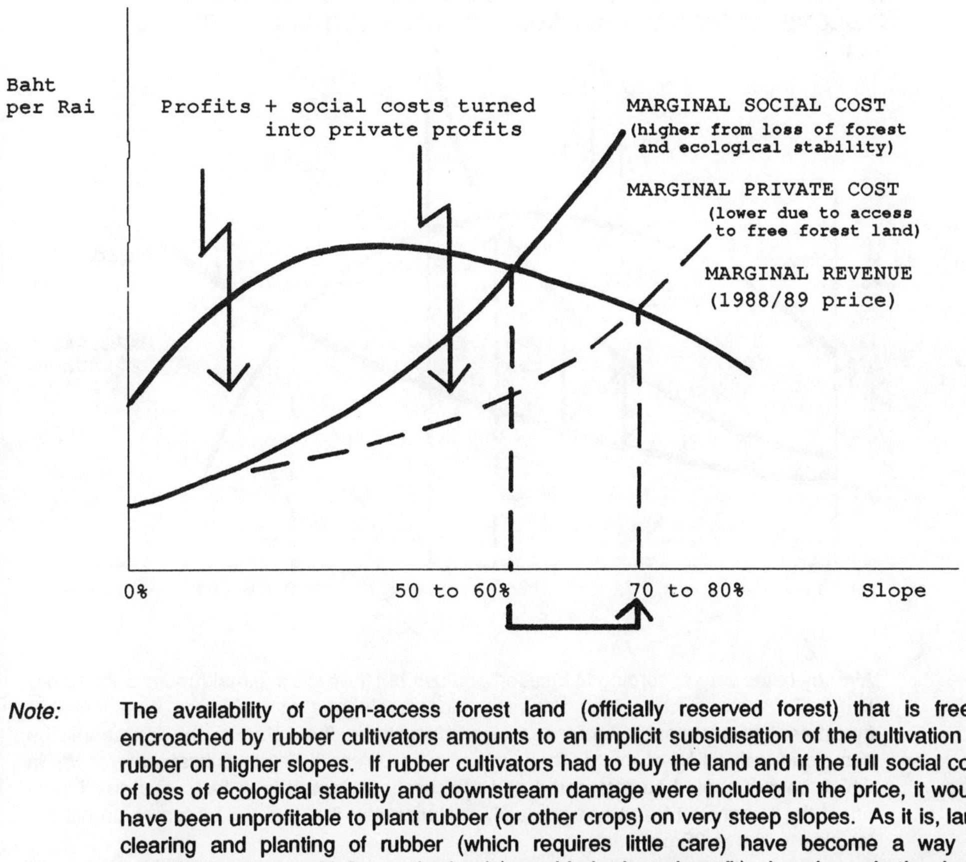

Note: The availability of open-access forest land (officially reserved forest) that is freely encroached by rubber cultivators amounts to an implicit subsidisation of the cultivation of rubber on higher slopes. If rubber cultivators had to buy the land and if the full social cost of loss of ecological stability and downstream damage were included in the price, it would have been unprofitable to plant rubber (or other crops) on very steep slopes. As it is, land clearing and planting of rubber (which requires little care) have become a way of establishing "ownership" over the land (an added private benefit). Logging, whether legal or illegal, has further lowered the marginal private cost curve by reducing the cost of clearing and access. The damage from the recent landslides and floods is no more than the accumulation of unpaid social costs by loggers, shifting cultivators, and upland rubber "owners".

Source: Panayotou, T., "Economics of Man-Made Natural Disasters" in *Safeguarding the Future*, by NOC/NESDB/USAID, Bangkok, 1989.

Figure 3

INTERNALISING THE SOCIAL COST OF CULTIVATION FOR RUBBER ON STEEP SLOPE THROUGH A PROGRESSIVE LAND TAX VARYING ACCORDING TO SLOPE (AND/OR VULNERABILITY), LOCATION AND LAND USE

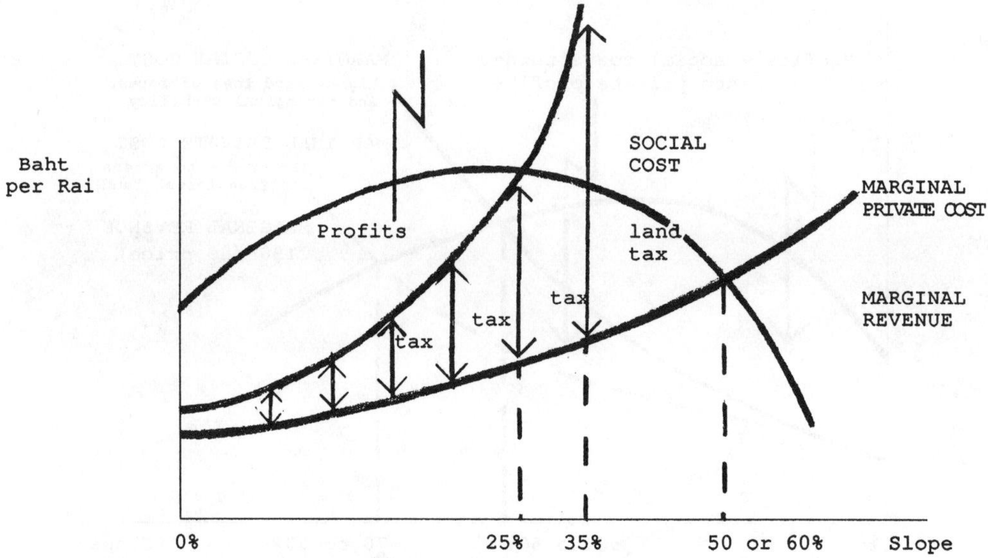

Note: Already taxes vary according to location and use but they are minimal (under Baht 10 per Rai). To make such a land tax more acceptable and at the same time increase investment in sustainable increases of productivity in the uplands, the tax should be combined with titling of encroached upland land unless it lies in critical watersheds in which case it should be reforested and effectively protected (see text). To cushion its effect the tax should be raised gradually. (Notice that the land tax becomes prohibitive for slopes above 35 per cent).

Source: Panayotou, T., "The Economics of Man-Made Natural Disasters", in *Safeguarding the Future,* by NOC/NESDB/USAID, Bangkok, 1989.

Figure 4

A HYPOTHETICAL EXAMPLE OF LAND TAXES VARYING ACCORDING TO USE AND SLOPE (VULNERABILITY)

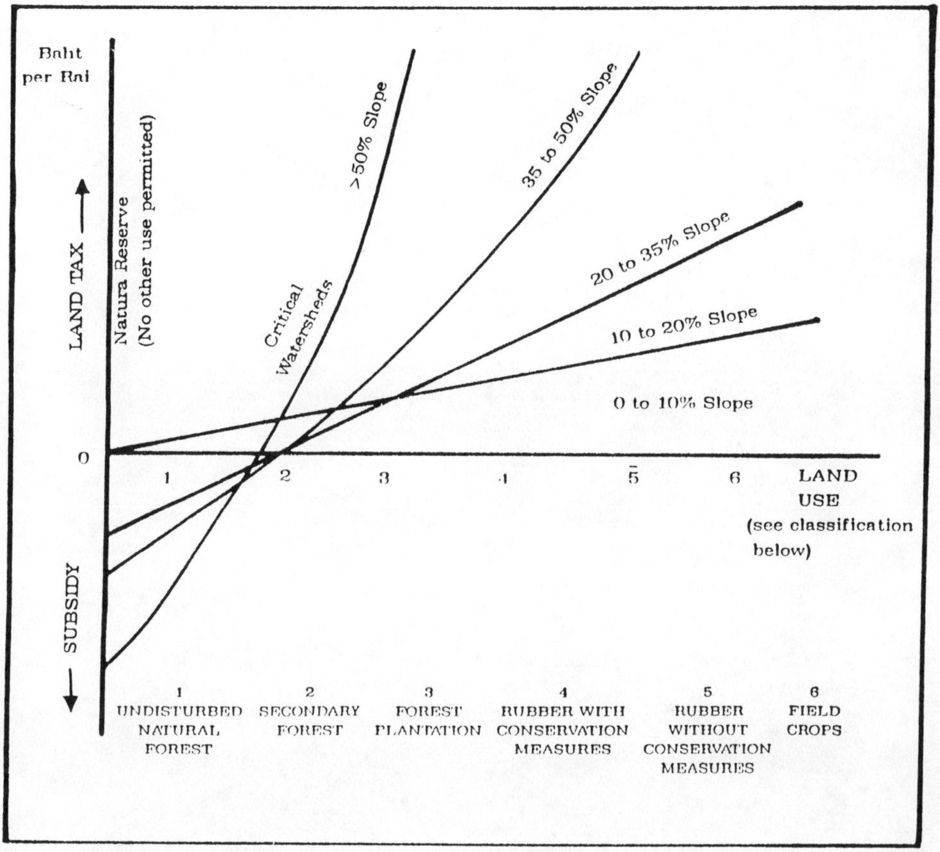

Note: Notice that there is no discrimination against any land uses for flatlands and there is total discrimination for natural reserves. Since people inhabiting the uplands are usually poorer such taxes may turn out to be regressive. This is why they should be progressive in terms of size and value of land holding and should be combined with land titling for squatters.

Source: Panayotou, T., "The Economics of Man-Made Natural Disasters", in *Safeguarding the Future,* by NOC/NESDB/USAID, Bangkok, 1989.

BIBLIOGRAPHICAL REFERENCES

AGENCY FOR INTERNATIONAL DEVELOPMENT (AID)

Environmental and Natural Resource Management in Central America: Strategy for AID Assistance, Washington, D.C., AID, 1988.

Development and the National Interest: US Economic Assistance into the 21st Century, Washington, D.C., AID, February 1989.

"The Economics of Man-Made Natural Disasters" by T. Panayotou in *Safeguarding the Future: Restoration and Sustainable Development in South Thailand*, USAID Team Report, Bangkok, AID, May 1989.

Environmental and Natural Resource Management in the Asia and Near East Region: Strategies for AID in the 1990's, Washington, D.C., AID, 22nd September 1989.

AHMAD, Yusuf J., Salah El SERAFY and Ernst LUTZ

Environmental Accounting for Sustainable Development, Washington, D.C., The World Bank, June 1989.

ANDERSON, Dennis

The Economics of Afforestation. A Case Study in Africa, Baltimore, John Hopkins University Press, 1987.

ASIAN DEVELOPMENT BANK (ADB) AND INTERNATIONAL IRRIGATION MANAGEMENT INSTITUTE

Irrigation Service Fees: Proceedings of the Regional Seminar on Irrigation Service Fees, Manila, ADB, 1986.

AUSTRALIAN UNESCO COMMITTEE FOR MAN AND THE BIOSPHERE

Ecological Effects of Increasing Human Activities on Tropical and Sub-Tropical Forest Ecosystems, Canberra, Australian Government Publishing Services, 1976.

BARBIER, Edward B.

Economics, Natural Resource Scarcity & Development, London, Earthscan Publications, 1989.

BINSWANGER, Hans P.

"Brazilian Policies that Encourage Deforestation in the Amazon", Washington, D.C., World Bank, April 1989.

BOOTH, Anne

Agricultural Development in Indonesia, Sydney, ASAA Southeast Asia Publications Series, 1988.

CLARK UNIVERSITY PROGRAM FOR INTERNATIONAL DEVELOPMENT

Renewable Resource Trends in East Africa, Worcester, Massachusetts, Clark University, 1984.

CONWAY, Gordon R., Ibrahim MANWAN and David S. McCAULEY
The Sustainability of Agricultural Intensification in Indonesia: A Report of Two Workshops of the Research Group on Agro-Ecosystems, Ford Foundation and Agency for Agricultural Research and Development, Ministry of Agriculture, Indonesia, December 1984.

COOTER, Robert D.
"Inventing Property: Economic Theories of the Origins of Market Property Applied to Papua New Guinea", undated.

DAVIS, Gloria
Indonesia Forest, Land and Water: Issues in Sustainable Development, Washington, D.C., World Bank, 1989.

DHANASETTHAKARN, Apisak
"More Deforestation Since Logging Ban", *The Nation*, 29th June 1989.

DIXON, John A. and Maynard M. HUFSCHMIDT, eds.
Economic Valuation Techniques for the Environment, Baltimore, Johns Hopkins University Press, 1986.

DUNKERLY, Harold B., Alan A. WALTERS and John M. COURTNEY
Urban Land Policy Issues and Opportunities, Volume II, World Bank Staff Working Paper No. 283, Washington, D.C., World Bank, May 1978.

The Economist
"The Extended Family -- A Survey of Indonesia", 15th August 1987.

"Traffic Jams: The City, the Commuter and the Car", 18th February 1989.

"City Lights", 18th February 1989.

"The Environment Survey", 2nd September 1989.

ERLANGER, Steven
"Indonesia Takes Steps to Protect Rain Forests", *The New York Times*, 26th September 1989.

FALLOUX, F.
"Land Information and Remote Sensing for Renewable Resource Management in Sub-Saharan Africa: A Demand Driven Approach", Washington, D.C., World Bank, 26th June 1989.

Far Eastern Economic Review
"Win Some, Lose Some", 27th October 1988.

FEDER, Gershon, Tongroj ONCHAN, Yongyuth CHALAMWONG, and Chira HONGLADAROM
Land Policies and Farm Productivity in Thailand, Baltimore, Johns Hopkins University Press, 1988.

FOOD AND AGRICULTURE ORGANIZATION (FAO)
Integrated Pest Management in Rice in Indonesia, Jakarta, FAO, May 1988.

GILLIS, Malcolm
"West Africa: Resource management policies and the tropical forest", in Robert Repetto and Malcolm Gillis, eds., *Public Policies and the Misuse of Forest Resources*, New York, Cambridge University Press, 1988.

GOODLAND, Robert and George LEDEC
"Environmental Management in Sustainable Economic Development", *International Association of Impact Assessment*, Spring 1987.

GORSE, Jean Eugene and David R. STEEDS
Desertification in the Sahelian and Sudanian Zones of West Africa, Washington, D.C. World Bank, 1987.

HARVARD INSTITUTE FOR INTERNATIONAL DEVELOPMENT (HIID)
"The Case for Multiple-Use Management of Tropical Hardwood Forests" Cambridge, MA, Harvard Institute for International Development, January 1988.

The Jakarta Post
"Government to Abolish Subsidy for Utilization of Pesticide", 2nd December 1988.

JOHNSON III, Sam H.
Physical and Economic Impacts of Sedimentation of Fishing Activities: Nam Fong, Northeast, Thailand, Urbana-Champaign, University of Illinois, 1984.

LEDEC, George and Robert GOODLAND
Wildlands: Their Protection and Management in Economic Development, Washington, D.C., World Bank, 1988.

LEONARD, H. Jeffrey
Natural Resources and Economic Development in Central America, New Brunswick, Transaction Books, 1987.

MAHAR, Dennis J.
Government Policies and Deforestation in Brazil's Amazon Region, Washington, D.C., World Bank, 1989.

McCOY-THOMPSON, Merl
"Sliding Slopes Break Thai Logjam", *World Watch*, September/October 1989.

McNEELY, Jeffrey A.
"Protected Areas and Human Ecology: How National Parks Can Contribute to Sustaining Societies of the Twenty-first Century" in David Western and Mary C. Pearl, eds., *Conservation for the Twenty-first Century*, Oxford, Oxford University Press, 1989.

Economics and Biological Diversity: Developing and Using Economic Incentives to Conserve Biological Resources, Gland, Switzerland, International Union for Conservation of Nature and Natural Resources, 1988.

"How Dams and Wildlife Can Coexist: Natural Habitats, Agriculture, and Major Water Resource Development Projects in Tropical Asia", *Journal of Conservation Biology*, Volume 1, No. 3, 3rd October 1987.

MIRANTE, Edith
"A 'Teak War' Breaks Out in Burma", *Earth Island Journal*, Summer 1989.

NATIONAL RESEARCH COUNCIL PANEL ON COMMON PROPERTY RESOURCE MANAGEMENT, BOARD ON SCIENCE AND TECHNOLOGY FOR INTERNATIONAL DEVELOPMENT, OFFICE OF INTERNATIONAL AFFAIRS
Proceedings of the Conference on Common Property Resource Management, Washington, D.C., National Academy Press, 1986.

ORGANISATION FOR ECONOMIC CO-OPERATION AND DEVELOPMENT (OECD)
Economic Instruments for Environmental Protection, Paris, OECD, 1989a.

Renewable Natural Resources, Paris, OECD, 1989b.

PANAYOTOU, Theodore
"Economics, Environment and Development", Development Discussion Paper No. 259, Cambridge, MA, Harvard Institute for International Development, December 1987.

"Thailand Management of Natural Resources for Sustainable Development: Market Failures, Policy Distortions and Policy Options", Cambridge, MA, Harvard Institute for International Development, May 1988.

"Natural Resource Management: Strategies for Sustainable Asian Agriculture in the 1990's", Cambridge, MA, Harvard Institute for International Development, September 1988.

"An Econometric Study of the Causes of Tropical Deforestation: The Case of Northeast Thailand", Development Discussion Paper No. 284, Cambridge, MA, Harvard Institute for International Development, March 1989.

"Natural Resources and the Environment in the Economies of Asia and the Near East: Growth, Structural Change and Policy Reform", Cambridge, MA, Harvard Institute for International Development, July 1989.

"The Economics of Man-Made Natural Disasters: The Case of the 1988 Landslides in South Thailand", Washington, D.C., Agency for International Development, August 1989.

PEZZEY, John
"Economic Analysis of Sustainable Growth and Sustainable Development", Washington, D.C., World Bank, March 1989.

PROGRAM FOR INTERNATIONAL DEVELOPMENT
Clark University in Co-operation with National Environment Secretariat, Ministry of Environment and Natural Resources, Government of Kenya, *Resources, Management, Population and Local Institutions in Katheka, A Case Study of Effective Natural Resources Management in Machakos, Kenya*, Worcester, MA, Clark University, October 1988.

REPETTO, Robert

Skimming the Water: Rent-seeking and the Performance of Public Irrigation Systems, Washington, D.C., World Resources Institute, December 1986.

Economic Policy Reform for Natural Resource Conservation, Washington, D.C., World Bank, May 1988a.

The Forest For the Trees? Government Policies and the Misuse of Forest Resources, Washington, D.C., World Resources Institute, 1988b.

ROGERS, Peter

"Fresh Water", in Robert Repetto, ed., *The Global Possible: Resources, Development and the New Century*, New Haven, Yale University Press, 1985.

ROSS, Lester

Environmental Policy in China, Bloomington, Indiana University Press, 1988.

SCHRAMM, Gunter and Jeremy J. WARFORD, eds.

Environmental Management and Economic Development, Washington, D.C., World Bank, 1989.

SOUTHGATE, David and David PEARCE

"Agricultural Colonization and Environmental Degradation in Frontier Developing Economies", Washington, D.C., World Bank, October 1988.

SPEARS, John

"Containing Tropical Deforestation: A Review of Priority Areas for Technological and Policy Research", Washington, D.C., World Bank, October 1988.

SPEARS, John and Edward S. AYENSU

"Resources, Development and the New Century: Forestry" in Robert Repetto, ed., *The Global Possible: Resources, Development and the New Century*, New Haven, Yale University Press, 1985.

SRIVARDHANA, Ruandoj

The Nam Pong Case Study: Some Lessons to be Learned, Environment and Policy Institute, Honolulu, East-West Center, 1982.

SZULC, Tad

"Brazil's Amazonian Frontier" in Andrew Maguire and Janet Welsh Brown, eds., *Bordering on Trouble: Resources & Politics in Latin America*, Maryland, Bethesda, Adler & Adler Publishers, 1986.

THAILAND DEVLOPMENT RESEARCH INSTITUTE (TDRI)

National Resources Profile, TDRI, 1987.

THOMAS, Vinod

"Pollution Control in Sao Paulo, Brazil: Costs, Benefits and Effects on Industrial Location", World Bank Staff Working Paper No. 501, Washington, D.C., World Bank, November 1981.

WATSON, Peter L. and Edward P. HOLLAND
"Relieving Traffic Congestion: The Singapore Area License Scheme", World Bank Staff Working Paper No. 281, Washington, D.C., World Bank, June 1978.

WORLD COMMISSION ON ENVIRONMENT AND DEVELOPMENT
Our Common Future, New York, Oxford University Press, 1987.

WORLD RESOURCES INSTITUTE
The World Bank and The United Nations Development Programme, Tropical Forests: A Call for Action, Parts I and II, Washington, D.C., World Resources Institute, October 1985.

WORLD RESOURCES INSTITUTE AND INTERNATIONAL INSTITUTE FOR ENVIRONMENT AND DEVELOPMENT
World Resources 1986, New York, Basic Books, 1986.

World Resources 1987, New York, Basic Books, 1987.

World Resources 1988-89, New York, Basic Books, 1988.

INCENTIVES FOR CONSERVATION:

THE EXAMPLE OF KAFUE FLATS, ZAMBIA

by

C.A. Drijver and A.B. Zuiderwijk *

* Centre for Environmental Studies, Leiden University, The Netherlands.

RÉSUMÉ

Les individus, dont le comportement influe sur l'environnement, sont sensibles à toutes sortes de stimulations externes autres que les incitations économiques. Les trains de mesures d'incitation dans lesquels les facteurs socio-culturels ne sont pas pris en compte s'intègrent mal au contexte et ne font pas évoluer les comportements dans le sens souhaité. Ainsi, la population locale peut considérer les réserves d'animaux sauvages créées par le gouvernement central comme une ingérence, car cette population ne tire pas suffisamment profit du développement du tourisme et considère les animaux comme son bien propre. Dans une situation de ce genre, le braconnage sera inévitable. Dans certains cas, par contre, des incitations non matérielles (faire appel aux valeurs traditionnelles) peuvent être plus efficaces que les signaux donnés par les prix. Pour atteindre les buts visés, il sera probablement préférable de se référer aux structures socio-économiques existantes (organisation traditionnelle, chefs de tribu) pour assurer la mise en oeuvre et le suivi des mesures de protection de la nature, plutôt que de s'y opposer. Les auteurs illustrent (4ème partie) le fonctionnement des divers systèmes encourageant la conservation et l'exploitation des ressources naturelles dans la plaine de la Kafue en Zambie. Ils insistent sur la notion de "train de mesures d'incitation" combinant des instruments divers qui font appel à des motivations matérielles et non matérielles, et sur l'importance des processus de participation à la conception et à la mise en oeuvre de ces trains de mesures.

SUMMARY

Individuals, whose behaviour affects the environment, are responsive to a wide range of external stimuli aside from economic incentives. Incentive packages that do not take account of socio-cultural factors appear out of context and fail to change behaviour in the desired direction. For instance, game reserves set up by the central government may appear as an outside intrusion to local people who do not sufficiently benefit from the associated tourism scheme and who consider the game as their own property. In this case poaching would be the inevitable result. Conversely, in some cases non-material incentives (appealing to traditional values) can achieve more effective results than price signals. Using, rather than confronting, existing socio-economic structures (traditional order, tribal chiefs) for the implementation and monitoring of conservation efforts is more likely to achieve the aim of such efforts. The authors illustrate (Part 4) the work of different incentive schemes for conservation and natural resource use in Zambia's Kafue flats. They stress the concept of the "incentive package", combining a variety of instruments acting upon material and non-material motivations, and the importance of participatory processes in the design and implementation of these packages.

1. *General Introduction*

A major factor contributing to the over-exploitation of natural resources in developing countries is the fact that people can earn the immediate benefits of exploiting natural resources without paying the full social and economic costs of resource depletion (Repetto, 1987). Instead, these costs are transferred to other people, either in the present (to downstream communities, to society as a whole) or in the future (to next generations).

Government policies generally support activities to open up forests, to reclaim wetlands or to intensify land use in sensitive areas through tax exemptions, institutional support and legalized free access to these areas (Blaikie, 1985 and Moris, 1987). However, these privileged incentives for resource depletion are not in accordance with the scarcity of these natural resources. Areas with great biodiversity for instance are becoming increasingly scarce.

In an important step towards sustainable development, some governments are reviewing their present policies in order to reduce incentives that favour environmentally unsound practices and to create incentives for the conservation and sustainable use of natural resources. Such a change of policies is being promoted in the sector of national parks and nature conservation.

This article discusses the concept of incentives and illustrates their application to the conservation and sustainable use of nature in a recent example from the Kafue flats in Zambia.

2. *The Concept of Incentives*

2.1 Incentives act upon motivation

With regard to conservation goals an incentive can be defined as "an inducement that motivates individuals and/or organisations to undertake activities that conserve natural resources". A disincentive, then, can be defined as "an inducement that de-motivates individuals and/or organisations to undertake activities that deplete natural resources". Incentives thus are to be conceived as stimuli, that act on the motivation of private or corporate actors.

2.2 Senders' and receivers viewpoint

In most of the literature about the use of economic instruments in environmental management these instruments (e.g. subsidies or taxes) are automatically seen as incentives and often also named as such. The equating of instruments and incentives is typical for a policy-makers' view on the concept. Below we will explain that this view hampers our understanding of the working of incentives in reality.

Incentives can be looked at from the point of view of those who send them (*senders*, e.g. policy makers/implementors) as well as from that of the *receivers* (actors at different levels of society, including the direct users of resources). The first thing to acknowledge from the latter point of view is that individuals are subject to the influence of a much wider range of external factors than those (price) signals alone, that originate from government policies (see Figure 1). A new policy instrument is not an isolated factor; for the local actor it is just one element of his/her socio-economic context. The new instrument will only lead to new behaviour when it is compatible with existing societal forces.

The second point to acknowledge is that external factors are clearly not interpreted by every actor in every culture or context in the same way; consequently policy measures do not always bring the expected and intended results. A set of incentives that appears to be a consistent "incentive package" from the point of view of a government agency may thus be inconsistent or irrelevant from the point of view of the local actor, and will create no motivation to act according to the policy-makers' intentions. The receiver's point of view is thus essential if one wishes to understand the actual working of incentives.

2.3 Economic and socio-cultural incentives

Economist sometimes reduce the concept of "incentives" to "economic incentives", reflecting the view that people ordinarily are motivated only or largely by economic considerations. In our view people's behaviour is also guided by socio-cultural considerations. Incentives must therefore be broadly defined, comprising two kinds: material (economic) incentives and non-material (socio-cultural) incentives (see also Goulet, 1989).

Socio-cultural incentives spring from financial/economic considerations on the part of the actor. They may be realised in terms of money (e.g. salaries, subsidies or income from the market) and in kind (e.g free housing or access to land).

Moral incentives spring from social and cultural rewards and penalties. Man wants to be respected and accepted by the community, and especially by those people who have a special value to him. Rewards from these so called "significant others" may include: praise, appeal to patriotism or the prospect of fulfilment from having done one's "duty". Penalties are e.g.: the threat of disgrace and the loss of status (Goulet, 1989). These penalties make people fear being reported as not behaving in a socially acceptable way.

2.4 Perverse Incentives

The promotion of biological diversity and the sustainable use of natural resources is not only a matter of creating new incentives but also a matter of modifying existing incentives for over-exploitation. Referring to incentives for over-exploitation, McNeel (1988) speaks of perverse incentives. He defines a perverse incentive as "one which induces behaviour which depletes biological diversity".

Some perverse incentives arise from market failure. However, other perverse incentives spring directly from government policies. Numerous policies not only fail to reflect the true opportunity cost of resource use, they perversely encourage more rapid and extensive degradation of soils, water, and biota than market forces alone would (Repetto, 1987).

Perverse incentives influencing the way natural resources are managed often spring from policies on land rights. Appropriation by the state of natural resources like agricultural land, forests and wildlife, involving the transfer of responsibility and decision power regarding natural resource use from village to state, often led to the breakdown of traditional structures of incentives and disincentives, ultimately leading to the over-exploitation of these natural resources.

Figure 1

THE RELATION BETWEEN EXTERNAL FACTORS (INCLUDING POLICY MEASURES), ACTIVE INTERPRETATION, (INCENTIVES AND MOTIVATION FOR BEHAVIOUR)

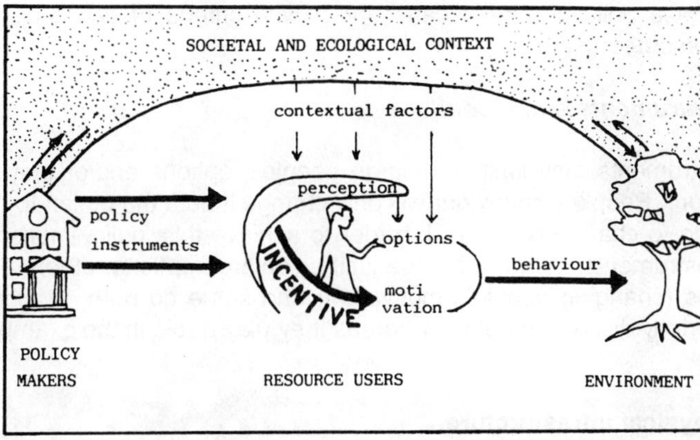

Figure 2

DIFFERENT TYPES OF INCENTIVES

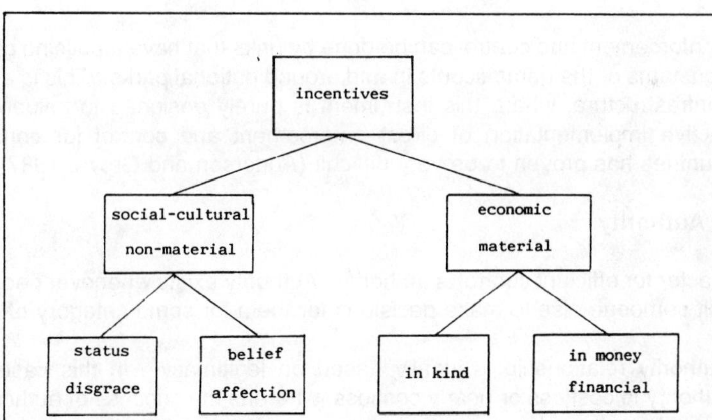

Modifying the perverse incentives resulting from government policies is, however, not easy. An important reason for this is that these policies, irrational as they may seem in economic and ecological respects, often have a strong political and/or social rationale. All too often public (government) resources in general, and natural resources in particular, are used as *political resources*, to be allocated according to political criteria (see Bates, 1981 for Africa). It is clear that these political criteria can conflict with criteria of economic efficiency and sustainability of resource use.

3. Policy Instruments and Incentives

Policy instruments may limit or enlarge people's options and/or they may influence people's motivation. People's behaviour will only change if both the option to change is open and the motivation to change is there. In order to achieve this, policy-makers make use of different policy instruments. Some of these limit or enlarge options, others are designed to provide incentives (changing people's motivation) and some do both. Major categories of instruments are briefly discussed below, whereas they play a role in the example of the Kafue flats in Zambia.

3.1 Physical Infrastructure

The creation of physical infrastructure can be used to provide people with alternative options of resource use or of income generative activities in general. A road or a bridge may, for instance, enable people to take part in off-farm employment opportunities. The removal of a road or a bridge may, on the other hand, prevent people from migrating into sensitive areas and thus reduces their options.

3.2 Direct enforcement and control

Direct enforcement and control can be done by units that have a policing capability like the army, the customs or the game scouts in and around national parks. This is also the case with physical infrastructure, where this instrument is purely designed to influence people's options. Effective implementation of direct enforcement and control for conservation in developing countries has proven to be very difficult (Anderson and Grove, 1987).

3.3 Authority

A key factor for efficient control is authority. Authority exists whenever people explicitly or tacitly permit someone else to make decisions for them for some category of acts.

The authority relationship is ideally based on legitimacy. In this case any single exercise of authority is costless or nearly costless, whereas the success of authority is based on a non-material incentive. However, if legitimacy is absent, authority must necessarily be backed by some degree of coercion. The success of authority is then clearly based on the material incentive (e.g. the fear of penalties or the hope of rewards). Maintaining authority in the absence of legitimation can be expensive and is sometimes impossible.

The weakness of *legitimate* government authority in developing countries can partly be explained by the existence of traditional authority structures. So called "traditional" authorities also claim and obtain authority and in this way challenge the authority of the government).

These traditional authorities offer both possibilities and limitations for sustainable natural resource management, as the Zambian case-study shows.

3.4 Economic Instruments

Economic (material) incentives are what most economists have in mind when referring to incentives. Economic instruments that create economic incentives can take numerous concrete forms: taxes, subsidies, changes in agricultural output prices, etc. Economic instruments can show results in a relatively short time, if the material benefits are clearly perceived as such by the actors. However, the maintenance of economic incentives often implies high financial costs in the form of tax deductions, subsidies, etc. Because every act of "good" behaviour has to be rewarded, the marginal costs of control by economic instruments do not diminish. Economic incentives stem not only from market-based instruments, but also from instruments that increase local managing responsibility over natural resources and the security of access rights. Generally, people are more motivated to invest in the sustainability of their resource use, if secure rights to the proceeds of their property and labour exist. When access rights to natural resources (e.g. forests or agricultural land) are conditional on the sustainability of the use of these resources then, clearly, an economic incentive is created for wise use.

3.5 Communicative Instruments

Communicative instruments can be either "normative", i.e. aiming to strengthen certain existing values or to introduce new values, or "cognitive", aiming to provide information.

Strengthening the value of existing institutions may contribute to conservation, especially when these institutions were effective in regulating access to resource use. The season for floodplain-fisheries by the Kotoko in North Cameroon is, for instance, regulated with the help of a local ritual that prevents fish from being caught before spawning has taken place (Van der Zee, 1988). Often, however, new values or institutions will have to be introduced.

It is clear that "normative" communicative instruments (e.g. awareness building) do not lead to results overnight; changing people's norms and values is a time-consuming undertaking, whether they refer to social relationships or to the value of nature. On the other hand, when norms and values are eventually internalised and institutions function, they can be expected to operate for a long time. Just as in the case of legitimate authority, the marginal costs of social control through norms and values tends to be nil or almost nil.

Furthermore, mention should be made of "traditional" values or institutions that offer possibilities for promoting the sustainable use of these resources. These types of "traditional" institutions may sometimes be strengthened or reintroduced as part of a communicative strategy in conservation projects.

Awareness-building also has an informational aspect; people can be made more aware of the real costs and benefits of their acts. Likewise, individual and social benefits to be achieved with sustainable natural resource management can be emphasized. In this case communicative instruments complement economic instruments, thereby strengthening the material incentive.

Other communicative instruments like education and extension imply the transfer of information, thereby providing the local community/actors with more options. Examples of these include the communication of alternative crops and cropping techniques and techniques for soil and water conservation.

3.6 Combining Instruments

Environmental policies and projects aim to change people's behaviour in order to promote restoration of degraded ecosystems and to prevent the occurrence of new degradation. Generally, a combination of instruments is used for this aim. In theory such a package may be designed to:

-- build or enlarge people's resource use options;

-- remove existing perverse incentives; and

-- create incentives for conservation.

In our example of the Kafue Flats the working of such a package of instruments in practice is explained.

4. Instrument and Incentives at Work at the Kafue Flats

Southwest of Lusaka, between Itesitesi in the west and Kafue Gorge in the east, the Kafue river meanders over 240 km. Every year discharges of the river show a distinct peak corresponding with the wet season rains. Excess water spills over and inundates an area of about 2 000 km^2 in dry years up to 6 000 km^2 in very wet years. This area is called the Kafue flats (see Figure 3).

Figure 3

**MAP OF THE KAFUE FLATS AND SURROUNDINGS.
THE SHADED AREA REPRESENTS THE FLOODPLAIN AREA. SOME 6 000 KM^2, INUNDATED IN EXTREMELY WET YEARS**

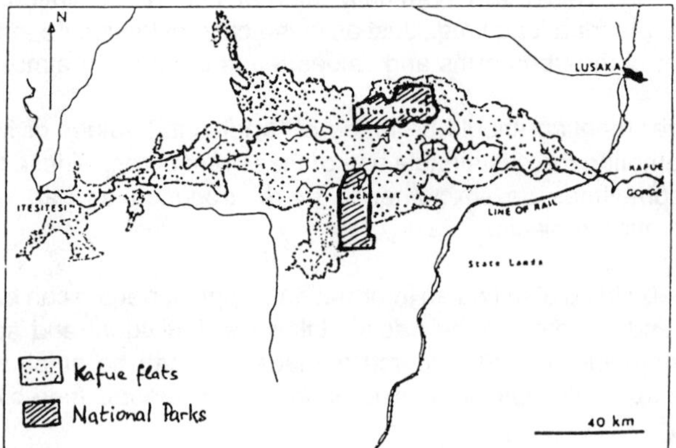

For centuries, herding, fishing and traditional hunting have been practised in the flats by local communities. Two tribes are traditionally involved in herding, the Ila and the Tonga. Most of the 250 000 head of cattle grazing on the flats each season belong to them (Jeffery and Chooye, 1989). The impact of overgrazing can be seen in the flats; the herdsmen are aware of this problem and confirm the rapid growth of the number of cattle during the last decades (private communication).

Preferential access to land and water has been given to outside interests such as large-scale cattle farming, irrigation schemes, safari hunting and hydro-power development. This has reduced the surface area for traditional cattle and has accelerated the problem of overgrazing.

By providing extensive and fertile nursery grounds for fish, the Kafue flats support one of the most productive fisheries in Zambia. Average annual fish production between 1966 and 1985 was 7 700 metric tonnes (Subramaniam, in preparation). However, production has declined over this period due to overfishing (Jeffery and Chooye, 1989).

Owing essentially to its richness in fish and grass, the Flats support some 400 species of birds. This wetland is therefore an area of international standing as waterfowl habitat.

The Kafue Lechwe, a species unique to this floodplain, is the most conspicuous wild ungulate living off this rich resource. The Lechwe population has declined from 100 000 in 1976 to 50 000 in 1983 (Chabwela, 1987). Other important wildlife species include hippopotamus, zebra, wildebeest and buffalo. Nowadays, the wildlife can be found almost exclusively in and around the two national parks located in the flats, Lochinvar and Blue Lagoon.

Up to 1988 wildlife was in danger even in these areas. Poorly armed regular scouts, without adequate means of transport, have to stop poachers who sometimes enter the parks with vehicles and automatic weapons. Moreover, they have the task of protecting wildlife against surrounding communities. These local people had obvious economic incentives to poach or to assist poachers from outside -- this was the only way for them to benefit from the park.

As can be learned from other park areas in Africa, the exclusion of local communities from wildlife utilisation and management produced situations of conflict and has frustrated the potential co-operation between governments and people in the field for sustainable resource management (Anderson and Grove, 1987).

4.1 Objectives and approach of the WWF-Zambia Wetlands Project

Against this background the WWF-Zambia Wetlands Project was established with WWF-I support in 1986. This project covers two important Zambian Wetland Areas: the Kafue flats and the Bangwenlu Swamp. The project aims to establish an equitable partnership with local communities and the Zambian Government in order to jointly conserve natural resources, enhance their productivity and improve the standard of living of the wetlands' local communities through the sustainable exploitation of resources. The project has identified the sustainable utilisation of wildlife for safari hunting, as an innovative income generating development option for local communities in the Kafue flats. However, the realisation of this option requires that poaching is largely controlled and legal hunting is properly organised.

Moreover, it requires a transfer of management responsibilities and benefits from the central government to local communities. Thus a new management structure is needed which requires co-operation between people and institutions at different levels of the traditional and modern society. A new management structure will only have a chance of being sustainable if key actors at the different levels feel that the new management is in their specific interest or at least not against their interest. *Sustainable resource management, therefore, requires the provision sufficient incentives for the key actors to participate now and in the future.*

4.2 Instruments and incentives at the national and international level

"Debt for nature swap"

The Government of Zambia and the World Wide Fund of Nature were the first supporters of the Zambian Wetland Project (ZWP). In August 1989 they agreed upon a "debt for nature swap" that involved $2.27 million (Allen, 1990). In simple terms, this means that WWF pays part of Zambia's foreign debt in US dollars to an international bank under the agreement that the Zambian Government allocates a corresponding sum in its national currency (Kwatchas) to conservation and development activities.

For WWF there is an economic incentive to support projects in developing countries through the "debt for nature swap" model. They do not pay the full debt sum to the international bank but profit from the discount rates at the secondary loan market. They need, so to say, less dollars to fund projects that use local currencies. For the National Treasury of Zambia there is a clear economic incentive for co-operation too as it is easier for them to pay in local currency than in dollars.

Two important shifts in bureaucratic procedures

Within the Zambian Government the project is implemented through its National Parks and Wildlife Service (NPWS). Two important shifts in bureaucratic procedures that occurred early in the 1980s have been major preconditions for the successful implementation of the new approach. One change was that NPWS secured permission to go beyond the civil service in its quest for the best employees to help conserve wildlife and enforce the law. This meant that NPWS could now begin to involve local people in wildlife management.

The experiences of the experimental integration of villagers in anti-poaching actions proved to be very successful and provided an incentive for NPWS to consolidate this approach by training villagers so that they could be employed as village scouts (Dale Lewis in Stone, 1989).

The second important change of procedure was the decision to allow the wildlife department (NPWS) to establish its own revolving fund for wildlife conservation. Before that, the NPWS had to pass its earnings from hunting and tourism to the Ministry of Finance. The new financial autonomy was a positive incentive for the Department: from that moment on the Department could present itself to donor organisations and to the local communities as a partner with authority to decide upon the allocation of the revenues to local communities. Also a material incentive was created because the Department's financial welfare now was more directly related to the success of the hunting and tourism industries.

These two major changes of procedure and the fact that the new approach of wildlife management and revenue generation had already been tested in three Game Management Areas in the eastern part of the country (Lupande Development Project), were convincing arguments for the US Agency for International Development and the WWF to fund a nation-wide programme through which the new approach could be implemented in all GMAs in Zambia. Together with the National Parks, this comprises about 30 per cent of the country's territory. This programme is known in Zambia as ADMADE (Administrative Management Design for Game Management Areas).

Under the ADMADE Programme the revenues from the sustainable utilisation of wildlife through hunting and cropping are collected by the Wildlife Conservation Revolving Fund of the NPWS and reallocated according to the following formula:

1. 40 per cent goes to wildlife management costs for that particular game management area, approximately half of which is used to employ local residents as village scouts to protect and manage the wildlife resources in their own chiefdom;

2. 35 per cent for community development projects to improve the welfare of local residents;

3. 15 per cent for the management and needs of the adjacent national park.

4. 10 per cent for the Ministry of Tourism to promote international tourism in Zambia.

Recognising the ruling authorities of both traditional African leadership and governmental units, ADMADE has designed an administrative structure that enables local leaders to decide upon the use of the 40 and 35 per cent, after having received advice and proposals. Furthermore, ADMADE provides training opportunities for villagers to become village scouts as well as various forms of institutional and organisational support.

The existence of ADMADE can be classified as an important supporting instrument for the Zambian Wetlands project because the Project profits from the institutional pioneering and achievements of ADMADE. At the same time, ADMADE benefits from the Zambian Wetlands Project, because it applies the ADMADE principles in the extensive area of Zambia's wetlands and thereby supports ADMADE's legitimacy.

4.3 Set-up of the WWF-Zambia Wetlands Project and Incentives at the local level

In order to illustrate the impact of incentives at the level of local people and local organisations, we will briefly outline the set-up of the Zambia Wetlands Project, thereby focusing on the southern part of the Kafue flats in and around the Lochinvar National Park.

Lochinvar National Park is a very diverse and fertile environment. Thanks to the fact that no settlement and cattle herding are allowed, it forms a stronghold for the still significant numbers of Lechwes in the flats (including the GMAs).

If poaching in the Park and the GMAs can be controlled, a 20 per cent annual growth of the Lechwe population will be possible. Also other wildlife populations like zebra and buffalo will grow. For 1991 a very conservative assessment of the sustainable yield of wildlife for the GMAs in the Kafue Flats amounts about $150 000. Before 1990 all this money was collected by the Government in Lusaka. Since 1990 the Government has approved a reallocation according to the ADMADE-percentages.

The project pursues the following activities:

-- Yearly aerial survey and counting of wildlife numbers in different parts of the Kafue flats;

-- Providing yearly advice to NPWS on the maximum number of animals per species for which they should give a hunting permission and the distribution of these quotas over sub-areas of the flats;

-- The strengthening of legal enforcement through assistance to the Park ranger and his scouts and to the GMA unit manager on wildlife issues and the training of village scouts through the ADMADE Programme;

-- Awareness-building through community meetings and visits to organisations, administration and individual villagers, explaining the necessity and benefits of conservation and anti-poaching, especially the way by which sustainable use of wildlife can contribute to community development;

-- Promotion of the establishment of a sustainable management structure that enables local people and local authorities to decide jointly on:

 * the way their wildlife quota will be used during that particular year (e.g. how many animals will be sold to safari hunters, which safari-tour operator will be used, how many animals will be cropped, when and what will be done with the sterns and the meat, etc.);

 * the management and allocation of earnings from wildlife utilisation;

 * the identification of community needs, the allocation of funds for community development actions and the co-ordination of support to these actions;

 * the ways by which local communities and local authorities in the Kafue flats could act in order to tackle environmental issues like poaching, overfishing, overgrazing, flood reduction and land reclamation.

This management structure is formed around two types of organisational bodies. The first, closely linked to the local level and the authority of chiefdoms, is called a Community Development Unit (CDU). About 20 villagers from that particular chiefdom are represented. They are mostly people who already have some power and/or authority in their village, like a village headman or someone who is active in the church, the party or the school. In addition to the 20 villagers, the chief has a direct representative. Moreover, some local government officials in fishery, veterinary, forestry and agriculture are co-opted members; almost all members are men. The secretariat of the Zambian Wetlands project has played an active role in establishing the CDUs.

The second type of organisational bodies comprises more chiefdoms and corresponds more or less with the regional level, the district Wetland Management Authorities (WMAs). Although the Kafue flats is one Wetland, for practical reasons two WMAs were established in the Kafue flats, one on either side of the river.

More than 50 per cent of the WMA members are CDU representative; other members comprise: the chiefs, Provincial Government representatives like the Governor and part of his staff, an MP, representative of NWPS and a few technical officers (like agricultural or fisheries-development officers). Being the local level units, the CDUs are designed to play the leading role in the identification of community needs, the determination of priorities, and the submission of plans and budgets to the WMA for development actions, including education and training. Even so, the CDUs play a pivotal role in the actual management and control of environmental problems and better protection of the wetland's resources. [During a CDU meeting, for example, it was decided with a herding group to plan an extra watering place just outside the National Park in order to change the (illegal) track by which they used to cross through the park area]. The role of the WMA is to select and approve proposals from the CDUs and link all management and development initiatives to the governmental planning level. Moreover the WMAs manage the funds and submit requests for funding or logistic support to the Government and international donor agencies.

Incentives for chiefs and village headmen

Chief Hamusonde is the oldest and most respected Tonga chief. At the beginning of this century, when he was a young boy, wildlife used to be abundant in the area, including lions and elephants. (Nowadays neither species can be found in the flats). In spite of the obvious economic disadvantages of lions attacking cattle and elephants destroying crops, Hamusonde is a convinced supporter of their reintroduction (private communication with Udo de Haes). His cultural background inspires him to say: "My grandchildren should know what a lion looks like", and so he expresses a moral incentive for wildlife conservation.

The CDUs were originally designed as new structures. However, the project staff became aware of the potential conflicts between this new local structure and the existing local authority of the chiefdoms. The authority of the chiefdoms in the area seems to function well and quite sustainably. After discussions it was decided to present the idea of using chiefdoms as CDUs, thereby totally relying on the traditional structure. For the chiefs and the village headmen this decision was a positive incentive since they now knew that the project would not undermine their traditional authority; instead it was now going to use and thus strengthen their position and prestige.

Stronger position and authority not only give prestige but may also give access to economic benefits for the individual and his or her family. For instance, the place for a new borehole for drinking water can be claimed by the chief for his village. Another more individual economic incentive is the fact that community management of wildlife gives opportunities to reintroduce free hunting rights for chiefs for a certain number of animals.

Incentives for the local community

Since the Zambian government took over command of the National Park area and the wildlife management in the GMAs in 1965, there was no longer any incentive for the local residents to protect these resources or to promote their wise use. On the contrary, there was a clear economic incentive to poach or to assist poachers that came from outside. It was a way of making money with hardly any costs. Moreover, the poaching was justified by the perception of local people that these animals used to belong to their fathers and grandfathers and were taken away by white men and Government in order to ensure privileged access to the game.

The project had the task to remove these combined economic and socio-cultural perverse incentives and to create wise use incentives instead. It was realised that a basic precondition for success would be to gain sufficient credit and trust. Therefore, in its communications with local people the project has been very clear about its objectives (see above) and its roles. From the beginning the project staff has underlined that the project will not take over communal land and will not impose unwanted development on the community but seeks full community participation. These statements were meant to remove two general disincentives for co-operation.

Secondly the project staff has stressed the legal responsibility to respect and promote the integrity of the National Park (e.g. no settlement and cattle in the Park) and to support the statutory rules for the GMAs (e.g. no hunting without a licence). They explained that enforcement of these rules would be improved and co-operation from the community was required in anti-poaching actions.

Closely linked to this, ample attention has been given to explain the promising economic benefits of sustainable utilisation of wildlife (without poaching). Furthermore, the government's new policy was explained, which was to institutionalise the decentralisation of management responsibilities to the local communities and the allocation of more than 50 per cent of these benefits to employment and community development projects, to be decided upon by the community itself. From this moment the image of the poacher changed; under the new arrangements poacher not only steals from the state, he steals from the community and so becomes an enemy of the community. As a result, traditional authority of the chiefs and social control by the community were mobilised for anti-poaching.

We see here a clear example of the combined working of different instruments:

-- The enforcement of existing statutory rules and sanctions in order to give an economic disincentive for resource depletion;

-- The creation of decentralised rules and benefits in order to give a socio-cultural and economic incentive for the mobilisation of social control by the community;

-- The use of training (village scouts), education and awareness-building in order to ensure the correct understanding and perception of the new rules and opportunities and to stress the acting power and responsibility of individuals.

For a lasting appreciation of these incentives and an actual change of people's behaviour it is of utmost importance that some of the expected benefits are realised within a short period and are perceived as such by as many people as possible. Therefore, the project has given full support to a number of community development activities that would be beneficial for the community as a whole instead of for individuals.

Next it was discussed with the people that part of these benefits could be used for income generating activities that would increase the community's self-sufficiency and decrease its dependency on wetlands' resources only (Jeffery and Chooye, 1989).

A fifth crucial element of the project's approach is that it does not focus on wildlife alone, but that it promotes the productivity and wise use of all wetland resources including agricultural crops, pastures, cattle and fish. This makes sense from an ecological viewpoint, and it also demonstrates to the community that participation and development are not used here as an instrument for wildlife conservation, but as part of a fully integrated conservation development project, a project that is directed to the improvement of the resource base for a number of different (wet)land users (e.g. fishermen and cattle owners). This integration of different resource users in the project is very important, because it is known from other resource management projects in Africa that the exclusion of user groups may lead to serious conflicts.

From some fishermen it was learned that their reasons for co-operating in anti-poaching and wise use are two-fold. In the first place they hope that the project can assist them in improving their access to government services like schools and teachers, as well as medical services and transport facilities to the fish markets and limit their dependency on a few traders. In this respect their women complained about the high prices they had to pay for soap, matches, wood and the like. Secondly, they expect that the project will stop the immigration of outsiders who contribute (disproportionately?) to (over)fishing in their area.

The area of Nyimbe is part of the best fishing zone in the Kafue river because it is very close to the National Park. The vast lagoon in the Park is an important fish breeding ground for the whole river. The CDU member of Nyimbe thinks that the current number of fishing groups is 10 times too high. In the 1960s every fisherman had to apply for a licence at the Provincial Government. The latter would turn down applications for fishing camps that were already overcrowded. According to the original inhabitants of the camp this regulation has helped them a lot in the past. However, for reasons yet unknown the Government has failed to keep it up.

The fishermen are directly concerned with resource depletion. They have seen what has happened over the last twenty years and now experience a decrease in catches and a resulting increase of working hours. For them there are direct economic reasons to support a reinforcement of an existing statutory rule.

For the Tonga herding families as a whole the participation in revenues and resulting community development activities, like the setting up of clinics, schools and watering places, provide a positive incentive to co-operate with anti-poaching policy. It is not clear whether this is the same for those young Tonga boys that for longer periods stay out in the flats with the herds, far from schools and clinics and close to the game.

Although many cattle owners are aware of the overgrazing problem, they do not consider reducing the number of cattle. In the first place there are perverse incentives that spring from the cultural function of cattle in Tonga society. Examples are the slaughtering of cattle at initiations and funerals and the so called "Shimunenga ceremony", which includes a yearly parade where all owners select and show their best bulls and cows. Secondly, there are economic disincentives related to the use of cattle as exchange. Wedding gifts are given in the form of cattle, and major payments are made by selling cattle. The high inflation rate of the local currency and the absence of a decentralised and reliable alternative form of investment and banking create economic disincentives for the Tonga to reduce cattle numbers. When questioned about the problems of overgrazing many of them suggest opening up the Park for cattle in order to lower the pressure in the GMAs.

5. Discussion

Experience with the creation of incentives for conservation purposes have been gained fairly recently. Interpretation of the results should therefore be done with caution. There is still a lot to be understood, especially about the way in which different approaches work in the long run. Nevertheless a number of intermediate conclusions emerge from this paper.

1. In the literature on environmental policy and management one finds many examples of poor performance of top-down enforcement and control. As a reaction to this there is a danger of expecting too much from the use of incentives. One should however not forget that the use of incentives is only one possible field of environmental policy and management. Its focus is to increase the actors *motivation* for environmentally sound behaviour. Limiting or increasing actors *options* is another field and increasing *the capacity of natural resources* to "carry" human activities is again another field.

2. In the first section of this paper we have explained the importance of analyzing incentives from the viewpoint of the actors (institutions or individuals resource users) to whom policy instrument are directed and not from the viewpoint of policy-makers.

A misconception of the policy-makers' view-point is the use of the word "incentive" as if it represents a category of policy/instruments, while there is in fact a fundamental difference between incentives and instruments.

3. The receivers' viewpoint on incentives leads us to the issue of *competition.* For local actors a new policy/measure will usually result in a change of one or a few factors that act upon her/his motivation. This will not necessarily lead to a real change of her/his preference for the present method of resource use. A real change of motivation will only occur when the newly given inducement is comparable with the existing incentives.

4. A direct consequence of the preceding point is the need to analyze the existing incentive structure beforehand. Such an analysis should however be carried out within the framework of an *actor oriented analysis* of the environmental problem and its causes. In such an analysis the question: "who loses and who benefits as a result of the occurrence of the problem concerned?" has to be answered. Next to these *stakeholders* all *actors* who contribute to the occurrence or maintenance of the problem are identified, including not only the direct users of resources but also the *actors behind actors.* A crucial step is the question "why these actors do what they do?" What are their options and their motivations and which factors are limiting their options? Are these factors of a technical, financial, economic, societal or cultural nature?

5. The non-material or *socio-cultural incentives* (like social or religious status) may be of equal or more importance for environmental behaviour than economic (material) incentives. In the case of the Kafue flats this is illustrated by the relatively successful authority of local chiefs that is based on moral incentives at the level of the local community.

6. In this paper we have distinguished between different categories of instruments and incentives and we have stressed the importance of combining these into *packages*. The idea is that a combination of instruments, when carefully tuned to each other and to the problem situation for which it is designed, can produce mutually supportive incentives.

Before the Zambian Wetlands Project (ZWP) the package of instruments used for conservation around the National Park was almost exclusively based on one category of instruments and one organisational level: direct regulation through enforcement and control by the government.

In Figure 4 the direct regulation through enforcement and control by the government has been visualised by an arrow that starts from the organisational level of the government and goes down to the people and by-passes the level of chiefdoms. At the international level there are two arrows that indicate the use of communicative instruments and *ad hoc* subsidies by international organisations designed to create awareness at the level of the Zambian government.

The picture totally changes with the realisation of the ZWP: there is still direct enforcement and control by government. However, the government is now assisted by members of the community (see the small arrow below chiefdom level).

Secondly a structural economic instrument has been introduced, which is the decentralisation of revenues from the national to the chiefdom level and from there further down to the people. So far however most economic benefits have been created at the level of the communities (schools, clinics, boreholes).

The introduction of this new economic instrument has been backed by awareness-building and education on an *ad hoc* basis at the level of chiefdoms and people, by training of village scouts through the ADMADE programme (structural) and by organisation of people and representatives at the chiefdom level to ensure a structural basis (CDU's and WMA's) for the sharing of benefits, responsibilities (costs) and between the government and communities. Part of the package is that the traditional authority of the chiefs is now also used to combat poaching and promote sustainable use of not just wildlife but also of other resources in the area.

In the case of the ZWP this combination of different instruments so far seems to be a promising approach in producing *a package of mutually supporting incentives* for conservation. Further research is necessary to determine which arrows of the combination are of major importance for different groups of local people and how negative interaction between instruments that are based on a totally different approach of people can be prevented. One could imagine, for instance, that the creation of material incentives (payment for "good behaviour") could hamper the development of norms and values that give rise to normative incentives or the fact that use is made of traditional authority structures will limit the possibilities for participation for certain socio-economic groups.

Another possible example of problematic interaction is the negative influence of direct regulation (and its often coercive mode of implementation) on the general attitudes of people towards a resource conservation programme or project; in this way positive attitudes enhanced by awareness-building are likely to be hampered.

In the Kafue flats the limits of participation that were set from above are directly linked to the survival of the National Park and its wildlife which are considered as assets of national and even international importance. This rationale and the fact that these limits where clearly set from the very beginning, contribute highly to their acceptance by participants.

The instrument package of the ZWP clearly shows the involvement of different levels in the society and the attempt to create incentives at all levels. In general it is not enough to produce incentives for the direct users of resources only. A new management structure will only be sustainable if key actors at different levels of the traditional and modern society feel that the new management is in their specific interest or at least not against their interest. Sustainable resource management thus requires the development of a management structure that provides sufficient incentives for the key actors to co-operate now and in the future.

Figure 4

PACKAGES OF MAJOR INSTRUMENTS FOR CONSERVATION BEFORE AND AFTER THE START OF THE ZAMBIAN WETLANDS PROJECT

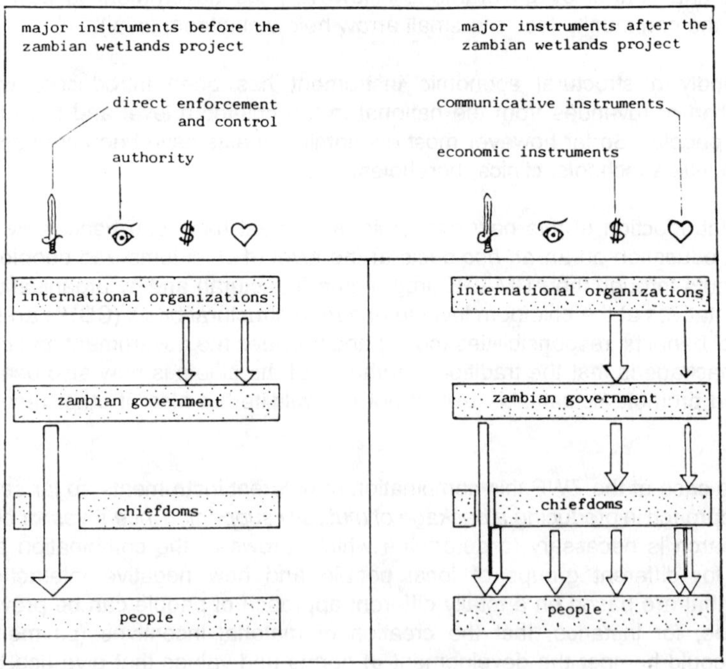

However, this implies that projects must accommodate and benefit people who are likely to be amongst the more powerful. This strategy, which we may call "working with the system", runs the danger of strengthening existing inequalities and creating disincentives for the co-operation of the affected people.

7. A crucial element in designing and sustaining a successful package is the direct linkage between on the one hand privileged access to resources (and the benefits from them) and on the other hand the responsibility of managing these resources sustainably. In order to meet this condition the wildlife in the chiefdoms in the Kafue flats are carefully assessed from aerial counts which are then used as the basis for the hunting quota per chiefdom, during the next year. When one of the chiefdoms fails to control poaching then the same chiefdom will have less income from safari hunting during the next year.

BIBLIOGRAPHY

ALLAN, L.
Debt for Nature Swaps Work!, WWF-feature, Gland, Switzerland, WWF, February 1990.

ANDERSON, D. & R. GROVE
Conservation in Africa: Peoples, Policies and Practice, Cambridge, Cambridge University Press, 1987.

BATES, R.H.
Markets and States in Tropical Africa: The Political Basis of Agricultural Policies, Berkeley, University of California Press, 1981.

BLAIKIE, P.
The Political Economy of Soil Erosion in Developing Countries, Essex, Longman, 1985.

CHABWELA, H.N.
"Protected Areas and Community Based Wildlife Harvesting as a Component of Wetland Conservation Strategies: Zambia", Paper, National Parks and Wildlife Service, Zambia, 1987.

DRIJVER, C.A. & M. MARCHAND
"Taming the Floods: Environmental Aspects of Floodplain Development in Africa", *Nature and Resources*, Vol. 22, No. 4, 1986.

FREEDMAN, J.L.
Social Psychology, London, Prentice Hall, Inc., 1978.

GROOT, W.T. de & M. MARCHAND
"Kafue Flats, Zambia: Floodplain Planning on a Cross-road", *Papers from an International Symposium on the Polders of the World*, Vol. 1, Wageningen, IZRI, pp. 276-287, 1982.

GOULET, D.
Incentives for Development the Key to Equity, New York, New Horizons Press, 1989.

JEFFERY, R.C.V. & P.M. CHOOYE
"The People's Role in Wetland Management: The Zambian Initiative", *Proceedings of the International Conference: The Peoples Role in Wetland Management*, Leiden, The Netherlands, 1989.

LINDBLOM, C. E.
Politics and Markets: The World's Political and Economic Systems, New York, Basic Books, 1977.

NcNEELY, J.A.
Economic and Biological Diversity: Developing and Using Economic Incentives to Conserve Biological Resources, Gland, Switzerland, IUCN, 1988.

MORIS, J.
"Irrigation as a Privileged Solution in African Development", *Development Policy Review,* No. 2, Vol. 5, June 1987, pp. 99-123.

REPETTO, R.
"Economic Incentives for Sustainable Production", *Annals of Regional Science,* Vol. 21, No. 3, 1987.

RICHARDS, P.
Indigenous Agricultural Revolution: Ecology and Food Production in West Africa, London, Hutchinson, 1945.

STONE, R.D.
Zambia's Innovative Approach to Conservation, Wildlife Fund Letter, No. 7, 1989.

SUBRAMANIAM, S.P.
"A Brief Review of the Status of the Bangwenlu Basin and Kafue Flats", Proceedings of the WWF-Zambia Wetlands Project Workshop, 1986, in preparation.

GOVERNMENT OF THE REPUBLIC OF ZAMBIA AND IUCN
The National Conservation Strategy for Zambia, Gland, Switzerland, IUCN, 1985.

ZEE, Van der
Les pêcheurs Kotoko dans les yaéréres au Nord du Cameroun, Serie : Environnement et Développement au Nord du Cameroun, Centre for Environmental Science, Leiden, The Netherlands, 1988.

ENVIRONMENTAL MANAGEMENT IN INDONESIAN AGRICULTURAL DEVELOPMENT

by

Faisal Kasryno*

Ning Pribadi*

Achmad Suryana*, and

Jamil Musanif*

---

* Faisal Kasryno is the Director of, and Ning Pribadi, Achmad Suryana, and Jamil Musanif are Agricultural Economists at the Bureau of Planning, Ministry of Agriculture, Government of Indonesia.

RÉSUMÉ

Depuis plus de dix ans, le gouvernement indonésien s'efforce de conjuguer le développement de l'agriculture et la protection de l'environnement en axant la planification sur les régions agricoles, les systèmes d'exploitation pour la conservation des terres, l'action phytosanitaire intégrée, la suppression des méthodes de culture itinérante et la régénération des zones agricoles dont l'environnement est dégradé. L'exposé présente certains résultats obtenus en ce domaine dans la période 1984-1989. Il décrit aussi la procédure de l'étude d'impact sur l'environnement (EIA) appliquée au cycle des projets tant gouvernementaux que privés. Toutefois, dans la mise en oeuvre des EIA, un certain nombre de problèmes demeurent, notamment les insuffisances ou les lacunes concernant l'objet de l'étude, la résistance de la collectivité qui voit dans l'EIA une entrave bureaucratique, une administration défectueuse et le manque de formation. De nouveaux progrès seraient réalisables, suggère l'auteur, si la procédure était simplifiée et si elle était rendue obligatoire.

SUMMARY

The government of Indonesia has been trying for over ten years to relate agricultural development to the conservation of the environment by focusing planning on agricultural regions, land conservation farming systems, integrated pest management, elimination of shifting cultivation practices, and rehabilitation of environmentally damaged agricultural areas. The paper presents some achievements in this area for the period 1984-1989. It also describes the procedure for environmental impact assessment (EIA) as applied to both the government and the private project cycle. A number of problems in EIA implementation persist, however, among which are poor or non-existent terms of reference, community resistance because EIA is seen as a bureaucratic hindrance, a weak administration and lack of training. It is suggested that further progress could be made by simplifying the procedure and making it compulsory.

1. Introduction

Agriculture remains an important sector to the Indonesian economy. In 1988/1989 it contributed approximately 20.1 per cent of GNP (1983 constant prices), absorbed 56.1 per cent of the labour force, and accounted for 26.5 per cent of total non-oil exports.

Since at least the mid-1970s, Indonesia has been very much aware of the cost of environmental degradation and the impacts of development on the environment. Since then, conservation of natural resources and living environment has been one of the major concerns in agricultural development, along with production promotion, export enhancement, employment opportunity, income improvement and regional development objectives. To deal with those issues more seriously, Environmental Impact Assessment (EIA) in agricultural activities was formally endorsed in the third "Five Year Development Plan", started in 1978.

Based on experience in assessing, restoring, and mitigating the adverse environmental impacts of development, the government has taken further steps to strengthen EIA. The issuance of state law No. 4, 1982 and No. 29, 1986 make EIA a required element in project feasibility studies, especially for large projects which involve bank loans or external loans. However, the practice of EIA has encountered various problems and difficulties. These include: limited resources, lack of knowledge and experience among the staff, imprecise data and measurements. The questionable effectiveness of the procedures as implemented thus far shows a need for the country to work continuously to establish more firmly the principles of sustainable development in the agricultural programme.

2. Sustainable Agricultural Development

The degradation of the ecosystem and of both the quality and the quantity of natural resources constitute a very high indirect cost of the development programmes. Awareness of this has motivated the country to deal with the difficult task of assessing, mitigating, restoring and trying to prevent the adverse environmental impacts. It is increasingly recognised that agricultural activities are essentially a process of environmental and national resource management aimed at producing biological outputs needed by human beings. The size and sustainability of production very much depend upon the availability and the extent of natural resources and the quality of environmental management. Bearing that in mind, the government has decided to relate as far as possible agricultural development to the conservation of environment and natural resources. This concept is embodied in the notion of "Sustainable Agricultural Development". Sustainable agriculture development is characterized by the integration of optimal use, conservation and maintenance, replenishment and development of environment and natural resources. Optimal use is to be based on resource potential, on the maintenance of a productive ecosystem as input for agricultural production, and recognises the crucial role of the ecosystem in harmonizing regional development.

With reference to this "Sustainable Agriculture Development" concept, the reorientation of the development policies has been a leading responsibility of the Ministry of Agriculture, and we have emphasized, among other things, planning based on agricultural regions, land conservation farming systems, integrated pest management, elimination of shifting cultivation practices, and rehabilitation of environmentally damaged agricultural areas. These aspects of our approach are briefly discussed.

Agriculture Regionalisation

Agriculture regionalisation is closely related to the adoption of the criteria of appropriate land use planning. These criteria are determined by considering environmental sustainability, natural resource potential and other technical and non-technical factors. Based on these criteria, a region is basically divided into protected areas, in which most activities are forbidden, supportive areas (e.g. urban and other types of service activities), and various types of agriculture area. In regard to the last mentioned, an example would be the restriction of the practice of intensive agriculture in areas where the land is more than gently sloping, because intensive farming on steep slopes would accelerate erosion, which clearly reduces natural resource sustainability. Agriculture land use areas are also categorised in more detail under a Ministerial Decree, which is also based on the ecologically sustainable resource use criteria.

Land Conservation Farming System

This is a farming system which takes direct account of the maintenance of environmental sustainability and optimisation of farming activities. Monoculture and seasonal farming are allowed to be done in areas slopes less than 8 per cent. Areas with sloped between 8-15 per cent are recommended to be used for integrated farming involving a mix of seasonal and annual crops, but together with the conservation techniques such as terraces, farm-beds and small dike construction. Areas with a slope of more than 15 per cent is recommended for tree crops and with the use of more intensive conservation techniques, to promote land covering and terrace supporting plants in addition to constructed terraces and farm beds.

An example of land conservation efforts on steep sloped areas is a number of watersheds conservation programme in Java. Java is a mountainous island with limited level land for cultivation. Java comprises only 7 per cent of the total land of Indonesia but it is inhabited by two-thirds of the country's population. As Java's population continues to grow, farmers are being forced to clear and cultivate steep slopes. Upland Java faces very serious conservation problems involving soil erosion. Thirteen watersheds on Java are considered to have critical erosion problems. It is estimated that soil erosion rates range from 10 ton to 40 ton/hectare/year, and the rates are increasing.

Upland conservation programmes in Java supported by the government of Indonesia began in 1976. One of the programmes is located in the Citanduy watershed in the eastern West Java. The Citanduy conservation project established a model farm programme that consists of introducing a package of upland agricultural technologies, including bench terraces, new cropping patterns and rotations, and provides subsidies for the construction of terraces and purchased inputs. This package was introduced on land with slopes up to 50 per cent. Land with slopes of more than 50 per cent are eligible for an agro-forestry package. The programme was intended to create benefit both on-site and off-site of the watershed. On site, the new technology should improve farm incomes and land conservation, and there are off-site yield benefits due to the reduction of soil erosion.

Other upland agriculture conservation projects in Central and East Java provinces provide the farmer-participants with packages of agriculture conservation technology free of charge [including the provision of extension services], with the farmers having the responsibility to provide labour and crop care expenses. The projects have had some success: farmers outside the project are have also began to adopt the conservation technology and soil erosion in the project areas has significantly reduced.

To rehabilitate marginal agricultural land -- especially in the dry land areas -- the government has also distributed tree crops together with fertilizer to be grown on marginal land areas. The tree crops include cashew and cocoa. In addition, for some regions the government has also distributed king grass and other improved grasses, both for livestock feed and soil rehabilitation and conservation.

Integrated Pest Management

In the years following the first introduction of pesticides, they tend to become increasingly popular with the farmers who come to rely on them and to use them indiscriminately and excessively. This type of use has serious adverse consequences, however, since the biocides cause human health problems [for consumers of produce but especially for agricultural workers], plus negative impact on livestock, fish, wild animals, plants, and natural predators. Moreover through adverse impacts on the predators of pests, there may be a pest resurgence, development of secondary pests, etc., plus the emergence of resistance and cumulative impacts from residuals. Integrated pest management was first introduced in 1979 along with the intensification programme. The intensity of management practices is, of course, in accordance with the advancement of extension services on this matter and the rate of adoption of this particular technology by farmers. Along with integrated pest management, mechanical, physical and biological pest controls are practised, but still under irregular and case by case basis. The main part of the integrated pest management programmes promoted by the government is development of manpower capabilities, such as training of farmers, field observers, and extension personnel. At the end, farmers are expected to be able to carry out proper practices of integrated pest management in their own fields.

In Indonesia, in order to minimise these impacts, restrictions on the use of dangerous pesticides was effected through Presidential Decree No. 3, 1986. A further step has been in the establishment of an integrated pest management system. This system gives a first priority to the use of non-pesticide agents for pest and disease control. For example, this will involve taking into account the time of planting, the timing of irrigations, the farming pattern, the amount of fertilizer used, hand weeding, land sanitation measures, and the use of pest-resistant crop varieties in controlling pest population. Under such a system, insecticides are applied when the population of insects reaches a pre-determined limit or biological threshold which serves to trigger or to justify the application and it is a step that is taken when other measures could not give good results. There are also other measures such as mechanical, physical and biological pest control. Thus, mechanical pest control seeks to eliminate pests by hand, by traps or by other equipment. Physical pest control uses high or low temperature, moisture, light or sound waves. Natural pest predators are used in biological pest control.

Economic considerations are obviously important in determining which of these measures to use. The gradual reduction of pesticide subsidies has also been effected as part of the effort to promote the proper use of pesticide and to encourage farmers to think in terms of alternative methods. Efforts to enforce the presidential decree on pesticides are carried out (1) through licensing mechanism and (2) regulation on trade and distribution. Indeed, since 1988 pesticides and insecticides are no longer subsidized. With the promotion of the integrated pest management system and the elimination of the subsidy, the use of pesticides and insecticides in the last two years has declined. As presented in Table 1, the use of pesticides fell from 17 342 tons in 1987 to 10 840 tons in 1988 and 8 660 tons in 1989. Meanwhile, rice production steadily increased at a reasonable rate. This production growth was mainly from yield increase. In addition, since 1986, no serious or large-scale pest outbreaks were encountered.

Table 1

CHANGES IN THE USE OF PESTICIDES FOR FOOD CROPS IN INDONESIA,
1980-89

Year	Pesticide use (tons)	Rice fields (000 ha)	Production (000 tons milled rice)
1980	6 366	9 105	20 161
1981	9 006	9 382	22 286
1982	11 256	8 988	22 837
1983	13 887	9 162	24 006
1984	13 816	9 764	25 933
1985	14 980	9 902	26 547
1986	17 216	9 988	27 014
1987	17 342	9 923	27 253
1988	10 840	10 090	28 340
1989	8 660	10 531	29 072

Source: Ministry of Agriculture, Indonesia.

Elimination of Shifting Cultivation Practices

Shifting cultivation is an old farming system which is still being practised among the isolated tribes, especially in the outer islands. Farms are built by cutting and burning forest area. This system causes the degradation of productive ecosystem and the living environment, and affects land productivity through the destruction of top soil, the best part of the soil for agricultural purposes, and soil micro-organisms. It takes about a year for the land to be restored to its previous condition following the burning process.

In order to eliminate this practice, Indonesia has been implementing a resettlement programme since the late 1970s. Through this programme, the isolated tribes are given housing facilities along with farmyards, farm inputs and education on land conservation farming approaches. For this purpose, demonstration plots are established as learning media for the new settlements. This programme progresses gradually. Economic incentives such as free distributed land and housing are not always effective means. The difficulty in socio-cultural adjustment and lack of command on settled farming practices by isolated tribes are also becoming major constraints.

Rehabilitation of Deteriorated Agricultural Areas

This involves problem areas due to natural disasters or to the neglect over a long period, for example, as may be found on smallholder estate farms. The activities supported include replanting or new planting of smallholder farms, or public forest in upland areas, dryland and marginal land. Other activities involve the construction of control-dams for flood prevention and water storage. Except for very small reservoirs, these works are undertaken in co-operation with the Ministry of Public Works.

Besides the above policies, selective cutting in timber production is practised under strict controls in order to maintain production in the long term. A contribution to a reforestation fund at the rate of US$10 per cubic metre of timber is mandatory. This is regulated through Presidential Decree Nos. 29 and 30, 1990. Collection of the fund is done by the Ministry of Forestry through its representative in the wood industry association. Management of the fund is organised by the Ministry of Forestry, while reforestation and forest rehabilitation can be carried out by third parties or in co-operation with other agencies, both private and governmental institutions.

3. Environment and Natural Resource Management in Indonesia

At a national level, environment and natural resource management is a responsibility of the State Minister of Population and Environment. The Minister manages programmes related to environmental affairs, such as Inventory and Evaluation of Natural Resources and Environment; Forest, Soil and Water Reservation; Rehabilitation of Forest and Critical Land; and Environmental Pollution Management and Coastal Area Development. These programmes are implemented by the ministries who deal with the various projects.

As an illustration, Table 2 presents the work done under environmental and natural resource management at the national level during the fourth Five Year Development Plan (1984/85-1988/89).

The Ministry of Agriculture during the fifth Five Year Plan 1989/90-1993/94 is implementing three of the above mentioned environmental programmes through six projects. Three research projects are dealing with Forest, Land and Water Resources rehabilitation, two projects are for Environmental and Natural Resource Management and one project concerns Coastal Area Management. Rp. 870.3 million (US$ 470.5 thousands) is allocated for these projects during the 1990/91 fiscal year.

Table 2

ACHIEVEMENTS ON ENVIRONMENTAL AND NATURAL RESOURCE MANAGEMENT PROGRAMME IN INDONESIA,
1984/86-1988/89

Items	Fiscal year				
	1984/85	1985/86	1986/87	1987/88	1988/89
Construction of control dams:					
-- Number	345	267	280	138	55
-- Area under service[1]	86.25	65.00	72.75	34.50	13.75
Establishment of demonstration farms:					
-- Number	707	710	474	165	153
-- Area under service[1]	109.92	236.83	175.51	40.75	38.25
People's forest area rehabilitated[1]	4.83	11.48	19.77	-	2.50
Damaged farm area rehabilitated[1 2]	2 669.77	2 975.18	3 243.76	3 319.01	3 373.51
Area reforested[1 2]	1 164.50	1 237.72	1 326.59	1 342.43	1 355.35
Natural resource conservation sites[2 3] -- Number	314	320	328	328	342
-- Area[1]	12 242.50	12 454.50	12 687.70	13 612.10	13 659.10
National Parks: [2]					
-- Number	19	19	19	20	21
-- Area[1]	4 665.30	4 665.30	4 665.30	4 776.30	4 866.00
EIA Training (persons)	545	610	855	1 174	988

[1] Thousand hectares. [2] Cumulative number. [3] Wildlife, natural forest, tourism parks, sea parks.

Source: Speech by the President of Indonesia, Jakarta, August 1989.

4. Environmental Impact Assessment (EIA) in Agricultural Development

EIA Procedure

Subject to State Laws No. 4 and No. 29, described earlier, within the Agriculture sector, Ministerial Decrees have been released concerning the implementation of EIA procedures in regard to agricultural development. An Agriculture Commission and a Technical Team for EIA have also been established to provide technical guidance and to monitor the implementation of EIA. Technical guidance documents for EIA preparation have been released for food-crops, livestock, fisheries and estate-crops. Each Directorate General and Agency within the Ministry of Agriculture has an EIA working group, who evaluate EIA documents, and make recommendations to the commission regarding further action. The main steps are as follows:

Environmental Information Presentation (EIP). This is an outline review of a project plan (for a new project) or project activities for the early identification of probable environmental impacts. It includes an outline of a plan or actions for controlling of the negative impacts. Based on the possibility of causing adverse environment impacts, the EIP evaluation determines whether or not the project will need to be further reviewed at later stages. Circumstances under which EIPs need to be presented have been established through ministerial decree.

Environmental Impact Assessment (EIA). This is intended to be a careful and deep analysis on important environmental effects caused by the planned project, including the possibility to prevent or offset the negative impact. For ongoing or completed project EIA is known as Environmental Evaluation Presentation (EEP). Evaluation of these document also determines the need of further actions.

Environmental Management Plan (EMnP). This describes in detail the activities or efforts to prevent, mitigate or restore the negative impacts caused by project activities. The approval of the document also indicates the feasibility of the project based on sustainability of natural resources and environmental aspects. The project will incorporate and be responsible for the implementation of the approved plan described in this document.

Environmental Impact Monitoring Plan (EMtP). This document describes in detail the monitoring plan of the environment impacts. Schedule, standard and procedure of monitoring are essential information contained in this document, also the agent responsible for monitoring process. The project can be started upon approval of this document.

In general, this environmental analysis is an important component in the project planning process, but economic considerations are equally important. The use of economic criteria such as IRR, B/C and NPV indicates the economic feasibility of the project. The rate or degree of economic feasibility measured by IRR or B/C could be lowered by incurring cost of environmental management. Final decision for project approval, of course, should not only be based on economic feasibility or environmental management, but should consider all factors and how it (the project) may finally contribute to national development objectives. The government may also exercise its power in promoting EIA through providing economic incentives or penalties such as imposing no tariff for importing machinery to be used in reducing impact on the environment or imposing higher taxes on firms who do not comply with EIA. An illustration of the EIA project cycle is presented in **Figures 1 through 3** which indicates that all projects done by the government, externally assisted and private, are subject to EIA processes in each step of the project cycle. EIP is done preceding pre-feasibility study. Environmental monitoring and management plans must be prepared before approval of the project or project implementation. Environmental evaluation is done as feedback during project implementation, monitoring and evaluation.

Training and Community Aspects

Human resources development is an important factor in the development of EIA. The Ministry of Agriculture has been conducting EIA training; however, the number of trained officers is still limited, because of inadequate expert resources and training funds. Since EIA is a relatively new concept for Indonesia, improvement on training materials and the concept of EIA itself is an ongoing process and is continuously conducted by the National Commission and Agricultural Commission for EIA.

The Agriculture Commission for EIA has been conducting EIA appreciation meetings for the MOA officers in the central and provincial offices. The same training is also conducted for private and government enterprises. There were four such training sessions during 1989-90. Community appreciation is encouraged to conduct social controls on the implementation of environmental management by firms. This is proven to be effective and complements the monitoring done by the government. Through this community awareness, more legal cases on this matter have been brought through courts. This helps the government in controlling and monitoring firms. The government also creates non-monetary incentives to firms by giving honours, medals or certificates for their recognisable achievements in environmental management.

5. Problems In EIA Implementation

Although there is an increasing awareness of the need of EIA and efforts have been made toward the implementation of EIA, a number of problems are being encountered in implementation. Four deserve special mention:

-- Community perception of the EIA. There is resistance because EIA is seen as a bureaucratic hinderance, as a source of additional costs, and because it is argued that the problem could be dealt with during implementation;

-- Bureaucratic problems. The terms of reference for EIA are sometimes poorly drafted, the EIA is not always done to schedule, and there are inter-departmental disputes over evaluation criteria. Because of the last-mentioned, terms of reference are sometimes absent;

-- Technical problems. Because of the paucity of trained officers, the quality of EIA documents is questionable, including the basic evaluation, cost estimates, etc. Also, there are still few adequate consultants and experts to assist in EIA document preparation. As a consequence, there is a real difficulty in preparing the documents for some projects.

-- Incomplete Processes. Some existing agricultural industries, such as palm oil or sugar processing plants, have been planned along with an environmental monitoring plan and an environmental management plan (EMtP & EMnP). However, the Environmental Impact Assessment and Environmental Information Presentation, to be carried out after implementation is completed, are still rarely done.

6. Conclusion and Recommendations

In Indonesia, government development policies are increasingly based on the sustainability of environmental and natural resources. Also, government institutions have been established for the purpose of environmental and natural resource management. Progress has been made to increase the awareness of environmental damage. While these are real achievements, the implementation of the programmes has not been without problems.

The problems reflect a still significant lack of technical expertise, a lack of training facilities and expertise for the training of the staff responsible for the implementation of the policies. The funds available for the implementation of the programme as a whole are not yet adequate. As well as more training, improved inter-sectoral co-ordination could be helpful in increasing the flow of information about the experience of other sectors in dealing with these problems. Also, improved co-ordination would help with inter-sectoral disputes. Similarly, as well as more funds for EIA, we also need to review the procedures carefully to see if economies and efficiency gains might not be made, for example, through making the preparation of the EIA, EmtP and EMnP compulsory, and to be done with one document.

Indonesia has to work on these issues so that the better implementation of the EIA procedure will promote and speed up the achievement of the Sustainable Development Programme that has now become such an important part of the development strategy.

Figure 1

EIA STATUS ON GOVERNMENT PROJECT CYCLE

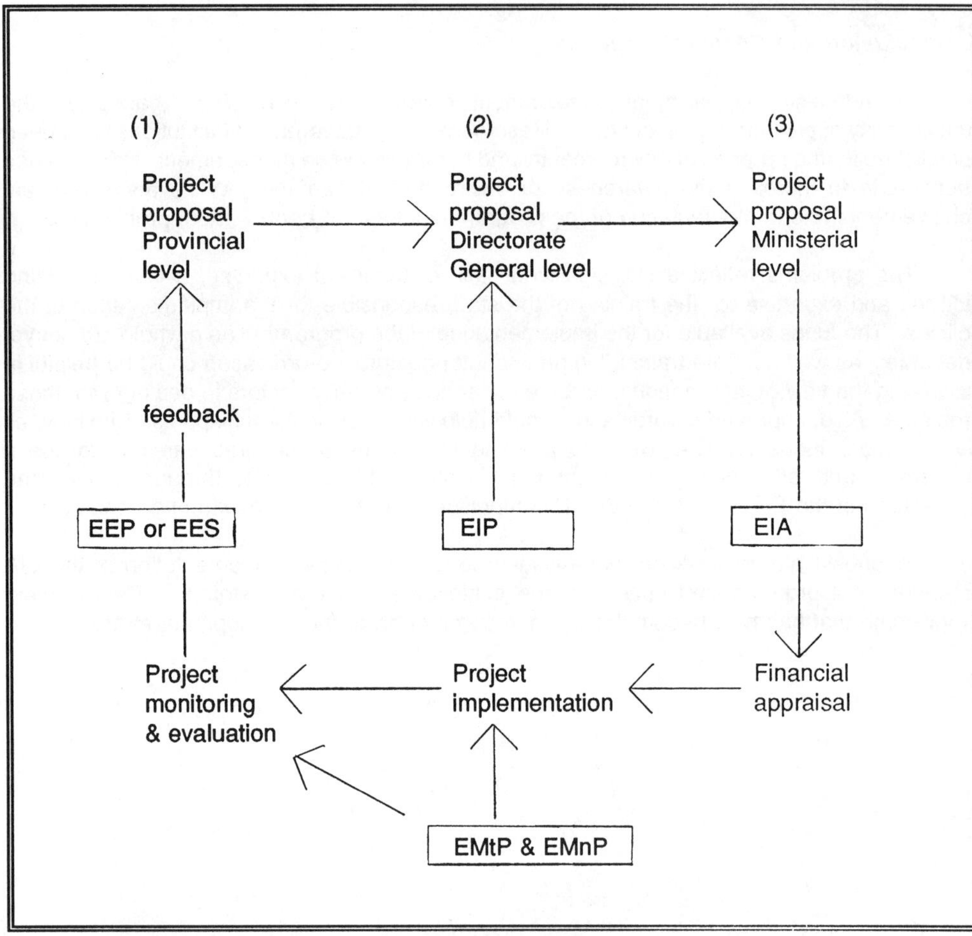

Notes:

EIP	=	Environmental Information Presentation
EIA	=	Environmental Information Assessment
EMtP	=	Environmental Monitoring Plan
EMnP	=	Environmental Management Plan
EES	=	Environmental Evaluation Study
EEP	=	Environmental Evaluation Presentation

Figure 2

EIA STATUS ON EXTERNALLY ASSISTED PROJECT CYCLE

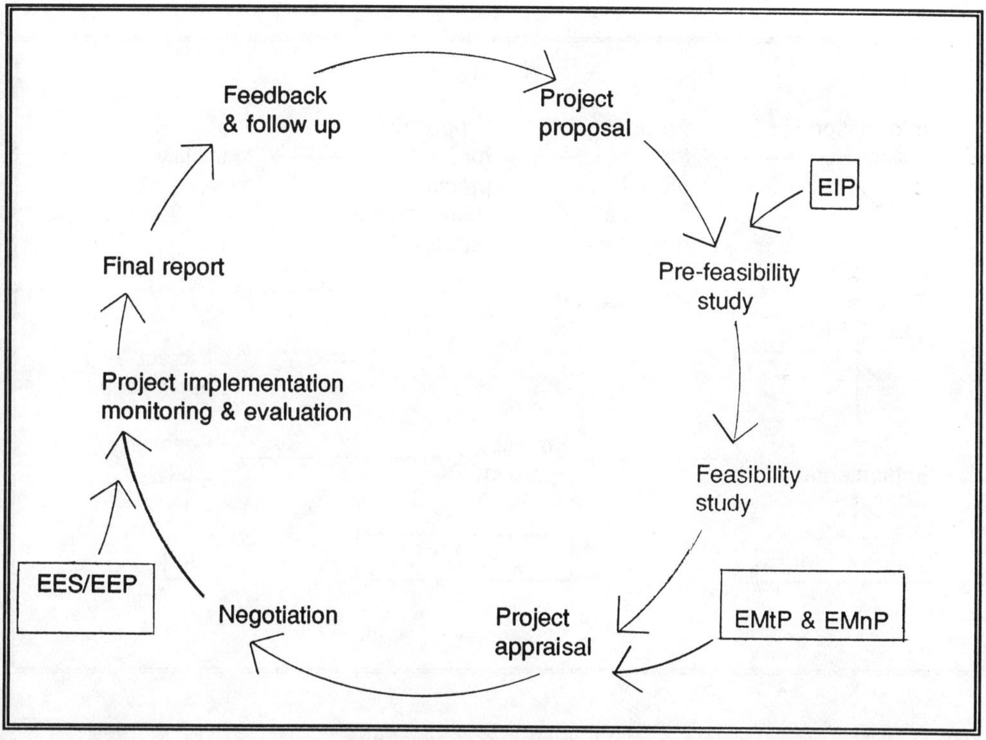

Notes: EIP = Environmental Information Presentation
EIA = Environmental Information Assessment
EMtP = Environmental Monitoring Plan
EMnP = Environmental Management Plan
EES = Environmental Evaluation Study
EEP = Environmental Evaluation Presentation

Figure 3

EIA STATUS ON PRIVATE PROJECT CYCLE (NATIONAL AND FOREIGN INVESTMENT)

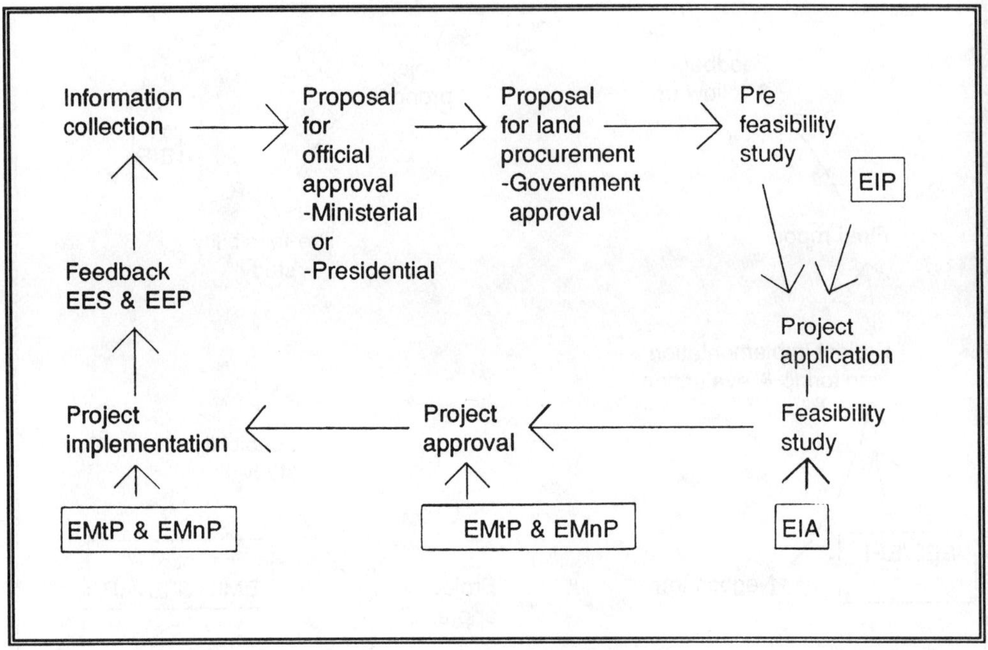

Notes:

EIP	=	Environmental Information Presentation
EIA	=	Environmental Information Assessment
EMtP	=	Environmental Monitoring Plan
EMnP	=	Environmental Management Plan
EES	=	Environmental Evaluation Study
EEP	=	Environmental Evaluation Presentation

BIBLIOGRAPHY

COCHRANE, Harold C. and Paul C. HUSZAR, *Economic Analysis of the Model Farm Program and Its Subsidization Under The Citanduy II Project*, USAID, Indonesia, 1988.

GAJAH MADA UNIVERSITY, *Integrated Pest Management for Onion Plants,* Bulaksumur, Gajah Mada University, 1989.

MUSANIF, J., *Procedure and Obstacles of Environmental Impact Assessment in the Agriculture Sector,* 1988.

PRASETIO, M., *Environmental Impact Assessment in the Ministry of Forestry,* Jakarta, 1988.

TAMPUBOLON, S.M.H., *An Economic Analysis of Soil Conservation Practices in the Citanduy River Basin, Java, Indonesia,* 1988.

USAID/Indonesia, *Technical Assistance to Upland Agriculture and Conservation Project, USESE, Indonesia,* 1989.

AN ECONOMIC PERSPECTIVE ON MANAGEMENT IN THE PUBLIC SECTOR

by

Dennis Anderson *

* University College London and St Antony's College, Oxford University.

RÉSUMÉ

Convaincu qu'une bonne gestion de l'environnement repose sur des principes économiques sains, Dennis Anderson esquisse les meilleurs moyens par lesquels le secteur public pourrait améliorer sa propre gestion de l'environnement et parvenir à une meilleure économie (en réduisant les coûts externes) tout en produisant les ressources financières nécessaires pour réaliser les améliorations souhaitées dans l'environnement et dans l'économie. Il étudie de plus près les domaines dans lesquels l'introduction d'*incitations obéissant aux lois du marché (MBIs)* (par exemple dans la tarification de l'encombrement des villes ou dans la réduction des émissions des véhicules et de l'industrie) ou la suppression des subventions existantes (produits agrochimiques, par exemple) serviraient plus efficacement l'économie et l'environnement. La suppression de subventions préjudiciables à l'environnement et l'abaissement du coût administratif de mise en conformité amélioreraient aussi les équilibres financiers du secteur public. La réglementation directe, autre solution possible, s'est révélée impraticable dans de nombreux pays, en raison de faiblesses institutionnelles touchant la législation et l'administration. L'auteur termine sur une mise en garde, à savoir qu'il ne suffit pas de bien calculer quelques prix pour améliorer la gestion de l'environnement si les conditions macro-économiques agissent à l'opposé des incitations économiques mises en place. Toutefois, se conformer plus strictement à l'efficience économique dans le secteur public est aller dans le sens d'une saine gestion macro-économique. L'étude du professeur Anderson lève bien des doutes sur le degré d'amélioration qu'il est possible d'atteindre dans la gestion de l'environnement relevant du secteur public en respectant simplement les principes généraux de l'efficience économique.

SUMMARY

Convinced that good environmental management originates from good economics, Dennis Anderson outlines the best possible ways in which the public sector can improve its own environmental management and achieve an economic improvement (by reducing external costs) while at the same time generating the financial resources required to bring the desired environmental and economic improvements about. He looks in greater detail into a number of issue areas where the introduction of *market-based incentives (MBIs)* (eg in urban congestion pricing or vehicle or industrial emission control) or the removal of existing subsidies (as in agro-chemicals) would serve the economic and environmental aims more efficiently. The removal of environmentally harmful subsidies and the lowering of administrative cost of compliance would also improve the public sector's financial balances. The regulatory approach, which is the alternative to MBIs, has proven unworkable in many countries due to institutional weaknesses regarding law and administration. He warns in the end that putting a few prices "right" will not suffice to improve environmental management if macro-economic conditions work in the opposite direction to the economic incentives put in place. However, stricter observance of economic efficiency in the public sector is a movement towards sound macroeconomic management.

Professor Anderson's paper clarifies much doubt on how improvements can be achieved in public sector environmental management by simply abiding by the general principles of economic efficiency.

1. Introduction

This paper concentrates on two questions:

- How best to raise public financial resources to provide for the environmental management activities of governments, and

- How governments might best appraise their own environmental management activities.

The paper follows the economic principle that environmental policies ideally have two aims, not one, which is to achieve an environmental *and* an economic improvement, the latter being achieved by a reduction of the external social costs of environmental damage. For this reason the terms "best appraise" and "best ways of raising resources" can usefully be assessed by reference to familiar social and economic criteria for decision making, namely the social rate of return to investment and the social efficiency of prices.

Before turning to the above questions explicitly, two points of continuity with other papers in this Conference might be noted. The *first* concerns the *scale* of public sector involvement in environmental management. Any management -- in government as in business, and whether economically or environmentally related -- has to deal with the awkward question of how far responsibilities are best delegated to others. This is essentially at the core of the current debate on the use of market based incentives (MBIs) vs command and control (CAC) measures in environmental policy, discussed in this Conference by Pearce, whose analysis will not be repeated here. But the point is perhaps worth noting that a greater use of MBIs, by the nature of the approach, would delegate far more of the investment decision making and financial responsibilities away from the public sector -- though not, it should be emphasized, responsibilities for the setting of environmental standards and the general directions of policy. Self-evidently this would reduce strains on public financial and administrative resources, the first of the two questions this paper is to address.

Second, related to this, MBIs (which in most cases would amount to a tax on pollution or a user charge for an environmental service) would often be a significant source of revenue while pollution persists, and this too would help to defray the costs of public sector management. However, if MBIs were environmentally successful in their aim, the revenues would ultimately decline as pollution is abated (Figure 1), hence some provision in the tax structure must be made to keep the policies intact, e.g. for administration, monitoring, R&D. Experience shows that one environmental problem frequently follows another, much as photochemical smog and acid deposition issues surfaced in the industrial countries after "the great stinking smog" had been addressed by the Clean Air Acts of the 1950s and 1960s[1], and there is a continual need for revenues to provide for continuity and development of policy, independently of the amount of pollution abatement. This suggests that provisions in *indirect taxes* related to the public costs of implementing environmental policy would usefully complement MBIs (Figure 1)[2].

Figure 1:

Pollution Taxes and Pollution Abatement

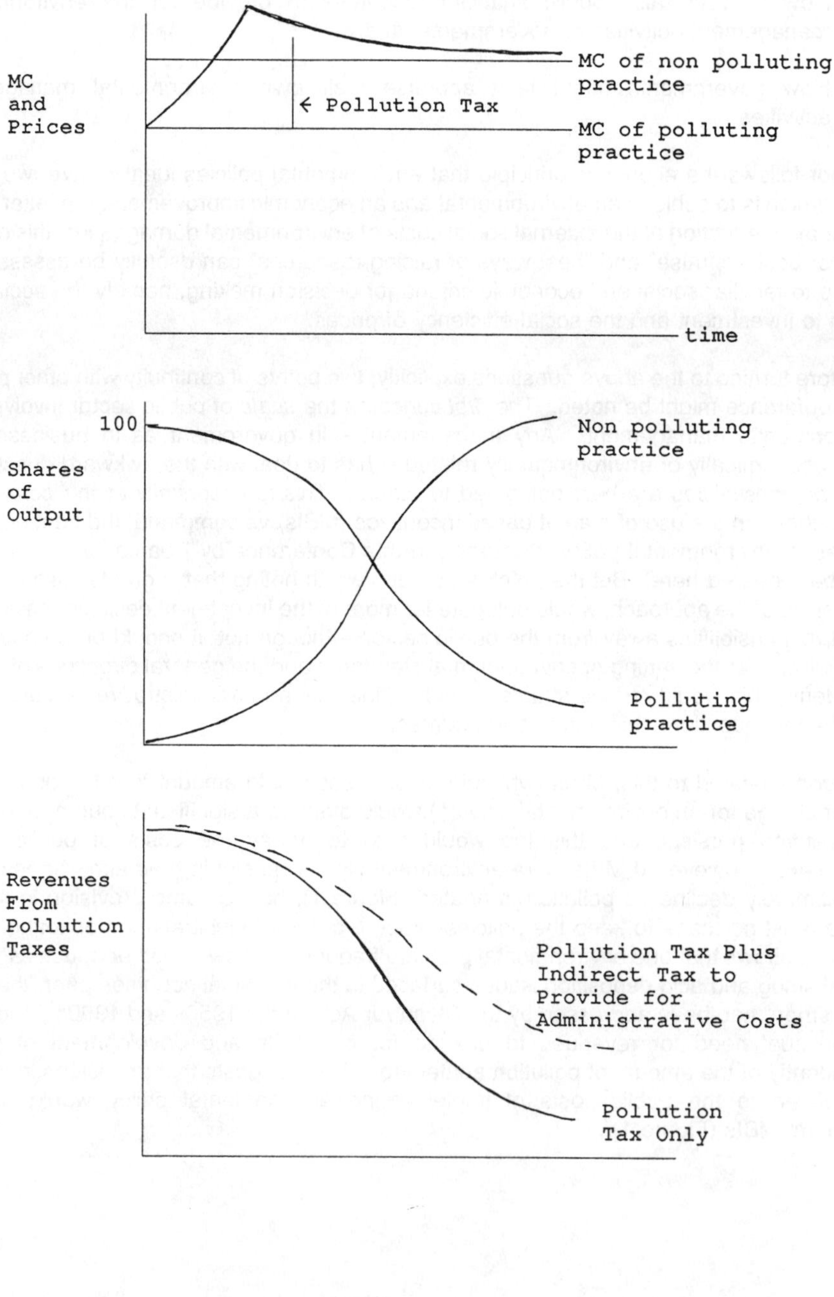

2. Raising Revenues

It is rare to find an environmental problem that should be dealt with exclusively privately (once MBIs are in place) or exclusively publicly. Table 1 presents a matrix of environmental problems, instruments and issues in developing countries[3]. It is noticeable how many problem areas that could usefully be delegated to private investment once MBIs are in place still need to be complemented by public investment; and in all cases expenditures of one form or another are required from the public sector, for instance for R&D, administration and the monitoring of compliance with policy. Conversely there are some public investments -- soil erosion control policies and gaining the environmental benefits from social forestry are two examples -- which require appreciable private commitments of labour and capital by farmers.

At the top of the table are listed some of the issues to be addressed in the course of weighing the policy options: the effects on costs and output (efficiency criterion); whether there will be an "innovative response" in terms of low-polluting technologies being introduced; how the regulatory alternatives compare with market-based incentives; the costs of administration and enforcement; the impact of the policies on revenues and expenditures; whether to subsidise certain policies (e.g. R&D into non-polluting technologies); how trade and investment will be affected; whether the pricing system is subsidising pollution or not; how different income groups might be effected by the policies, and whether offsetting or compensating arrangements can be found if the costs are borne unduly by one group; and whether macroeconomic conditions are working against environmental policy. Some of these issues are dealt with in other papers in the workshop. The present paper is concerned with two of them: the problem of raising revenues, and the effects of policies on costs and output (economic efficiency). There is inevitably some duplication between two sections since, as will be seen, to solve one problem is often to solve the other.

Now consider the revenue-raising problems associated with the various problem areas listed.

Urban congestion pricing. This is still a widely ignored policy despite its considerable promise for reducing congestion, fuel consumption and emissions levels in urban areas, and despite the considerable success of the Singapore Area Licensing Scheme, which reduced urban traffic densities by 50 per cent[4]. The sizeable revenues from congestion pricing would probably make the policy financially self-sufficient; they would provide for the costs of administration, of monitoring, and of electronic tolling schemes if these were preferred to the technically simpler alternatives of area licensing. (Not the least merit of the original Singapore Area Licensing Scheme however was its administrative and technical simplicity.) They would also provide a financial surplus[5], sufficient in many cases to finance urban infrastructure improvements such as roads, drainage, the repair of public buildings damaged by vibration and acid deposition, the provision of public transport services, and improved traffic management. At the same time, the surplus could be used to neutralise any adverse distributional effects of congestion pricing policies, e.g. by tax relief elsewhere or expenditures on public transport[6]. It is hard to think of a policy which would simultaneously solve an environmental problem, an economic problem (the waste and inefficiencies of congestion), a social problem and a financial problem so readily. It is a good example of the principle noted at the outset regarding the coincidence of environmental and economic interests in environmental policy.

Table 1 Matrix of Problems, Instruments and Issues

ISSUES
Economic Efficiency and Innovation
The Regulatory Alternatives
International Trade and Investment
Administration and Compliance Costs
Revenues and Expenditures
The Use of Subsidies
Second Best Issues
Income Distribution
The Macro-economic Context of Environmental Policy

PROBLEM AREAS	ECONOMIC INSTRUMENTS			
	Pollution Tax	User Charges	Conservation Incentives	Public Investment
Urban Transport				
- congestion	x --->	x		x
- noise	x			
- vehicle emissions	x --->	x	x	
Water & Sewerage	x	x		x
Greenhouse Gases				
- emissions	x		x	
- carbon sinks (afforestation)				x
Waste Disposal Industry		x	x	x
- effluents	x --->	x		
- gases: (SO_2, NOx, CO, particulates)	x --->	x	x	
Agriculture				
- chemicals	x			
- fertilizers	x			
- soil erosion				x
- soil quality[1]				x
Forestry				
- watersheds		x		x
- rainforests		x		x
- social forestry				x
CFCs	x --->	x		
Wildlife Reserves		x		x

(----> denotes "evolving into.")

[1] E.g. arising from desiccation, losses of nutrients, salination or other, depending on the area.

It is sometimes said that the problems of applying the Singapore scheme to other cities would be too great -- they are often sprawling, multi-centred cities, with too many points of entry to monitor, political opposition may be fierce, the lead-times for introducing public transport may be long while the distributional effects of congestion pricing may be immediate, and so forth. But this is to admit that the problem is complicated, not that it is unsolvable. In fact there are many ways to address such issues. Phasing is one approach, beginning with simpler systems (e.g. parking taxes and vehicle licences) and introducing the changes in small steps over a suitably long period, to give people time to adjust and the authorities time to monitor and modify policies as required. There is an abundance of research available which suggests that such problems would be tractable.

Vehicle and Industrial Emission Charges. Much the same can be said about taxes related to environmentally offensive vehicle and industrial emissions, although the revenue impact -- with the singular exception of carbon taxes, if they were introduced -- would be less. The revenue impact would also be more transient. E.g. we know from the range of technological options available[7] that sulphur taxes and taxes on leaded fuels would have quite dramatic effects on SO_2 emissions and lead pollution provided they were sufficient to stimulate the introduction of the low polluting options (scrubbers on power stations, catalytic converters and unleaded fuels). Nevertheless, the lags associated with the introduction of some technologies (e.g. of scrubbers or a greater use of gas for power generation) would be quite long, and there would be significant revenues from emission tax policies for some time.

Carbon Taxes. Developing countries have understandably resisted any policy initiatives on global warming, questioning the fairness and affordability of any restrictions -- whether induced by taxes or regulations -- on their use of fossil fuels. They have also (as have others) questioned the evidence on global warming. Yet it is not too soon to ask, what would they stand to gain or lose from introducing a carbon tax if it becomes necessary to use this as an instrument of policy to reduce global carbon accumulations in the atmosphere? On further inspection, it is a tax developing countries could profitably consider.

To begin, it would be more than three decades before such a tax would have any fundamental effect on the structure of energy supplies -- in particular, in effecting a shift towards low carbon technologies. Figure 2 shows one such scenario based on some recent simulation studies[8] of world energy demand and supply. (The figure shows a "global" supply structure, though we have also broken it down by developing and industrial country groupings.) Given the long lead-times involved in developing the low carbon "backstop" technologies, the size of the fossil fuel industry, and the long lags associated with changing energy supply structures, the transition to a low carbon emissions scenario (lower part of figure) would take perhaps 50-100 years. The main effects of carbon taxes in developing countries would be

- To raise revenues. For two-to-three decades they would essentially be acting as an indirect tax.

- Low deadweight losses if it turned out that global warming was not serious and the tax were converted from tax on fossil fuels according to their carbon content to an indirect tax on energy. (Energy demands are fairly price inelastic, which makes energy consumption a good candidate for indirect taxation on efficiency grounds.)

- To create an incentive for private investment in the renewables industry -- hydro, biomass and solar in particular -- in which developing countries may have a long-term comparative cost advantage. (E.g. solar insolation is 1.5 to 2.0 times those of the industrial countries, which makes the costs per watt-peak of solar capacity 30 to 50% lower.) It would also provide an added incentive for the development of natural gas resources.

Once again we have an example of an environmental policy (if the MBI route rather than regulation were chosen) being potentially an important source of revenues. As Smith and Pearson (1990) have shown for the UK, there is also no obvious reason why the revenues from such taxes could not be used to neutralize any adverse distributional effects of the taxes while leaving a surplus, although this is clearly an issue that can only be sorted out by local analysis.

Agro-chemicals. Large subsidies for agro-chemicals in developing countries seem to be more the rule than the exception (Table 2). Economic considerations would argue for removal of the subsidy -- and possibly a tax if pollution is significant -- and environmental considerations the same. This would also raise significant revenues, as the second column of the table suggests, again sufficient perhaps to provide for the costs of administration of environmental policy in this area.

Table 2

Pesticide Subsidies in Selected Countries

	Subsidies as a percentage of retail costs	Annual value ($ million)
China	19	285
Columbia	44	69
Ecuador	41	14
Egypt	83	207
Ghana	67	20
Honduras	29	12
Indonesia	82	128
Senegal	89	4

Source: World Resources Institute, 1985, quoted in Repetto, 1989, Table 6-3, p. 74.

Figure 2

The Renewable Energy Scenario Revisited

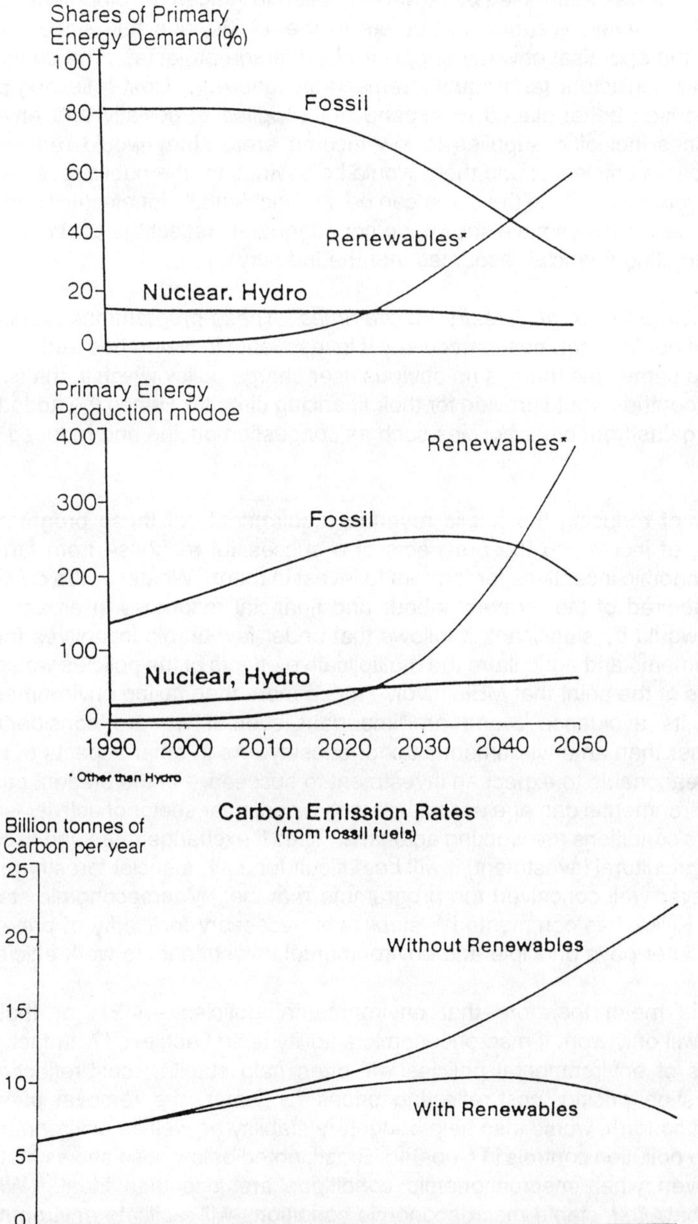

Water, Sewerage and Waste Disposal. These are activities in which appreciable public investments are involved. Public policies towards these services in developing countries have widely erred in favour of subsidising investment and, often, operating and maintenance costs. The long-standing question still arises, what would be the gains from the adoption of cost-reflecting prices? It was addressed by Lewis in relation to African development more than two decades ago, by Turvey, Warford and others in the 1970s, and has since been routinely encountered in the appraisal of water supply and sewerage projects[9]. The conclusions have been remarkably consistent (and equally remarkably ignored). Cost-reflecting prices would leave the authorities better-placed to expand the supplies of socially and environmentally important services including supplies to low income areas; they would reduce waste and losses, and improve efficiency; and there would be savings for the public revenue in the form of reduced subventions. (Much the same can be said incidentally for electricity pricing policies which, as the recent surveys have shown, do not adequately reflect the cost of capital and the problems of attracting financial resources into the industry[10].)

Soil Erosion and Social Forestry Programmes. These programmes require significant commitments of public resources, particularly if investments in watershed and windbreaks are involved. At the same time there is no obvious user charge policy which in the circumstances of developing countries would provide for their financing directly. Hence the added importance of the revenue gains from other policies such as congestion pricing and reduced subventions for the utilities.

One way of reducing the public revenue requirements of these programmes -- and, simultaneously, of increasing the prospects of a successful response from farmers -- is to improve the economic incentives for farmers to invest in them. Whatever the public policy, the commitment required of the farmers' labour and financial resources in erosion control and social forestry would be significant; it follows that under favourable incentives for investment in land improvements and agriculture the multiplicative effects of the policies would be greater. This reminds us of the point that MBIs involve much more than taxing environmental damage or subsidising its avoidance[11], and are important even if we are considering a public investment rather than an environmental tax or subsidy. As in other aspects of public policy, it would be unreasonable to expect an investment to succeed -- in the present case, the price of avoiding environmental damage associated with a particular sector of activity -- if prices and macroeconomic conditions are working against it. Thus if exchange rates and fiscal incentives work against agricultural investment, it will be difficult for, say, a social forestry programme to succeed, however well conceived the programme may be. Macroeconomic stability is also important. As Killick has commented[12], stability is necessary for clarity of price signals and thus for the polluter pays principle and environmental investments to work efficiently.

Does this mean therefore that environmental policies -- MBIs or their regulatory alternatives -- will only work if macroeconomic stability is first achieved? In fact, the revenue raising aspects of environmental policies will often help stability; cost-reflecting prices for energy, congestion pricing, cost-reflecting prices for water, the removal of subsidies for pesticides, and so forth, would also help budgetary stability as well as environmental policies. The example of pollution controls in Cubatao, Brazil, noted below, also shows that policies can be effective even when macroeconomic conditions are less than ideal. What is being suggested is that, *first*, stable macroeconomic conditions will facilitate environmental policy-making, and *second* that environmental policies will often contribute to macroeconomic stability; there is often mutually beneficial association between the two.

Forest and Wildlife Reserves. Much is rightly made of the importance of user charges for the services provided by forest and wildlife reserves (including licensing and stumpage fees in the case of forestry). Nevertheless, significant public resources are required for their protection. Two points carry over from the above remarks on other sectors. The first is that the revenues raised from MBIs elsewhere would leave the authorities better placed financially to implement those environmental investments that by their nature are less capable of being financially self-sufficient. The second, once again, is on the importance of macroeconomic and fiscal conditions for a sustainable management of these resources. These issues have been much discussed in relation to tropical forestry[13]; the only additional point to make is that a reduced stress on the resources brought about by improved macroeconomic and fiscal conditions would self-evidently make public management and protection of them less costly and more effective.

This brief review of the possibilities for raising financial resources to address environmental problems in developing countries shows that taxing pollution and introducing cost-reflecting user charges for environmentally-related services would make the policies financially self-sufficient in important cases. Indeed in some cases (congestion pricing and emissions taxes) they would be likely to earn a considerable surplus for a period, while in others (utility rates) they would reduce the requirements on the public revenue. In situations where revenues eventually fall as pollution is successfully addressed, there may still be a good case for indirect taxes on the (then environmentally unoffending) sector in order to maintain policies intact and provide for the costs of administration. Recalling the economic principle stated at the beginning of this paper, it is therefore not to overstate the point to propose that environmental policies should have three aims, not two: to achieve an environmental improvement, an economic improvement (by reducing external costs) and to generate the financial resources required to bring the environmental and economic improvements about.

3. Appraising Environmental Management Activities

There are several issues under this heading: the criteria used for the setting of standards and for expenditure decisions; the cost-effectiveness of a policy and the responses of private agents to it; and whether distributional and employment issues are dealt with effectively.

3.1 Criteria

Intangibles, and considerations of health, safety, heritage, wildlife habitats and beauty of the landscape all of course have had a major bearing on environmental policies. In addition, the old idea that environmental policies have important economic effects is gradually winning acceptance.

Approaches to the monetary evaluation of environmental benefits in OECD countries have recently been reviewed by Pearce and Markandya (1989). The US Environmental Protection Agency (EPA) (1987) has also undertaken a review of its experiences with cost-benefit analysis in the period 1981-86, when a number of policy initiatives were being reviewed with respect to the Clean Air Act, the Clean Water Act, toxic substances, resource conservation and recovery, hazardous substance contingency plans in the event of accidents, and the use of insecticides, fungicides and rodenticides.

There is a good case for developing countries to begin to address the questions, what would be the economic benefits of various types of environmental improvement? and how would these compare with costs? The following considers some of the problem areas listed in Table 1 and the economic benefits and costs that would be worth weighing.

Urban Congestion Pricing. The main benefits would be reduced travel times (valued by reference to wage data), reduced fuel consumption and vehicle emissions, reduced accident rates and loadings on health services, and a significant source of public revenue. When combined with traffic free zones, there are also the benefits to business activities in central areas to be weighed. The costs would be increased loadings on public transport and private passenger vehicles; these would in principle be self-financed through private fares and increased demands for passenger services. The revenues from congestion pricing would also provide for improvements in infrastructure and traffic management schemes, as discussed above.

Vehicle and Industrial Pollution. The costs of the technologies required to reduce emissions and effluents have been examined in a large number of studies, and reviewed at various times by the OECD, 1987, 1988, 1990. The benefits of improved health and reduced acid deposition on property, water, agriculture and forests are more difficult to estimate, though a number of attempts have been made based on analysis of property prices, the costs of illness and other approaches[14]. As Markandya and Pearce conclude "environmental pollution in the form of air pollution, noise nuisance and water quality deterioration have significant effects on ... property values. The overwhelming evidence of the empirical studies supports this conclusion." Given the damage to property, life and health experienced by the industrial countries from vehicle and industrial pollution in the course of urban-industrial expansion, analysis of the economic benefits of pollution abatement in the developing countries would not seem misplaced. The following comments by Findley (1988, p. 67) on pollution in Cubatao, Brazil are particularly telling:

> "The case of Cubatao demonstrates, perhaps more dramatically than any other in the world, the most extreme results of unregulated occupation of land by mixed uses in a sensitive ecological setting: a large nation's most important and most polluting factories concentrated in a small area subject to atmospheric inversions and interlaced with thousands of homes; tens of thousands of people bathed in toxic effluent and sleeping directly over pipelines carrying flammable and explosive substances; acid rain defoliating adjacent mountainsides and causing landslides that threaten not only the factories and residences but the highways, railroad, pipelines, and the harbour connecting the community to the outside world; and public officials at all levels seemingly in a state of paralysis, obsessed with the goal of economic development and striving to ignore the environmental catastrophe they have allowed....
>
> "Since 1985 there has been real progress toward ameliorating some of the worst aspects of the environmental fiasco in Cubatao. A tremendous amount of pollution control equipment is being installed in industrial plants, which also have been switched to less-polluting fuel, thousands of residents are being assisted in relocating to more suitable living areas, [enforcement agencies have] become more aggressive in using fines and temporary plant closures to deal with recalcitrant polluters, and the Ministerio Publico has initiated public civil actions seeking restoration of damaged wetlands, waterways, and hillsides. Moreover, through extensive national newspaper and television coverage of the agony and progress of Cubatao, all of Brazil has received an environmental education."

Water, Sewerage and Waste Disposal. These investments too have important effects on health, life and property. But interestingly they can be justified very often by the economic criterion of willingness-to-pay for the services, quite apart from these important intangibles. Surveys can be undertaken to estimate the costs of not providing the services, e.g. of the costs of water provided by vendors and tankers when public supplies are not available, or to people having to fetch and carry water over long distances[15]. The costs to people of services not being available are very often appreciably greater than the costs of public services, as might be inferred from the survey of water supplies in Lagos summarised Table 3.

The finding that consistently emerges from such surveys is that people are often willing to pay for improved services. If tariffs reflected the costs of their provision, the services would also generate satisfactory returns, and there would be an incentive for the reduction of losses and wastes. These are long-standing and (to economists) familiar arguments[16], which however remain relevant. Once again we have an example of a policy which brings good environmental benefits, good economic benefits and which (under the right tariffs) could provide for much of its own financial requirements. Any appraisal of public sector management activities in the area of water supply, sanitation and waste disposal must be judged against this possibility.

Carbon Taxes. It seems too soon to be able to contemplate estimating the long-term benefits of halting global warming, if indeed it is occurring, though some attempts have been made[17]. The scientific evidence is much in dispute. As noted earlier, it may be preferable to consider the question instead of the gains and losses associated with carbon tax policies, if these need to be introduced for precautionary reasons. Paradoxically, because they would be a fairly efficient form of indirect taxation for some decades, there may be some economic gains from the policy even if global warming turns out to be less serious than thought and the taxes were to be reduced or revoked.

Agro-chemicals. The economic benefits of reducing pollution from agro-chemicals, like those of reducing industrial emissions and effluents are also difficult to estimate. A minimum estimate of the benefits of removing the above-noted subsidies for agro-chemicals can be estimated in the usual way by looking at the allocative effects on farm inputs and outputs.

Soil Erosion and Social Forestry. The benefits can be measured in terms of the long-run effects on agricultural output[18].

The economic analysis of the benefits of environmental improvements can also be extended to other areas, such as wildlife and forests. It is beyond the scope of this paper to review the various approaches and results obtained so far. Suffice it to say that they can be important influences on the design of policies, in particular for the setting of standards and appraising expenditure decisions. They may also serve to remove commonly held doubts in policy-makers' minds that environmental policies are only a cost; very often, it is the *absence* of policies that is more costly to an economy.

3.2 Cost-Effectiveness and the Response of Private Agents

Two further criteria by which public policies should be assessed, in addition to the benefit-cost criteria, are the cost-effectiveness of policies and the responses of private agents to them. The two are related in ways which are familiar, but which may be worth restating by reference to the situations in developing countries.

Table 3

Costs of Alternative Sources of Water Supply In Lagos, 1985
(Naira, N)

		Naira/m^3
Marginal Costs of Public Supplies[1]		1.5
Alternatives to Public Supply:		
Tankers	40 gallons for N2	11.0
	200 gallons for N10	11.0
	1000 gallons for N20	4.2
Vendors	8 gallons for N.40	11.0
	40 gallons for N1.0	5.5
	1000 gallons for N20.0	4.4
Household Expenditures[2]		
Low income households (30 lcd[3])		1.6 to 2.4
Average (50 lcd)		1.9 to 2.8
Household Expenditures Plus Labour Costs[4]		
Low income households		2.2 to 3.0
Average		2.2 to 3.1

1. In border prices.

2. Applies to 515 households without access to public supplies.

3. lcd: litres per capita per day.

4. Assumes N2.5/day for labour costs, and low income households spending three hours per week, the average household 1.3 hours, carrying water (based on survey results). The average amount of water carried by low income households was 6.3 tons per month over distances of 100 to 300 metres.

Source: Appraisal documents for the World Bank-financed water supply project, 1988. Surveys of 800 households were undertaken by the water supply engineers of the Lagos Water Supply Corporation as part of project preparation, with the help of Diane Reedy.

The first is in the *choice of instruments*. It is nearly twenty years since Baumol and Oates (1971) in a still much cited paper demonstrated that MBIs, in the form of taxes on pollution, lower the costs to polluters in complying with policy. Polluters facing high costs of pollution abatement would prefer to pay a charge or a tax while those facing low costs would prefer to avoid it by installing the necessary equipment or changing practices. Hence the least-cost forms of abatement are introduced first, and there is a better ranking of priorities. The analysis has stood the test of time and of applied work[19].

Does the argument have any merit in developing countries? In fact, it probably has even greater merit than it has in industrial countries. In addition to (a) lowering the costs to the polluters in complying with policy, MBIs (b) would lower the costs of administration and (c) in some circumstances may be the only operational approach available given the institutional difficulties -- and added public financial requirements -- of implementing the "command-and-control" approach.

Environmental taxes e.g. on commercial energy and agro-chemicals could be grafted onto existing indirect taxes on such commodities. Indirect taxes have long been favoured forms of taxation in developing countries because of their administrative convenience. For many problem areas environmental taxes would work through existing administrative arrangements and would be operationally feasible. By being levied at wholesale or bulk supply points, problems of non-compliance with policy as well as administrative costs would be minimised. In addition, they would feed through to informal sector and small-scale activities, in so far as these activities used polluting products. Such activities easily escape the regulatory net, as they often do with income taxes[20].

Chronic institutional weaknesses with respect to law and public administration in some countries must also raise doubts about any policy that rests heavily on regulation. Aside from reducing costs and the occurrences of non-compliance as just noted, taxes can also achieve useful effects *even if* the levels of pollution and the parties responsible for it are not precisely known: polluters still pay (as they would, for instance, with taxes on agro-chemicals or on polluting fuels) and there is the incentive for pollution reduction by demand changes, substitutions and innovation. The regulatory approach, in contrast, is much more exacting on matters of damage measurement, monitoring compliance with standards, and so forth; its administrative burden is greater, and it would be more prone to problems of bribery and default when administration and laws are weak.

Lastly, it was noted earlier that cost-effectiveness and a good response from private agents will also depend on macroeconomic conditions and the general structure of macroeconomic incentives. A good example is erosion control. However well conceived erosion control programmes might be, they will be unlikely to succeed if macroeconomic conditions are working against agricultural investment. Conversely, favourable conditions may not only encourage private investment in what have come to be called sustainable forms of cultivation, but by doing so reduce the onus on the public sector. Again the practical conclusion is that the appraisal of public sector environmental management programmes must-needs take account of the macroeconomic context.

This conclusion is reminiscent of that which has emerged from operational experience with the use of cost-benefit methods in developing countries over the past 20 years, whether the investments in question were environmentally related or not. In the 1960s and 1970s project appraisal using shadow or accounting prices was a boom industry in economics, and many highly regarded texts on the subject emerged[21]. As the authors were at pains to point out, there was no good substitute for bringing actual and shadow prices into alignment ("for getting prices right") if efficiency and growth were to be achieved. Nevertheless, projects were widely appraised in a shadow world, often neglecting the problems that the huge disparities between shadow and actual prices would present for the projects in question. Since the actual world was, on account of distortions in the general structure of macro- and micro-economic incentives, very often a good deal harsher on the projects than the shadow worlds, making numerous well-conceived projects non-operational, it is not surprising (with the wisdom of hindsight) that many projects failed, and that the emphasis on economic reform and structural adjustments later emerged as a necessary condition for projects to succeed. This is essentially the point Warford has made[22] in emphasising the importance of the links between general economic policies and the environment, and in broadening the definition of the term market-based incentives. Environmental policies and investments are unlikely to succeed without favourable macroeconomic and fiscal policies to support them, and it will be important to reflect this concern in the criteria used for appraising public sector management activities.

3.3 Income Distribution and Employment

Issues under this heading also need to be examined when appraising the environmental management activities of the public sector. These are large subjects, on which little research has been done in the developing countries[23]. There are three questions to be addressed:

- The effects of the programmes or policies on labour demand and productivity;
- The *incidence* of the benefits, e.g. on health and living conditions; and
- The design of compensating policies where a programme or policy may affect employment or distribution adversely.

Environmental policies are often unthinkingly criticised (and even more strongly opposed) on the grounds that they may create unemployment or reduce the productivity of labour. There are however significant examples of where they would raise the demands for labour in economically productive ways: in social forestry programmes; in watershed plantation and management programmes; in the planting and maintenance of windbreaks, and the extraction of timber from them; in areas threatened by erosion and desertification; in the protection and maintenance of wildlife and forest reserves; in the construction and maintenance of water supply, sewerage, storm drainage and waste disposal systems; and in the supply of public and private passenger transport services if congestion pricing and associated urban improvement schemes were introduced. Besides being labour-demanding, such activities would satisfy another basic requirement of public expenditure policy, which is that they would have good social returns to investment.

Some environmental policies would ostensibly reduce employment, e.g. Clean Air Acts may reduce employment in coal and lignite mining. Even here, however, it would be desirable to examine the employment possibilities in the alternatives, e.g. in the provision of clean fuels and of their supporting infrastructure, household appliances and industrial equipment.

The connections between environmental policies, employment and earnings opportunities are thus an important aspect of the policies which could be turned to good advantage. Where there are reasons for thinking that the effects on employment and income distribution might be adverse, consideration might be given to the use of the revenue gains or savings from the various MBIs discussed above to promote more labour demanding programmes. There are many possibilities here, in the infrastructure services in particular.

However, it is also important not to lose sight of the *incidence* of environmental improvements and their effects on living standards: of reduced congestion and travel times for low income workers in cities (probably the group most inconvenienced by congestion); of improved water supply, sanitation, storm drainage and waste disposal systems in low income areas; of reduced depositions of pollutants; of cleaner air; of improvements of the level and long-term security of rural earnings arising from erosion control programmes, and so forth. Formal surveys are still lacking which would provide evidence on these matters, though they are surely a requirement for the preparation and appraisal of public policies and expenditures on the environment.

4. Conclusion

The adoption of environmental taxes and cost-reflecting user charges for environmentally-related services in developing countries could go a long way towards addressing the question, how might environmental programmes best be financed? In important cases (congestion pricing and, for a period, emissions taxes) there would be financial surpluses, in others (utilities) a reduction of public revenue requirements. They would also be administratively less burdensome and costly than the regulatory approach to environmental policies.

As to the appraisal of public programmes and policies, the use of cost-benefit analysis would help in the preparation and design of policies and investments, and to address questions as to their affordability and importance. The danger to avoid is that of taking too narrow a view of, say, a market-based incentive to reduce pollution or of a public investment to achieve an environmental improvement. It is not sufficient to appraise investments in a shadow world, whether the investment is environmentally related or otherwise, or to assume that putting one or two prices "right", say, by introducing an environmental tax to reduce pollution will have the intended effects. However well conceived an initiative may be, it may not succeed if macroeconomic conditions and the general structure of economic incentives are working against it.

NOTES AND REFERENCES

1. Brimblecombe (1987), Ashby and Anderson (1981) and Parker (1989) provide fascinating historical reviews.

2. See also my paper on Environmental Policy and "The Public Revenue in Developing Countries", Anderson (1990).

3. The classification follows a suggestion by David Pearce.

4. Goodwin and Jones (1989), and Jones (1989).

5. See Goodwin (1989).

6. For a further discussion of approaches, see the Institute for Fiscal Studies (IFS) research proposal on "Tax Reform and the Environment", IFS (1989).

7. See OECD (1987, 1988 and 1990).

8. By Catherine Bird and myself; at the University College London (UCL) and the Oxford Institute for Economics and Statistics. It is to be presented in a forthcoming paper on "Renewable Energy and Carbon Accumulations".

9. Lewis (1969), Warford (1966), Warford, *et al.* (1974). I also revisited the issues in my paper on infrastructure pricing policies in Africa (Anderson, 1989).

10. Munasinghe *et al.* (1988). See Diaz (1985) on Mexico on the contribution of subventions for the public utilities to inflation and the likely contribution of their removal to price stability.

11. Schramm and Warford (1989).

12. At a conference at the Overseas Development Institute, London, March 1990.

13. E.g. Gillis and Repetto (1988), Mahar (1989), Binswanger (1987).

14. Again see Pearce and Markandya (1989) and US EPA (1987).

15. See World Bank (1988) the Lagos Water Supply Project, for a recent example (summarised in Table 3 below).

16. See e.g. Warford (1966) and Saunders *et al.* (1977).

17. See Nordhaus' review. Nordhaus (1990).

18. See Anderson, Chapter 10 in Schramm and Warford (1989).

19. For an early illustration, see the World Bank study on water pollution policy in Finland, by Warford, Pellegrini, Kneese and Maler (1974).

20. Point made by David Turnham in the preparatory notes for this Conference.

21. The OECD "manual" of Little and Mirrlees (1968, 1974), Squire and van der Tak (1975) were three influential texts, later delightfully complemented by Ray (1984).

22. Warford (1987, 1989a) and Schramm and Warford (1989)

23. See my review for the World Bank. Anderson (1990).

BIBLIOGRAPHICAL REFERENCES

ANDERSON, Dennis, "Infrastructure Pricing Policies and the Public Revenue in African Countries," *World Development,* Vol. 17, No. 4, 1989, pp. 525-542.

Environmental Policy and the Public Revenue in Developing Countries, Environment Working Paper, No. 36, Washington, D.C., World Bank, 1990.

ASHBY, Eric and Mary ANDERSON, *The Politics of Clean Air,* Oxford, Oxford, University Press, 1981.

BAUMOL, William J. and Wallace E. OATES, "The Use of Standards and Prices for Protection of the Environment," *Swedish Journal of Economics,* Vol. 73, March 1971.

BINSWANGER, Hans, "Fiscal and Legal Incentives with Environmental Effects on the Brazilian Amazon," Agriculture and Rural Development Department, World Bank, Processed, 1987.

BRIMBLECOMBE, Peter, *The Big Smoke,* London and New York, Routledge, 1987.

DIAZ, Fransisco Gil, "Mexico's Path From Stability to Inflation," Chapter 12 in Arnold C. Harberger, *World Economic Growth,* San Fransisco, ICS Press, 1985.

FINDLEY, Roger W., "Pollution Control in Brazil," *Ecology Law Quarterly,* Vol. 15, No. 1, 1988, pp. 1-68.

GILLIS, Malcolm and Robert REPETTO, *Deforestation and Government Policy,* Occasional Paper No. 6, San Francisco, International Center for Economic Growth, 1988.

GOODWIN, Peter B., "The Rule of Three? A Possible Solution to the Political Problem of Competing Objectives for Road Pricing," *Traffic Engineering and Control,* October, 1989.

GOODWIN, P.B and P.M. JONES, "Road Pricing: The Political and Strategic Possibilities," A Report of the Transport Studies Unit, Oxford University, Oxford OX2 6NB, TSO Ref. 40, 1989.

INSTITUTE FOR FISCAL STUDIES (IFC), *Tax Reform and the Environment: A Research Proposal,* London, Institute for Fiscal Studies, November 1989.

JONES, Peter M., *The Restraint of Road Traffic in Urban Areas: Objectives, Options and Experiences,* Discussion Paper No. 3, Transport Studies Unit, Oxford University, 1989.

LEWIS, Arthur, *Some Aspects of Economic Development,* Tema, Ghana Publishing Corporation, 1969.

LITTLE, I.M.D and MIRRLEES, J., *Manual of Industrial Project Analysis,* Paris, OECD Development Centre, 1968.

Project Appraisal and Planning for Developing Countries, New York, Basic Books, 1974.

MAHAR, Dennis J., "Deforestation in Brazil's Amazon Region: Magnitude, Rate and Causes," Chapter 7 in Schramm and Warford, 1989.

MUNASINGHE, Mohan, Joseph GILLING and Melody MASON, *A Review of World Bank Lending for Electric Power,* World Bank Industry and Energy Department Paper, March 1988.

NORDHAUS, William D., "To Curb or Not to Curb: The Economics of the Greenhouse Effect," paper presented to the annual meetings of the American Association for the Advancement of Science, New Orleans, February 1990.

ORGANISATION FOR ECONOMIC CO-OPERATION AND DEVELOPMENT (OECD), *Emissions Control,* Paris, OECD, 1987.

Emission Controls in Electricity Generation and Industry, Paris, OECD, 1988.

Energy and the Environment: Policy Overview, Paris, OECD, 1990.

PARKER, Andrew N., "Environmental Policy: Case Studies in Water and Air Pollution," University College London, Processed, 1989.

PEARCE, David W. and Anil MARKANDYA, *Environmental Policy Benefits: Monetary Valuation,* Paris, OECD, 1989.

RAY, Anandarup, *Cost-Benefit Analysis: Issues and Methodologies,* Baltimore, MD, Johns Hopkins University Press, 1984.

REPETTO, Robert, "Economic Incentives for Sustainable Production," in Schramm and Warford, eds., 1989.

SAUNDERS, Robert J., Jeremy J. WARFORD and Patrick C. MANN, *Alternative Concepts of Marginal Cost for Public Utility Pricing,* World Bank Staff Working Paper No. 259, May 1977.

SCHRAMM, Gunter and Jeremy J. WARFORD, eds., *Environmental Management and Economic Development,* Baltimore and London, Johns Hopkins University Press, 1989.

SMITH, Stephen and Mark PEARSON,
Taxation and Environmental Policy: Some Initial Evidence, IFS Commentary No. 19, London, Institute for Fiscal Studies, 1990.

SQUIRE, Lyn and Herman G. van der TAK, *Economic Analysis of Projects,* Baltimore MD, Johns Hopkins University Press, 1975.

U.S. ENVIRONMENTAL PROTECTION AGENCY (EPA), *EPA's Use of Cost-Benefit Analysis: 1981-86*, EPA-230-05-87-028, Washington, D.C., EPA, August 1987.

WARFORD, Jeremy J., (1966), "Water Requirements: The Investment Decision in the Water Supply Industry," *Manchester School,* Vol. 34, pp. 87-112, reprinted (with revisions) as Chapter 6 in Ralph Turvey ed., *Public Enterprise,* Penguin Modern Economics, 1968.

"Environment, Growth and Development," Paper No. 14 for the Development Committee of the World Bank and the IMF, Washington, D.C., World Bank, August 1987.

"Environmental Management and Economic Policy in Developing Countries," Chapter 22 in Schramm and Warford, 1989a.

"World Bank Support for the Environment: A Progress Report," Staff Report No. 22 of the Development Committee, Washington, D.C., World Bank, 1989b.

WARFORD, Jeremy J., A. PELLEGRINI, Allen V. KNEESE and K.G. MALER, *Finland's Water Pollution Control Programs,* World Bank Public Utility Department Research Paper, 1974.

WORLD BANK, Staff Appraisal Report of the *Lagos Water Supply Project,* 6375-UNI Washington, D.C., 1988. Restricted.

WORLD RESOURCES INSTITUTE (WRI), *Paying the Price: Pesticide Subsidies in Developing Countries,* Washington, D.C., WRI, 1985.

RECENT EVOLUTION OF ENVIRONMENTAL MANAGEMENT IN THE BRAZILIAN PUBLIC SECTOR: ISSUES AND RECOMMENDATIONS

by

Ronaldo Serôa da Motta *

* Instituto de Pesquisa Ecônomica Aplicada (IPEA), Ministry of Economics, Brazil.

RÉSUMÉ

Les problèmes d'environnement du Brésil sont nés du développement rapide, dans le passé, d'activités du secteur moderne, de la présence d'une importante population à faible revenu, conséquence de la disparité des revenus, ainsi que d'une frontière agricole où l'accès aux terres est libre. Dans les premiers temps de la planification du développement, on s'est peu préoccupé de l'environnement ou de la pauvreté, et nombre des énormes problèmes écologiques du Brésil dans les zones à réaménager et à coloniser, où l'accès aux terres est libre, illustrés par le cas de la région amazonienne, sont issus de programmes et de situations qui remontent à cette époque. De même, l'organisme responsable de la protection de l'environnement ne s'est pas renforcé, aussi une législation a bien été adoptée pour remédier aux problèmes de pollution liés à l'urbanisation et à l'industrialisation mais cette législation n'a pas été véritablement appliquée. Récemment, les préoccupations croissantes et les effets négatifs résultant des approches antérieures ont entraîné des changements, en particulier une utilisation plus générale et plus efficace de l'étude d'impact sur l'environnement comme instrument de référence dans la planification des projets. Il reste cependant beaucoup à faire pour changer la structure des mesures d'incitation afin de modifier les comportements privés, et pour influer sur la conception des projets de sorte que l'on prenne en compte les questions d'environnement et de viabilité, au lieu de s'en remettre à des mesures d'atténuation et de rectification prises après coup. Il est recommandé d'utiliser plus souvent une analyse coûts-avantages qui attribue un prix à l'environnement, de comptabiliser les ressources naturelles et d'appliquer des instruments économiques.

SUMMARY

Brazil's environment problems stem from the past rapid development of modern sector activities, the presence of a large low income population, due to income inequality, and an open access land frontier. Early development planning gave little attention to the environment or to poverty, and many of Brazil's considerable environmental problems relating to the open access areas of new development and settlement, as illustrated by experience in the Amazon region, stem from programmes and developments begun during this era. Similarly, the environmental agency remained weak, so that while there has been legislation to correct the pollution problems associated with industrialisation and urbanisation, legislation was not effectively enforced. Recently, rising concerns and adverse impacts from past approaches have led to changes, particularly in a much wider and more effective use of environmental impact assessment as a standard tool in project planning. Much however remains to be done to change the incentive structures so as to modify private behaviour, and to influence project design to take account of environment and sustainability considerations, rather than reliance on *ex post* mitigation and corrective measures. More use of cost-benefit analysis that incorporates environmental pricing, plus environmental accounting and the use of economic instruments is indicated.

1. Introduction

It is now widely accepted that economic development is often accompanied by increasing stress on natural systems and negative effects on environmental quality.

Although many of the current environmental problems are shared by all nations, in the newly industrialised countries these problems have been exacerbated due to radical changes in their society and economy as a result of fast and recent industrialisation. This feature differentiates the environmental problems faced by NICs from those commonly attributed to developing countries.

Industrialisation has not only been causing the degradation problems of a modern industrial society. Despite the NICs' high rates of growth, part of the population in these societies still relies significantly upon their natural resources. This situation creates other kinds of environmental problems when the resource availability is threatened.

In the case of Brazil, this duality is bound to persist longer since economic growth has been almost nil during the last decade. Furthermore, apart from the mentioned environmental degradation, fast industrialisation and urbanisation have accentuated serious social problems which are far from being immediately solved.

Bearing this in mind, economic growth in Brazil has led to distinct environmental problems which can be analyzed according to the nature of their underlying economic activities, as follows:

i) the open access activities;

ii) the low income activities; and

iii) the modern sector activities.

The modern sector activities generate the same problems as those commonly shared by the industrialized countries, such as: industrial pollution, waste disposal, motor car emissions and so on. As will be seen in the following sections, though some improvements have been achieved, the expansion of these problems is far from being effectively controlled.

The same is true for the open access activities in the frontier area. The Brazilian economy is no longer a rural society but almost 30 per cent of its population, 44 million people, still live in rural areas. Although market-oriented agriculture is the main source of income, there are 15 million subsistence farmers. Land tenure is highly concentrated. Ten per cent of all farms are larger than 100 ha and occupy 79 per cent of total land under cultivation and pasture in the country. Moreover, gathering is still an important activity in some regions of the country, occupying almost 1 million people. In that number one may also include about 100 thousand indians who can only survive in their natural habitat. As will be discussed later, the development programmes attempting to expand agriculture in open access frontier areas have indeed exacerbated the dispute for natural resources without succeeding in terms of income generation and distribution.

In fact, these programmes reveal another kind of environmental problem caused by the inequality of income in Brazil. Almost 50 per cent of the Brazilian work force earn no more than US$ 150 per month. Income is highly concentrated and it has not changed in the last two decades. The Gini coefficient is estimated at around 0.5. No more than 42 per cent of the urban active population consists of registered workers, that is, informal activities are predominant in the Brazilian cities. Only 15 per cent of the youngsters between 15 and 19 years are in secondary education. Moreover, living conditions, particularly in the big cities, are extremely precarious. Thus the lack of housing, education opportunities, water supply, sewage system and mass transport exacerbate the social distortions. This situation is still more accentuated in the Northeast region where average income is half of the national average. Therefore, the opportunities offered in the frontier area appear more attractive than those low income level activities in the urban sectors. Thus when governmental programmes designed to create job opportunities are developed in the frontier areas, the open access activities are stimulated due to the labour availability from urban low income level activities. The resultant dispute for the use of natural resources increases the adverse effects on the environment.

The next section presents a brief description of the evolution of environmental management in the Brazilian public sector in frontier areas and in the sectors controlled by state-owned enterprises. The recent experience of the Brazilian Environmental System will also be analyzed. The last section points out the main issues and makes some recommendations for feasible improvements.

2. Environmental Management in Brazil

2.1 Government participation in the Brazilian economy

Although economic, social and environmental planning have been universally regarded as governmental duties, the need of pursuing a high rate of growth has led the governments of the NICs to assume other economic functions. In the case of Brazil, this governmental participation in the economy covers a wide range of functions and was developed under authoritarian rule. Therefore, the commonly accepted function of planning was conducted following social objectives which were chosen without scrutiny by the society. If some benefits in terms of efficiency can be accounted to that, it is also recognized that important social and environmental concerns were neglected. The same applies to other economic functions under governmental control.

Even if one can blame this previous political situation for the major social and environmental distortions, those problems will not disappear in the current democratic period without radical changes in the way the government acts as planner, regulator and producer.

In this section some economic activities developed by the Brazilian government are briefly described. For each activity the main resultant environmental problems are pointed out. The way they were considered in the past and the current behaviour towards the reduction of these problems' extension and expansion is also analyzed.

Some activities analyzed here are well known and were subject of extensive research, therefore, it is not intended to review these studies covering all the aspects of each case. On the contrary, attention will be given to a few points which are helpful to distinguish the nature of the environmental problems being analyzed. In doing so, it will be possible to make some recommendations for better governmental performance on the environmental dimension.

The activities are analyzed with examples according to three environmentally sensitive functions assumed by the government in the Brazilian economy, as follows:

i) development planner;

ii) energy and mineral producer, and

iii) environmental regulator[1].

2.2 Government planning and policies

a) In the absence of environmental concern

In the last three decades the Brazilian government has designed and implemented many programmes and policies to spur economic development in the Amazon[2]. The actions were based on import substitution industrialization and commercial agriculture according to the mainstream national development model at that time. This national model had no concern with environmental matters. In fact, it assumed that economic growth in Brazil should disregard environmental costs and consider them as granting comparative advantages instead.

This first plan of Amazonia integration included:

i) road-building programmes to link the region to other parts of the country;

ii) agricultural colonization schemes to absorb the surplus labour from other depressed regions; and

iii) fiscal incentives to create a tax-free industrial zone in Manaus (capital city of the Amazonas state) and also to make agricultural activities more attractive in the region.

As could be expected, millions of migrants in search of land and employment opportunities flew to the region. So did enterprises to take advantage of fiscal incentives and to appropriate large areas of land.

The tax-free zone in Manaus is fully established, though it made no contribution to creating a technology capacity in the region.

The result in terms of agricultural expansion is unquestionable. Taking into account only the Classic Amazonia (The North Region) in the period 1970-85, the cultivated area almost doubled while in the country as a whole the increase was 28 per cent. In number of people employed in agricultural activities the increase in the region during this period reached 140 per cent which was much higher than the national average of 32 per cent. However, land tenure in the region followed the same concentrated pattern of the rest of the country. In the North region almost 17 per cent of the farms are larger than 100 ha and occupy 78 per cent of land used for agricultural and pasture activities.

The region's occupation is led by rural farmers who usually abandon their plots after years of use due to declining yields. Consequently, they move further into the forest and in their place come the large landowners to convert the areas into pasture. Therefore, logging has also sharply increased, almost four times in the last two decades, as an activity linked to the clearing need of the farmers.

The regional agriculture is then characterised by increasing occupation of the forest, that is, deforestation. The environmental consequences of this development pattern are well known. Not only biodiversity is at stake but also the traditional and sustainable activities of the region based on gathering and fishing. However, unsustainability exists not only in environmental terms. The poor condition of the roads to the consumer markets associated with the ascending cost of the inputs needed to make agriculture possible in the region, have made this activity financially less attractive for these small-scale farmers.

The failure of the small-scale agricultural model plus the pressing need of foreign currency to pay the increasing oil bill and external debt services changed the governmental development strategy for the region. Now the main concern is the creation of export-oriented poles of development for livestock, forestry and mining. Although these plans were made in the mid-1970s, it was only during the 1980s that the first results appeared.

Mining prospecting activity was responsible for the discovery of enormous gold, cassiterite and iron fields. The high unit value of the first two makes extraction by prospectors viable, and therefore these fields became spontaneous poles of attraction of migrants drawn from the depressed regions of the country as well as those peasants of the region who did not succeed in small-scale agriculture. Gold prospectors are widespread all over the region living in precarious settlements. They practice "aluviao" mining in the river banks using a highly polluting rudimentary technology.

The planned official poles were concentrated in the great Carajas Programme, created in 1980, which is a mining-oriented project. Another main pole project was POLONOROESTE programme created in 1981 to organize the fast and chaotic development taking place in the western Amazonia.

Both programmes were designed with close attention to environmental problems in order to avoid the mistakes already made in the previous experience in the region. Unfortunately, they did not succeed.

b) Mistargeting the environmental problems

b.1 POLONOROESTE

The main aim of POLONOROESTE was to promote the necessary investments to assure a long term development of the northwest region of Brazil which includes the western amazon states of Rondônia and Mato Grosso. Resources of US$ 1.5 billion would be spent, of which 34 per cent would come from the World Bank. The programme conception was based on the assumption that sustainable agricultural activity in the region was a matter of rational planning. In other words, by reproducing the infrastructure of the richest regions of Brazil, the region's development could be sustainable and oriented towards small farmers. The Programme's budget breakdown clearly reveals this commitment. Half of the budget is devoted to road construction and paving (BR-364 highway, see Map), 25 per cent to agricultural settlements, and 15 per cent to agricultural research and extension. Health, protection of indian areas, land acquisition, administration and environmental services are covered by the remaining 10 per cent. It is not the small size of the share of the resources devoted to social and environmental services which reflects the mistargeting but the high share of road and settlement costs.

Without intending to revive either the Todaro or Lewis surplus labour models in their urban-rural and rural-rural versions, it can be recognized that all the conditions to attract low income and natural resource dependent activities were reinforced with the POLONOROESTE programme. At the same time, institutions and infrastructure failed to cope with this situation. As a result, deforestation was intensified in the Northeast region and in other neighbouring regions due to the migration flows stimulated by the Programme investments. They pushed gold and cassiterite prospectors to more distant places in the forest. The threat on indians and communities of gatherers increased enormously.

b.2 Great Carajas Programme (PGC)

PGC was launched in 1980 to develop five economic activities: mining, metallurgy, forestry, agriculture and livestock. To accomplish that, government offered fiscal incentives and subsidised credit. A huge hydroelectric plant was built to provide cheap energy for the region (see Map).

The iron mining and metallurgy projects are already operating. The forestry projects are now being implemented and the agricultural and pasture projects have been phased out.

The whole programme is run by an inter-ministerial council. But the mining project is under responsibility of a state-owned enterprise, Companhia do Vale do Rio Doce (CVRD), and was initiated in 1983 with an estimated cost of US$3.5 billion. At that time CVRD had developed some capacity of controlling the negative effects of mining on the environment from their projects in the other regions of Brazil and it was concerned about the environmental consequences occurring in the development process of western Amazonas. The World Bank financing of US$300 million was also conditioned on an environmental assessment of the project. Therefore, the iron project was implemented following a very detailed environmental study covering many aspects relative to impacts and mitigative actions to be undertaken by CVRD. In fact, this study has been a bench mark in environmental impact assessment in Brazil as will be discussed in Section 2.3.

The study recommendations were entirely followed regarding the iron ore project and the railroad which links the mining sites to the port at Sâo Luis city (see Map). Although the study had also shown some concern with the metallurgy programme, the implementation of the charcoal and pig iron projects was outside CVRD's responsibility since they are private initiatives. The PGC council however set strict reforestation requirements which were never followed in practice. The resultant deforestation is now reaching alarming levels and it is not clear that these metallurgy projects would remain financially feasible if reforestation requirements are followed[3].

The mining project can be considered an example of a well-conceived programme in environmental terms and the metallurgy projects as the opposite. However, both have failed when the entire PGC programme is taken into account. Once more the nature of the region's environmental problems was ill-perceived. Even if the metallurgy programme had succeeded in reducing deforestation, the number of migrants drawn to the area to be engaged in open access and low income activities would not be drastically reduced. Ironically, making the region more attractive was the main programme's main contribution to the environmental degradation which is taking place there. Without taking this in consideration, the environmental procedures adopted in the mining project were, for the region as a whole, insufficient.

Nevertheless, the phase-out of the agricultural and pasture poles in the PGC programme can be envisaged as a change in the development approach to the region. Another turning point is the Environmental and Indian Communities Protection Project (PMACI I) later undertaken to assess the environmental and social impacts caused by the paving of the road from Porto Velho to Rio Branco in the same western Amazonia (see Map).

c) The conservation perspective

The paving of the Porto Velho-Rio Branco highway was a strong demand of the local population engaged in commercial activities. This highway is a northern extension of the Cuiaba-Porto Velho highway which was paved as part of the POLONOROESTE programme (see Map). The 1988 environmental impact assessment was assigned to IPEA and IBGE which are, respectively, a research institute of applied economics and an institute of statistics and geography. Both are subordinated to the Ministry of Economy.

If on one hand the assessment study was particularly aware of the environmental consequences caused in the region when access roads are built, on the other, the study assumed that the paving could generate economic benefits for the region. The region's environment was studied according to a holistic approach. Demands and suggestions from local and indian communities were taken into account. The project intended to accommodate all the economic activities in the region. Thus the proposed mitigative actions were towards the forest preservation and protection of gathering and indian communities. To accomplish that the study prioritizes the creation of four gatherers' reserves, three national forests, one ecological reserve and the demarcation of the indian areas. For the small-scale farmers in colonization settlements the project recommended more financial and technological aid to make agriculture sustainable. The study also recognized the need of compensating and relocating the people living in the areas devoted to these reserves, forests and indian communities.

As can be seen, PMACI I introduces a new dimension in the planning of the Amazon region. It follows a conservation perspective where a compromise between preservation and development is assumed to be possible in the region.

It is not surprising that environmentalists considered the project too development-oriented while the direct beneficiaries of the road paving regard it too environmentally concerned. Monetary costs have not been estimated for the environmental components, nor for the relocation costs. There is no sound study on the financial and economic viability of the gatherers' reserves. The debate still goes on and the paving work is being postponed[4].

2.3 Governmental productive sector

a) Learning by doing

Although the governmental productive sector is overwhelmingly engaged in modern sector activities, the main three state-owned companies have changed their environmental performance with the lessons learnt from their Amazon projects. One example is the mining activities discussed in the previous section. As was mentioned, CVRD, a state-owned enterprise which is the world's major iron ore exporter[5], has successfully implemented environmental procedures and actions for the mining and the railway projects of the Great Carajas Programme. Despite the environmental side effects on the region, the CVRD environmental study[6] can be regarded as a bench mark for the company's environmental activities which are now internationally recognized.

Another important state-owned company is *Electrobras* which controls the electricity monopoly. Since Brazil's main electricity primary source is hydroelectricity, the company has developed in the last thirty years a respectable technology on dam engineering from plants built in the south and northeast regions of the country. Apart from the damage on environment, dam flooding causes a social problem when communities living in the plant area have to be moved elsewhere. Thus the company has acquired some knowledge in dealing with these matters which, however, were far from being equitable or environmentally satisfactory. With the construction of Tucurui hydroelectric power station in the Great Carajas Programme area (see Map) in the beginning of the 1980s, the company started to face these problems in much higher degree. The biological diversity at stake was richer and singular. Not only rural workers but also the indians had to be moved out. Moreover, Tucurui plant presents the highest ratio of output to flooded area in Brazil and also the timber to be harvested in the inundated area was lost because of mismanagement of the firm commissioned for that. In a period of growing concern on Amazon issues and democratic winds in Brazil the company found itself exposed to public opinion.

In 1986 the company published its first *Environmental Master Plan* which was also part of the requirements of a World Bank loan to the Brazilian electricity sector. Since then the company has drastically changed its way to deal with these social and environmental issues. As will be discussed in Section 3, a recent version of this plan contains some radical changes in energy planning.

Another energy monopoly run by the government is the oil company *Petrobras*. This company also had an experience in Amazonia which drastically changed its behaviour in environmental questions. With the increase in the mid-1980s of oil and gas exploration in the Juruá river basin in the Amazonas region (see Map), the company's managers started to be aware of certain environmental consequences of its activities. Although the resulting deforestation from oil prospecting is negligible compared to other activities, the presence of the company has worked as a pull factor to attract migrants to the area being explored. The consequences are the same as discussed in the preceding section, though in the case of oil exploration they occurred in lesser degree due to the project scale.

In 1987 a group of ten experts was commissioned by *Petrobras* to undertake a study to analyze and guide the company's procedures in dealing with the region's environment. The resultant report was the company's first acknowledgement of its responsibility for an environmental assessment. Until then, *Petrobras*, as many other oil companies in the world, had very little concern for environmental matters. Although it is still very incipient, following the report's publication in 1988, the company's environmental concern sharply increased. A preliminary *Environmental Master Plan* is being implemented and the company is also more conscious of the need for fuel quality programmes to make emission control of combustion processes possible.

b) Learning by law enforcement

One of the most effective environmental laws issued in Brazil requires an environmental impact assessment of projects considered environmentally sensitive. As environmental impact the law defines "any change which affects the physical, chemical and biological properties of the environment caused by any materials or energy resulting from human activities which, directly or indirectly, may bring harm to health, safety and well-being of the population; social and economic activities, wildlife and vegetation; the aesthetic and sanitation conditions of the environment; and the quality of natural resources".

Undoubtedly the reinforcement of the EIA law in 1986 initiated a new phase of environmental management in Brazil[7]. Most of the firms operating in the modern sector of the Brazilian economy had their first contact with environmental issues due to the EIA requirements. Obviously, the resulting change in behaviour varies in each case according to many aspects which will be discussed in the following section.

Nevertheless, the major state-owned enterprises have been pressed to correctly fulfil the EIA requirements which has certainly contributed to their better performance in environmental matters. In the examples analyzed above, CVRD and *Electrobras* have in fact dictated the general procedures for the rest of the sector.

2.4 Governmental agencies on environment

a) The institutional and legal evolution

The current National Environmental Policy (*PNMA*) was basically defined by a 1981 law in order to make social and economic development compatible with the preservation and quality of the environment. The same law created the National Environmental System (*SISNAMA*) to implement this policy.

The policy aims were strengthened by the 1988 Brazilian Constitution which also considered the Amazon Forest and four other Brazilian singular ecosystems as national patrimony.

The PNMA provides four policy tools:

i) environmental standards;

ii) environmental zoning;

iii) environmental impact assessment; and

iv) environmental data base.

The current SISNAMA is comprised of a government council formed by representatives of all ministries; an advisory and deliberating council (*CONAMA*) formed by representatives of the states, unions, NGO's and experts; a central agency (*SEMAM*) which is a secretariat linked to the Presidency and also chairs the CONAMA; and executive agency (*IBAMA*) linked to SEMAM; other public agencies concerned with environmental matters, and the state and province environmental agencies. Since 1989 the resources to carry out the PNMA have been financed by the Environmental National Fund under SEMAM administration[8].

As many governmental structures in Brazil, SISNAMA is somewhere between the unitary and the federal systems. States and provinces have seat in CONAMA and play an important role. Moreover, they often have specific environmental laws and very active environmental agencies which share with the federal government the assessment and evaluation of many environmental aspects. Nevertheless, policy and budgetary control remain in central government hands.

SISNAMA only started to function in 1984 when CONAMA had its rules set up. The first radical change occurred in 1988 with the creation of IBAMA to integrate all federal executive agencies. However, the system was still controlled by a ministry in which environment was not the only concern. The autonomous current structure was formed in 1990 with the new administration. The change was undoubtedly welcome since the previous structure did not allow the system to work properly due to its political fragility within the responsible ministry. On the other hand, CONAMA which had an important role in EIA introduction and was a forum to solve policy conflicts, is facing, to some extent, a political vacuum due to the new SEMAM status and responsiveness. It has also been recognized that IBAMA has become more effective in its enforcement duties in the Amazon region.

At the upper levels of the system, there are still some constraints to make the superior council perform its function of intervening in the national planning process and standardizing governmental actions in environmental matters and other related issues.

So far the Amazon occupation has been the dominant issue in SEMAM actions in domestic and international affairs. However, some important and related issues have been also highly demanded by the other system components.

b) The environmental policy results

As already mentioned the system was not able to participate effectively in the planning process of the economy. For example, the formulation of the main development programmes and projects has not been scrutinized within the SISNAMA. So far it has failed either to set up or review environmental standards. Also pollution control policies were completely disregarded. Apart from the creation of forest, ecological reserves and areas of environmental interest, an effective zoning effort to organise economic activities according to environmental parameters was not attempted. The environmental data base is still far from being systematically organised.

However, as discussed in Section 2.3, the EIA procedures have been increasingly implemented and they have fairly succeeded in the modern sector of the economy. Until December 1988, i.e., three years after their enforcement, a total of 140 EIA studies were already analyzed and another 85 studies were being evaluated[9]. Almost half of the projects were in the state of Sao Paulo which is the most developed state of Brazil representing a third of the country's GDP. However, only 15 projects were carried out in the Amazon region. Although none of them used any economic criteria in their analysis, there is no doubt that they have largely contributed to ameliorate the pattern of investments in the modern sector of the country in environmental terms. The analysis and approval of EIA studies is decentralized at the state environmental agencies. Only a few cases of high-impact projects need also to be considered by the central agency. Therefore, the efficacy of EIA procedures depends largely on these agencies' capability. As can be expected, the more developed is the state the more capable is the agency. Some states have already recognized that they are unable to undertake the evaluation studies unless the applicant firm pays for the expenses of contracting a consultant group to do it.

In the states where capability is more developed, there are, as they also recognize, many constraints to be overcome. Some have a technical nature such as insufficient knowledge of assessment methodologies and environmental standards, and the lack of environmental zoning and data base. Other complaints relate to the absence of environmental concern in some provincial governments and state enterprises who tend to regard EIA studies as another red tape barrier, and to the fundamentalist position of some NGOs without taking into account other social and economic considerations.

Summing up, despite their widespread adoption and relatively successful results, the fragility of EIA procedures is becoming very apparent.

3. Recommendations

the previous sections of this paper have briefly described the environmental management within the Brazilian public sector. In the context of Brazilian development, government's influence over the economy has been highly significant. It was also shown that environmental concern in government actions increased significantly in the last decade.

In fact, socially unsustainable economic growth has been the main source of the environmental problems in Brazil. Trying to reduce the social inequality with development programmes in the frontier areas, the government policies not only exacerbated these problems but also promoted a waste of natural resources. Every part of the public sector, including the productive branch, participated in the development actions. The environmental consequences of these experiences drastically modified the government approach to the region and changed state enterprise behaviour towards environmental matters. These changes were more sound particularly in modern sector activities with the introduction of eia procedures, though there still are some important constraints to be overcome.

There is no doubt that Brazil has moved from a "development at any cost" situation to an attenuated development path. Will the current improved environmental awareness assure any kind of sustainable development in the future?

Instead of answering this question, this section will only try to discuss the use of economic criteria in the Brazilian public sector environmental management which could enable it to improve its performance. The focus will be on the main economic issues which have already been proposed in the literature concerning developing countries. However, there is no intention to go in details into the theoretical and methodological background of the implementation process of the suggested actions.

It is also acknowledged that other issues pointed out in the previous sections, such as environmental education, institutional strength, and community and NGO participation are equally relevant, but they will not be specifically discussed.

3.1 The use of economic criteria

As can be noted from the description presented in the previous sections, there has been in Brazil a complete disregard for economic analysis when environmental issues are evaluated. This situation is not particular to Brazil; even in developed countries that issue is still at a preliminary stage. In the Brazilian case there are at least three management levels where economic criteria would be helpful and, as will be shown, they will need a coherent approach.

a) In the use of natural resources in frontier areas

Economic theory tells us that the use of resources in open access areas leads to extinction when the harvesting effort is costless or takes place at levels above the natural rate of regeneration. In the case of the Amazon region both conditions prevailed. The benefits of fiscal incentives made economic activities in the region very attractive at microeconomic levels. The facilities of roads and settlements drew a growing migratory flow of low income activities in the rural and urban areas of the country, increasing the demand for land which presents, in most areas of the region, a low rate of regeneration. Thus deforestation occurred to allow continuous agricultural harvesting. The pressure on the forest was increased by fiscal rules which use cleared land as a condition for entitlement of the farmers to it. The same process is underway in the mining activity in the region. Fiscal benefits are not offered for prospectors but the individual's false expectation of large profits in gold and cassiterite prospecting activities, associated with the surplus of low income labour drawn from the agricultural projects, is spreading the activity all over the region. Although mineral reserves being depleted are a minor part of the total availability, the environmental consequences in terms of water pollution and degradation of wetlands are not negligible. Timber production also increased in the region without proper management which contributes to the wasting of the region's natural resources. Thus it seems plausible that government policies in the region should be based on economic criteria which take into account the opportunity cost of the region's natural resources.

In the literature we can find several studies[10] proposing valuation approaches and estimates for the social opportunity cost of the region's natural resources, in terms of biodiversity and potential gathering activities, to stimulate the use of a benefit-cost approach for the current economic activities being carried on in the region. However, no attempt was undertaken to develop a set of policies and economic incentives, taking into account the magnitude of the migration flows to the region, which could make feasible such environmentally minded activities. Furthermore, there still is insufficient knowledge on the microeconomic behaviour of the current activities in the region and their demographic and spatial distribution. That is, sustainable development in the region will demand more economic research, in particular, field surveys to fix economic parameters and determinants.

Needless to say those studies on opportunity costs are essential to orient the current local communities' demands in the region for gathering reserves and sustainable agricultural practices. This is more relevant if one is to prove that these costs represent the case of an infinite quasi-option value.

b) In the management of the productive sector

As already mentioned, most of the major state-owned enterprises have their own Environmental Master Plan. They are filled with environmentally oriented actions but, at the same time, are not able to guide effectively the investment selection according to other firm's goals. This is particularly true when preventive actions are expensive or when, which seems to be the major problem, these actions demand a change, even a minor one, in their engineering technology. Perhaps due to their lack of financial accountability, they usually tend to spend on compensation or mitigative projects rather than engaging in changes at the project design. Despite the commitment stated in these plans, most of the effective changes derive from EIA evaluation or local and NGO pressure. This process is not only expensive but also spoils the firm's image.

Therefore, much has to be done in order to make these plans more effective in environmental terms. Apart from the internalization of environmental concerns in the behaviour of the firms' staff, the plan conception must also be modified. That is, an approach is needed in which environmental considerations are given standing in the planning process.

Recently, the Brazilian state-owned electricity company, has proposed a Plan with the following interesting modifications[11]. First, the selection of the company's project ranking for its expansion programme will consider some environmental indicators along with the usual financial ones. Thus the initial company's project selection already reduces environmental impacts at the project level. Of course, the definition of these environmental indicators will deserve a significant research effort. It could be an environmentally sensitive economic indicator or a set of indicators based on ecological features or even both.

The second modification in the company's planning procedure consists of analyzing the implementation of a group of highly ranked projects. In this phase a cost-benefit analysis is proposed which includes an estimate of environmental costs due to the project impacts. Some of these costs are already defined in the environmental legislation and others will be revealed in prior examination with affected local communities and interested NGOs. Tangible costs will be counted and internalized in the calculation of the project's net present value. In the case of a project with positive NPV associated with significant intangible costs, other agents--and not the company alone--will decide on its implementation. Based on specific environmental accounting the company intends to make explicit the part of the electricity price due to environmental costs.

The analytical development of this and any other equivalent proposal will rely upon the implementation of the environmental policies.

c) In the environmental system

As pointed out in Section 2, the National Environmental Policy is far from being fully implemented. EIA enforcement is the major attainment, however its effectiveness is at stake when other policy tools like zoning, standards and a data base are not used since they will provide the necessary technical parameters needed for the elaboration of the EIA. In all three areas economic criteria have an important role to play.

As was discussed before in the case of frontier areas, some kind of environmental economic valuation will be needed to elaborate an environmental zoning if a conservation perspective is to be adopted. Any attempt to apply cost-benefit analysis in EIA procedures will fail if zoning is not already defining basic economic and ecological parameters.

Assuming that market-oriented approaches require more technical capability and other resources still to be developed and implemented, it seems that regulation based on standards may still have a role in environmental policy in Brazil. On the other hand, such an assumption cannot be generalised and some market incentives or mixed forms can be attempted as, for example, in river basin management. Whatever the option, much has to be done in policy designing for pollution control in Brazil.

Environmental statistics is another promising area. Brazil has developed a fair capability in producing statistical data which has not been employed to collect and process specific economic data such as defensive expenditures. Only now an attempt is under way to include some environmental satellite-accounts into the Brazilian national accounts.

This lack of economic criteria can be understood in so far as macro-economic planning has not fully incorporated environmental considerations. This is also valid for other social aims since, as has been discussed elsewhere, the specification of a social welfare function is arbitrary.

However, the absence of environmental considerations in macro-economic and sectoral planning is the main reason for public sector mistargeting of environmental management, a common problem in all countries whatever their degree of development. How to make this integration possible, and what are the resulting structural changes in the economy, seems to be nowadays one of the major challenges in environmental management.

3.2 Global Issues constraints

Newly industrialized countries like Brazil will depend very much on better environmental management to pursue a sustainable development path. All kinds of environmental, social and economic problems are calling for coherent solutions. But the political and popular will, that now in Brazil seems to be committed to find a compromise between growth and environment, will not be sufficient to overcome these problems. Brazil will also need to count on fair relationships with developed nations.

It seems that the international agenda on environment has forgotten the lessons of the Brundtland Commission. Development issues and not global issues should fill this agenda. To restrict the Brazilian environmental problems within the greenhouse effects and the ozone layer parameters is also a mistargeted policy. Turning Brazil into an environmental debtor instead of a supplier of environmental services will not help Brazilian and global environmental quality improvement. That will only place another burden on the country's development in addition to its external financial debt. Not surprisingly, economic incentives, as for example an earmarked fuel tax, do not play an important role in the discussion of global issues.

Changing the world development pattern would be more effective than aiming at global issues which probably rely on unattainable solutions to open access problems. Therefore, any resolution of these problems will eventually require concessions by the industrialised countries on development-related issues, such as external debt, trade, and technology transfer.

Legal Amazônia

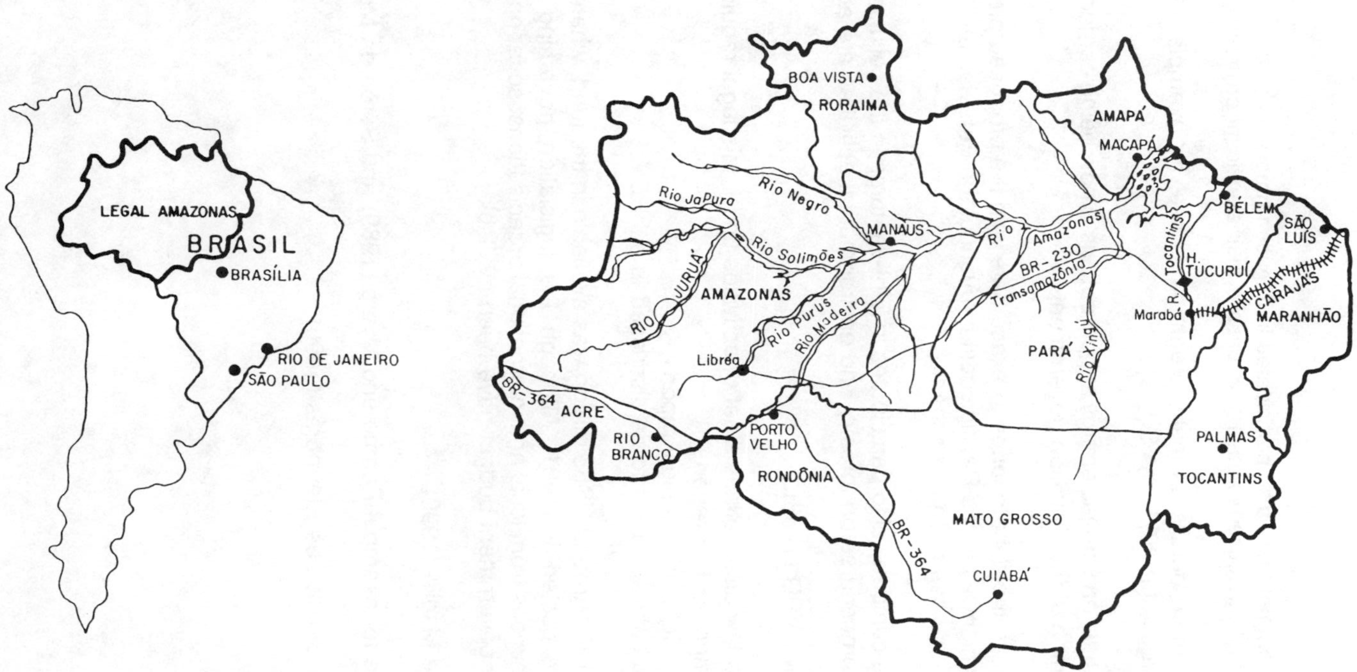

NOTES

1. Government has also participated in irrigation programmes and steel projects which are not addressed in this paper despite their significant environmental impacts.

2. For more details on these programmes see, for example, Mahar (1989) and Margulis (1990).

3. A study on Carajas energy supply options is now being carried out by the World Bank and the Brazilian government.

4. In fact, the debate tends to exacerbate with the proposed project of extending the highway to the Pacific coast throughout the Peruvian amazon region under a Japanese financing scheme.

5. The company also participates in joint-ventures in the cellulose industry where its procedures on forestry and environmental activities are adopted.

6. See CVRD (1986).

7. The law also defines a set of activities under this legal requirement. The EIA comprises two reports:
   i) a detailed technical report,
   ii) a concise report to be discussed in public.

8. In 1990 around US$5 million was available in the fund, whereas, US$8 million is expected in 1991. Although the legislation governing the fund allows donations from local and international organisations, so far only resources from the government budget have been available.

9. See Maglio (1990).

10. See for example Pearce and Myers (1989) and Serôa da Motta (1989).

11. For details see Eletrobras (1990).

BIBLIOGRAPHICAL REFERENCES

CVRD,

"Metodologia de avaliação ambiental aplicada para um caso de enfoque preventivo. Projeto Ferro Carajás," *Série Espaco, Ambiente e Planejamento,* CVRD/GEAMAN, Vol 1, No 1, January 1986.

ELETROBRAS,

Plano Diretor de Meio Ambiente do Setor Elétrico 1990/1992, Preliminary Draft, 1990.

MAGLIO, I.C.,

"Questões verificadas na aplicação do EIA/RIMA: a experiência da Secrétaria do Meio Ambiente de Sâo Paulo," *I Simposio Nacional de Análise Ambiental,* Rio Claro, Sâo Paulo, May 1990.

MARGULIS, S.,

O desempenho do governo brasileiro, dos órgãos contratantes e do Banco Mundial com relação a questão ambiental do Projeto Ferro Carajás, IPEA, mimeo, 1990.

MAHAR, D.J.,

Government Policies and Deforestation in Brazil's Amazon Region, World Bank, 1989.

PEARCE, D. and MYERS, N.,

"Economic values and the environment of Amazônia," in D. GOODMAN and A. HALL, eds. *The Future of Amazonia: Destruction or Sustainable Development,* Macmillan Press, 1989.

SERÔA DA MOTTA, R.,

Análise de custo-benefício de projetos amazônicos, course on *Impactos Ambientais de Investimento na Amazônia: Problemática e Elementos Metodológicos de Avaliação,* PNUD, Manaus, September 1989.

TOWARD MORE EFFECTIVE ENVIRONMENTAL REGULATION IN DEVELOPING COUNTRIES

by

Faith Halter *

* Faith Halter is a consultant in international environmental policy, law and programme implementation, based in Arlington, Virginia, USA. Ms. Halter spent more than ten years with the US Environmental Protection Agency. She specialises in pollution management, natural resource conservation and pesticide management.

RÉSUMÉ

Dans les pays en développement, la faiblesse des institutions, dans leur capacité et dans leur fonctionnement, pose un grave problème lorsqu'il s'agit de faire face aux périls pour l'environnement. Même s'il existe des lois d'habilitation et une certaine forme de mécanisme institutionnel pour la protection de l'environnement, les gouvernements, pour la plupart, doivent affronter les plus grandes difficultés pour tenter d'assumer les responsabilités inscrites dans leur mandat. Les gouvernements des pays en développement doivent renforcer les fonctions institutionnelles "traditionnelles" qui commandent directement les activités affectant l'environnement ; ils doivent aussi prendre des mesures économiques afin de faire changer les comportements qui nuisent à l'environnement. Cette double approche devrait calmer certaines anticipations déraisonnables quant à ce que les contrôles directs permettent de faire, accroissant ainsi les chances de succès des programmes de réglementation. Les normes de protection de l'environnement fixent le cadre et la portée de moyens économiques plus larges permettant de promouvoir la protection de l'environnement et la productivité à long terme, buts indissociables d'un développement durable. De plus, ces approches sont étroitement imbriquées : une réglementation efficace tend à promouvoir, à entretenir et à compléter les incitations économiques. Cet exposé analyse les informations de base appropriées sur la réglementation de la protection de l'environnement mise en place par les institutions des pays en développement, et propose un cadre analytique qui peut être utile aux gouvernements lorsqu'ils conçoivent des stratégies pour élaborer et mettre en oeuvre des programmes de réglementation plus efficaces. L'auteur recommande aussi certains mécanismes d'assistance pour soutenir ces efforts. Une place privilégiée est faite aux programmes de gestion de *la pollution urbaine et industrielle*, domaine relativement nouveau dont l'importance croît rapidement.

SUMMARY

Weak institutional capacity and performance in the developing countries poses a major problem in coping with environmental challenges. Many governments, even if they have enabling laws and some form of environmental institutional arrangement, face daunting challenges in trying to carry out their designated responsibilities. Developing country governments need to strengthen the "traditional" institutional functions that directly control activities affecting the environment, and to institute economic measures to change environmentally detrimental behaviour. This dual approach should relieve some of the unrealistic expectations of what direct controls can accomplish, and thus increase the chances for more successful regulatory programmes. Environmental standards provide the context and measure for broader economic means of promoting environmental protection and long term productivity, the twin goals of sustainable development. Moreover, these approaches are intertwined; effective regulation tends to drive, support and supplement economic incentives. This paper reviews pertinent background information on environmental regulation by developing country institutions, and suggests an analytic framework that governments can use in devising strategies to design and implement more effective regulatory programmes. It also recommends some assistance mechanisms to support these efforts. The specific focus is on programmes to manage *urban and industrial pollution*, a relatively new area of rapidly growing importance.

1. Introduction

1.1 Objective

The objective of this paper is to identify: (a) important background information for designing environmental regulations in developing countries; (b) key elements and effective strategies for government regulatory programmes to implement environmental laws and policies; and (c) measures to enhance responses by international donors and recipient governments.

1.2 Definitions

"Institution" refers to formal and informal organisational arrangements, rules and procedures within government to establish and implement environmental policies through regulatory programmes. The emphasis will be on government institutions at the national level, but the same general principles would also apply to decentralised regional and local government activities.

"Pollution management" includes efforts both to prevent and control environmental pollution and its physical impacts (air, water and soil), biological impacts (plants and animals) and social impacts (human behaviour).

"Urban" includes settlements on the fringes of urban centres that bridge urban and rural areas. "Sanitation" encompasses both garbage (solid waste) and sewage (human waste).

"Developing country" refers to any country that lacks policy, regulatory and technical environmental capabilities comparable to those of most OECD member countries. This definition includes countries that are rapidly industrialising, such as Chile, Indonesia and Thailand, countries with emerging economies, such as Singapore and Taiwan, and countries that have industrialised intensively under socialist economies, such as Eastern Europe and the Soviet Union.

These governments and others in similar positions will need to follow the same steps as less industrialised countries in advancing their environmental regulatory programmes, even though they may be able to progress faster through greater financial resources and better access to skilled professional staffs. The same is true for differences of size; while governments in countries such as Brazil, China and India must operate on a much larger scale, basic principles of sound environmental regulation will still apply.

2. *Background*

2.1 Environmental pollution and natural resource conservation

Natural resource conservation and environmental pollution pose special complexities because the issues are multidimensional and require an interdisciplinary approach. Although industrial activity tends to be more easily and highly regulated than either natural resource use or urban sanitation, government institutional programmes in both areas have the same general needs and constraints.

The differences stem from the nature of the issues and the relative newness of environmental pollution as a major phenomenon and source of concern in developing countries. Natural resource use often involves long-standing rights and behaviours that are entrenched in a society's cultural and legal systems. There is usually a (sometimes huge) variety of government entities, at all levels, with at least nominal responsibilities for management of the resources in question. These factors can exponentially increase the inevitable problems in operating regulatory programmes.

In contrast, the industrial activities that are a major source of environmental pollution are comparatively recent. Neither industrial polluting nor poor sanitation practices in densely populated urban areas are regarded as an established "right" in the same sense that natural resource use is often viewed. Also, there is usually much less existing government responsibility for managing pollution, and therefore less occasion for resistance to new regulatory programmes from entrenched bureaucratic interests.

These factors may make analyzing regulatory issues and structuring government authorities somewhat easier and less controversial for pollution management than for natural resource conservation. On the other hand, the close links between industrial growth and government plans for economic expansion can cause environmental regulation in this area to trigger strong political sensitivities. This is a major reason for the need to identify concrete economic advantages from better pollution management.

Another potentially significant difference lies in the fact that in natural resource management, the targeted activity is usually the actual exploitation of the resources, whereas pollution is usually an unwanted byproduct of an otherwise legitimate activity. The fact that pollution is one step removed from productive economic activity may present extra challenges in devising economic policies to influence polluting activities, and therefore increase the importance of direct government regulation, especially for large industrial and sanitation sources.

The geographic distributions of natural resource degradation and environmental pollution are also different. Key natural resources tend to be concentrated in specific areas, such as tropical rain forests. Environmental pollution, on the other hand, is globally recurrent -- it occurs in virtually every city, every industrial area, every place where agricultural chemicals are applied. The scale is certainly greatest in rapidly industrialising countries and major urban centres, but it poses serious health and environmental problems in every country.

Despite the differences outlined above, pollution and natural resource damage are often connected. The worldwide threats of ozone depletion (from chemical emissions) and global warming (largely from burning fossil fuels) underline this point. Harm to coastal fisheries from industrial and municipal discharges, and damage to lakes and forests from acid rain are other examples of common links.

2.2 Urbanisation and industrialisation in developing countries

Trends. Accelerating urban and industrial growth in many developing countries poses critical threats to human health and child survival, labour productivity, the success of economic investments, and the quality of life. Environmental problems include: insufficient quantity and quality of water supplies; severe inadequacies in the collection, treatment and disposal of human, solid and hazardous wastes; rapidly worsening air quality; and broad public exposure to dangerous chemicals. In some areas, including Eastern Europe, the magnitude of these problems is far greater than in OECD member countries[1].

Environmental problems are closely linked to population pressures. Human population has doubled since World War II, with approximately 85 per cent of the increase occurring in developing countries. Population will double again by the middle of the next century, to 10 billion people, and most of the growth will again be in developing countries[2].

By the year 2000, almost 40 per cent of the population in developing countries will live in urban centres; a projected figure for Latin America is 76 per cent[3]. Most mega-cities (having populations greater than 10 million) are already in developing countries. Their numbers will more than double by the year 2000, and 18 of 22 projected new mega-cities will be in developing countries[4].

Cities in developing countries are currently unable to collect about 30 to 50 per cent of their garbage. This problem will increase as urban centres grow. Moreover, as countries become more affluent, the volume of solid waste increases at a higher rate than population growth, and the waste contains larger amounts of non-biodegradable and toxic components[5]. Every $1 billion in Gross Domestic Product is estimated to generate about 100 tons of hazardous waste from the manufacture of pharmaceuticals, paints and dyes, chemicals, pulp and paper, and fossil fuels, as well as small enterprises such as electroplaters and tanneries[6].

Adequate collection of sewage is also severely lacking in developing countries. For example, only 217 of 3 119 towns and cities in India have any sewage systems, and these serve less than one-third of the urban population. The Ganges, one of the most polluted rivers in the world, receives direct discharges of urban and industrial wastes from 115 cities[7].

The World Health Organization (WHO) estimates that worldwide, 600 to 1 200 million people live in cities where the air pollution levels do not meet its current health criteria[8]. Urban centres in some developing countries, especially mega-cities, suffer from extreme air pollution[9]. Mexico City experienced a 50 per cent increase in levels of air pollution in 1979 alone[10]. Recent air pollution rates in Beijing, as compared to Tokyo, the largest city in East Asia, were 5-17 times higher for particulate matter, 3-6 times higher for sulphur oxides, and 4 times higher for nitrogen oxides[11].

Industrial production in developing countries is diversifying and growing, particularly with respect to heavy and capital-intensive industries, such as metal products, chemicals, and machinery, which tend to pollute more heavily than light industries. Even though developing countries represent only about 18 per cent of the world manufacturing output, their production and exports have been growing faster than those of industrial countries since the 1960s[12]. Here, too, waste management is a growing problem. In Hungary, 80 per cent of the 5 million tons of the hazardous waste generated annually is disposed of improperly[13].

Illegal economic activities which are not ordinarily counted can also be significant sources of pollution. For example, refining paste from coca leaves to make cocaine involves the use of chemicals such as sulphuric acid, kerosene, lime, acetone and carbides. The waste materials from this process are a significant source of pollution in areas of Columbia and Bolivia where cocaine is manufactured[14].

Pollution from urban and industrial growth is likely to rise sharply in coming years. For example, the Asian Development Bank estimates that regional air and water pollution will multiply by 5 to 10 times over the next 15 years, based on an expected 150-200 per cent increase in industrial and mining activity, and a 300 per cent increase in the number of motor vehicles[15].

Consequences. While there is insufficient data to accurately quantify the extent of harm to human health and the environment from urban and industrial pollution, ample evidence exists of serious impacts. The environmental horror stories from Eastern Europe and the Soviet Union graphically illustrate the dangers of unchecked urban and industrial growth[16]. Cost estimates for tackling their pollution problems are astronomical. For example, just to refit East German industry to Western standards -- not including cleanup plans -- will take 15-20 years and cost estimates range from $20 billion (East German estimate) to $200 billion (West German estimate)[17]. The USSR projects that government funding for environmental protection will rise from $24 billion in 1990 to $46.4 billion by 1995[18].

WHO estimates that three-quarters of all illness and 80 per cent of child deaths in developing countries are associated, directly or indirectly, with unsafe sewage disposal, poor hygiene, and poor water supplies[19]. This includes both urban and rural areas, but the statistics on urban growth noted above indicate that the scope and degree of these problems is likely to be greater and to increase more rapidly in urban centres.

Air pollution is another major source of death and debilitating disease. In Bombay, breathing impairment is the single largest cause of death; sulphur emissions from industrial facilities are a major factor[20]. Lead emissions from the combustion of fuels in motor vehicles are another cause of severe health problems from air pollution. A study of 102 babies born in Mexico City during 1987-89 found that half of them had concentrations of lead in their blood that are associated with mental retardation[21]. A recent study of environmental health in Bangkok has also identified lead contamination as an extremely serious problem, both particles suspended in the air and deposited on soil[22].

Burgeoning urban growth may lead to the presence of residential areas, especially informal settlements, adjacent to industrial facilities. This was the situation in Bhopal, India, where an explosion in a pesticide formulation plant resulted in more than 200 000 injuries, and estimated deaths ranging from 2 500 to as high as 15 000[23].

Urban and industrial pollution may also harm rural populations and fragile ecosystems through water- and airborne pollution. Nearly 9 per cent of agricultural land in East Germany has been ruined in this fashion[24]. Some areas in Poland are uninhabitable because of soil contamination from industrial emissions of sulphur dioxide and other air pollutants[25]. Poor waste disposal practices can also threaten key coastal resources, endangering important economic activities such as fisheries and tourism[26].

2.3 Setting a theme and priorities for pollution management

Theme. A fundamental theme should be the integration of pollution management into planning activities, with an emphasis on the concepts of pollution prevention and integrated pollution management.

Pollution prevention and integrated pollution management are two fundamental concepts that should underlie any effort to manage pollution[27].

Pollution prevention refers to efforts to minimise the occurrence of pollution, as opposed to cleaning up pollution after it occurs. Evaluating all the inputs and outputs of a polluting activity facilitates deciding how best to maximise production efficiency and minimise pollution. Some pollution prevention measures, such as reducing evaporation of solvents or reusing waste products, can provide cost savings, as well as environmental benefits. Once stated, the concept of pollution prevention seems self-evident. However, it is often difficult to persuade companies to act on this philosophy, particularly without concrete examples that have direct application and will provide short-term economic benefits.

Integrated pollution management involves considering the overall effects of specific pollution management measures upon the affected ecosystem. For example, in deciding the "best" way to dispose of a hazardous waste, one would compare the environmental impacts of various alternatives, such as incineration, land filling, and ocean dumping. This is an important departure from the way the United States and other industrial countries have often analyzed pollution problems. Previously, there has been a tendency to regulate environmental media, such as air and water, separately. A growing consensus finds this approach inadequate because it tends to shift environmental problems from one medium to another, without sufficient evaluation of overall impacts (a phenomenon sometimes called "cross-media pollution").

Priorities. The following priorities for urban and industrial pollution will apply in many developing countries: improving water quality; reducing industrial pollution; safe management and disposal of pesticides; and reducing emissions from motor vehicles. How to balance these priorities will vary substantially from country to country.

Improving water quality. As discussed above, contaminated and inadequate water supplies are the major cause of health and productivity losses from pollution in developing countries. Assistance should concentrate on improving urban sanitation infrastructures and targeting major industrial activities that endanger water quality, such as textile dyeing, leather tanning, food processing and metal manufacture. Reducing dependence of pesticides and fertilizers, and improving their use and application, can also produce major improvements in water quality in urban and rural areas.

Reducing industrial pollution. As compared to most urban sanitation problems, major industrial sources of pollution are relatively easy to identify and regulate. Since it is cheaper and easier to incorporate improvements at the planning stage, assistance in this area for rapidly industrialising countries should be a priority, to minimise future problems of the magnitude now facing Eastern Europe. One area to concentrate on is planning for new industrial zones, including free trade zones.

Besides the sources of water pollution noted above, other important industrial categories include: sources of air pollution, such as chemical processing plants and cement factories; thermal power generation (often addressed in energy programmes); and facilities at high risk for major technological accidents, such as the pesticide factory in Bhopal. Industrial pollution management is related to concerns about occupational health, as well as public health.

Safe management and disposal of pesticides. The international community has only recently begun to focus on the enormous problem of outdated pesticide stocks in developing countries, especially those with large programmes to control grasshopper and locust infestations, or to control diseases borne by insects and rodents. Safe management and disposal of pesticides is closely linked both to traditional agricultural development activities and to growing concerns about similar problems involving a much broader range of hazardous chemicals and wastes.

Reducing emissions from motor vehicles. Air pollution from industrial sources and from burning fossil fuels and biomass can be addressed through programmes to reduce industrial pollution, improve energy efficiency, and reduce deforestation and global climate change. However, emissions from combustion in motor vehicles is a special category of air pollution that will mushroom in many developing countries. Given the limited progress in reducing vehicle emissions in many industrialised countries, one can expect this problem to prove as intractable as it is serious for developing countries[28]. In addition to reducing the lead content of gasoline and introducing alternative fuels, urban planning in developing countries must focus on improved transportation systems, especially for large urban centres.

2.4 Overview of Government Environmental Institutions in Developing Countries

Surveys. As in other activities, strengthening and building institutional capacity is a critical element in improved environmental management. International experience suggests that institution building is among the most difficult and elusive of objectives just as it is among the most important causes of development programme failure. In 1985, WHO completed a worldwide survey that highlighted the lack of institutional capacity to manage pollution within developing country governments[29]. Of 59 moderately to rapidly industrialising countries, only 10 had most key programme requirements[30]; 29 had some, and 20 had little or none. Not one of the 76 less industrialised countries had any significant institutional capability in this area.

These findings are consistent with the experience of international donors. For example, according to a 1988 report of the World Bank's Operations Evaluation Department, almost 75 per cent of the Bank's projects include institutional development as a goal, but only 30 per cent of the projects achieve substantial success. In 1985, the success rate was only 17 per cent for the subcategory of agricultural projects[31] for more than ten years. Moreover, World

Bank reports evaluating agricultural projects (a category that also includes forestry and land and water management) have most often identified problems with institutional design, capacity and implementation as key reasons for poor performance[31].

Principles of institutional development. Efforts to strengthen developing country institutions in environment and other fields have been the subject of considerable study in recent years[32]. The general principles outlined in these studies apply to pollution management and other environmental concerns. Key principles include the following:

-- governments should try to improve implementation of existing laws and institutions, rather than creating new ones as a response to problems;

-- consideration should be given to the broader economic, social and other contexts, as well as to the governmental context in which a law or institution must operate;

-- the location of responsible authorities within the government can play a key role in determining their potential influence;

-- it is crucial to balance responsibilities and co-ordination among national, regional and local government authorities in order to achieve a dynamic interaction of policy and operations;

-- when trying to strengthen government institutions, it is important to include parties from the public and private sector who can help to design and implement feasible programmes;

-- staff training and development is at least as important as other government resource needs;

-- examples from national governments in industrialised countries are often inappropriate to developing countries because they would require more financial, technical and human resources than are available; better examples can often be found within developing countries, and from local and regional governments within industrialised countries;

-- programmes should be structured to achieve some early successes, however modest, that can be replicated; and

-- both tangible and intangible benefits should be used as criteria for evaluating programme success; standards for evaluation also need to recognise that many years may be necessary for programme benefits to become apparent.

Experience also seems to indicate that an authoritarian style of government may increase the reluctance of institutions to acknowledge substantive problems and programme weaknesses, even though such an acknowledgement may be a necessary prelude to begin making improvements. Authoritarian governments however, may have something of an advantage in an ability to make needed changes outside official institutional channels.

Special considerations for pollution management. There are also institutional considerations that apply particularly to pollution management and other environmental issues in developing countries.

Since responsible environmental authorities frequently lack power within the government, they need to adjust their expectations of what their regulatory programmes can accomplish. Often, they have to rely on negotiation and compromise in order to build coalitions and work effectively with other government agencies, the private sector and the public.

An important tool is reliable information, especially about the scope and economic costs of environmental harm to human health and key natural resources. Information like this, from environmental impact assessments and other sources, must be translated into concrete terms so that senior policy makers can apply them in familiar modes of decision making. To support these efforts, government officials need to establish networks with professionals in other countries, as well as within domestic channels, to exchange information, ideas and experience.

Developing country institutions need domestic and international support for addressing otherwise overwhelming issues in gradual increments. Trying to adopt and implement impossible environmental goals can lead to regulatory paralysis. It would often be more productive for governments, donors and the public to accept reasonably expeditious measures that involve delays in meeting standards equivalent to those in industrialised countries, rather than insisting on attaining the unattainable.

Valid reasons for setting less (or more) stringent standards than other governments could include different priorities regarding public health problems, such as placing a higher priority on reducing malaria than on reducing cancer. Another instance would be differences in economic or technical resources that may dictate different choices. For example, some of the pesticides preferred in industrial countries because they are more environmentally benign are relatively expensive and dangerous to use, and may therefore be less attractive to the governments of developing countries.

Many common pollution sources in developing countries are too small and numerous to regulate efficiently. A government should not expect major environmental improvements from direct regulation of such sources, unless it is prepared to carry out an intensive implementation programme; otherwise, social and economic measures to induce life-style changes will be more likely to obtain necessary improvements. Sources in this category include small-scale, private commercial activities, such as textile dyeing and metal working; informal housing settlements; and pesticide use by small farmers.

Besides obvious improvements in human health and natural resource conservation, there are other potential economic benefits from effective environmental regulation. Environmental requirements can increase production efficiency and generate markets for new products and services. In developing countries that are seeking massive foreign investment, such requirements may improve environmental planning for new ventures and provide more certainty for investors about their legal obligations and possible liabilities.

Some institutional considerations apply broadly to international assistance activities. Recipient governments may sometimes lack enough experience with pollution management to formulate requests for help that will produce the most effective results. There may be a corresponding problem within donor agencies, whose staffs may also be unfamiliar with these issues, and therefore find it harder than usual to evaluate the feasibility of assistance requests. Extra caution may be necessary to avoid the ever-present danger of overly ambitious planning and inflated expectations from development projects.

3.5 International Context For Environmental Regulation[33]

The US experience. The United States is widely regarded as a world leader in environmental regulation, and is often looked to as a model. US pollution control programmes rely heavily on a "command and control" approach[34].

The government establishes stringent, detailed requirements for all relevant aspects of potentially polluting activities. Failure to meet these requirements subjects a polluter to liability under a rigorous legal enforcement programme of civil and criminal sanctions, including penalties and corrective actions that can lead to permanent closure of the offending operation if it does not come into compliance.

The national government establishes general targets and detailed programme requirements. Local governments are then strongly encouraged to enact equivalent programmes, at which time they receive primary implementation authority. The national government provides support in terms of policy direction, funding, information and training.

These programmes have resulted in substantial improvements in environmental quality. Their effectiveness has been due in large measure to strong public and political backing for the government's use of a sophisticated legal system that grants substantial power to government environmental institutions. A driving force has been almost unlimited public access to the government's environmental information, which has supported continuing media coverage and specifically authorised citizen lawsuits to force the government and polluters to comply with their legal obligations.

The United States is now undergoing a widespread re-evaluation of its regulatory approach to pollution management. There is a growing belief that to make further advances, the government needs to modify its conceptual basis for managing pollution. This will require integrating environmental factors earlier and more pervasively in planning activities and incorporating principles of pollution prevention and integrated pollution management. It will also involve shifting some of the regulatory emphasis from command and control to more consensual approaches[35] and to market-based economic incentives for compliance[36].

It is easier to articulate these principles for change than it is to translate them into effective action. There is a search for examples at the local level, and for ways to apply these examples generically. Besides seeking domestic examples, the United States is looking more toward other OECD countries to learn from their experiences. The movement to revise US regulation of pollution management is still in its early stages, and is likely to continue for many years.

Recent European developments. At the same time that the United States is rethinking its environmental command and control approach, other OECD countries have been going through a similar process, and in many cases have made significant advances[37]. The most innovative, comprehensive programmes may be developing in the Netherlands[38].

In addition to the efforts of individual governments, the European Community as a whole is wrestling with questions of harmonization, establishing new, more rigorous and far-reaching environmental regulations, and experiencing a "green" revolution with growing public demand and citizen activism for better environmental protection[39]. The sudden spotlight on the devastating pollution in Eastern Europe has added another important dimension to these activities.

Implications for developing countries. The rising call for more effective environmental institutions and regulatory programmes in developing countries comes at a time when industrialised countries with more experience are themselves in a state of flux. This situation offers opportunities for innovation to help developing countries avoid some of the pitfalls experienced by industrial countries. However, it could also generate confusion and frustration, with developing country governments being urged to implement systems based on evolving principles that are not yet fully worked out at the operational level.

The following discussion on programme requirements assumes that for the foreseeable future, most efforts to strengthen environmental regulatory programmes in developing countries will draw heavily upon "traditional" Western approaches to pollution management. The following discussion, based on a good deal of field and case study experience, emphasizes options that may be most useful to developing countries, and suggests modifications to make them more appropriate to local conditions and constraints.

3. Establishing Major Requirements for Environmental Regulatory Programmes

3.1 National policies, empowering laws and institutional arrangements

Much of the initial effort in pollution management, as in natural resource conservation, is likely to concentrate on including pollution management issues in country environmental profiles and national conservation plans, enacting or revising general empowering laws, and setting up some initial stage institutional arrangements.

By its nature, enabling legislation is usually too general to be implemented effectively without more detailed programmes and procedures established by a responsible government authority. This section suggests a framework for developing regulations and institutional programmes to implement enabling laws on environmental pollution. It addresses: environmental quality standards; analyzing pollution problems; research and monitoring; developing core regulations; compliance; and pilot projects[40].

3.2 Environmental quality standards

One of the initial steps for shaping a regulatory scheme to manage pollution is setting environmental quality standards. These standards, based on health and environmental criteria, establish acceptable baseline limits for pollutant concentrations in specific environmental media, such as air, water and soil. The same standards may apply generically, or they can be tailored according to projected use. For example, standards for drinking water quality would be stricter than standards for water intended for industrial use.

For developing countries that lack adequate capability to design their own environmental quality standards, the guidelines established by WHO provide a convenient starting point. They are intended to provide broad protection to human health, with a considerable margin of safety. Besides general guidelines for the various environmental media, there are recommended limits for concentrations of many specific pollutants[41].

In most cases, meeting even the WHO guidelines (which are less stringent than the standards set by some industrialised countries) will be far beyond the means of a developing country that has adopted them. One approach recommended by WHO is to set interim goals[42]. For example, a government might aim to achieve 70 per cent of key standards for potable water in designated areas within 10 years, and then phase in additional improvements.

One of the advantages of environmental quality standards is that they can function as a regulatory "safety net". A general rule requiring regulated sources to meet applicable environmental quality standards can provide a legal mechanism for government to respond to pollution problems, even in the absence of more specific regulatory standard.

This is not to suggest that environmental quality standards alone are an adequate basis for regulating pollution; in fact, regulating pollution by specific environmental media can be counterproductive, as discussed above. Even so, using environmental quality standards as a target for pollution management efforts, in the absence of core pollution management regulations, can serve as a stopgap measure during the extended time that will be necessary to develop and implement a complete regulatory programme.

3.3 Analyzing pollution problems

One important result of the analytical approach chosen for pollution management will be the selection of examples or models to help strengthen institutional programmes. For instance, many of the pollution management programmes in the United States would need substantial modification to work in developing countries because they are extremely complex and require extensive government resources for implementation. Also, they often fail to incorporate adequately pollution prevention and integrated pollution management.

As discussed above, applying the complementary concepts of pollution prevention and integrated pollution management tends to discourage regulating pollution problems by environmental media such as air, water and soil. More environmentally sound approaches for setting core programme requirements include regulation by substance, by source, and by geographic area[43].

Regulation by substance is common with regard to pesticides, toxic chemicals and hazardous waste. Substances are often classified for regulatory purposes according to their chemical structure (e.g., organic solvents), their function (e.g., pesticides) or their effect on human health (e.g., carcinogens). Besides controlling the licensing of new pesticides and chemicals, this approach is commonly used to set requirements for domestic and international manufacture, transport, use and disposal of regulated substances.

For many of these purposes, regulation by substance has proved very effective and is now widely used both domestically and in some instances, internationally[44]. However, as a means of managing pollution, this approach poses similar problems to regulation by environmental media; its focus on a single issue tends to limit opportunities for pollution prevention and integrated pollution management[45].

Regulation by source. Requirements for specific sources and categories of sources will be at the heart of most government environmental regulatory programmes for pollution management. Large industrial and sanitation facilities are relatively easy to regulate and provide the most readily achievable reductions in pollution. Also, they can better afford necessary process and equipment changes because of economies of scale and better financing. After establishing regulation of such major sources, a government can extend similar requirements to smaller facilities.

In countries experiencing rapid industrialisation, it may be advisable to concentrate more on planning for new facilities than on expensive capital improvements to existing facilities. One common approach is to make new requirements applicable immediately to new facilities, and phase them in more gradually for existing operations. For example, this is the approach being taken with regard to industrial regulation in East Germany. Stringent rules apply to new construction, effective July 1, 1990; the requirements will be phased in more gradually for existing facilities[46].

Ideally, the entire activity to be regulated should be viewed as a single complex source of potential pollution. Evaluating relevant inputs and outputs for the overall activity makes it much easier to maximise pollution prevention and to manage polluting activities as cost-effectively as possible. This type of review is sometimes called an environmental audit. When working with companies in developing countries, it can be helpful to characterise these audits in terms of increasing production efficiency, rather than stressing environmental protection[47].

Regulating a polluting facility as a single source is a relatively new concept. Many industrial countries, including the United States, tend to regulate specific types of equipment, or specific emission points at a facility, which sometimes leads to the kinds of problems already described from other "single viewpoint" approaches. Indeed, this may be a late comer advantage to be enjoyed by developing countries. In any event, it is worth underlining once again that regulatory examples from industrial countries have to be carefully screened for their appropriateness.

One potential drawback of looking at a source holistically for regulatory purposes is that this approach can require detailed consideration of each source, and allow considerable discretion to individual officials in setting applicable requirements. To minimise this possible problem, the government can set regulatory goals and then allow companies broad discretion in deciding how to meet them. The goals may be fixed emission limits, reducing total emissions by a certain percentage, or a combination, which may also be mixed with certain process or equipment specifications. (The company's approved plan can serve as the basis for a permit to construct or operate.)

Regulation by geographic area has been used most commonly in efforts to clean up bodies of water, both domestic and international, and watershed areas. It can also apply to specially protected areas, such as national parks and key agricultural land. The broadest of all are new international efforts to curb stratospheric ozone depletion and global warming. Environmental regulations for designated geographic areas may apply to both categories of sources and to specific substances.

3.4 Research and monitoring

It is hard to design effective pollution management programmes or to evaluate their success without adequate baseline information, research and monitoring. However, developing country governments may have little choice but to initiate some programmes without much data, where they perceive a great threat to human health or the environment. In some countries, universities or nongovernmental organisations may be able to help collect and evaluate environmental data.

For example, Fundacion Natura, a nongovernmental organisation in Ecuador, is conducting an environmental survey of about 2 000 industrial facilities, as part of a larger environmental education project funded by the US Agency for International Development. The survey will identify the principal industries in Ecuador, and collect information about potential environmental effects and appropriate process and control options. The results will be used to help stimulate follow-up actions by public authorities and the private sector.

Another way to supplement limited government research and monitoring capabilities is to require regulated entities to, in effect, monitor and inspect themselves and report the results to the government. (A programme of periodic government inspections can help to uncover any inaccuracies in the reports.) This however, can only be expected to work in the case of large companies. This kind of regulatory monitoring and reporting also facilitates government compliance efforts and can be helpful to responsible companies. Points to consider in setting monitoring and related requirements include: availability of necessary equipment and testing facilities; cost; strengthening of agency staffing required to build up the capacity to maintain good records; and company record keeping capacities.

3.5 Developing core regulations

Environmental quality standards and monitoring requirements should apply broadly and can serve as underpinnings for any regulatory programme on pollution management. How best to proceed in establishing the more specific requirements at the core of a regulatory programme and designing appropriate institutional arrangements is a question that each country may answer differently. This section discusses that next level of implementation.

Formal promulgation. With respect to the preliminary matters of national law and institutional organisation, a common procedure has been for a donor organisation to provide a foreign expert to assist a government team for a few weeks in designing a law and/or a corresponding institutional arrangement. This has the advantage of producing a system, at least officially, but there may be disadvantages.

If the project focuses on national law, the resulting product will almost surely lack sufficient detail to be implemented without more specific regulations. No matter how intensively the team works, there is rarely enough time to investigate thoroughly the local ramifications of the new requirements or to evaluate alternative approaches. Also, the programme's scope probably far exceeds the government's ability to implement it and regulated entities' ability to comply with it. These factors, not surprisingly, all too often result in a programme that exists primarily on paper. This has been the case in Eastern Europe, where extensive laws and institutional authorities were wholly ineffective in averting the current state of environmental crisis[48].

The government risks losing credibility and undermining public respect for its policy goals when it has laws without meaningful implementation. Also, this situation may unfortunately provide more temptations to corruption than opportunities to protect the public. But there is some advantage to having formal legal requirements even where a government cannot implement them. The requirements may guide responsible parties, and they will already be in place should a time come when implementation is more feasible. The system at least provides a tangible benchmark and offers some certainty about the governments's intentions to the community that will become subject to the regulations.

How to balance these realities becomes increasingly important as a government moves from a general legal and organisational framework to actual programme implementation. The goal, of course, should be to reduce pollution and its negative impacts on human health and the environment. Formalising a detailed regulatory scheme within a relatively short time in a government with little or no experience in pollution management is unlikely to produce this result.

One approach that may be more productive is using a regulatory roundtable. This approach can apply to any of the regulatory issues discussed above. The following examples focus on regulation by source because it is likely to be more difficult; it is most dependent on local conditions, and there are fewer readily applicable examples that can assist developing country officials.

Regulatory roundtables. The purpose of a regulatory roundtable is to foster an open, constructive dialogue between the government and potentially affected parties. Where a government needs to develop regulations, a roundtable can serve as a forum for negotiations with interested parties, leading to promulgation of new requirements. Where a regulatory programme already exists, the government can work with roundtable members to improve implementation and identify any need for formal revisions[49].

The key roundtable participants in most developing countries will be government environmental officials with direct regulatory responsibility and representatives of the targeted source or category of sources. It may also be advisable to invite government officials from outside the central environmental authority, if co-operation from their departments will be necessary to successful implementation. These might include representatives from the national planning authority, or local officials who will be responsible for detailed implementation. Other groups that should be considered, if they exist in the country and their participation is politically feasible, are workers' unions or co-operatives, relevant nongovernmental organisations, such as environmental or community development groups, and members of the technical and research communities.

Almost invariably, regulatory requirements established through a regulatory roundtable will be less stringent than the government might have initially wished. The benefit should be that whatever is agreed upon, can be implemented and will produce real environmental improvements, however modest.

To help address government concerns about progress, it may be possible to develop a graduated programme of incremental improvements that allows more time and/or flexibility in attaining the government's environmental goals. Ultimately, if the roundtable participants are unable to reach an acceptable compromise, the government has the option of setting (and trying to enforce) whatever rules and programmes it believes are necessary.

One benefit of a successful regulatory roundtable is that it can serve as an ongoing forum, or at least foster a network, that interested participants can continue to use. This could be particularly helpful to encourage co-operation among small- and medium-sized companies on issues such as improving production efficiency, waste reduction, recycling and waste treatment.

For example, in response to new national and state legislation, tanneries and the local government in Vaniambaddi, near Madras in southern India, worked through a committee to establish a central waste treatment facility for a few dozen tanneries that recovers and properly disposes of chromium salt from tannery wastewater. Industry pays 75 per cent of the costs, and government pays the other 25 per cent[50].

The same general approach can also apply to pollution problems that do not readily lend themselves to formal regulation. For example, small vans owned and operated by independent private individuals are a major source of vehicle emissions in many urban centres[51]. A roundtable approach could help in addressing issues such as allocating transportation routes and vehicle maintenance.

Some industrial countries, such as the Netherlands, have used co-operative approaches extensively in establishing new environmental programmes. In the United States, where federal laws often restrict the government's authority to compromise on achieving environmental goals, this is still at the experimental stage.

There are several reasons why the use of regulatory roundtables should be suitable for establishing specific pollution management programmes in many developing countries. First, many countries have a cultural tradition of seeking consensus and building compromise. Second, if the government's resources are limited, other participants may be able to provide valuable supplementary information or expertise.

Third, the information developed through these roundtables can help to make difficult, sometimes unpalatable but important decisions about how a government can set achievable goals for pollution management. Finally, extremely limited enforcement capabilities elevate the need for many developing country governments to obtain as much voluntary compliance as possible.

3.6 Compliance

Stressing potential economic benefits from pollution prevention and integrated pollution management, and using approaches such as regulatory roundtables can improve the likelihood of compliance with pollution management requirements. Nevertheless, it is a fact that compliance will only be partial. In limited circumstances, legal enforcement can be a powerful tool; on many more occasions, developing country governments will have to rely on a broader array of mechanisms.

Legal enforcement. Governments that embark upon legal enforcement of environmental requirements should be prepared to build a programme gradually[52]. This section will highlight a few of the issues that may be of particular concern for developing countries.

Building the necessary elements in a successful enforcement action requires special skills and experience. Besides adhering to applicable legal procedures, the government will have to satisfy substantive requirements, such as standards for the sufficiency of evidence. Also, regulatory authorities are not the only ones who need to develop the necessary skills and experience; the same is true of the judicial community, which will probably have to be educated on both the seriousness and the technical complexities of environmental pollution.

Officials and the public may think first about assessing penalties, particularly where violations have led to notable public harm. However, a penalty should be a tool to obtain compliance, not an end in itself. The government should also ensure that the violator will take the necessary measures to comply with environmental requirements on an expeditious timetable. In extreme cases, the government may decide to require a violator to cease operations until it has achieved an acceptable degree of compliance.

The initial targets of environmental law enforcement are likely to be multinational companies and joint ventures that include foreign investors because of their size, their financial standing, and the tendency to hold them to a higher standard of behaviour and culpability than domestic operations. However, environmental authorities should not overlook domestic activities that are major sources of pollution.

Government involvement in a polluting activity may often prove a complicating factor in the case of both domestic and internationally-affiliated violators. This is a problem in industrial countries, too[53], but it may be exacerbated in developing countries because of the pervasive nature of government economic interests. For example, many key production activities in developing countries, such as processing export crops, tanneries and mining, are owned or managed at least in part by the government or a quasi-governmental entity. The same may be true for municipal sanitary facilities, such as landfills and sewage treatment plants. Taking effective action against such violators is often more a political than a legal issue.

To run an effective enforcement programme, the environmental authority must be perceived as likely to prevail in legal proceedings. However, formally prosecuting a case to its ultimate conclusion is time-consuming and expensive for all parties involved; most cases will probably be resolved through negotiation and settlement. In these instances, the final agreement should be documented in a legally enforceable manner, so that the government will have prompt recourse if the violator does not comply.

The settlement process is very flexible. Settlement discussions may range beyond the narrow question of a specific violation to encompass more general issues of environmentally sound operation. This can provide an opportunity for the government to educate a violator and to obtain commitments toward improved pollution prevention and integrated pollution management through procedures such as environmental auditing and follow-up planning.

Efforts to settle a case may fail for any number of reasons. If so, the government may reactivate formal proceedings. However, government officials should also consider whether other alternatives are available, such as arbitration or environmental mediation[54]. In arbitration, both parties agree to submit the disagreement to an arbitrator, who then makes a decision. That decision may have the effect of a recommendation or of a binding opinion, depending on the terms of arbitration.

In environmental mediation, the mediator's role is to help the parties find common ground for resolving their differences. Familiarising environmental officials with the concepts of this approach might help them not only in resolving enforcement actions, but also in working with other government departments in the general course of their duties.

Other compliance mechanisms. There are many routes a government can pursue, besides legal enforcement, to encourage compliance with pollution management requirements. Some are specific incentives and disincentives within the direct purview of environmental authorities, such as accelerating the issuance of permits for complying facilities, barring repeat violators from obtaining government contracts, and publicising particularly good and bad environmental behaviour. Other approaches to foster compliance would require co-ordination with other government authorities. These include economic measures such as user fees to encourage efficient use of scarce resources, and tax reductions on the import of pollution control equipment. Technical measures, such as encouraging the establishment of co-operative disposal facilities or recycling operations, would also depend on co-operation between government and industry.

3.7 Pilot projects

A pilot project can serve as a relatively painless, low cost means of determining which regulatory approaches will work best. It can provide invaluable experience to a government contemplating major new administrative procedures or institutional arrangements. Pilot projects can incorporate elements of both regulatory and compliance programmes. Local governments in industrialised companies can often provide useful examples of pilot projects and other innovative approaches that may more easily applied in developing countries than larger, nationally oriented programmes.

For example, in 1990-91, the US state of Massachusetts is conducting a pilot project to test implementation of a new law requiring sources to reduce their emissions of toxic pollutants[55]. The project focuses on manufacturing facilities that make intensive use of metals.

Project elements include: training inspectors to conduct multimedia inspections; developing enforcement approaches that will use source reduction as the primary means of compliance; co-ordinating activities between the government's regulatory and technical assistance programmes; and evaluating the pilot project itself as a model. The government will make more formal decisions about the best institutional arrangements for this new programme after it evaluates the results of the pilot project and discusses them with interested parties.

4. *International Assistance Mechanisms*

The recommended methods for analyzing pollution and developing regulatory programmes favour a more incremental approach to environmental institutional development. The emphasis would be on building from a base of modest operational innovations; broad changes in law and government institutions would grow more from the continuous process of a government's gaining experience through its interactions with the regulated community and the public. Trying to implement this approach will require changes in the attitudes and operations of developing country governments. It will also require corresponding changes in the international assistance efforts to support environmental regulatory programmes.

Many donors have begun to recognise that developing country officials will need more assistance in planning and implementing the kinds of analyses and activities described in this paper. Virtually all the multilateral development banks and several U.N. agencies are putting more emphasis on environmental institutional development. The same is true for some bilateral donors[56]. This section will discuss: policy dialogue; technical assistance; education and training; public education; and internal donor operations.

4.1 Policy dialogue

Applying the concepts reviewed in this paper may affect policy dialogues between international donors and recipient governments countries in several ways. Raising the substantive issues of pollution prevention and integrated pollution management should help to provide a focus for discussions on sustainable development in the context of managing pollution. Measures to improve institutional performance in these areas should be included in programme and project design and loan conditions.

Donors can help developing countries to take a more practical approach to implementing pollution management programmes by highlighting these ideas in policy dialogue and in the kinds of assistance they offer for institutional development. This process can work in two directions; recipient governments can suggest using these principles to design assistance programmes that are more likely to strengthen their institutional capabilities for sound environmental management.

The cost of these efforts would probably be somewhat higher than is presently allocated to environmental institutional development because they would in some instances require continuing assistance, at least on an intermittent basis, to be most effective. However, they would not necessarily require funding that would be orders of magnitude higher than present levels.

4.2 Technical assistance

National environmental planning. Pollution impacts on environmental health and natural resource degradation should be included in new country environmental profiles and action plans, and added to existing ones[57]. This will be crucial to heighten awareness of the problems, improve prevention and planning, and to build baseline data for future evaluations and decision making.

Information resources. Developing countries need access to existing international materials and databases. They also need to generate and use domestic environmental information.

Abundant information exists on pollution management that would be helpful to developing countries, but it is difficult to provide the information in a useful form to the people who need it. Donors can help to develop and disseminate checklists and key examples of appropriate laws and regulations on pollution management. This might be more helpful than simply providing access to regulatory packages from industrial countries or large legal databases[58].

For governments that have basic computer capabilities, donors could identify a few particularly important and useful databases to be shared. For example, the U.N. Environment Programme's (UNEP) International Register of Potentially Toxic Chemicals maintains a database with worldwide scientific and regulatory data on pesticides and other toxic chemicals. It was recently adapted to a user-friendly PC system for use in developing countries.

Many developing country governments could benefit from "starter" libraries with basic technical and regulatory information and guidance. There have been some efforts to provide such libraries that could serve as examples[59]. Several U.N. agencies, such as WHO, UNEP, and the Food and Agriculture Organization, have technical materials designed for use in developing countries and available in several languages that could serve as some of the core materials; so do other international organisations and some bilateral donors.

Developing environmental guides for key economic activities is another fruitful area for improving information resources. For example, a group of bilateral donors and multilateral banks will be collaborating with several developing countries to produce a guide on environmental planning for energy projects[60].

Environmental economics. Environmental planners in developing countries need relatively simple methods of calculating and comparing the positive and negative economic impacts (both short and long-term) of different environmental strategies, especially for specific project proposals. General arguments about the benefits of sustainable development will not be sufficient to influence economic development activities without this kind of information.

Regional co-operation and planning. Donors can also assist developing countries by helping to address shared pollution problems that can benefit from regional or sub-regional co-operation. For example, fulfilling international obligations on restricting movements of hazardous substances may require co-operation among neighbouring countries on issues such as notification and transport. Some problems, such as establishing facilities for recycling and hazardous waste disposal, will require joint solutions in regions where it would not be economical for each country to maintain separate facilities.

Consultancies. By their nature, regulatory and institutional development are matters that require attention over an extended period of time. Donors may need to offer more consultancies lasting from several weeks to a few months, to allow time for exploring implementation options more thoroughly, and conferring with a wider circle of people outside the government.

Where recipient governments can demonstrate that they are actively pursuing implementation, donors could try to structure consultancies so that they can provide supplementary support. It might be best to design such arrangements so that the government receives ongoing periodic assistance, rather than basing foreign advisers in-country for lengthy periods. This could help to foster local self-sufficiency and reduce project costs.

In some cases, donors can provide relatively low cost ongoing institutional support through co-operation with bilateral voluntary organisations. For example, the US Peace Corps is training volunteers who will assist local governments in Poland with environmental management.

Long-term pilot projects. Donors should consider instituting a small number of pilot projects, lasting a minimum of three to five years, to help a few countries develop and implement more effective government environmental regulatory programmes. Several donors could jointly design a "package" of assistance whereby each would provide specific types of support, and all could use the pilot to improve donor co-ordination on environmental management, and strengthen institutional development. To create a strong likelihood of success, any governments selected would need sufficient policy commitment, resources, political stability, and ability to work with the public and private sectors.

4.3 Education and training

In all education and training activities, emphasis should be given to "training the trainers," selecting participants who in turn can teach their new skills to others.

Workshops and courses. Countries that already have at least a minimal institutional base for pollution management could benefit from local workshops or courses that draw together members of the public and private sector, identify necessary actions, and plan follow-up (which in some cases could be supported by donors). For example, in 1988, the US Agency for International Development and the US Environmental Protection Agency cosponsored a workshop on hazardous and toxic waste management for government and industry officials from Indonesia and Thailand. Participants reviewed technical information, plans for a hazardous waste management facility, and a draft Indonesian regulation. In at least one case, the workshop led to short-term technical assistance for a participating company.

For governments that lack an institutional base, or where international donors are not active in pollution management, it might be more feasible to sponsor workshops and courses at the regional or sub-regional level for several countries to work on generic problems or try to harmonise their approaches to common issues. This could facilitate building valuable regional networks, as well as familiarising government officials with important regulatory matters.

In-country or regional educational sessions on pollution management could address any number of topics, such as: options for building institutional infrastructure; examples or guidelines for laws, regulations and implementation programmes; procedures for issuing permits (emphasizing cross-media approaches); key elements of an inspection programme; regulating key industries or sanitation facilities; environmental health; and risk assessment. Intensive training on legal enforcement would be most productive in countries that already have a reasonably well-developed regulatory infrastructure.

Pollution prevention and integrated pollution management should be prevailing themes in all workshops and courses, as well as being appropriate topics themselves. Workshops and courses on regulatory implementation should concentrate on addressing specific problems with examples, and stress contributions from participants. Exercises such as role-playing could prove helpful to attendees in areas such as processing permit applications or conducting an enforcement negotiation.

Gaining practical experience. A recurring problem seems to be that many environmental officials in developing countries have advanced degrees but little practical experience. One response has been for universities and training centres in industrial countries to design programmes for developing country officials that include class projects with immediate application, such as designing a landfill for a neighbouring town, or temporary work assignments with a local government agency or environmental consulting firm[61].

Donors and developing country officials should explore opportunities for establishing similar programmes in developing countries. Regional training centres at local universities or research institutions would be more accessible, cost less to finance participation, and could provide more direct benefits to nearby countries. They would also encourage developing country officials to look to each other more for guidance, and help to foster interpersonal networks for sharing information and experience.

4.4 Public education

It will take generations for developing countries to resolve urban and industrial pollution, and as well as other difficult environmental problems. Well-informed citizens and leaders will be central to motivating social change and the political will to make concepts of sustainable development operational. Public education at all levels is a necessary component to this process. Post-secondary school education and community awareness programmes are especially important for influencing the development of government regulatory programmes on pollution management.

Higher education in disciplines such as engineering, urban planning, architecture and sociology should integrate fundamental concepts of sound pollution management into general courses of study. Community awareness efforts should include sponsoring public education campaigns, strengthening local abilities to prevent and respond to industrial accidents[62], supporting community action groups, and educating the news media. In all cases, it will be important to link principles of pollution management with concrete health and economic benefits. Donor support to universities and nongovernmental organisations can play a key role in these areas.

4.5 Internal donor operations

Implementing the measures discussed above for strengthening developing country environmental institutions will require modifications to some donor operations.

Internal policies and staff training. The needed changes in policy dialogues between donors and recipient government described above must first occur within donor organisations. They need to incorporate the concepts of pollution prevention and integrated pollution management into their own environmental ethic of sustainable development. They will also have to place a higher priority on carefully designed efforts to enhance implementation of environmental laws and institutional programmes. These modifications will often require additional staff training, as well as internal policy changes[63].

Co-ordination among donors. The widespread impacts of environmental pollution on human health and natural resources are receiving more attention from many donors, and many of the countries they work with require similar kinds of assistance. Improved donor co-ordination will be important for leveraging limited resources in order to strengthen government capabilities in pollution management. The preceding discussion of assistance mechanisms noted some possible areas of collaboration.

5. Conclusion

The growing international urgency about accelerating environmental threats at global, national and local levels is placing increasing demands on government environmental institutions in developing countries. Moving beyond the creation of laws and institutions for environmental management, to actual implementation, is an essential part of making sustainable development work.

The special complexities of environmental issues make the challenges to institutional development in this area particularly daunting. Nevertheless, it should be possible to increase the effectiveness of these institutions by applying recent insights into the process of institutional development, particularly by taking a more functional and incremental approach.

One of the keys to any successful programme to strengthen the regulatory capabilities of environmental institutions will be a recognition of the areas where they can and cannot be effective. Direct environmental regulation is much better suited to addressing large, discrete operations than small, dispersed activities. In the latter situation, broader economic and social programmes can be far more effective in inducing needed changes. In many cases, the distinctions between "traditional" regulatory approaches and new economic incentives to curb environmental harm will be less clear in practice than in theory. Devising the most effective strategies in developing countries will be a gradual process of experimentation and learning[64]. There are few clear answers, and the lessons learned can often benefit the governments of developing and industrialised countries.

This paper has suggested ways to strengthen regulatory programmes for pollution management in developing countries. The same principles of analysis and gradual programme building would apply to a much broader range of environmental issues, at all levels of government. In some cases, maximising the effectiveness of these approaches will require significant changes in the philosophy and operation of both domestic programmes and international assistance programmes.

NOTES AND REFERENCES

1. H. Jefferey LEONARD, ed., *Divesting Nature's Capital: The Political Economy of Environmental Abuse in the Third World*, New York, Holmes and Meier, 1985, p. 264.

2. WORLD RESOURCES INSTITUTE (WRI), *Development and Pollution in the Third World*, Washington, D.C., WRI, May 1989, p. 5.

3. WORLD COMMISSION ON ENVIRONMENT AND DEVELOPMENT, *Our Common Future*, Oxford, Oxford University Press, 1987, Table 9.1, p. 236.

4. WRI, supra n. 2 at p. 5.

5. S.J. COINTREAU, *Environmental Management of Urban Solid Waste in Developing Countries: A Project Guide*, Washington, D.C., World Bank, 1982, p. xii.

6. WRI, Centre for International Development and Environment, *Toward an Environmental and Natural Resources Management Strategy for ANE Countries in the 1990s*, Washington, D.C., WRI, January 1990, p. 37.

7. CENTRE FOR SCIENCE AND ENVIRONMENT, India, "The Environmental Problems Associated with India's Major Cities", *Environment and Urbanization*, Vol. 1, No. 1, April 1989, p. 10.

8. WORLD HEALTH ORGANISATION (WHO), *Assessment of Urban Air Quality*, Geneva, WHO, 1988.

9. U.S. AGENCY FOR INTERNATIONAL DEVELOPMENT (USAID), *Environmental and Natural Resource Management in Developing Countries: A Report to Congress*, Washington, D.C., USAID, Vol. 1, February 1979, p. 109.

10. D. RILEY with Chris KERREBROCK, *Environment Latin America: Facing the Realities of Rapid Growth*, New York, World Environment Center, 1981, p. 27.

11. V. SMIL, "China's Environmental Morass", *Current History*, Vol. 88, No. 227, September 1989, p. 287.

12. WORLD BANK, *World Development Report 1987*, New York, Oxford University Press for the World Bank, 1987.

13. *The Washington Post*, "Eastern Europe Faces Vast Environmental Blight", 20th March 1990, p. A1.

14. HENKEL, R., "The Bolivian Cocaine Industry", in *Drugs in Latin America*, Studies in Third World Societies, Publication No. 37.

15. WRI, supra n. 4, p. 37.

16. E.g., *New York Times*, "Pollution in Eastern Europe Described as Grim", 17th January 1990, p. A11; *Washington Post*, supra n. 13, p. A1; *TIME*, "The Greening of the U.S.S.R.", 2nd January 1989, p. 68.

17. *The Washington Post*, supra n. 13, p. A23.

18. *TIME*, supra n. 16, p. 69.

19. CENTRE FOR SCIENCE AND ENVIRONMENT, supra n. 7, p. 10.

20. *Ibid.*, p. 10.

21. WRI, *Development and Pollution in the Third World*, for the Tokyo Conference on the Global Environment and Human Response, September 1989, p. 17.

22. Information provided to the author by S. HAMMAM, Assistant Director, Office of Housing, Private Enterprise Bureau, USAID.

23. A. AGARWAL, J. MERRIFIELD and R. TANDON, *No Place to Run: Local Realities and Global Issues of the Bhopal Disaster*, New Market, Tenn., Highlander Center and Society for Participatory Research in Asia., 1985, p. 1.

24. *The Washington Post*, supra n. 13, p. A23.

25. *Ibid.*, p. A1.

26. For example, industrial sources of marine and coastal pollution are an important focus of the Regional Seas Programme, sponsored by UNEP and the U.N. Industrial Development Organization.

27. For a general discussion of these issues, see, N. HAIGH and F. IRWIN, ed., *Integrated Pollution Control in Europe and North America*, Washington, D.C., Conservation Foundation, 1990; D.W. PEARCE and R.K. TURNER, *Economics of Natural Resources and the Environment*, Baltimore, M.D., Johns Hopkins University Press, 1989.

28. See generally, J.A. DOELEMAN, *Public Reflections on Private Motorcars in the Urban Environment*, Occasional Paper No. 15, Department of Economics, University of Newcastle, N.S.W., Australia, May 1985.

29. WHO, *Preliminary Assessment of National Programs for Health Protection Against Environmental Hazards*, Doc. No. PEP/85.8, 1985.

30. The indicators selected as key program requirements were: enabling legislation; comprehensive environmental health strategy; regulatory standards; laboratory facilities; enforcement and compliance monitoring; staffing; research and forecasting; national inter-sectoral coordination; involvement of health authorities; and vertical delegation to government authorities at the sub-national level.

31. B. LAUSCHE, *Environmental and Natural Resource Management Institutions in Developing Countries*, World Bank, Environment Department, Background Paper, p. 10, (Draft, 10th October 1989).

32. E.g., OECD Development Centre, *A Model for Environmental Administration in Third-World Countries*, Doc. No. CD/R(88)31 (revised), Paris, OECD, January 1989; W. ASCHER and R. HEALY, *Natural Resource Policy-making in Developing Countries: Environment, Economic Growth, and Income Distribution*, 1990; R. BAKER, "Institutional Innovation, Development and Environmental Management", *Publ. Adm. & Dev.*, Vol. 9, No.1, p. 29, January-March, 1989; J. SHANE, "Environmental Law in the Developing Nations of Southeast Asia", in *Developing Economies and the Environment: the Southeast Asian Experience*, McGraw Hill, 1979; B. JOHNSTON and W. CLARK, *Redesigning Rural Development: A Strategic Perspective*, 1982; A. ISRAEL, *Institutional Development: Incentives to Performance*, 1987. For a more radical perspective on the same issues, see, H. DE SOTO, *The Other Path: The Invisible Revolution in the Third World*, New York, Harper and Row, 1989.

33. The author cited supra n. 27 provide a good overview of this subject.

34. For a critical review of federal pollution management programs in the United States, see M. LANDY, M. ROBERTS, S. THOMAS, *The Environmental Protection Agency: Asking the Wrong Questions*, Oxford, Oxford University Press, 1990.

35. This topic is addressed in the discussion of compliance, under the following section on establishing major program requirements.

36. E.g., R. STAVINS, "Harnessing Market Forces to Protect Our Environment: Initiatives for the New President", *Environment*, Vol. 31, No. 1, January/February 1989, p. 4; Editorial, "Grime and Punishment", *The New Republic*, 20th February 1989, p. 7 (advocating market-based incentives for better pollution management).

37. Germany, France, the Netherlands, Norway, Sweden, and the United Kingdom are among the European countries taking innovative measures to control pollution. So is Canada. See generally, HAIGH and IRWIN, supra n. 27; PEARCE and TURNER, supra n. 27; DOCTER, Institute for Environmental Studies/Milan, *European Environmental Yearbook*, London, DocTer International, 1987. For a discussion of some of the ways that these activities could be helpful to developing countries, see M.S. ADISESHIAH, ed., *Economics of Environment*, New Delhi, Lancer International, 1987.

38. See generally, GOVERNMENT OF THE NETHERLANDS, Second Chamber of the States General, *To Choose or Lose: National Environmental Policy Plan*, session 1988-89, 21 137, nos.1-2; and GOVERNMENT OF THE NETHERLANDS, National Institute of Public Health and Environmental Protection, *Concern for Tomorrow: A National Environmental Survey 1985-2010*, 1989.

39. E.g., DOCTER, supra n. 37; A. HAAGSMA, "The European Communities' Environmental Policy: A Case Study in Federalism", *Fordham International L.J.*, Vol. 12, No. 311, Winter, 1989.

40. This is not a complete catalogue of the major functions of a government environmental institution. There are other important functions not addressed in this article, such as finance and administration, and external affairs.

41. E.g., H.W. de KONING, ed., *Setting Environmental Standards: Guidelines for Decision-making*, Geneva, WHO, 1987.

42. Information provided to the author by H.W. de Koning, Regional Adviser on Environmental Pollution Control, Pan American Health Organization.

43. See generally, HAIGH and IRWIN, supra n. 27.

44. A well known international example of this approach is the 1989 *Basel Convention on the Control of Transboundary Movements of Hazardous Wastes and Their Disposal.*

45. For an example of how the OECD is trying to address this issue, see, OECD, Environment Directorate, Chemicals Group and Management Committee, *The Cross-Media Approach to Pollution Control and Its Incorporation into the Project on Coherent Approaches for Controlling Hazardous Substances,* Doc. No. ENV/CHEM/CM/87.8 (Draft, 16 July 1987).

46. *The New York Times International,* "West Germans Get Ready to Scrub the East's Tarnished Environment", 27th June 1990, p. A6.

47. While there are many handbooks on theory and techniques of environmental auditing, there seems to be a need for more materials designed for use in developing countries.

48. E.g., *Statement of Dr. Zbigniew Bochniarz, Official Representative to the United States of the Polish Ecological Club, before the U.S. House of Representatives, Committee on Energy and Commerce, Subcommittee on Transportation and Hazardous Materials,* Washington, D.C. (23rd April 1990).

    Preliminary findings in a World Bank case study of environmental institutions indicate that even in developing countries viewed as having relatively strong environmental laws and institutions, implementation has been weak at best. Information provided to the author by B. Lausche, Environment Department, World Bank.

49. See generally, M. PRITZKER and D. DALTON, *Negotiated Rulemaking Sourcebook*, Administrative Conference of the United States, 1990.

50. The treatment facility has been operating for about five years. Despite its success, there have not been many other similar programs developed in this region of India. This highlights another problem of institutional development -- how to effectively implement the results of successful activities on a larger scale. Information provided to the author by Dr. S. Padmanabhan, Consultant, Energy and Environmental Policy, Innovation and Commercialization Program, USAID.

51. For example, in Lima, Peru, 95 per cent of public transportation is estimated to be operated by independent private individuals. DE SOTO, supra n. 32, p. 93.

52. A brief review of some statistics on enforcement actions of the U.S. Environmental Protection Agency (USEPA) illustrates the gradual strengthening of its enforcement programs. In 1972, USEPA instituted one enforcement case in federal court; in 1989, it initiated 364. During that same period, new annual administrative enforcement

proceedings grew from 860 to 4136. USEPA, *Enforcement Accomplishments Report: FY 1989*, Office of Enforcement and Compliance Monitoring, Doc. No. 20E-2001, February 1990.

From 1977 to 1989, annual penalties assessed in federal court and agency administrative proceedings rose from less than $5 million to nearly $35 million. Id. In 1984, twelve years after USEPA began operating its enforcement program, the agency issued a new penalty policy that built upon its previous experience. Penalties collected within the first year after the new policy became effective totalled $21 million, four times greater than penalties collected during the previous year. C. JONES, Penalties on the Rise, *EPA Journal*, Vol. 13, No. 2, p. 8, March 1987.

53. In the United States, more than 15 000 sites at federal facilities have been cited for violations of federal and state environmental requirements. Most of these are military and energy facilities. National Governors' Association, *National Association of Attorneys General, From Crisis to Commitment: Environmental Cleanup and Compliance at Federal Facilities*, Report of the NGA-NAAG Task Force on Federal Facilities, January 1990. The problem of federal facility compliance with environmental laws is so pervasive that there is a new U.S. periodical devoted to this subject, *Federal Facilities Environmental Journal*.

54. See generally, G. BINGHAM, *Resolving Environmental Disputes: A Decade of Experience*, Washington, D.C., Conservation Foundation, 1986; F.P. GRAD, "Alternative Dispute Resolution in Environmental Law", *Col. J. Env. Law*, Vol. 14, No. 157, 1989. For an analysis of the problems of introducing alternative dispute resolution at the U.S. Environmental Agency, see, R.H. MAYS, "Alternative Dispute Resolution and Environmental Enforcement: A Noble Experiment or a Lost Cause?", *Env. Law Reporter (News and Analysis)*, Vol. 18, No. 10087, March 1988.

55. A recent interim report concludes that the program shows great promise. MASSACHUSETTS DEPARTMENT OF ENVIRONMENTAL PROTECTION, *FY 90 Report on the Blackstone Project*, 23rd July 1990.

56. For example, USAID is making environmental institutional development one of the centrepieces of the agency's revised environmental strategy.

57. A recent review of country environmental studies conducted on behalf of USAID indicates a need for more in-depth consideration of institutional and economic policies and measures to implement them. The OECD's Development Assistance Committee is reviewing these findings. LAUSCHE, supra n. 31, pp. 9-10.

58. In developing these kinds of information resources, it would be useful to consider the experience the Food and Agriculture Organization (FAO) has had in developing guidance materials for pesticide legislation.

59. For example, the USEPA, Region 9, has worked with some Asian countries on developing basic environmental libraries.

60. The Environmental Manual for Power Development is a collaborative project sponsored by the African Development Bank, Asian Development Bank, Gesellschaft fuer Technische Zusammenarbeit, Kreditanstaet fuer Wiederaufbau, Overseas Development Administration, USAID, and the World Bank.

61. For example, the University of California at Los Angeles has been operating an expanding program of this sort in the field of waste management.

62. One potential resource is a program administered by UNEP's Industry and Environment Office that trains communities in emergency preparedness and helps them to develop local action plans. The program is called Awareness and Preparedness for Emergencies at the Local Level (APELL).

63. USAID is about to embark on an ambitious staff training to support its revised environmental agenda. See generally, USAID, *Initiative on the Environment, Working Group on the Environment*, May 1990. One of the training goals is to have an officer in every mission who can review environmental impact assessments within three years.

64. A helpful discussion of this point appears in PEARCE and TURNER, supra n. 27, p. 160.

EFFECTIVE ENVIRONMENTAL REGULATION: THE CASE OF THE PHILIPPINES

by

Delfin J. Ganapin, Jr. *

* Delfin J. Ganapin, Jr. is Director, Environmental Management Bureau at the Department of Environment and Natural Resources, the Government of The Philippines.

RÉSUMÉ

Delfin Ganapin brosse un tableau frappant de la manière dont la capacité d'un gouvernement à gérer l'environnement peut être, et a été, renforcée dans un pays en développement lourdement handicapé par le remboursement de sa dette extérieure et disposant de moyens techniques et financiers limités. Son exposé met en lumière le rôle capital joué par une structure politique démocratique pour susciter un élan dans la société et dans les organismes officiels afin d'améliorer la capacité de résoudre les problèmes prioritaires de protection de l'environnement. Sa démarche est celle d'un décideur convaincu qu'il faut obtenir un large appui de tous les participants à l'application des mesures de protection de l'environnement, et non les heurter. Après avoir passé en revue la situation politique et économique des Philippines, l'auteur consacre l'essentiel de son propos (troisième partie) à analyser les composantes particulières d'un programme visant à renforcer la capacité de gestion, l'illustrant de nombreux exemples tirés de l'expérience acquise par les Philippines. Il s'agit notamment de susciter une volonté des citoyens et des pouvoirs publics, d'assurer l'infrastructure technique, de mettre en place des mesures d'incitation, de transformer les structures bureaucratiques et les traditions existantes, etc. En conclusion, l'auteur indique que, dans les pays en développement, pour élaborer et appliquer une politique de l'environnement avec une efficacité grandissante, il faut, non plus disséquer davantage la difficulté de l'entreprise, mais surtout mobiliser des individus très capables et pleins d'imagination.

SUMMARY

Delfin Ganapin gives a vivid picture of how the government's environmental management capacity can and has been be strengthened in a developing country heavily constrained by foreign debt repayments and limited by technical and financial means. His paper highlights the crucial role of a democratic political structure in building a momentum in the society and within the public agencies towards improving the capacity to deal with environmental priorities. His approach is that of a policy maker who recognises the need to enlist broad support of, rather than confront, all parties involved in the application of environmental policies. After a overview of the Philippine economic and environmental situation, the main body of the paper (Part 3) discusses the specific ingredients of a programme to strengthen management capacity giving frequent examples from the experience of the Philippines. These include, creating a will on the part of the public and the government, securing the technical infrastructure, putting incentives in place, transforming the existing bureaucratic structures and traditions, etc. The conclusion suggests that making and implementing environmental policy in an increasingly more effective way in developing countries needs no further discussion of how difficult that is but essentially the commitment of highly capable and imaginative individuals.

1. Introduction

Environmental regulation in the Philippines started as almost a carbon copy of the US model. This is perhaps to be expected since the local environmental movement emulated the American environmental movement and has strong linkages with it. Early training in environmentally related courses as well as support consultancies in environmentally related projects also came from US institutions and agencies.

Over the years, however, experience has shown that unique Philippine situations call for equally unique environmental regulatory mechanisms. There are wide differences in the level of supportive resources and technology as well as in the socio-political milieu.

While linkages with US -- based environmental agencies and non-governmental organisations (NGOs) continue and have even expanded to embrace those of other countries especially in Europe and the ASEAN countries, the fact remains that the Philippines will have to adapt or create innovative environmental regulations that satisfy its peculiar circumstances.

2. Overview of the Philippine Situation

The Philippines is a country in transition. Whether it is developing, which connotes a positive transition, or not is debatable. What is clear is that compared to many industrialised countries of the West, the Philippines is economically underdeveloped.

Therefore, one of the country's foremost preoccupations is economic development. Unfortunately, past colonial exploitation and the more recent decade of dictatorship left the country with political and economic problems of crisis proportions. The Philippines is starting its recovery not from zero but from a negative balance sheet.

The country's massive foreign debt continues to grow, eating up almost half of the annual government budget in debt service, which is seen by some as an environmental problem in itself.

Funds shifted to servicing debt are taken away from basic services, one of which is environmental protection. About half of the operational budget of the Department of Environment and Natural Resources (DENR) cannot be met by local funds. Important environmental and natural resource conservation projects have to be supported by external grant or concessional loan sources. The DENR's Environmental Management Bureau laboratory, the focus of environmental research and monitoring, is housed in an old condemned building so shaky that sensitive balances do not give accurate readings when heavy vehicles pass by. Only half of the regional environmental units have laboratories, with incomplete equipment at that.

Much effort has already been expended to request additional budget from government, at least to meet the basic equipment and infrastructure requirements for environmental research, training and monitoring. Either there are no funds available or funds have to be allocated to economic projects given greater priority. The development of a well trained and well equipped environmental programme in the Philippines in the near future is thus largely dependent on external support.

The more problematic aspect of poverty, however, has to do with its effect on the population at large. Poverty makes immediate survival the dominant problem for people, forcing them to be destructive towards the very resources that sustain them. For the Philippines the numbers are staggering: an estimated 8 million slash-and-burn cultivators within forest lands. The rest of the 60 per cent of the population below the poverty line (more than 30 million people) ends up as dynamite and cyanide fishermen, small-scale miners, illegal loggers, garbage scavengers and slum-dwellers.

The government itself is being forced by economic prerogatives to compromise environmental priorities. It is often argued by those agencies and officials charged with promoting local and foreign investment that the Philippines cannot be too strict in its environmental regulations as it cannot afford to turn away or delay projects that could provide employment and raise much needed foreign exchange. Industrialisation is being aggressively pushed to meet the needs of the masses of people seeking employment. The numbers involved are again staggering, roughly an estimated million new job seekers a year.

With the push for industrialisation comes the demand for more energy projects. The push for geothermal and coal-fired power plants as well as other sources of energy is so aggressive that its planners have expressed in no uncertain terms their impatience with environmental impact assessment requirements.

The Philippines is trying to create a more democratic society and there have already been important strides in this direction. But political structures built over centuries cannot be reformed in a few years. A powerful elite segment of society still clings to traditional politics and in fact seeks to strengthen such a political system. As a result, much needed socio-economic reforms remain difficult to pursue. The ensuing political tug-of-war between traditionalists and reformers has turned the policy reform into a slow process. In the last three years, the Philippine Congress, because of continuous acrimonious debate has not been able to pass any one of the many environmental bills drafted for consideration.

The use of political influence to by-pass stringent regulatory procedures is still pursued by big business. In many cases, regulatory procedures get enmeshed in a complex array of political considerations. Getting the right decisions implemented requires playing the political game.

The whole political field is made much more complicated by the actions of a disgruntled right wing of the military establishment. There have already been six military coup attempts. While all of these attempts failed to wrest political power, every one has caused further economic deterioration and has weakened government resolve to make the needed radical reforms.

On the positive side there is the flowering of an environmental movement in the Philippines. Only in the last several years there have been hundreds of new environmental NGOs formed all over the country. Many of the major developmental NGOs and civic organisations have also started incorporating environmental programmes into their activities. The media, from print to radio and television, has begun to give greater attention to environmental concerns. Media personalities such as popular movie stars and singers have joined the environmental cause.

The increase in the number of environmental NGOs is not without problems. All of them demand special attention. All of them demand that they and the concerns they espouse be given priority.

In many cases this is problematic. For one, governmental agencies are not equipped with enough manpower, equipment and budgetary resources to deal simultaneously with all of the concerns raised by hundreds of environmental NGOs. In some cases, governmental employees do not have the experience and the inclination to deal with what they perceive as noisy, emotional environmental activists. There is a wide gap between public expectations and government capability at both the technical and the psychological levels.

In truth, many NGOs and environmental activists, for lack of training and experience, see environmental issues in a simplistic manner. In certain cases the problem is contextualised in a highly localised setting. Thus, they expect solutions to come easily. Government, on the other hand, tends to take sometimes too rational a view that is biased in favour of broader national considerations.

An additional problem also has to do with separating the genuine environmentalists from those riding on the growing environmental awareness for business and political purposes. NGOs have been hastily organised to be able to catch the growing number of negotiated contracts reserved for NGOs. Defeated political candidates as well as those hoping to run for the next elections have joined community protests and coalitions on controversial environmental issues. While they get free newspaper or television space, their dramatics often befuddle the facts and confuse the issues involved.

3. Towards an Effective Regulatory Mechanism

The effort at developing effective environmental regulations in the Philippines began in the late 1970s with the formation of the National Environmental Protection Council and the National Pollution Control Commission. At the time the country's environmental movement was still young and thus could not provide enough pressure for more stringent environmental laws. The authoritarian government of the time also made the implementation of environmental laws a subject of power politics. As a result, certain basic environmental laws exist but without good precedents of implementation to guide future decisions. The situation is made even more difficult by the fact that many environmental regulations contain only general principles and do not yet have problem-specific operational guidelines. As the country marches towards democratisation with an increasingly conscious and vigilant citizenry, there still remains a lot to be done as regards efforts to develop effective environmental mechanisms.

Present efforts can be grouped according to the following strategies. For presentation purposes they are discussed separately although in actual practice, each one complements and strengthens the others.

3.1 Developing Public and Government Political Will

The development and implementation of environmental regulations can only be as strict as the willingness of society to abide by them. Lack of political will has always been identified as a key reason for the non-implementation of good environmental regulations. The development of a strong political will to make and accept difficult environmental decisions therefore forms the basis for environmental regulation.

For a poverty stricken country like the Philippines, even a small increase in outlays is a serious sacrifice to the government and the public. For certain businesses it could mean bankruptcy. The costs may even be cultural and psychological in nature. While laws exist against slash-and-burn cultivation and against fishing in marine reserves, farmers and fishermen reason that they and their forefathers have done these types of resource exploitation since time immemorial. For every improvement in environmental quality, there will definitely be some cost involved. The question is whether those sectors of society that will be affected are willing to bear such costs.

The massive destruction of certain resources will necessitate radical solutions. With less than a million hectares of virgin forests left, the Philippines is considering a total ban on logging. Without the support of the communities within and adjacent to forest areas, the military, powerful politicians and even the loggers themselves, such a total ban could only lead to increased illegal logging and smuggling as prices of wood skyrocket. For these types of radical solutions, no less than total support from all sectors of society is needed.

The effort at developing political will for environmental protection in the Philippines has taken several complementary approaches. Basically, these efforts involve public environmental education and the provision of higher political/legal authority in the implementation of environmental protection strategies.

Environmental education programmes, using all available forms of modern and traditional mass media, both from government and the NGOs, are increasingly being put on line. The main message is that environmental protection is now a matter of survival and not only from an ecological perspective but also from an economic and political one. The Church and some NGOs have even raised environmental protection to the level of a religious duty. As the public develops such awareness and in the process strengthens their commitment to make the necessary sacrifices, environmental regulations can be more strictly implemented. It was in this way that the Department of Environment and Natural Resources was able to get away, without too much protest from the affected public, with its imposition of very stiff fines for smoke-belching.

Protests from environmentally aware communities have also enabled government to utilise its full potential as mediator and judge of pollution cases. Such protests make even the most politically influential business concerns abide by the procedures and decisions of the government's environmental agency. The alternative for business is a long, drawn out fight with communities and NGOs, putting its public image at stake and risking violence.

The strength of environmental commitment does not have to be developed from an emotional angle. For some sectors of society such as the business community and the country's development planners, the emotional approach taken by grassroots NGOs is considered irrational. The support of such segments of society should thus be recruited using their own language of rationality. This means using economic arguments for environmental protection. Studies that show that certain environmental regulations over certain areas and activities actually redound to overall economic benefit have been very useful in convincing an otherwise uncooperative segment of society. The incorporation of environmental considerations in the national system of accounts would go a long way in dispelling the misconception that environmentalism is a concern fit only for radicals.

The provision of greater legal authority to responsible units of the government, and even to NGOs, as well as upgrading the environmental guidelines of line agencies into basic national legislation have been helpful. The issuance of an Executive Order creating a special Pollution Adjudication Board with the power to issue *ex parte* closure orders to polluting firms has made the implementation of pollution control laws much easier. When the evidence is strong that air or water quality standards have been violated, the Pollution Adjudication Board can immediately order closure of the pollution source without going through lengthy court hearings. Reconsideration of that decision is made only when the polluting firm commits itself to solving the pollution problem, by showing specific pollution control plans and by filing a surety bond equivalent to 25 per cent of the total cost of setting up the pollution control facility. The tendency is for the polluting firm to hurry up with the solution of the problem, or at least committing itself to such a solution, because to do otherwise means continued closure. In the past there was no such authority and the practice of polluting firms was to lengthen hearings with legal technicalities. As such, hearings as well as the pollution, continued for years.

With the advent of the Philippine Congress the task of creating the needed environmental legislation was passed on to the Senate and the House of Representatives. Environmental legislation passed by Congress is important because it has permanency and a higher level of authority than regulations created by the administrative orders of agencies. Regulations and guidelines passed by executive agencies would most likely change after the election of a new President or Cabinet.

A piece of Congressional legislation is an expression of political will at the higher levels of government. It will help settle questions of authority and even interpreting which decisions are more important in the implementation of environmental regulations. This is especially important given the fact that the authoritarian Marcos government had the power and the penchant for creating bodies with overlapping jurisdictions during its time. Unfortunately, the Philippine Congress, saddled as it is with too many priorities is too slow in enacting the needed environmental legislation. In three years, numerous bills have been filed but none has been passed yet. The environmental agency and supportive NGOs have also to be constantly vigilant to assure that environmental legislation does not become too compromised.

3.2 Strengthening the Human and Technological Infrastructure

The Philippines, compared to many developed countries, is a relative newcomer to the environmental field. Currently, the academic institutions that are supposed to provide the training grounds for professional environmental officers are just starting to develop their environmental science programmes. So far, no academic institution is yet ready to offer graduate courses beyond the master of science level in the field of environmental science and management. There is also no such thing as a B.S. in Environmental Science. The few good environmental experts the Philippines has were the ones who were able to avail of academic grants or scholarships for specialised training and graduate studies abroad. Until of late there was very little of this type of training.

The Philippines therefore has a dire shortage of environmental professionals. In the Environmental Impact Assessment (EIA) section of the Environmental Management Bureau, for example, a sensitive section that receives as many as 150 submissions a month for review, there are only 10 full-time staff. Only three had some sort of formal training in EIA, the rest have obtained their training through actual practice.

This lack of highly trained professionals was further exacerbated by the regionalisation of the environmental management service. The country now has a full spread of offices for environmental management but the pool of trained professionals that was formerly centralised is now too thinly spread. In one region, for example, of five provinces where pollution cases are rampant, there are not more than three truly qualified persons to carry out the proper work on environmental education, monitoring and problem-solving.

There is also a strong need to develop a capability to handle environmental regulatory activities at the community level, especially for those communities adjacent to potentially pollutive activities. A general awareness of problems is not enough. That has been found to create public frustration as it leads to increased demands for a cleaner environment but does not give the public the necessary ability to respond positively on their own. Affected communities thus become dependent on government response which by itself is seriously limited by lack of needed resources. The focus should be not only on getting communities to learn to spot environmental problems but also to act on them.

For both government and the public, there must develop an adequate level of literacy regarding environmental regulations. Too often, complaints cannot readily lead to decisive action by regulatory agencies because of legal infirmities in the complainants', and sometimes in the government's investigation and preparation. Charges of dilly-dallying and collusion are hurled by the public when cases grind slow not knowing that such infirmities or serious legal complexities exist. In such cases, resolutions are made more difficult as the public becomes non-co-operative or worse, easily succumbs to the machinations of those who have personal or political interests in seeing that controversies continue.

There should also be training for members of the business community. Too often their resistance to environmental regulations stem from an ignorance of such regulations. Lack of knowledge regarding available technology for solving environmental problems creates an irrational fear of environmental regulations. The Philippines is trying to correct the situation by requiring industrial firms to assign duly accredited pollution control officers which would be required to undergo periodic training on environmental regulations and developments in environmental protection technology.

The most difficult skill to learn, but one that should be developed in those involved in implementing environmental regulation, is that of arbitration and negotiation. The many considerations to be taken into account before decisions on controversial environmental issues could be made require that conflicts be resolved through a conflict resolution process. Government officials, community and NGO leaders and representatives of the business community should be given a good basic foundation in the principles of conflict resolution followed by a continuous strengthening of theory through actual practice.

A crash training programme is necessary. Learning from those countries more advanced in regulatory experience could enrich such training. There is no way by which this crash training could be done by one government agency alone. Allied government agencies should initiate their own in co-ordination with the Environmental Management Bureau. Existing academic and other training institutions which have already started their environmental programmes should also be strengthened and utilised.

The technological infrastructure for environmental monitoring, a most critical aspect of existing environmental regulations dependent on the measurement of deviations from set standards, is also lacking. Much of the equipment is due to be retired. Even for very basic equipment only half of the fourteen regional offices have been able to set it up in a semblance of a laboratory. Some reports that come in are thus based on visual observations. Such observations, however, are useless for adjudicatory purposes since laws call for quantitative measurements. Visual monitoring may serve to warn. But it falls short even at this since many pollutants become "visible" only when the pollution has become very serious.

The acquisition of enough top-of-the-line environmental monitoring equipment is only one aspect of the solution. Such equipment must be complemented with properly constructed laboratory rooms and buildings, the right vehicles for transport, and local capability for effective use and for proper repairs and maintenance. Another consideration is the performance and hardiness of the equipment to be acquired given the difference in climatic conditions between the receiving and exporting countries. In the Philippines, electrical power fluctuations must be considered specially in the acquisition of sensitive equipment.

One direction the Philippines is taking is the acquisition of top-of-the-line automatic monitoring equipment. The present system of sending government staff to sample and analyze air and water effluents entails too much time and resources that government does not have. Such monitoring is also prone to graft and corruption.

Another direction is the computerisation of data management. This will allow easy storage and retrieval of the expected deluge of data as monitoring is intensified. Computerisation is also seen as an anti-graft and corruption measure. It would allow a more intensified tracing of cases and their proper documentation. An access code system could also prevent unauthorised storage and retrieval of sensitive data. In the case of plans to improve the EIA system, user friendly computer programs are being developed to help laymen review or conduct EIAs.

A programme to strengthen the use of remote sensing, an important monitoring strategy for a country of scattered and often inaccessible islands, is on-going. This involves use of satellite imagery and small-format aerial photography for specific uses such as the environmental programme in Palawan. A supportive Geographic Information System is also being developed using regional pilot areas.

3.3 Organising Networks and Linkages

The practice of passing piecemeal environmental protection regulations according to sectoral concerns has resulted in the implementation of these regulations being placed under different agencies. While much of the authority over protection of the environment has been placed under the Department of Environment and Natural Resources, other agencies were able to retain management over key ecosystems. The Department of Agriculture, through its Bureau of Fisheries and Aquatic Resources, has jurisdiction over marine areas except marine parks and mangroves. Environmental protection over a large part of Metro Manila is under the Laguna Lake Development Authority since the watersheds and surroundings airsheds of Laguna Lake and not just the lake itself form part of the area under its management mandate. Zoning regulations are under the Housing and Land Use Regulatory Board. Analysis of the body of laws that can be interpreted as environmentally related shows that there are many other agencies involved as well.

There is no alternative to coordinating and establishing agreements for joint efforts. To solve the problem of jurisdictional overlaps that have led to delay, which in turn has caused endorsement of public complaints to other agencies, memoranda of agreement have been signed between the DENR and the Laguna Lake Development Authority authorising joint investigations and resolutions of pollution cases.

Similar efforts are being started for agencies involved in processes of issuing permits, including those for permits not directly related to environmental regulations. The Department of Tourism and the DENR, for example, have agreed that the former will withhold permits allowing tourism development activities such as resort construction until the latter provides the proponent the required Environmental Clearance Certificate. A similar agreement has been reached with the National Economic and Development Authority. Major government and private projects will not be given endorsements for funding until such projects have gone through the EIA process and have been given an Environmental Clearance Certificate. Major donor institutions such as the Asian Development Bank, the World Bank, USAID and OECF are likewise implementing a similar policy.

There are at least two very clear advantages to all this. The government's environmental agency is relieved of the burden of guarding against the implementation of many projects that could have a negative impact on the environment. Since many of the supportive agencies and institutions deal with projects at the planning level, corrections can be made at an earlier stage before government and private proponents could sink in substantial investments.

The organisation of networks and linkages for environmental protection is of course part and parcel of the effort to develop a strong political will for environmental protection. Such networking provides the necessary organisational structure to create and wield political will in an organised and constructive manner. Resources can be pooled. Areas or concerns where the environmental agency have no jurisdiction can still be managed through the authority of the linked agency or institution.

Linking with affected communities through their leaders, support for NGOs and local government officials is a must. Communities directly bear the costs of environmental degradation and should thus be heard for practical and ethical reasons. The experience so far shows that local residents are able to identify problems and observations that escape experts sent to investigate and resolve cases.

The importance of linkages with the business community in the implementation of environmental regulations has been shown in the critical support they are giving to a rivers revival programme in Metro Manila. The creation of VOICE (Voluntary Organization of Industries for Cleaner Environment) along the Navotas-Malabon-Tullahan-Tenejeros rivers has helped the government in creating an awareness about the need for immediately stopping the discharge of pollutants into the river. This has taken the edge off the very strict implementation of closures and penalties on polluting firms. Having accepted their responsibility for cleaning up the river, the resistance of industrial firms to the necessary impositions of government has decreased. There are still some which use political pressure, threats and bribery but they have been reduced to a manageable number.

A task force of key business leaders and government has also been formed. These responsible business leaders have offered what they are good at: organisation of profitable ventures, marketing of ideas and products and the raising of funds or capital. The business community is recognised as having a pool of funds and expertise much larger than that of the government. This could substantially expand the government's environmental protection capability by direct infusion of such resources or indirectly by lessening government regulatory burdens through such strategies as self-environmental code of conduct for industries.

Linkages with academic institutions, especially those with environmental programmes and laboratories, have been also been developed. The mutual objective of the linkages is the expansion of training programmes, provision of EIA technical review support for regional offices, and the inter-calibration of laboratories for multipartite monitoring.

It also has to be emphasized that the ease with which environmental regulations can be implemented depends on factors outside the traditional concept of environmental protection. It is virtually impossible to require people not to burn forests or use dynamite fishing when to do so would mean hunger for themselves and their families. It is very difficult to require small companies to set up pollution control facilities if to do so would mean immediate bankruptcy. Factors arising out of the people's extreme poverty must be dealt with by socio-economic programmes that are normally under the purview of development-oriented agencies and business organisations. They have to be linked to the efforts of environmentally-oriented agencies. This is a requirement of the now popular sustainable development approach, one that developing countries cannot help but follow.

For the Philippines, efforts at this have been initiated through the development of a Philippine Strategy for Sustainable Development or PSSD. Cabinet level approval was sought to force the traditionally individualistic executive agencies to co-ordinate with others in shifting their present and future programmes so as to be supportive of the principles and strategies of the PSSD. The critical aspect of PSSD operationalisation, however, will be in transforming its general strategies into agency-relevant policy reforms and incorporating the shifts into each agency's annual and medium term budgetary submission.

It is clear that what is to be done to protect the Philippine environment is beyond existing capabilities. The problem is that for certain environmental concerns, the need for solutions is very urgent and cannot wait for the slow type of regulatory developments the country is capable of. The only recourse is to request support from external institutions.

In addition, external linkages have worked well as a component of an early warning system regarding trans-boundary pollution, such as attempts to dump toxic and hazardous wastes. Linkages in the ASEAN region between each country's environmental agency is leading to a greater sharing of knowledge and resources and the harmonization of approaches and methodologies. External linkages should be strengthened to provide a comprehensive approach to regulatory practices beyond the local context.

3.4 Strengthening Preventive Approaches

Environmental regulations in the Philippines are especially weak in preventive approaches. Copying environmental regulations from other countries has created a body of legislation consisting of regulation at the operations level rather than at the planning stage. Perhaps one difficulty with developing regulations at the planning stage is that they require more difficult projective techniques and skills. One also deals with potential violations rather than actual ones which are much easier to establish.

Preventive regulations also require the development of certain basic tools or materials. The Environmental Impact Assessment system of the Philippines, the country's key preventive approach, exemplifies this. The Philippine EIA system is based on the identification of environmentally critical activities and sites. The listing of environmentally critical activities is clear and straightforward. For environmentally critical sites, however, the listing does not include clear delineations. There is a need for the identification and clear delineation of such sites, if possible down to the smallest planning units, to guide planners and the country's environmental officers as to which activities, because of their siting, must be required to pass through the EIA process.

An effort in ecoprofiling is therefore needed. Basically, the concept is similar to land use planning and zoning but adds more ecological parameters as decision points in assigning use of environmental resources. Some attempts are now being started on developing a methodology for assessing carrying capacities. A Strategic Environmental Plan for the province of Palawan was developed using ecoprofiling and carrying capacity assessments and is now pending in the Philippine Congress as an environmental bill. More of these types of work are needed within the immediate future.

A proposal is also being developed for industrial restructuring. The basic concept is that if industries are restructured so that the proper pollution control considerations are integrated into the process and construction of facilities, and not as an add on forced upon them, then industries can easily abide by environmental regulations in a cost effective manner. This is very important especially for those pollutive industries that are still using old and outdated industrial technology.

Another preventive approach under consideration refers to agreements against pollution transfer from developed countries to developing ones. Such transfers can occur as developed countries, due to pressures from a more environmentally aware public and their rapid development of clean technology, dispose of the more pollutive aspects of production and of old machinery. Developing countries like the Philippines, given their serious economic problems, are most susceptible to accepting such transfers.

The problem is that the Philippines does not yet have clear guidelines as well as mechanisms for dealing with such pollution transfers. Even now, banned products easily escape scrutiny by relevant government bodies and are dumped in Philippines markets. The absence of protective guidelines and mechanisms cannot, however, be used as an excuse for such dumping or transfer. It is now increasingly being argued that exporting countries should utilise their own strict and high level set of standards and rules in such transactions. The development of agreements to deal with this matter is of high priority. Efforts at improving environmental regulations become useless when controls are strong for locally sourced pollution but weak for externally sourced pollution.

3.5 Creating Incentives

Environmental regulations are best implemented when those who are the subject of regulation voluntarily abide by them. For such a situation to occur, there must be clear advantages and profit for supporting environmental regulations. Penalties, in a developing country situation, are becoming too costly not only on the part of the business community but also on the part of government. Penalties are disincentives that a government desperate for investments can ill afford. Environmental regulations should therefore contain substantial incentive mechanisms.

Environmental protection in the Philippines, because of the lack of locally available expertise and technology, is very expensive. The tendency of industry is to economise and this often leads to inadequate pollution control facilities. One possibility to get industry to abandon this practice is the promulgation of a policy recognising industrial firms investing in the latest pollution control technology or spending substantial investments for environmental protection as pioneer firms with the right to enjoy specific tax incentives, credit support and technical assistance.

Incentives are also psychological necessities in a situation where certain firms or activities are caught while the majority go free. This will be a reality which has to be faced until the country acquires enough resources to increase its environmental manpower complement and upgrade its monitoring equipment. If those caught are forced to construct pollution control facilities but in exchange are given tax incentives, then the sense of unfairness is dispelled or at least minimised.

There is also a preponderance of small businesses causing pollution in the Philippines. Without incentives they cannot set up the necessary facilities to meet environmental quality standards. But perhaps the more difficult problem has to do with artisanal fishermen, small scale miners and slum dwellers who are forced by a desperate need to survive to be destructive of their environment. They need incentives in the form of alternative livelihood systems to shift away from their presently destructive practices.

One successful incentive system is the practice of giving a certain percentage of the value of logs confiscated from illegal loggers to the source of information that led to the confiscation. What could have been purely a risk is counterbalanced by the profits from the reward system. The only problem with this approach is that it appeals mostly to people's mercenary values, the same values that promote illegal logging and other environmentally destructive practices.

Incentives that cater to and strengthen positive values should therefore be developed. The giving of awards for the most pollution control conscious industrial firm, for example, can reinforce the environmentally positive values of that firm's owners and managers. It is important, however, that the prestige attached to such awards be maintained by making such awards highly selective and recognised by what society considers as prestigious institutions.

One other possible incentive for the business sector is support for the growth of local firms that specialise in environmental technology. Government could privatise many aspects of its monitoring and technical assistance work to stimulate such growth.

3.6 Searching for Relevant Methods and Approaches

There has come a realisation that certain unique situations exist in the Philippines that render straight copies of environmental methods and approaches from western developed countries difficult or even counterproductive to implement. There is a need to adapt rather than adopt.

In the training of local environmental professionals it is now being realised that a good grounding in the realities of the Philippine situation, from the biophysical and technological to the socio-economic and political, is necessary. Training programmes and trainers, especially those that come from external technical assistance, must have the same strong grounding. Too often, trainees are sent abroad and learn what is ideal and come home only to be disappointed. Training programmes and technical assistance should have strong components for priming foreign experts and counterpart trainees about the need to adapt to local conditions and limitations as well as contain planning strategies that could help overcome some of those limitations.

The immediate problem has something to do with the lack of introspective analysis of environmental situations and capabilities at the country level. There are strong feelings of what the country lacks but not yet at the level where an operational plan pinpointing critical interventions for each unit of the environmental agency and allied agencies involved, at the national and regional levels, can be developed and implemented. This has to be developed if the Philippines is to be deliberate and effective in its efforts to improve the situation. This is also needed if Philippine partnerships with foreign institutions are to result in relevant projects and programmes.

The search for relevance is also hampered by the lack of even basic research on ecosystems that have to be protected. Environmental regulations regarding river pollution, for example, depend on river classification and characterisation. Yet only about half of the total number of major rivers in the country have been classified as to best use. Many of those that are in the classified category have not even been properly characterised as regards parameters related to flushing or dilution capacities. Standards thus set, either locally set or borrowed, are basically on an experimental basis. Basic research and monitoring, ideally on the basis of highly localised situations, must therefore be a major activity if environmental regulations are to be made more relevant.

Relevance also has something to do with the mind set. Environmental regulations to be relevant must not only truly protect the environment but must be seen by all sectors involved as truly protective. It has thus become important that refinements or reforms in environmental regulations take a highly consultative approach. As most of those that are to be potentially affected belong to the grassroots and are laymen, the search for relevant environmental regulations should include the transformation of legal and highly technical language into forms that the layman could easily understand. Community organising and pre-consultation groundwork have been found to be important in creating the environment for informed decision-making.

Some examples of shifts toward more relevant approaches include the organisation of communities for multipartite monitoring around destructive or potentially destructive activities. A people-powered system is being set up rather than a system based on sophisticated technology which the Philippines does not yet have. Another approach is passing the expense of monitoring to the firms being monitored since government cannot come up with sufficient resources to do this on its own. The set-up, however, has to involve automatic monitoring equipment sealed against manipulation, with regular periodic validation of readings by the government environmental agency or an accredited third party of experts.

3.7 Streamlining the Bureaucracy

One of the important directions in improving the effectiveness of environmental regulations is to make bureaucratic processes so easy to follow that it becomes definitely more advantageous to do so than to resort to legal contests and the traditional use of political influence, threats and bribery. A first step in this direction is decentralisation of environmental services. Some of the capable environmental staff have been taken from their central assignments and sent to regional offices. Training programmes are being speeded up to further build regional capability. The next phase will be to build capability at the provincial and community levels. In the long run, applicants and project proponents will not have to travel to a distant Manila to get necessary permits and clearances. It is also hoped that with decentralisation, environmental regulations can be handled with more dispatch and relevance by locally based environmental units.

Decentralisation efforts, however, have to be supported by simplification efforts. This is important at the initial stage when local units are still building up their capability and support resources. Regulatory decisions must therefore be categorised in terms of difficulty and complexity of procedures. Authority over the easiest and more local ones have been immediately given to local units. The more difficult ones will follow in line with the progress in capacity building of the local units. In the Philippine EIA process, for example, the review for small sand and gravel mining and the provision of the environmental compliance certificate have been given to the regional offices. In addition, the EIA procedure has been transformed into a simple matter of answering a checklist of questions.

The existing Philippine bureaucracy for environmental protection may be bloated at the central level but is actually very much understaffed at the local levels, especially considering the dire lack of training and equipment. It therefore could not act quickly on complaints or requests for support. Massive backlogs also reduce the efficiency of work and cause the regulatory units to lose credibility. A strategy that has had some initial success is the deputisation of responsible local government officials, NGOs and community leaders. Emphasis must, however, be on the term "responsible" as the transfer of authority could easily be abused and utilised for selfish ends.

Streamlining the bureaucracy is never complete without an aggressive campaign against graft and corruption. A salary standardisation programme that increased salaries in the hope that this would be an incentive for more efficient graft-free work has already been implemented. But such economic incentives are never enough. Basic values must change. This could be initiated by providing officials and employees alike a proper vision of where their work and that of their organisation should lead. There must be a clear understanding of the importance of their work, no matter how small, within the context of the country's serious economic and political problem and comprehensive efforts to do something about them. Better monitoring and documentation of decisions made on every case, the participation of NGOs and community leaders to provide checks and balances, and a strict implementation of anti-graft regulations are also needed.

3.8 Managing a Transition Period

The Philippine situation cannot for now afford radical shifts in regulatory policies. Poverty in its many senses is such that even small shifts entail major costs and sacrifices. Old practices and those that have benefited from them are still so well entrenched that their full transformation will require efforts beyond present capabilities.

A transition period is required. The management of this transition period is perhaps the most challenging task faced by Filipino environmentalists today. This difficult task requires that compromises be made but never to such a point that public welfare is unduly sacrificed or that ecosystem values suffer irreversible damage. It also requires a balancing act that takes into account various interlinkages and manipulates these interlinkages so that their sum always ends up positive for the environment.

The water quality standards for industrial effluents in the Philippines have been set so that the initial year's values are the lowest that can reasonably be agreed upon with the proviso that such values will progressively be more stringent in succeeding years until the ideal standards are reached. A jump to an ideal set of standards within the initial year would have meant closures of many industrial firms and a massive unemployment problem. Without such a transition strategy, improvement of the old water quality standards as well as others now on line will be practically impossible as the resistance from the industry sector, economic planners and political decision-makers would be too great.

A hotly debated issue in this transition period is what to do with the many firms and project proponents that have not followed environmental regulations, out of ignorance or ineffectiveness of the old system, but are now willing to abide by it. They are already required to pay enormous penalties if strict legal interpretation of the law is used. Yet to do so would again mean massive closures and serious economic and political problems. One idea is to set up an amnesty programme that provides forgiveness in exchange for commitments for rehabilitation and the establishment of pollution control facilities.

Ideally, environmental regulations should be seen and implemented in an integrated approach. Integrated approaches, however, are always conceptually difficult to grasp. It is also operationally difficult to get all sectors and needed resources together. Enough time must be given for certain prerequisites to be developed. Critical activities will have to be phased and organised in the proper sequence.

4. Conclusion

The effectiveness of environmental regulations in the Philippines cannot be taken out of the context of the social, economic and political conditions of the country. Improving the effectiveness of environmental regulations should therefore take a comprehensive approach. Improvements must be initiated not just on the regulatory aspects of environmental management but on others as well including even those that relate to economic development.

Sustainable development forms the philosophical framework for environmental regulation in the Philippines. With this, regulations have to be developed in such a way that they are supportive of both environment and development. This is very much like walking a tightrope.

Environmental practitioners must therefore be highly capable. They must be equipped not only with the proper technique but perhaps more importantly with the art of dealing with often complex social and political factors. Given the limitations and difficulties at hand, such practitioners must be imbued with a strong sense of mission and a willingness to make sacrifices for the sake of the future.

New efforts towards improving the effectiveness of environmental regulations in the Philippines are now much greater in number and magnitude than all efforts of previous years combined. But even that is not enough. The process must be speeded up through recruitment of local support, and where possible, of external assistance. External assistance, however, to be truly useful should recognise the uniqueness of Philippine conditions and join the search for relevant answers.

COUNTRY ENVIRONMENTAL STUDIES
A FRAMEWORK FOR ACTION

by

Walter Arensberg *

---

* Deputy Director, Center for International Development and Environment, World Resources Institute (WRI).

RÉSUMÉ

Au cours de la dernière décennie, les études par pays portant sur l'environnement (CES) sont devenues des instruments largement utilisés pour promouvoir une meilleure gestion de l'environnement et des ressources naturelles (ENR) dans les pays en développement. A mesure que l'on prenait conscience dans le monde entier des problèmes critiques liés à la dégradation de l'environnement, un nombre croissant de gouvernements de pays en développement, de donneurs internationaux et d'ONG se sont servis de ces études pour identifier et analyser les problèmes écologiques et pour définir de nouvelles stratégies en vue d'un développement durable. Vu leur popularité, le moment est venu de nous interroger sur ces études, de faire le point de nos connaissances. Est-on d'accord sur ce que devraient être les objectifs, la portée et la structure organique d'une étude nationale sur l'environnement ? Avons-nous une idée de ce qu'est la bonne méthode pour effectuer ces études ? Quel a été leur degré d'efficacité ? Comment peut-on les améliorer ? L'exposé est divisé en quatre parties. Tout d'abord, l'auteur fait le point de l'information existante sur le nombre et sur les types d'études réalisées ces dernières années puis, dans la deuxième partie, il donne une première évaluation de ces études, à partir des études de cas effectuées et d'un commentaire documenté. La troisième partie fait le point des connaissances en matière d'études par pays sur l'environnement, analysant ce que l'on considère être la bonne pratique dans ce domaine. Enfin, la dernière partie étudie les mesures qui pourraient être prises ensuite pour évaluer l'efficacité de ces études.

SUMMARY

During the last decade, Country Environmental Studies (CES) have become widely used instruments for fostering improved environment and natural resource (ENR) management in developing countries. As the critical problems associated with environmental degradation have gained worldwide recognition, a growing number of developing country governments, international donors, and NGOs have used CES to identify and analyze environmental issues and define new strategies for sustainable development. In light of their popularity, this is an opportune moment to ask what we know about the state-of-the-art of Country Environmental Studies. Is there a common understanding of what the objectives, the scope, and the organisational structure of a CES should be? Do we have a sense of what constitutes good practice in carrying them out? How effective have CES been? How can they be improved? The paper is divided into four sections. Following a review of existing information on the number and types of CES that have been prepared in recent years, Section 2 offers a preliminary assessment of CES, drawing from existing case studies and informed commentary. Section 3 presents the state of the art in CES, reviewing what is generally regarded as good practice in the conduct of these studies. And, the final section discusses what steps might be taken next to assess the effectiveness of Country Environmental Studies.

1. Background

The term Country Environmental Studies is designed to cover a variety of different types of studies that developing countries, donors, and NGOs have produced since the late 1970's. These include such studies as the World Bank's Environmental Action Plans, IUCN's National Conservation Strategies (NCS), USAID's Country Environmental Profiles, and others which share the common characteristics of being comprehensive, multi-sectoral analyses of national or regional environment and natural resources issues. According to the *Directory of Country Environmental Studies* (World Resources Institute 1990), over 220 CES of one type or another have been completed or were underway for 110 different countries during the last decade. Summary descriptions of the major types of CES appear in Part IV of the Directory. Individual descriptions of these are presented in Part III of the Directory, but it is useful here to categorise the types to clarify our understanding. Roughly, they fall into three general categories:

Comprehensive Multi-sectoral Studies. This is the category most commonly associated with CES. It covers the range of studies that are designed to foster sustainable development, identifying and analyzing environmental and natural resource issues and trends, and incorporating solutions to those issues into the country's planning, policy-making, and implementation for development. Some of these -- like the *Environmental Profiles* prepared by the Danish Department of International Development Co-operation (DANIDA) and the Dutch development assistance programme, the *Country Environmental Profiles* supported by the U.S. Agency for International Development (USAID); and the *State of the Environment Reports* (SOE) prepared by countries like India and Malaysia -- have concentrated primarily on descriptive assessment of environmental conditions and issues rather than on the development of strategic action plans. Others -- like the World Bank's *Environmental Action Plans* (EAP); the *National Conservation Strategies* promoted by the International Union for the Conservation of Nature and Natural Resources (IUCN); and, Canadian International Development Agency (CIDA)'s *Environmental Strategies* -- have embraced strategic proposals as well as descriptive analysis. These distinctions should not be drawn too strictly as the state of the art of CES is evolving rapidly and more and more supporters of CES view them as strategic planning processes and documents.

Sectoral Resource Assessments and Plans. CES falling into this general category may be similar in terms of organisation and methodology to those described above, but they concentrate on a single resource sector or issue such as forestry, marine resources, or biodiversity. Some examples of this type are the FAO's *Tropical Forestry Action Plans* and *Forest Sector Reviews*, the *Biological Diversity Profiles* of the World Conservation Monitoring Centre (WCMC), and the *Tropical Forest and Biological Diversity Assessments* conducted by USAID Missions in response to new requirements of the U.S. Foreign Assistance Act.

Special Regional Studies. This last category covers a number of CES that don't quite fit into the other two categories. These include CES which address a particular environmental problem in a broad geographic region, such as the *National Plans to Combat Desertification* of the CILSS and the Club du Sahel and the regional action plans to control marine pollution and manage marine and coastal resources supported by the United Nations Environment Program (UNEP)'s Regional Seas Program. The *Country Profiles* prepared by USAID's Office of Foreign Disaster Assistance can also be placed in this category.

Through a joint effort with the International Institute for Environment and Development (IIED) and the International Union for the Conservation of Nature and Natural Resources (IUCN), WRI will be up-dating the *Directory of Country Environmental Studies* during the coming year (1991).

2. Preliminary Assessment

Despite the numbers of CES that have been produced around the world, the information we have about their effectiveness is primarily impressionistic. At this point, no field-based, comparative evaluation of CES has been done, and all we have to draw from are several studies of individual cases and two general reviews prepared by the Center for International Development and Environment of the World Resources Institute and the Africa Region of the World Bank. These two reviews, however general, do offer some insights into the kinds of problems CES must overcome if they are to become more effective instruments for change.

The Center's CES Review

The Center for International Development and Environment of the World Resources Institute started its CES Review at the request of USAID's Bureau of Science and Technology, Office of Forestry, Environment and Natural Resources (S&T/FENR). Recognising an increased demand for Country Environmental Profiles and resource assessments from USAID missions, S&T/FENR wished to determine how effective past efforts had been and how they might be improved in the future. WRI's Center was asked to conduct the review because it had participated in or financially supported the preparation of a number of profiles and National Conservation Strategies through a Co-operative Agreement it maintains with S&T/FENR.

Purpose. The fundamental purpose of the CES Review was to help fashion new approaches to CES in the future. The review sought to address three broad objectives:

1. Identify the fundamental objectives and requirements which CES should be designed to achieve as perceived by international development assistance agencies, developing country governments, NGOs and other experts and practitioners dealing with the issue of sustainable development in developing countries.

2. Evaluate the state of the art of CES analyzing and comparing a selected number of them chosen from Latin America, Africa, and Asia to determine how effectively they met their objectives, how they were organised and conducted, how they were used and what impact they may have had.

3. Provide practical guidelines for the preparation of future CES to policy-makers, planners, managers, and researchers at donor agencies, and to developing country governments, NGOs, and other appropriate institutions.

Organisation. The organisation of the CES Review sought to involve academic experts, as well as practitioners in the study process. WRI's Center directed the project and formed a team composed of members of its own staff and collaborators from the Energy and Environmental Policy Center (EEPC) at Harvard University's Kennedy School of Government.

The EEPC group drew upon experts from Massachusetts Institute of Technology (MIT), as well as Harvard in the review process.

An informal Advisory Committee was also established to guide the work of the Center/EEPC team. It was composed of representatives from USAID, the World Bank, the Inter-American Development Bank, and the Canadian International Development Agency (CIDA). Representatives of the United Nations Development Programme (UNDP), the Economic Commission for Latin America, and the Organization of American States also participated in the review.

Study Process. The CES Review was based on a comparative assessment of six CES cases. The basic steps in the process involved selecting and developing the cases, doing a comparative analysis of them, and preparing final conclusions and recommendations.

The selection of the cases was based on considerations of variety in the type of CES, regional and geographic diversity, characteristics of the CES process, and availability and access to information and expertise on the CES. Two cases were selected from Latin America, Asia and Africa, each. They included:

1. *Dominican Republic: Country Environmental Profile* (July 1981);
2. *Natural Resources and Economic Development in Central America Regional Environmental Profile* (1987);
3. *Thailand Natural Resources Profile* (January 1989);
4. *National Conservation Strategy for Nepal* (1988);
5. *National Conservation Strategy for Zambia* (July 1985);
6. *Ruhengeri and its Resources: an Environmental Profile of the Ruhengeri Prefecture of Rwanda* (1987).

These cases were then assessed by interviewing experts who had participated in the CES. Although by no means comprehensive, the assessment questions examined issues related to the objectives of the CES, the process by which the CES was organised and conducted, the coverage and analytical content of the study, strategies for disseminating and using the CES, and the potential influence that the CES may have had on decision-making for natural resource management in the country. The results of this assessment were presented to a final brainstorming workshop of experts from Harvard, MIT, Canada's Institute for Research on Public Policy, and the organisations represented on the Advisory Committee. The findings and recommendations of the review were drawn up following this workshop.

Major Findings. The review was not designed to provide a definitive evaluation of the state of the art of CES and their impact on policy-making in developing countries. Such a study would have required looking at a broader sampling of different types of CES, and conducting extensive, in-depth comparative analysis and field surveys. Instead, the less ambitious approach described above, while not comprehensive or quantitative did offer relatively solid experience for making qualitative judgments about the CES cases. With this in mind, the outcome of the review should be viewed as the considered observations of informed experts rather than the conclusions of scientific surveys and field evaluations.

There are a number of general findings having to do with the overall success, organisation, and coverage that emerged from the review. In addition, some specific recommendations were identified that will be mentioned below and discussed further on in this paper in the section on good practice.

1. Even without the hard evidence of a field evaluation, the CES review concluded that the cases it covered had helped increase public awareness of environmental problems and contributed to improving environmental and natural resource policy and management in the countries they covered. In general, each in its own way, achieved what it intended to do.

For instance, the Country Environmental Profiles for Thailand and the Dominican Republic both had an immediate impact on the public policy debate in their respective countries. In the first case, the CEP defined the framework and established the information base for formulating resource management policy in Thailand. In the second case, the Dominican government used the Profile as an instrument for educating the public on environmental problems and as the basis for an integrated source of information on national trends and institutional issues.

The National Conservation Strategies for Zambia and Nepal also achieved their immediate objectives of establishing the framework for future conservation action. In both cases, the national governments endorsed the NCSs which had emerged from a highly participatory process of planning and analysis.

The other two CES covered by the review also appear to have been influential. The detailed survey, mapping, and environmental data base prepared for the Ruhengeri Prefecture established a new basis for natural resource planning and policy-making in that region, and became a critical element in the National Environmental Action Plan (NEAP) which the government of Rwanda is now developing with the assistance of the World Bank, USAID and other donors. The Regional Environmental Profile for Central America also had a significant influence on public discussion of environmental issues in that region. The report has provided the analytical and factual basis for USAID's Regional Natural Resource Management Strategy and is one of the main intellectual underpinnings of the new Central American Commission on Environment and Development. It has also been distributed widely among NGOs and government planners.

2. The CES covered by the review offered different ways of organising and managing the CES process. Although no case offered a perfect model, their collective experience does provide guidance for the future.

The structure of the two NCSs was quite similar, reflecting IUCN's long experience with the NCS process. In both cases, the structure drew heavily upon government sponsorship and participation in order to secure the long term commitment of government planners and policy-makers. Under the auspices of the appropriate ministries, special NCS Secretariats were established in both Nepal and Zambia. Guidance for the work of the secretariats was provided by Policy and Technical Advisory committees made up of government, NGO and private sector representatives. The Secretariat staff was very small leaving most of the technical work to be done by experts from other government agencies, the private sector and universities. In both cases a concerted effort was made to involve rural communities in the planning and analysis process by holding public meetings and discussion sessions in villages. The guiding principle behind the NCS approach was to create the conditions for government acceptance of the NCS by integrating appropriate officials into the process from the outset. It was also important that the NCS reflect the concrete concerns of the rural community. The public participation process was designed to achieve that aim as well.

The two CEPs took slightly different approaches. The Natural Resources Profile of Thailand was initiated by the National Environment Board of the Thai Ministry of Science, Technology and Energy, which, in turn, designated the Thailand Development Research Institute (TDRI) as the institution responsible for preparing the profile. TDRI is a research and policy analysis group. Although TDRI directed the study and drew on its own staff for technical work, it also enlisted the help of other government officials and scientists. Members of the National Environment Board, the Royal Irrigation Department, the Electricity Generating Authority, the Ministry of Agriculture and Co-operatives, and the Department of Labor and Health also were involved in the study. Public participation was through consultations with community representatives and NGOs rather than through village level meetings.

The case of the Dominican Republic reflected a more conventional approach. Under the general guidance of USAID and SURENA (the Under-secretariat for Natural Resources), a multidisciplinary team of expatriate consultants worked closely with Dominican counterparts to prepare the profile. The President of the Republic also took a keen interest in the profile once it was complete, urging his ministers to consider it as the basis for national policy. What public participation occurred was through the process of data gathering and analysis pursued by the team rather than through formal meetings. Along with many of the profiles prepared for USAID on Central American countries, the process followed in this case was the closest to a conventional consulting assignment.

The two regional profiles followed different paths, although, like the Dominican CEP, they were closely tied to USAID. The Ruhengeri Profile was prepared under the USAID sponsored Ruhengeri Resource Analysis and Management Project (RRAM) by a multidisciplinary team of expatriate and Rwandan experts. While the project was developed with the Rwandan Ministry of Agriculture and its Forestry Service, the forestry service apparently did not then give it as high a priority as other mainline forestry projects. However, it has become a key component of subsequent EAP work in Rwanda.

The Central American Regional Profile was initiated by the International Institute for Environment and Development (IIED) and USAID. Although the project did involve extensive collaboration and consultation with Central American and United States experts, the profile was compiled and written by one author with help from consultants. A technical review committee of Central American and US members did review the draft; and CATIE (the Central American Agricultural Research and Training Center) published and distributed Spanish versions of the final report. Aside from the quality of its analysis, the influence of the Central American Profile has been due primarily to the energetic efforts of USAID, IIED-North America (now WRI), and CATIE to promote it rather than to the way it was organised.

3. In general, the CES achieved their function as overview reports or profiles quite well. All of them contained thorough descriptive data on environmental and natural resources conditions and trends; and, to one degree or another, they each dealt with social and cultural factors effecting the use of natural resources, economic patterns of resource exploitation, and institutional responsibilities and barriers to effective resource management. For instance, the Thai Profile pays special attention to some of the economic, legal, and institutional dimensions of resource use; the Central American Regional Profile offers an insightful analysis of the relationship between economic growth and resource degradation; and the two NCSs, by design, detail the legislation that needs to be enacted to implement National Conservation Strategies in Nepal and Zambia.

Overall, however, little emphasis was given to in-depth analysis of basic policy issues. Even the NCSs, which were designed to produce legislative proposals, did not delve thoroughly into the analysis of alternative economic or institutional policies to achieve their aims. In the case of the NCS, this may be attributable to the fact that they are designed primarily to promote conservation strategies and did not emphasize other questions of sustainable development as much. The same type of analysis also is missing from the other CES. One reason for this is that most of the CES did not set out to be anything more than sophisticated overviews. Another may be that this kind of analysis often runs head on into delicate and controversial political questions. In the minds of the donors and the CES team, getting the environmental issues on the agenda in the first place may have been hard enough without burdening the discussion with volatile and often intractable political concerns.

4. One clear lesson to be drawn from all of these CES is that what happens after the CES is published is a vital concern. Even the product of a perfectly structured process may gather dust on a bookshelf if a well-thought out strategy is not in place to launch it into the public arena.

There are examples of different approaches to follow-up in each of the cases. In all instances, efforts were made to publish enough copies of the CES report to distribute it widely (in the local language, as well as English). Efforts also were made to provide the reports to the media and to feature them at conferences and workshops. As mentioned earlier, legislative proposals also were put forward as a result of the NCSs for Nepal and Zambia.

In one form or another, the sponsors of these CES also have sought to tie their recommendations to subsequent development assistance programmes. Multi-donor meetings were proposed following the completion of the Zambia and Nepal NCSs. The Thai Profile has been used by the government to shape current policy and programmes and it provided the substantive underpinnings for USAID's natural resource management programme for the country. And, finally, explicit steps were taken by USAID to use the Central American Regional Profile to substantiate the need for its major new resource management strategy for the area.

These kinds of follow-up activities can obviously make a CES markedly more effective. But what must be borne in mind is that the objectives and strategy for follow up need to be thought out early in the CES process. Without such forethought, the right amount of funding cannot be set aside, and, more important the CES process itself cannot be shaped to respond to opportunities that may arise for expanding its influence.

Recommendations. The recommendations of WRI's CES Review found their way into the guidance on good practices which the Working Party on Development Assistance and the Environment of the OECD's Development Assistance Committee recently published. They covered four general themes each of which is elaborated upon in the section of this paper on the state of the art. The first is that CES should be viewed as processes aimed at developing and implementing strategies for sustainable development. The second is that they should be organised in ways that enhance the opportunities for public sector and private sector participation, co-ordination and training in the process. Third, they should seek to define and implement policy reforms which will improve natural resource and environmental management. And, fourth, they should develop conscious outreach and follow-up programmes as part of long term strategies for promoting sustainable development. Many of these general themes are recognised now in the basic principles that shape the objectives, organisational structures, and processes of the World Bank's National Environmental Action Plans.

World Bank's NEAP Review

In April 1990, World Bank's Africa Region issued a preliminary review of its experience with National Environmental Action Plans. Its brief report, entitled *National Environmental Action Plans in Africa: Early Lessons and Future Directions* (AFTEN, Technical Department, Africa Region, 13th April 1990) defined the salient features of NEAPs and examined the effects they have had on environmental policy and management in those countries of the region where they have been completed. At that point, the NEAP process was underway in Rwanda, Ghana, Guinea, and Burkina Faso, and had been completed formally in Madagascar, Mauritius, and Lesotho. The report did not pretend to be comprehensive or definitive, but it did clarify the purposes and components of the NEAP process and some of the major results it appears to have produced to date.

Purpose. The purpose of an National Environmental Action Plan is to make environmental considerations an integral part of a country's planning and decision-making processes for national development. The premise underlying the NEAP process is that sustainable development can only be achieved once environmental and natural resource factors are viewed as a common element of all policy-making rather than separate elements imposed from outside. With this in mind, the NEAP process has a number of distinguishing features having to do with their organisation, the nature of the study process, and the role of the donor community.

NEAP Organisation. Above all, an NEAP is a process, rather than a final product. Although the specific analyses, reports and programmes that emerge from it are important, the primary aim of a NEAP is to structure a process for environmental planning, policy-making, and project implementation that involves the full gamut of public and private actors who have traditionally been part of the development process, as well as those who often have not, such as environmental NGOs and village level groups. The basic NEAP process is by definition multi-sectoral and highly participatory.

Although the structure of NEAPs have varied from country to country, they have generally had three common features:

1. A Steering Committee has been created to set and co-ordinate policy. This committee has involved non-governmental as well as governmental organisations;

2. A technical secretariat has been established to direct the work and ensure multi-sectoral co-ordination and participation;

3. Working groups have been formed to analyze specific sectoral and environmental issues. These groups have been drawn from NGOs and universities, as well as participating public agencies.

A fourth feature of the organisation is that the donor community-led in these cases by the World Bank -- has played an organised and active role from the beginning of the NEAP. The World Bank has provided a task manager to assist with donor co-ordination, various donors have provided funds and technical support to the process as it unfolded, and multi-donor round-tables have been held to co-ordinate investment policy and funding for countries that have completed their NEAP.

Study Process. The NEAP study is designed to be flexible and focus on those issues of highest priority to the country. As described in the AFTEN report, the process usually involves four basic phases of work:

1. Identification of critical environmental issues and a ranking of the priority to be given them;

2. Problem analysis and the formulation of alternative solutions;

3. Preparation of the NEAP report; and

4. Preparation of NEAP implementation strategies, including government action plans, the implementation of corrective measures in existing development projects, and new investment programs.

In the World Bank's experience to date, NEAPs have given considerable emphasis to examining the causes underlying environmental degradation. Although they have analyzed trends in deforestation, soil loss, desertification and other major issues confronting the countries involved, they have also sought to examine root causes such as population pressures on the land and the effects of traditional practices and governmental policies on natural resource management. Exploring these causal interrelationships has permitted the NEAP planners to formulate policy reform packages and new investment programmes that can correct existing disincentives for better natural resource management.

Although the scope of each NEAP has varied according to the issues prevailing in each of the countries, the NEAPs carried out to date have addressed a number of issues common to most African countries. These have included:

1. The need to establish environmental policy and incentives that embrace multiple sectors of the economy;

2. The need to develop effective institutions to formulate environmental policy, co-ordinate inter-governmental action, build environmental awareness in public agencies, involve NGOs and private sector interests, and maintain effective contact and co-ordination with local community organisations;

3. The need to create or strengthen a national capacity to carry out environmental assessments of policies and projects;

4. The need to establish environmental information and monitoring systems that are effectively tied to planning and decision-making processes; and,

5. The need to train human resources through increasing public understanding of environmental problems and developing specialised environmental training programmes for government and private sector personnel.

These common concerns have been treated with varying degrees of success by the countries involved in preparing NEAPs.

Results of the AFTEN Review

Recognising that the AFTEN Review was not a detailed ex-post evaluation, its findings, nevertheless, offer a preliminary assessment of the effectiveness of the NEAP process in Madagascar, Lesotho, and Mauritius, the three countries in which NEAPs have been completed. The review also draws some examples from the other countries in which NEAPs are now underway.

Increased Environmental Awareness. The process of developing NEAPs has increased awareness of the importance of environmental issues on the part of governmental officials, leaders of the private sector, NGOs, community groups, and the public, in general. This has been a direct result of the conferences, workshops, media coverage, and community consultations involved in the process, as well as of the experience government personnel have gained from working on specific NEAP studies.

Strengthened Environmental Policy and Institutions. In each of the countries, the NEAP has generated new environmental policies and institutions. Lesotho, Mauritius, and Madagascar have adopted new comprehensive national policies, and each country also has adopted sectoral policies for coastal resources, pollution, biodiversity, and land use which have explicit environmental purposes. Environmental protection is one of the specific objectives of Lesotho's new National Settlements Policy. Each of these countries has also established new institutions, such as a ministry or inter-governmental co-ordinating commission to deal with issues of environmental policy formulation and programme co-ordination. In all these cases, the NEAPs have called for new environmental legislation and changes in existing legislation.

Environmental Assessments. The NEAPs also produced new governmental requirements calling for environmental assessments of new development projects. Training programs to increase local capabilities for carrying out these projects have also been instituted as a result of the NEAPs.

Development of Human Resources. The NEAPs have also offered a vehicle through which local ministerial staff, representatives from NGOs, community leaders and local professionals could be trained and/or gain experience with environmental issues and analytical methodologies. Leaving a competent staff in place to implement its initiatives is one of the main objectives of the NEAP process.

Strengthened Local NGOs. One of the clearest achievements of the NEAPs in Madagascar and Lesotho, as well as Rwanda and Ghana is the degree to which it involved non-governmental organisations in the process. Local village leaders participated in the international environmental conference associated with the NEAP in Lesotho, and NGOs and universities in all of the countries contributed to the work of NEAP task forces. The NEAPs also facilitated new relationships between local NGOs and international NGOs with particular interest in environmental issues in the countries. This was especially true in Madagascar where the international conservation community has played a very active role in monitoring and formulating strategies for the protection of that country's rich biodiversity.

Strengthened Donor Co-ordination. NEAPs have contributed to strengthening donor co-ordination on a number of fronts. They have offered a forum for dialogue among donors, and between donors and governments, on environmental matters. They have provided the means to assess the environmental issues associated with existing development assistance projects, and they have provided the means to develop co-ordinated investment programmes for new environmental initiatives. The NEAPs have also given host governments detailed planning documentation for presentations to UN Donor Roundtables and other UN meetings.

3. State of the Art

Introduction

This overview and preliminary assessment of Country Environmental Studies provides the basis for describing the current state-of-the-art for CES. Even though CES may vary from country to country, there are central elements common to them all that can guide us in designing and implementing new studies. These concern the fundamental goals of CES, their organisational structure, their scope, and the strategies donor and host governments pursue to follow-up on them. As stated earlier, much of the discussion of the state of the art that follows is reflected in the note prepared by the World Resources Institute for the DAC's Working Party on Development Assistance and Environment entitled: "Good Practices for Country Environmental Studies" (DAC/ENV(89)3 2nd November 1989).

Goals and Objectives

A general definition of the fundamental objectives of a CES can be drawn from our experience to date. Although variations will exist among different types of CES, there appears to be a general consensus among practitioners and governments alike that CES should be viewed primarily as a dynamic component of a long-term strategy for bringing about sustainable development through improved environmental planning, policy-making and management. Although they are essential as instruments for developing sound information on environmental conditions and trends in a given country, CES should move beyond this descriptive profiling function to pose practical policy solutions that confront the underlying causes of resource degradation and environmental contamination. This will involve analyzing and designing policy reforms for complex, and often delicate, political institutional and economic situations. With this in mind, the CES process must be extremely sensitive and responsive to the political and social context in which it occurs. Viewed within this general framework, CES seek to meet four fundamental objectives:

1. Identify and assess fundamental trends in environmental quality and natural resource use. This objective includes establishing an integrated baseline of data and information on the condition of a country's environment and the socio-economic factors and activities that influence natural resource use and environmental quality. Although developing such basic data should not be seen as an end in itself, it can be especially useful in countries where such

information may not exist or has never been compiled in a comprehensive form. A key aim of developing such a profile of conditions and trends should be that it be based on types of data, indicators and other information that is useful to future planning and policy-making.

2. Formulate plans and policy responses to reverse environmental degradation and mismanagement of resources and incorporate sound management practices in future policy and programmes. Achieving this objective will require a thorough understanding of the linkages between existing policies (fiscal, economic, etc.) and resource use, and will require the development of the political and institutional means to change policies which may be misdirected.

3. Strengthen public and private institutional capabilities for environmental planning and management. This will involve designing strategies for incorporating environmental and natural resource management considerations into the practices of existing development institutions as well as influencing the private sector and strengthening NGOs. Achieving this objective should also include leaving institutional mechanisms in place for gathering data, monitoring environmental trends and conducting analytical studies which can assist planners and policy makers.

4. Increase public awareness of environmental conditions trends and critical issues, and build public support for initiatives to improve environmental quality and the management of natural resources.

Organisation and Processes

Considering these fundamental objectives, it is clear that the central thrust of a CES is to strengthen the capacity of public and private institutions to define and implement policy for sustainable development. All the strands of an effective CES -- whether they entail accurate profiling of trends, public education, training for NGOs, or policy and legislative work with official government agencies -- should come together to strengthen the institutional framework for environment and natural resource management in a country. Seen this way, a CES is a strategic process involving a variety of interrelated, carefully timed activities, all of which aim toward policy and institutional reform. This concept was put clearly by DAC Chairman Joseph Wheeler in a statement cited in the World Bank's review of Environmental Action Plans (Falloux, *et al.*, 1990, p. 2):

> "The process of working with developing countries on environmental planning needs to benefit from full co-ordination from institutions and donors. The purpose, of course, is not simply to produce a piece of paper called a Conservation Strategy or an Environmental Action Plan, but rather to work with developing countries to implement a process of environmental planning and decision-making as a permanent and institutionalized aspect of societal decision-making. The process must be part and parcel of overall development decision-making and must involve the private sector actors who, in the end, must support the political process involved and who are often the key implementing partners."

Obviously, these objectives have a direct bearing on how a CES is organised and conducted. There are several critical concerns to be taken into account when organising a CES, defining its technical coverage, and devising strategies for disseminating CES publications and following up on CES recommendations.

CES Start-Up

The complexity of the CES process places a special premium on negotiating clear agreements beforehand about the basic objectives of the CES, its organisational structure, the forums and procedures for intergovernmental co-ordination and public participation in the process, the technical coverage of the study, and the obligations and commitments of the participating donors and the government to follow through on the implementation of the recommendations of the CES. Before starting the formal CES, a preliminary assessment should be undertaken which defines these basic policy and institutional parameters and sets the scope of the study. This preliminary "scoping" study should examine the critical trends and policy issues the CES should concentrate on, as well, as establish the institutional arrangements for the project and the basis for private sector and NGO participation in it. It should also deal with such essential questions as the commitment of funds, technical staff requirements, in kind services, schedules, and other administrative matters.

CES Structure and Organisation

Fulfilling the fundamental institutional objectives of the CES will require organising the study process with particular care. On one level, strengthening the government's capacity to engage in effective environmental planning and management will require introducing critical environmental issues, data, and policy approaches into the formal decision-making processes of government agencies which traditionally have not taken environmental considerations into account in their policy-making. Doing this demands political support as well as the creation of forums for effective intergovernmental co-ordination and training for policy makers and public officials. On another level, it demands involving local community representatives and NGOs in the process in order to create new constituencies and new capacity on a level where environmental policy may be implemented.

Lead Agency. Bearing these considerations in mind, CES organisers should place special emphasis on selecting the lead agency for the CES effort. Ideally, this agency would have the political prestige, bureaucratic skill and technical expertise to manage the CES process and act as its advocate nationally and within the government. It would also have the authority and technical capacity to integrate environmental and natural resource factors into the national economic development planning process.

As the DAC Working Party's Note points out, the logical candidate for this rôle would be a national planning or economic development ministry, not an agency with a single sectoral interest or an *ad hoc* body with no permanent authority or status. In theory, at least, such a national development planning agency would have the mandate and the co-ordinating powers to convene the sectoral ministries of government and negotiate agreements on matters of policy and programme priorities. In cases where no such central integrative body exists, however, an environmental agency should have the lead responsibility as long as it also is given explicit authority to co-ordinate other sectoral interests in the process.

Co-ordination. One of the basic objectives of the CES is to achieve more effective co-ordination among the various governmental and non-governmental actors involved in development and natural resource management. From the outset, institutional mechanisms need to be established to facilitate co-ordination in a number of specific areas. A special *Steering Committee* should be created to provide intergovernmental co-ordination on policy, as well as technical matters. Chaired by the lead agency, this committee would include representatives of sectoral ministries, special agencies, private sector interests, and NGOs concerned with environment and development issues. The *Technical Secretariat* for the CES is also an instrument for co-ordination. Its multidisciplinary staff should be drawn from the participating agencies and also from NGOs and the private sector. Both the Steering Committee and the Technical Secretariat offer forums for introducing new approaches to ENR analysis and management through specialised briefings and training sessions.

The CES also should be co-ordinated with the programmes of the international donors assisting the country. Donor co-ordination can be achieved through early notification to the relevant donors in the country and the creation of a special donor committee to work with the CES. The CES should be designed to complement or supplement -- not duplicate -- donor activities so that the end result of the CES can provide packages of potential projects and investments that donors already may be predisposed to support.

Public Participation. As emphasized earlier, the CES process should be founded upon the maximum feasible participation of the local communities, NGOs, and the private interests effected by the study. Such participation will help identify priorities, assess alternative strategies, and develop consensus around the recommendations of the CES. NGOs, as well as private business interests, can bring specialised insights into the characteristics of environmental problems and the practical and cultural constraints underlying various policy options. With this in mind, the CES should establish a deliberate publicised process of public participation through the Steering Committee, technical review committees, and routine meetings at the community level. These meeting can be viewed as public information meetings, as well as working sessions for analysis, impact assessment, and the design of policy and programme options.

CES Technical Coverage

Traditionally, the scope of CES has concentrated on the description and assessment of conditions and trends in the use of natural resources and the quality of the environment. As CES aim more at strategic interventions for the reform of environment and natural resources policy and management, however, certain general approaches and avenues of analysis need to be given more consideration. These will vary from country to country, but there are a number of suggestions that can be put forth here.

Although the coverage of a particular CES will vary according to the characteristics of the country for which it is being done, generally speaking, CES will analyze trends and issues in the following environment and resource areas: soil/agriculture; forestry; mineral resources/mining; hydrology; marine and coastal resources; and biodiversity. It will examine issues in rural development and land use, urban environment, industrialisation, air and water pollution, sanitation and hazardous wastes. In analyzing the underlying causes of the mismanagement of natural resources, the CES will also examine social and cultural factors, sectoral economic practices and policies, and the legal, regulatory and institutional framework for environment and natural resources management in the country.

Scoping. When starting a CES, the importance of the "scoping" process described earlier cannot be emphasized enough. Through it CES participants can reach agreement on the focus of the CES work, determining the issues to be given priority and the level of detail at which they can be most usefully treated. There is always a tendency to avoid critical analysis by letting a CES become an encyclopedic inventory of environmental trends and the natural resource base. A carefully conducted "scoping" process can help avoid this by targeting central policy and management issues for analysis and sharpening the strategic focus of the CES.

Economic Policy Linkages. CES should examine the interrelationships between prevailing economic and fiscal policies and patterns of resource use and environmental quality. Existing market subsidies, taxes, export incentives, and regulatory techniques may provide disincentives to the sustainable use of resources which also may lead to environmental degradation. These factors and linkages need to be identified and analyzed so that development planners and policy-makers can fashion policy instruments that benefit rather than diminish the quality of the environment.

Institutional Dynamics. CES also need to assess the dynamics of the institutional relationships for environment and natural resource management in a particular country. A variety of institutional bottlenecks often impede effective ENR management in developing countries, including lack of inter-agency co-ordination, overlapping, confused, or contradictory legislative mandates and functions; insufficiently trained staff, and limited budgets. Although these issues are often identified, CES need to explore the processes of decision-making more closely to determine how these interrelationships influence the adoption of new policies and programmes, and how they might be changed.

Information Systems. One of the desired outcomes of CES is the establishment of systems for gathering and managing environmental data that are effectively linked to governmental planning and decision-making processes. With this in mind, the CES should inventory the sources of environmental and natural resource data in the country, design indicators of environmental trends, gather data to analyze those trends, and develop an institutional system of monitoring and reporting on those trends.

Strategies for Building Public Awareness and Education

One of the fundamental objectives of the CES process is to build public awareness of the role and importance of environmental and natural resource factors in sustainable development. A deliberate public education strategy should be pursued throughout the formal CES process and after that process is complete. Such a strategy could include conventional newspaper and television coverage; well-targeted distribution of interim and final reports; design and dissemination of popular versions of technical reports; community workshops; conferences, etc. Training programmes for policy-makers and planners can also be designed around the output of the CES process. These activities should be viewed as part of the regular CES programme and adequate funding for them should be built into overall project.

Deliberate Follow-up Strategies

The CES process should design a deliberate strategy for donors, host country governments, and participating national and international NGOs to follow up on the recommendations and proposals produced by the CES. The CES will generate a range of recommendations for policy reform, legislation, institutional restructuring, training, research, and monitoring, among others. Implementing these strategies will require long-term commitments of funds and technical assistance, as well as political support from a variety of donors, host governments, private sector interests, and NGOs. The process of securing these commitments needs to occur throughout the CES and a series of host country/donor roundtables should be held to design a detailed follow-up programme and reach agreements about the appropriate levels of support to be provided by the participating parties.

4. Next Steps

An optimist reading this overview might conclude that there is little more we need to do to improve CES. Consensus seems to exist about the fundamental objectives of the CES process; we have built up considerable experience with how CES should be organised and conducted; and, with the advent of NEAPs, some might even say that we have concrete, living models of the state of the art.

But there is still a good deal more we need to know about this approach to environmental reform. CES have not been in use long enough to have matured and been tested fully as instruments of change. While there may be agreement about their utility as a general approach, we still need to know much more about how effective they really have been in introducing lasting changes in institutional behaviour and policy in developing countries. It may be that it is still too early to draw any hard conclusions from a comparative evaluation, but such a look indeed is needed and, at the very least, would contribute a greater measure of certainty to the impressionistic findings we now have.

The comparative evaluation we are recommending should be aimed at one central question: has the CES process been institutionalised within the countries that have applied it. The main purpose of a CES is to change the way a country manages its use of natural resources and the quality of its environment. Improvements in the sustainability of the resource base and the quality of the environment are expected to flow from such changes in institutional behaviour. While it would be extremely interesting to jump directly to an examination of the impacts a CES may have had on the environment itself, the more immediate question to be answered is whether the institutional changes the CES intended have actually taken hold and become a permanent feature of the planning, policy-making, and implementation process in the country.

In determining how completely a country has institutionalised the CES approach, one should seek answers to a number of basic questions. What environmental policies have been adopted as a result of the CES and how are they being implemented? What governmental institutions have been created to formulate policy, plans, and investment programmes for the environment? How do these institutions relate to other sectoral agencies within the government? Do multi-sectoral co-ordination mechanisms exist to integrate environment into overall development planning and how well do they function? What institutions were created to collect data on environmental conditions and monitor trends? Is environmental assessment a functioning activity of government? What mechanisms exist for private sector and NGO participation in policy-making? These questions could be answered with relative ease, but they should be applied through a field study rather than a desk survey so that a more thorough evaluation of the circumstances and characteristics of each case can be obtained.

This overall review offers evidence that CES can provide a dynamic framework for action to improve environmental planning and management in developing countries. Through the comparative evaluation we propose, the Development Centre could help ensure that the framework would have a lasting value for developing countries, as well as the community of international donors.

BIBLIOGRAPHICAL REFERENCES

BAKER, Doug S. and Daniel B. TUNSTALL, eds., *1990 Directory of Country Environmental Studies: An Annotated Bibliography of Environmental and Natural Resource Profiles and Assessments*, Washington, D.C., World Resources Institute, 1990.

CENTER FOR INTERNATIONAL DEVELOPMENT AND ENVIRONMENT, *Country Environmental Studies Review*, Washington, D.C., World Resources Institute, 1989.

CONROY, Czech and Miles LITVINOFF, ed., *The Greening of Aid*, London, Earthscan Publications, Ltd., 1988.

DICKINSON, Joshua C., III *The Country Environmental Profile: Process and Product, An Evaluation of Profiles Conducted Prior to 1983 and Recommendations for Improvement*, Washington, D.C., International Institute for Environment and Development, 1984.

FALLOUX, François, Lee TALBOT, and Leif CHRISTOFFERSEN, *National Environmental Action Plans in Africa: Early Lessons and Future Directions*, Technical Department, Africa Region, The World Bank, 1990.

ORGANISATION FOR ECONOMIC CO-OPERATION AND DEVELOPMENT (OECD), *Development Assistance Committee, Working Party on Development Assistance and Environment: Good Practices for Country Environmental Studies*, Paris, Organisation for Economic Co-operation and Development, 1989.

VICTORIA FALLS WORKSHOP, *A Guide to Preparing Conservation Strategies, Conservation Strategies: A Means for Sustainable Development*, Gland, IUCN, 1988.

WORLD RESOURCES INSTITUTE (WRI), Centre for International Development and Environment, *Country Environmental Studies: An Annotated Bibliography of Environmental and Natural Resource Profiles and Assessments*, Washington, D.C., WRI with support from U.S. Agency for International Development, April 1990.

THAILAND'S EXPERIENCE WITH ENVIRONMENTAL PLANNING

by

Dhira Phantumvanit and Juliet Lamont *

* Thailand Development Research Institute Foundation (TDRIF).

RÉSUMÉ

Dans la planification de son développement, la Thaïlande a longtemps privilégié une politique de croissance avant tout. Cette stratégie est maintenant de plus en plus remise en question par la pollution grandissante et par les problèmes urbains auxquels s'ajoute l'épuisement rapide des ressources, forêts principalement, dans les zones rurales. L'aide a été fort utile dans le passé, notamment en assurant le financement et le soutien technique d'une série d'enquêtes et d'études de diagnostics, mais le moment est venu non plus de faire de nouvelles études mais d'agir. Dans l'action, il faut toutefois tenir compte de la force relative des divers participants ; le 7ème Plan, en particulier, devrait prévoir une importante contribution du secteur commercial privé et de la communauté des ONG qui se développe rapidement. L'aide peut jouer, là aussi, un rôle important en favorisant le jeu de nouvelles institutions, ou de nouveaux acteurs, dans la stratégie de protection de l'environnement et en contribuant à veiller à ce que les nouvelles priorités se traduisent en investissements et en mesures à prendre.

SUMMARY

For many years, Thailand emphasized a growth first policy in its development planning, but this strategy is increasingly challenged by growing pollution and urban environment problems plus rapid resource depletion, notably of forests, in rural areas. Aid has been quite helpful in the past, primarily through funding and technical support of an array of investigative and diagnostic surveys, but the need now is for action rather than more study. Action however, also needs to pay attention to the comparative strengths of the various participants and, in particular, the 7th Plan should look to a large contribution from the private business sector and from the rapidly growing NGO community. Here too, aid can have a significant role in promoting the roles of new institutions, or players, in environmental strategy and in helping to ensure that the new priorities are translated into investments and policies.

1. *Introduction*

Economic growth in Thailand over the past thirty years has been one of the highest and steadiest of the developing nations in the Asian region. In particular, growth during the last decade has been remarkable, increasing from 6-7 per cent per year to a rate averaging over 10 per cent per year from 1987-1989. Most analysts predict that the Thai economy will continue to grow at a rate exceeding 9 per cent this year.

The exceptional growth rates of the past three years have been primarily due to increases in exports, and a heavy influx of foreign capital. Concurrent to this growth, Thailand has been experiencing a rapid transformation from an agrarian society to an increasingly industrialized one, with some experts predicting that it will achieve Newly-Industrialised-Country (NIC) status by the middle of this decade. The share of agriculture in GDP has declined from 27 per cent in 1970 to current levels of about 16 per cent; forecasts indicate that this share will fall below 9 per cent by the year 2000. Meanwhile, the share of industry has increased from 26 per cent in 1970 to the current figure of 36 per cent, and is expected to exceed 40 per cent by the year 2000.

Much of the economic growth has depended, however, upon the consumption of Thailand's natural resource base, including forests, coastal zones, fertile agricultural lands, and an abundant supply of water.

Environmental Policy over the Past Thirty Years

The first three five-year Plans (1961-1976) emphasized economic growth as the primary objective in the country's development; the rich natural resource and environment base was viewed only in terms of its contribution towards maximising overall economic production. Development activities focused on the construction of infrastructure such as roads and railways, so as to improve access to natural resources, and thus to increase economic gains from the exploitation of these resources. The general outcome was an expansion of cultivable areas, but a rapid decrease in forest areas. In addition, large-scale irrigation projects were initiated throughout the country, including the construction of large dams and reservoirs. Growth and overall productivity in the short term were emphasized over the long term environmental impacts of natural resource exploitation.

However, rapid depletion of forest resources, deterioration of soil quality and fertility, and shortages in water supply sparked the introduction of resource protection and rehabilitation strategies under the Fourth Plan (1977-1981). In particular, the government began to gather data on various natural resource and environmental concerns, in an effort to develop background information which could be used for natural resources planning and management. However, activities relating to protection and conservation of natural resources appeared to be more investigative than functional at this stage.

Under the Fifth Plan (1982-1986), natural resource development strategies focused on an integrated approach to planning, based on activities that were implemented simultaneously in selected areas across the country. The aim was to coordinate planning strategies with local socio-economic development, and thereby increase the efficiency of natural resources utilization and restoration.

Natural resources and environmental planning under the Sixth Plan (1987-1991) has marked a turning point in the government's environmental strategies. While the first five Plans viewed the country's natural resources as a primary, and somewhat limitless, source of contribution to overall economic growth, the intensifying depletion and degradation of the resource base has forced a total revision of this perception to one in which the resource base may act as a constraint to economic development. Thus, the Sixth Plan emphasizes the development of alternative, non-agricultural sources of income to reduce dependency on increasingly unreliable productivity levels in natural resource areas. In addition, it has focused on decentralizing natural resources management to the local and provincial levels, in order to promote a sense of ownership, participation, and awareness among local residents.

Environmental Pressures From Inadequate Implementation

While natural resource planning has undergone several philosophical shifts over the course of the first to sixth plans, it is notable that the impacts of these shifts have remained at the planning stages only. Escalating environmental problems such as air pollution from growing industrial and auto emissions, water pollution arising from household and industrial wastewater, solid and hazardous wastes from industries and hospitals, coastal pollution, flooding and mudslides due to excessive deforestation, declining soil productivity, and degradation of the watersheds that maintain soil-precipitation balances, all present serious threats to the stability and sustainability of the Thai economy, and to the quality of life in Thai society as a whole.

In the urban sector, which accounts for over 80 per cent of GDP, lack of proper infrastructure has reached severe proportions. Bangkok, with a current population of over 7 million people, lacks an adequate sewerage system. Raw waste is dumped daily into the city's canals and the Chao Phraya River. Traffic in the downtown metropolitan area is crawling at an average speed of 13-15 kilometres per hour. Excessive groundwater pumping to meet growing demands has led to land subsidence of up to three to five centimetres per year, with subsequent costs for structural repairs.

The industrial sector, currently the major source of value added and export growth for the Thai economy, is facing problems such as inadequate water supplies, and lack of treatment and disposal facilities for solid and hazardous wastes. Not only do such problems impact growth within the sector, but issues such as improper waste disposal create public health hazards by contaminating open spaces and public waterways.

Finally, growing income disparities and structural imbalances throughout Thailand only aggravate, if not cause, many of the country's most serious environmental problems. While over 50 per cent of the population is employed in the agricultural sector, this sector produces only about 16 per cent of GDP. These figures suggest that a disproportionate share of earnings from Thailand's high economic growth fall to a limited sector of the population, an implication supported by prevailing rural poverty and landlessness. Landless and unemployed rural populations often encroach onto forest areas in search of cultivable land.

In short, the environmental problems currently facing Thailand present serious constraints to future economic growth and sustainability. Immediate policy measures and actions are required to mitigate negative environmental impacts, and to rehabilitate degraded natural resources, in order to avert the possibility of future economic decline.

Environmental Action Initiatives of the Seventh Plan

The upcoming Seventh Plan, now under the final stages of preparation, is one mechanism through which Thailand may initiate a more active approach to environmental management. Just as the First to Sixth Plans dictated much of Thailand's development over the past thirty years, the government is looking to the imminent Seventh Plan as its guide to meet the challenges imposed by impending NIC status, and to successfully negotiate the transformation from an agrarian to an industrial society. Active environmental management policy figures prominently in the new Plan, reflecting the rising concern over the long term impacts of environmental problems both here and internationally, and more importantly, the government's acknowledgement of the need for immediate, more effective environmental management in Thailand.

Broadly speaking, the Seventh Plan focuses on five major environmental management policy issues: natural resources management, environmental quality, energy and environment, industry and environment, and urbanisation and environment, all of which are viewed as constituting the central environmental concerns anticipated to accompany continued economic growth.

Beyond this anticipatory identification of priority concerns, the government is starting to put more weight and action behind its words. Consideration of a national electricity savings plan is already under way, indicating one of the government's first efforts to weave energy conservation into overall energy strategies, rather than simply trying to expand supply. Stricter industrial pollution regulations and parameters are also an anticipated effect of the Seventh Plan, while plans for water quality management systems in Bangkok have finally been mobilized. The Thai government recently launched a pilot project in joint government-private sector management of hazardous waste at the Bangkuntien Hazardous Waste Treatment Plant as one potential method for addressing the hazardous waste treatment issue. If these actions are any signs of the government's future strategies, it would appear that policies promoting active environmental management are a major component of the new path.

In essence, Thailand's race to NIC-dom, and the accompanying ecological, social, and political costs precipitated by this rapid development path, are finally forcing critical decisions in the environmental policy arena. Previously, extensive but inherently passive environmental surveys seemed sufficient in the environmental planning process. Currently, however, the severity of environmental deterioration across the country demands a shift towards policies that promote immediate and effective action. The Thai government is clearly initiating changes in its own sphere of influence. It is in catalysing a similar shift across all sectors of society that foreign aid may find its most effective niche.

2. *Strengths and Weaknesses of Environmental Plans*

Focus on Environmental Plans

International aid for environmental concerns has so far focused on the transfer of funds from industrialised to developing nations for the purpose of undertaking specific, topical study projects. In the case of Thailand, aid has been used primarily to support the development of extensive country environmental studies, or "master plans", which can then be used as tools for environmental and natural resources planning.

These plans tend to be either descriptive or analytical in nature, cataloguing data and information on current and historical trends in the country's natural resource base, the variables and forces acting to precipitate environmental deterioration, and the implications of this deterioration at the local, national, and increasingly, international levels. What is most lacking in the "master plans" is the financial feasibility element, linking recommendations with scarce resources at the disposal of the government. This has led, in many cases, to failure in implementing the formulated plans.

In Thailand, a grant from USAID was used to develop a *Thailand Natural Resources Profile*, which constituted the first comprehensive study of the country's natural resource base. The *Profile* presented both an overview of natural resource stocks and conditions, while providing detailed data on individual natural resource and environmental sectors such as water, forests, and land.

Funding from other aid organizations has promoted similar country profile efforts throughout Thailand, mainly relating to specific environmental and natural resource sectors. The result of such aid has thus been an extensive compilation of information about environmental trends, emerging issues, and comparative analyses of critical environmental concerns, which are then applied towards the development of policy and planning strategies in the government sector.

There are two significant characteristics of master plans. First, they emphasize data compilation and analysis, and are thus prescriptive rather than action-oriented. Secondly, due to traditional views of environmental management and planning as the realm of government agencies alone, many of these plans failed to include consideration of the broader scope of players now participating in or having an impact on environmental policy decisions. Both characteristics act as limitations to the effective implementation of any proposed environmental management strategies -- the first by continuing to channel energy and resources towards verbal rhetoric and paper analyses, and the second by ignoring the contribution and complementary strength offered by a broader, pluralistic approach to environmental management, as well as the potential delays imposed by interests that cannot be ignored any more.

Thailand also maintains a number of foreign aid-sponsored projects that can channel aid funds to address the current needs for promoting effective environmental management in Thailand.

MANRES: A Case in Point

One of the clearest examples of effective channelling of aid funds may be in the Management of Natural Resources and Environment Project (MANRES), launched in 1988 by the US Agency for International Development (USAID), acting through the Department of Technical and Economic Cooperation (DTEC). Scheduled to run through 1995, the goal of this US$ 44 million dollar-project is "to promote the economic and social development of Thailand through improved management of natural resources and the environment", with its main purpose being "to develop the capacities of Thai governmental and non-governmental institutions to define, analyse, and respond effectively to current and emerging natural resource and environmental problems, and thereby to build consensus and capacity for advancing policy options that will lead to sustainable development".

The hallmark of MANRES vis-à-vis previous aid efforts is in the Project's approach to achieving its stated objectives. First, it emphasizes a cross-sectoral program for the Development of environmental policy resolutions and environmental management responses, including increased participation of the private sector in environmental management, and inclusion of non-governmental organisations as equal voices in developing policy strategies.

Even within the government sector, MANRES stresses improved coordination among numerous government agencies -- the Department of Technical and Economic Cooperation, the National Economic and Social Development Board, the Office of the National Environment Board, the Tourism Authority of Thailand, and the Royal Forestry Department, to name just a few -- to build on the strengths of individual agencies, while attempting to reduce the tensions and obstacles to policy implementation that often arise due to overlapping or conflicting spheres of authority.

Another highlight of MANRES is its long term nature. The project, which was officially launched in 1988, has been structured to run over a seven-year period, thus confirming the necessity for long term planning as integral to the effective resolution of environmental problems.

Finally, the structure and objectives of MANRES stress in-country development of environmental management expertise and activities, so that individual agencies, and Thailand as a whole, will develop a self-sufficient and continuing system for effective implementation and enforcement of environmental management policies and techniques. In contrast to "one-shot" aid efforts of the past, MANRES focuses on developing capacities that can sustain themselves even after funding has ceased.

3. Towards a Multisectoral Approach to Environmental Management

Revising Aid to Ensure Action

Past aid efforts aimed at preparing broad, descriptive profiles and master plans of Thailand's natural resources and environment have run their course. Numerous studies have been completed, with good results. However, the complexity and urgency of current environmental and natural resource crises in Thailand demand a revision, or parallel evolution, in aid strategies.

Primarily, effective aid must encourage the active implementation of environmental management strategies, not merely reviews of current environmental conditions and paper plans. Aid must also reflect the expanded scope of players involved in environmental policy decisions; funding directed or focused only towards studies developed by government agencies may be ineffective at the grass-roots level. Aid institutions can no longer treat government as the only mechanism for environmental action; evidence in Thailand and abroad indicates that the public, NGOs, and the private sector can be equally effective at promoting sound environmental management, and have often been the catalysts for significant actions to date.

Government Sector

The traditional role of the government sector with respect to environmental management has been an all-encompassing one. Individual agencies have acted as planners, implementors, monitors, and enforcers of environmental policies and regulations. However, institutional constraints, overlapping authorities, ambiguous policy directives, and inadequate facilities, training, and manpower have presented continual obstacles to performing this role effectively.

A much more efficient strategy would be to strengthen government roles in areas where it has shown itself to be most effective in the past with respect to encouraging implementation of environmental policies at the ground level. In the government sphere, these areas would include: monitoring, laboratory research, and raising awareness.

The government is in a unique position to oversee environmental monitoring efforts because of its access to international environmental quality standards -- a structure which combines centralized agencies with local arms and field offices, and its coverage of numerous environmental sectors.

Government institutions in Thailand have also demonstrated considerable achievements in the development and promotion of laboratory research, primarily through the establishment of government laboratories which conduct high-quality, applied research across a range of scientific and technological fields. Given that these labs are already in operation, a logical direction for international aid would be to strengthen and tailor this existing capability towards environmental management.

Finally, government agencies possess both the resources and the position to raise awareness about environmental concerns across numerous sectors of Thai society. The Thai government possesses some of the most well-educated and capable specialists in the environmental field. It would be an appropriate and desirable direction to improve the communication of this expertise and knowledge to the public and private sectors. Not only would such actions draw on the talents and knowledge already available in the government sphere, but they would encourage better coordination and understanding between the government and non-government sectors, helping to build support and consensus for government decisions through a well-informed public.

Private Sector

Increasing participation from the private sector in environmental management is a significant trend emerging in response to more competitive international markets, and a changing global economic scenario.

Foreign aid could be directed towards encouraging the active participation of the private sector in environmental management. Specific aid targets could include helping to establish subsidies for businesses that implement clean technologies, the development of environmental quality standards in conjunction with industry so as to set feasible parameters, facilitating the flow of more efficient technologies from industrialised to developing nations, and tightening environmental impact assessment requirements and regulations so that companies employing proper environmental management techniques will not feel penalised by a system that fails to regulate the non-complying members of their respective industries. Businesses are an important source of environmental and natural resources data, technology, and management skills, all of which can be tapped more effectively both for environmental and economic gain.

Non-Governmental Organizations

NGOs constitute perhaps the fastest growing sectoral influence on environmental concerns in Thailand. In developing nations throughout Southeast Asia, NGOs have acted as a mobilising force for local communities and the public, initiating and supporting action at the ground level. Funding which supports NGO activities is thus a more direct and effective method of ensuring improved environmental management.

A fundamental feature of NGO activities is public education, which is used as a means to promote an awareness of environmental concerns, and thus to motivate grass-roots-level action. In Thailand, educational activities range from the publication of newsletters, to organised trips to national parks to community action programmes. Foreign aid could be channelled towards enhancing such awareness-raising activities through existing NGOs, which have already gained the confidence of the public. Funds could also support the launching of additional community programs modelled on successful predecessors.

A second significant feature of environmental NGOs is their increasing influence on governments and policy through active lobbying, and through their extensive expertise in specialized issues.

Independent Policy Research Institutes

Policy research institutes, by definition, are required to conduct technical and policy analysis across a range of policy issues to support the formulation of long term strategies for social and economic development. In Thailand and throughout Southeast Asia, these institutes are often consulted by national governments, as sources of information about critical policy issues, and as initiators of new policy strategies. Their influence is partly due to their autonomy; they can assume an objective role in the policy development process as a result of their independence, while bringing greater flexibility to their research and output since they are free from traditional bureaucratic constraints.

Specifically, there are four salient features which describe the nature and scope of existing policy research institutes. First, their access to existing, specialised knowledge in a number of fields both directly and indirectly related to the environment. Second, their suitability for handling the current complexities inherent in the resolution of environmental problems through their emphasis on multidisciplinary analysis, which allows for the integration and synthesis of large amounts of data in multiple areas of specialisation. Thirdly, their ability to transfer reliable, technical research information to both policy makers and the public, which is a necessary pre-requisite to the solution of environmental problems. And finally, their high level of influence on government policy decisions.

4. *Conclusions*

Thailand, like many other developing nations trying to balance economic growth with increasing pressures on the natural resource base, is facing a level of environmental deterioration that demands immediate, active steps towards mitigation and rehabilitation. While past aid from foreign sources has supported the development of master plans to guide such environmental management efforts, the plans have yet to be translated into pragmatic action.

Obstacles to effective implementation have in part been the result of traditional views regarding natural resource exploitation, and a failure to incorporate a broader, cross-sectoral approach to environmental management which is necessitated by the growing complexity of current environmental concerns. Therefore, future funding efforts should focus 1) on promoting the roles of new institutions, or players, in environmental management strategies, and 2) on the recognition of new priorities, such as the need for greater regional cohesion, emerging environmental concerns of developing nations, and the growing category of global environmental issues.

Directions for international aid must reflect the changes that have occurred in the environmental management sphere if it is to promote effective implementation at the ground level. Above all, aid must now focus on catalysing pragmatic action if environmental issues in developing nations are to be resolved.

BIBLIOGRAPHICAL REFERENCES

THE NATIONAL ECONOMIC AND SOCIAL DEVELOPMENT BOARD (NESDB), *Rural Natural Resources Management in Thailand*, Bangkok, NESDB, 1990.

PANAYOTOU, Theodore, David FOSTER, Malcolm BALDWIN, and Teerana BHONGMAKAPAT, *Environmental Issues for an Advanced Developing Country -- Final Report*, USAID/Thailand AMP Research Agenda, Bangkok, March 1990.

PHANTUMVANIT, Dhira, and Juliet LAMONT, *Regional Network on Sustainable Development*, Bangkok, Thailand Development Research Institute Foundation, August 1990.

PHANTUMVANIT, Dhira, Phanu KRITIPORN, and Tesrapon SOPONKANAPORN, *Business and Environment in Thailand*, Bangkok, Thailand Development Research Institute, March 1990.

THAILAND DEVELOPMENT RESEARCH INSTITUTE (TDRI), Macroeconomic Policy Program, 1989, *The Outlook for the Thai Economy*, prepared for the 1989 TDRI Year-End Conference, "Thailand in the International Economic Community", held in Chon Buri, Thailand, Dec. 16-17, 1989.

UNITED STATES AGENCY FOR INTERNATIONAL DEVELOPMENT (USAID), *Project Grant Agreement Between the Kingdom of Thailand and the United States of America for the Management of Natural Resources and Environment Project*, August 3, 1988, A.I.D. Project No. 493-0345.

COUNTRY ENVIRONMENTAL PROFILES: THE CASE OF COLOMBIA

by

Diana Pombo Holguin *

* Diana Pombo Holguin has directed the *Perfil Ambiental de Colombia.*

RÉSUMÉ

La Colombie souffre d'une dégradation environnementale qui s'accélère. Elle résulte principalement de la colonisation rapide des zones forestières qui sont soumises à des pratiques d'exploitation agricole non durables. En plus, cette dégradation est causée par l'inégalité d'accès aux ressources et par des politiques gouvernementales défavorables à l'environnement. Une réaction s'est fait jour en Colombie, notamment sous forme de création d'institutions, soutenue par l'aide extérieure. L'article résume de manière détaillée l'histoire institutionnelle du Profil Environnemental de la Colombie (CEP) et de sa mise en oeuvre à l'échelle régionale jusqu'à la date de la rédaction (septembre 1990). La mise en oeuvre comprend une réforme législative et la décentralisation des responsabilités de gestion de l'environnement ainsi qu'une réplique du CEP à l'échelle d'une des cinq régions de la Colombie (la région de la Côte Atlantique ou des Caraïbes). Pour la coordination de la gestion de l'environnement au niveau régional des "unités" doivent être créées pour chacun des cinq conseils régionaux de planification (CORPES); celle de la Côte Atlantique est la première à avoir été créée. L'article décrit également les difficultés rencontrées par les ONG, les organismes gouvernementaux et les acteurs du secteur privé, dont la coopération fut l'un des objectifs de cette initiative environnementale comme de beaucoup d'autres dans des zones en développement. Finalement, le cas particulier de la Colombie fait ressortir le rôle essentiel que joue l'agence d'aide extérieure, USAID dans ce cas précis, en fournissant un soutien financier et technique pour la création d'institutions.

SUMMARY

Colombia suffers from accelerating environmental degradation chiefly resulting from rapid colonisation of forest areas and their conversion to agricultural uses in an unsustainable fashion. The causes also include inequities in access to resources and certain environmentally harmful government polices. The response has been forthcoming in Colombia and has included an institution-building experience supported by foreign assistance. The article comprehensively summarises the institutional history of Colombia Environmental Profile (CEP) and related follow up action at the regional scale up to the date of writing (September 1990). The follow up includes a legislative reorganisation and regionalisation of environmental management responsibilities and a replication of the CEP at the scale of one of Colombia's five regions (the Atlantic Coast or Caribbean region). Environment "units" to coordinate management efforts at the regional level are to be created for each of the five regional Planning Councils (CORPES) -- the Atlantic Coast being the first to have come into existence. The account includes examples of difficulties encountered by NGOs, government agencies, and private sector actors -- the collaboration of which has been an objective of this and many other environmental initiatives in developing areas. In the end the particular case of Colombia reveals the crucial role played by a foreign donor agency -- the USAID in this case -- in providing financial and technical support for institution building.

The Colombia Environmental Profile (CEP) was undertaken between 1988 and 1990. It was coordinated by COLCIENCIAS (Colombian Fund for Scientific and Technological Research), a public institution related to the Ministry of Education, now being transferred to the National Planning Bureau. It was intended to be a cooperative effort of the different institutions involved with the management of natural resources and the environment. It was financed by USAID and technical assistance was coordinated by the Centre for Environment and Development of the World Resources Institute (WRI). The total budget of the project was around US$ 200 000.

1. *Rationale for Colombia Environmental Profile*

The decision to undertake the CEP was the result of an institutional recognition that serious environmental problems needed a stronger policy response. It was not the first effort to cope with environment and development issues, but the first one of national scope based on compiling and evaluating existing information. Previous efforts to devise a "National Strategy for Sustainable Development" had failed because of a lack of support by high level authorities.

The CEP was finally given the go-ahead in the middle of 1987, after an offer was made by USAID through the WRI (at the time the International Institute for Environment and Development -- IIED-USA) to support a CEP with a developmental perspective. The decision to proceed was made at the highest institutional level. The fact that COLCIENCIAS assumed responsibility for project coordination was decisive in getting other institutions involved. Still, certain of their representatives attached little importance to the project, as in the case of the National Planning Bureau, whose work is almost exclusively devoted to increasing national economic growth and living standards.

Besides these considerations, recognition of a number of major environmental problems gave impetus to the preparation of the CEP. These include:

- Rapid expansion of colonisation in forest areas;
- Under-utilisation of agricultural lands together with a rapid extension of the agrarian frontier into forest areas;
- Degradation and depletion of water ecosystems as a result of unplanned agricultural practices and urbanisation;
- Rapid process of soil erosion due to over-exploitation of soils and deforestation;
- Increasing social and economic conflicts occurring in critical ecological areas;
- Official government policies with negative environmental consequences.

2. *Project Design*

Several features were taken into account in the design of the CEP:

- There was already a large, albeit scattered, volume of specialised studies, as well as a lot of information concerning specific areas of the country. These studies were spread among official institutions and research centres. However, such studies had not been consolidated and evaluated.

- There was no comprehensive study integrating the ecological, social and institutional aspects of environmental management.

- The government had already begun a process of administrative decentralization. As a part of that process, several ministries had restructured their administrative organisation. The National Planning Bureau was responsible for the environmental management "sector", but decentralisation of this activity had not been started when the CEP began.

- There was a general consensus both among official institutions and non-governmental organisations (NGOs) about the urgent need to modernize and reorganize the institutional structure concerning the management of natural resources and environment.

3. *Process of Preparation*

An institutional Committee was created to assist the project and to coordinate the institutional contributions. A basic research group was organised which would be supported by specific institutional contributions. The financial administration was given to an NGO called "Fundacion Segunda Expedicion Botanica".

The institutional contributions were rather strong in terms of information, but extremely weak in terms of human resources. In the end, the bulk of the work was done by the basic research group. This fact was very significant for the project orientation and quality: there was no compromise with institutions or governments; we could freely evaluate and criticise the situation as we found it, particularly with regard to institutional behaviour.

On the other side, even though there was a deep interest among the professionals who made the institutional contributions, it was rather difficult to obtain a strong commitment from their superiors to the project and its follow-up. The situation improved as we could show partial results. The study was finished in November 1989. Publication followed in July 1990. Now there is a deep interest in the final project results.

4. *Objectives*

The main objectives of the CEP project were:

1. To evaluate the environmental situation and main tendencies of the country, integrating social, economic and ecological aspects, as well as the institutional resources and capability to cope with the main environmental issues.

2. To evaluate the state of the knowledge about the structure, function, uses and condition of various ecosystems.

3. To propose measures to change the non-sustainable tendencies and to solve the main difficulties of environmental management.

5. Major Findings

The following are the major highlights of the CEP's findings:

- The potential, limitations, and vulnerability of Colombian ecosystems strongly depend on the relations between the main ecological processes of different forest types and the related water systems.

- Almost none of the actual uses of land correspond to their desired uses.

- Economic growth has been based on the assumption that resources are unlimited. Therefore, the need for guaranteeing the sustainability of the natural resource base has not been internalised in Colombia. Forest and water resources have suffered first from this neglect.

- The country is self-sufficient in its food supply, but there is a strong inequity in social access to food.

- Despite the fact that most of the resource management systems are inadequate, the majority of ecosystems have not reached a breaking point of their regeneration and reproduction capacity. Still, important imbalances in hydric systems and a crisis in forest resources are foreseen in the near future.

- Strong processes of degradation (deforestation, erosion, loss of water and soil productive capacity) are concentrated in specific areas. What is foreseen for the near future is not an ecological disaster but a moderate and sustained deterioration process.

- There are important coincidences between social conflicts and ecosystem degradation. Also, institutional difficulties and a lack of interest in environmental issues are at the base of a great many environmental problems. The major environmental problems are to be solved firstly by means of changing social, economic and institutional conditions and secondly by technical means.

- Eight general processes of transforming natural ecosystems into cultural ones were identified in the country, together with the types of social and environmental problems appearing at each stage of a process. The processes are more advanced in some zones and in early stages in others. Prevention measures are to be promoted in places where these processes have just begun, and priority recuperation measures are to be set in place where processes have already reached undesirable levels.

6. *CEP Proposals*

The proposals emerging from the CEP are organised into four basic groups:

1. Guidelines for a rational and efficient use of natural resources, which include the following:

- Reorientation of non-sustainable tendencies;
- Increasing land use efficiency within the agrarian frontier;
- Improving food supply system;
- Promoting regional and local participation in export systems;
- Strengthening urban-regional linkages;
- Improving ecosystem and species conservation.

2. Improvement of the environmental management structure at the national and regional levels. This includes the creation of a National Environmental Management System and its lead institution, a decentralisation of duties and initiatives to organise environmental management at the regional level, and methods to integrate environmental management into the national planning system.

3. Fiscal, administrative and economic incentives for getting NGO and private sector actors involved in official environmental management programmes. Other incentives are proposed at the local level to promote certain types of sustainable agriculture, forestry, and fisheries practices.

4. Research and information priorities.

7. *Follow-up*

The official follow-up of the project was mainly conducted to have regional discussions about its orientation and results, to encourage the realization of further studies and to promote the inclusion of environmental management in regional planning processes.

Follow-up presentations were focused on the particular issues of each region. Special attention was given to rational resource use and management and to institutional strengthening to face the main environmental problems.

We had also agreed with COLCIENCIAS to evaluate further research needs and to include the definition of environmental investigation priorities as a part of the specific objectives of the project. These are now being used by COLCIENCIAS as the basis of a national environmental research plan. We are at present working on setting priorities in the use of official funds for scientific and technological research concerning environment.

Beyond the two activities mentioned above, there has been a good deal of unplanned activity. This has been related to the process of institutional strengthening, mainly involving the government.

Four main actions have been taken as a consequence of the CEP:

1. A law was formulated for the reorganization of environmental management at the national and regional levels;

2. A regional environmental profile -- modelled after the CEP -- was recently completed for the Colombian Caribbean region.

3. Following this profile, an environmental unit was created in one of the five major regional planning institutions (Atlantic Coast region). Finally,

4. A new environmental NGO was created.

7.1 Law project: National Environmental Management Reorganization

Since 1988, the National Planning Bureau (DNP) has been in charge of drawing up a project to reorganize and rationalize the entire national environmental management structure. After a number of difficulties, a piece of legislation was proposed at the beginning of 1990 according to which INDERENA, the institution currently responsible for the management and control of renewable natural resources was to be absorbed by the Administrative Department of Renewable Natural Resources and the Environment -- DARNAR.

This proposal had several weak points, especially its strong tendency to concentrate power and decision making in the centre, which runs counter to the general public administrative effort to decentralize. The proposal was discussed first by national institutions and later by the regional ones. The CEP itself had included a proposal to rationalise the administration of natural resources and the environment at the national and regional levels. Following the CEP, as a contribution to the reorganisation process, we prepared a draft new law which was based on regional and local management of environmental issues.

The basic points of our proposal were:

1. To maintain the shared responsibility of environmental management, organise the duties and levels of action, while strengthening their coordination; and

2. To create the National Environmental System, where the proposed administrative department would be the lead institution. Existing regional institutions would be in charge of regional coordination.

The regional environmental profile for the Caribbean Coast had already started (see next section). This enabled us to organize a study of the proposal among the various environment-related institutions of the Caribbean region.

A second version of the draft was finally presented by the Caribbean region environmental institutions to the other regions. After several months a final draft Law has been prepared by DNP to be sent to the National Congress. It includes the main content of our proposal.

7.2 Caribbean Environmental Profile

A few years ago the country was organized into five planning regions: Caribbean, Western, Central-Eastern, Orinoquian and Amazonian. For management coordination regional Planning Councils (CORPES) were created. The main tasks of these councils are:

1. To make regional planning policies and prepare the regional development plan. The national development plan is actually defined after the five regional plans prepared by the CORPES.

2. To prepare the regional investment plan.

3. To coordinate and supervise the execution of the activities of the different sector agencies.

These councils are made up of the Governors of the provinces (*departamentos*) of each region. They are supported by a technical committee and a technical unit.

After a workshop on the CEP held in Cartagena (Caribbean Region), the CORPES of that region (CORPES Costa Atlantica) extended an invitation to the group who had coordinated the CEP to work on a regional environmental profile for the Colombian Caribbean region. The main goals of this project are:

1. To provide more detailed information about the region;

2. To prepare a set of guidelines for environmental management plans relating to conservation, prevention, recuperation, promotion and risk;

3. To furnish some common guidelines to be used by institutions sharing responsibilities over natural or cultural units.

This project was started in February 1990 and finished on 15 September 1990.

7.3 An Environmental Unit in the Caribbean Regional Planning Council

The CEP proposal on environmental management identified the CORPES as the institution best able to coordinate and supervise environmental actions at the regional level. This proposal was based on two considerations:

1. The technical committees include representatives of most of the institutions which have responsibilities for managing natural resources and the environment; and

2. As subsidiary to the National Planning Bureau, the CORPES have great decision making powers with regard to the regional budget allocation.

In order to ensure the continuation of the efforts begun in constructing the regional profile, and to put into practice the proposals for regional environmental management, we prepared a small project for the setting up of an environmental unit within the CORPES. This unit is already functioning in Santa Marta, the location of the CORPES Costa Atlantica.

The proposal of creating this unit was based on two facts:

1. The creation of environmental units within the CORPES as regional coordinating extensions of the National Environmental System had effectively been included in the proposed Law.

2. The CORPES are called upon to exercise coordinating responsibilities in all issues related to regional development, therefore, in case the proposed Law is not approved in a short time by the National Congress, the coordination of environmental management at the regional level could still be organized and would contribute to the further strengthening of the national system once it comes into operation.

We have been invited by two other CORPES--for the Western and East-Central planning regions--to assist them in the creation of environmental units, together with the realisation of regional environmental profiles to give the necessary technical support to these units. One of the proposals for funding to support these efforts has already been approved, but there is still some further fund raising to be done before starting. There are also plans to organise a common information system for the three units.

7.4 Creation of an NGO

The group of professionals who coordinated first the CEP and recently the Caribbean regional profile have decided to continue working in the directions set by these two projects, if possible by assisting the planning regions in environmental management, and have created an NGO for that purpose. This new organization, named Estudio Ambiental, is already functioning in Bogota.

8. Main Project Difficulties

One of the project's most important objectives was to realize the CEP as a joint effort of private and official institutions. This objective has not been met in practice. The main problem was the lack of interest among non-environmental institutions. Also, bureaucratic limitations within official environmental institutions contributed to making their involvement in the project difficult.

Several cooperative agreements concerning the development of specific themes failed to be fulfilled by the relevant institutions. Some of the themes were intended to be part of larger programmes of work, the initiation of which was delayed and were therefore not available in time for use in the project. Some were prepared hurriedly at the last minute, without much regard to the quality of work. Others went well.

The project budget had been established on the basis of the availability of qualified human resources lent by various institutions. All institutions agreed to collaborate, but when time commitments were spelt out, they recognised the impossibility of dedicating high-level professionals to the project for the periods of time required.

The participation of the NGOs proved even more difficult. We asked for some proposals concerning specific areas, which the project budget could not afford to cover. Again, the project put too much strain on their resources. One NGO collaborated over several months but had to dedicate its human resources to other institutional priorities.

A further complicating factor was that the Colombian Forest Action Plan was being prepared simultaneously with the CEP. Some national institutions were already involved with and had committed resources to this plan and could not take on an additional burden. In the end, the CEP was done by the group of professionals and assistants included in the project budget, which was based on USAID resources, with a small contribution from COLCIENCIAS.

Therefore, one of the lessons is that the planning of foreign financial support for environmental projects in developing countries should seriously take into account the limitations of national institutions to dedicate human resources to more than one project at a time, in addition to ongoing institutional duties.

STRENGTHENING GOVERNMENT CAPACITY FOR ENVIRONMENTAL MANAGEMENT IN LATIN AMERICA

by

Kirk P. Rodgers *

---

* Kirk P. Rodgers is Director, Department of Regional Development at the Organization of American States (OAS).

RÉSUMÉ

Une assistance technique en matière de gestion de l'environnement est dispensée depuis plus de 25 ans en Amérique latine et l'on continue d'innover dans l'approche et dans les méthodes. Les leçons, positives et négatives, à tirer de cette expérience sont nombreuses. Au niveau régional et national, une bonne partie de la planification échoue, faute d'être liée à un financement et à un portefeuille d'investissements ; de même, la collecte de données est en grande partie inutile car les résultats sont dépouillés et présentés sous une forme qui les rend difficilement utilisables par les planificateurs et par les concepteurs ; dans tous les cas enfin, l'autorité politique doit venir compléter l'expertise technique. Il semble bien établi qu'une focalisation sur la région par une planification décentralisée facilite les tâches, décisives pour l'intégration, que sont le diagnostic, l'élaboration d'une stratégie et la planification des projets. Les mécanismes institutionnels assurant la capacité de faire exécuter les travaux méritent aussi une attention particulière ; à l'évidence, un financement spécial est une incitation puissante pour assurer la coopération des organismes, de même que les retombées financières, sous forme de taxes et de redevances à verser aux organismes qui supportent les coûts de fonctionnement des programmes. Il existe encore d'énormes possibilités pour utiliser efficacement l'aide extérieure dans la mise en place du soutien technique et du financement des projets au niveau régional et national.

SUMMARY

Technical assistance relating to environmental management has been provided for more than 25 years in Latin America, and innovation in the approach and method is continuing. There are many lessons to be derived from this experience, both positive and negative. At regional and national levels, much planning fails because it is not linked to finance and a portfolio of investments; similarly, much data collection is in vain because results are not processed and packaged in forms that facilitate their use by the planners and project designers; and in all instances, political authority needs to complement technical expertise. There is much evidence that a regional focus through decentralised regional planning helps with the key integrative tasks of diagnosis, strategy design and project planning. Institutional arrangements to ensure the authority to get the work carried out merits special attention; evidently special funding is a powerful carrot in assuring agency cooperation as is the feedback of finance through fees and charges to the agencies bearing the operating costs of the schemes. There are still considerable opportunities for an effective use of external assistance in the provision of technical support and project financing both at the regional and at the national level.

This paper attempts to distil from more than twenty-five years of experience in technical assistance related to environmental management in Latin America and the Caribbean, some lessons on how to strengthen national capabilities related to this crucial issue. It speaks frankly about what seemed to work and what did not. The focus of all of these efforts has been economic and social development, and the experience acquired flows out of efforts to assist governments in planning and managing their natural resources on a sustainable basis.

The experience of Latin America in environmental management pre-dates similar efforts in many other parts of the developing world and contains a wealth of lessons for other nations to learn from. This experience deserves wider attention from researchers and practitioners in international development than is the case at present. The region continues to innovate at an accelerating pace in response to growing environmental problems. Some of the experiences that will be described are so fresh that their success or failure can only be guessed at.

The paper deals not only with actions of government institutions which are directly involved in the environmental management but also the context of those actions which include national environmental policy, environmental legislation and the information base that supports government decisions on environmental management. It concludes with a range of examples of practical experience in strengthening government capacity for environmental management within the context of development planning and implementation.

1. National Environmental Policy

An important element in strengthening government capacity for environmental management is national environmental policy. While this subject is taken up elsewhere in our conference agenda I would like to briefly mention some experiences from Latin America on this important topic, particularly as it relates to strengthening environmental institutions.

The first experience of the Organization of American States (OAS) with helping a country develop its national policy on environmental management occurred in Peru in 1970-71 when, jointly with Peru's National Agency for Evaluation of Natural Resources (ONERN), the OAS undertook the preparation of "Guidelines for a Policy of Conservation of the Renewable Natural Resources of Peru" (ONERN/OAS, 1974). This study attempted not only to identify the country's principal resource management problems, but also to develop recommendations for a more unified and co-ordinated approach to natural resource management on the part of Peruvian public administration. The complex patchwork of overlapping administrative responsibilities of government agencies at the national, regional and local levels, and the ineffective implementation of a large body of legislation pertaining to the resources were identified as key obstacles, along with a lack of adequate staff training and underfinancing of the institutions involved. The study, published in 1974, eventually resulted in the drafting of a General Law of Conservation of Renewable Natural Resources of Peru which strengthened the co-ordinating role of the National Agency for Evaluation of Natural Resources and broadened its mandate. However, the policy guidelines which were established had a minimal impact on strengthening other institutions or improving government performance on resource conservation. The absence of any linkage between the report's broad policy statements and practical action through adjustments in the national budget became quickly apparent. Agency budgets and staff salaries are vital ingredients of an institutional strengthening programme. Policy recommendations must therefore be framed in accordance with the government budget when they direct government agencies to take specific actions.

Years later and with the experience of dozens of other Latin American environmental profiles, conservation strategies, and environmental action plans behind us we have come to believe that if government action is to be truly strengthened through policy planning efforts the latter must take on a different character. Currently, the OAS is assisting the government of Uruguay in the preparation of a National Environmental Study supported by the Inter-American Development Bank with more than $500 000 in grant financing (Government of Uruguay/IDB, 1988). The approach this time is different. While we are indeed identifying environmental problems and assisting the government in developing a wide range of policy ideas and recommendations, part of the effort is focused on helping the government to formulate investment projects to obtain loans or other kinds of financing to implement the recommendations. The investment projects are currently being formulated at the level of profile, and, in a few cases, at the pre-feasibility level. They are aimed at securing financing for efforts to address issues such as air and water pollution control, solid waste disposal, watershed management, forest exploitation, and eco-tourism. When the study is complete it will help to establish a national environmental policy, but more importantly it should constitute a *national environmental investment portfolio* -- the first of its kind in the Americas.

It is already apparent that the flow of external financing accompanying the implementation of these projects will have a significant effect towards strengthening national institutions which are responsible for environmental management. The fact that most of these projects turn out to be feasible from an economic standpoint is also significant for it challenges the widespread notion that few of the so-called "environmental projects" are bankable in the traditional sense of the word.

2. Environmental Legislation

As the previous section suggests, Latin America and the Caribbean are relatively advanced in terms of environmental legislation which is already on the books. The problems of resource conservation and environmental management were clearly identified many decades ago and legislation was one of the first acts taken by governments individually and collectively to address these problems. At the national level most governments have a multitude of laws addressing environmental management. In 1970 Peru already had more than 30 laws or presidential decrees pertaining to resource conservation with more in preparation.

In addition to the plethora of national legislation on resource conservation issues there is also a sizeable body of legal instruments which has been drafted in a multinational or regional context. One of the earliest was the 1940 Convention on Nature Protection and Wildlife Preservation in the Western Hemisphere. More recent legislation includes the Convention on the Prevention of Marine Pollution by the Dumping Wastes and other Matter (1972), the Treaty for Amazon Cooperation (1978) and the Convention for the Protection and Development of the Marine Environment of the Wider Caribbean Region (1983).

Existence of laws, as is well known, is no guarantee of action. An interesting example is the case of legislation pertaining to the establishment of marine parks and coastal protected areas in the Caribbean. A 1988 inventory of such areas carried out by the OAS (1988) revealed that of the 95 areas established by legal decree only 15 were fully protected. The remainder were all suffering from varying degrees of encroachment of development which in some cases had relegated them to the unhappy category of "paper parks". Legislation without enforcement in some cases is worse than no legislation at all. Legal decrees which establish government parks or protected areas without effective enforcement sometimes create a kind of no-man's land in which more serious abuses are permitted than would have been the case if the areas had remained in private hands or legally unprotected.

Some successful Latin American experiences in managing parks and protected areas will be given in a later section.

3. Natural Resources and Environmental Data

Practical actions of environmental management, whether they are carried out by governments at national, sub-national or local levels, as well as international assistance to support such efforts, all depend on the availability of data which measure different characteristics of the natural systems where development interventions are to take place. Serious Latin American efforts to obtain adequate data on the natural resource base probably predates efforts in most other developing countries. In many countries, systematic inventories of natural resources involving the use of modern technologies of aerial photographic interpretation began to be compiled in the early 1960s and, by the end of that decade, an integrated approach to the evaluation of land resources was widely accepted in the region.

These efforts received substantial international support and financing, strengthening the creation and rapid growth of Latin American institutions which today, in many cases, constitute some of the key agencies responsible for environmental management. Many of these institutions that began as data gathering and processing centres, later received wider mandates pertaining to environmental policy, monitoring of environmental conditions and in a few cases responsibility for certain aspects of resource management. For some, a preoccupation with the collection of more and more information and preparation of better and better maps took precedence over effective use of resource data in the planning of development and design of investment projects. A certain disillusionment with these mapping and data collection institutions set in during the late 1970s and, as government budgets shrank and international assistance dwindled, some resource survey institutions fell on hard times, lost qualified staff and sharply reduced their data collection efforts. Today many of these institutions are being called upon to take a lead role on the subject of environment. Old problems still plague them, however, including their traditional difficulty in producing scientific data in a form which facilitates its use in planning and managing sustainable development. They must also be helped to better understand their institutional role on the broad subject of environmental management.

A key issue for Latin America is not so much the availability of natural resource data as it is the effective use of such data by planners and economists. A particularly critical goal is the definition of resource development potential, such as land use potential, to be able to guide development along sustainable lines. The strengthening of natural resources data production in the Americas should now be focused on three major themes:

1. Improved data collection and monitoring of air pollution, water contamination, acid rain, toxic wastes, deforestation, soil erosion, biodiversity, etc.;

2. Better integration of data from different sectors in order to obtain a composite picture of resource potentials and limitations; and,

3. More effective incorporation of data about the conditions and trend of the natural resource base into development decisions taken by economists and planners.

Latin America is making progress on all of these fronts, but a great deal of outside assistance is required. Modern technologies of remote sensing and computerised geographic information system for data integration have much to offer, but there is a risk of overinvesting in hardware and sophisticated technologies which requires expensive training. Simpler techniques using existing data should not be overlooked. Countries such as Brazil have launched major efforts to define land use potential and carrying out "ecologic zoning" in the Amazon Region. Integrated river basin development planning has reached a generally high level of sophistication throughout the Americas supported by significant technical assistance efforts of such agencies as OAS, UNDP, and bilateral donors (OAS, 1978a).

4. The Case for Integrated Regional Development Planning

The case for decentralising of planning and implementing development as a means for promoting better environmental management is gathering momentum. The belief is that if you plan development with a clear understanding of the potentials and limitations of the natural resource base on which it depends, and if you identify early on in the process the possible conflicts that may occur between different uses of resources, you can plan development which is sustainable and resolve the potential conflicts which would otherwise come to be referred to as "environmental impacts" (OAS, 1987). Experience in Latin America has shown that for most countries such integrated development planning focused on the resource base is most practical when carried out at a sub-national level. The planning units may be physical regions such as river basins or political units such as states, provinces or even municipalities. A key to the success of such efforts is the existence of an institution which has the authority to implement the planned development, backed by a serious government commitment to decentralisation.

This approach, which incorporates the environmental dimension into development planning at its earliest stages, has come to be referred to as integrated regional development planning. The approach is the evolutionary product of twenty years of experience in Latin America and the result of much trial and error. In 1984, with financial support from the USAID, the OAS published a book: *Integrated Regional Development Planning: Guidelines and Case Studies from OAS Experience*" (OAS, 1984) in which it examined twenty years of its own experience through a series of case studies of regional planning in the Americas. The overall problem to be addressed had been laid down in the 1983 *Environmental Strategy* of the USAID which stated: "The common critical need in all regions is more effective management or renewable natural resources using integrated approaches to regional planning and project design. The goal of integrated planning is the preparation of a national plan in which all development sectors have been assessed for their effect on all the resources in a given geographic area. It implies significant co-ordination among sectors and flexibility to modify activities to avoid resource depletion and assure long term productivity".

The methodology of the OAS on regional development is, in essence, a phased approach to integrated planning with a systematic incorporation of environmental issues from the outset and the use of technical assistance to support institution building. The approach is characterised by distinct phases starting with an initial overview of the sub-national region within the context of the country's national development plan, followed by a more detailed analysis of promising development areas and sustainable development projects. The three essential elements are diagnosis, strategy and project development.

Diagnosis: A rapid analysis to determine the principal problems, potentials, and constraints of a region. The development diagnosis can include an evaluation of natural and other resources and socioeconomic conditions; delineation and analysis of sub-regions, identification of critical institutions, sectors, and geographic areas; generation of new information, and pulling together ideas for investment projects.

Strategy: Selection of pressing issues and opportunities for addressing them with the available resources. Those opportunities indicate actions that are politically feasible within a time frame short enough to maintain momentum. Alternative strategies should be presented so the government has a choice.

Projects: Preparation of interrelated and compatible investment projects to implement the selected strategy. These projects, developed usually through pre-feasibility, should provide a balance among infrastructure, goods production, and services. Collectively, their benefit-cost ratio must be acceptable to governments and donors. The projects should then be presented to the government, together with any ancillary actions required, in an action plan of short to middle-term duration.

The strengths of this approach are its integrative, multi-sectoral character, its potential to identify and minimise conflicts in resource use at an early stage, its effect of reducing the need of environmental impact analysis of the projects it identifies and formulates as well as its involvement of the beneficiaries of development and other affected parties at an early stage of the development planning process. The weaknesses of the approach are institutional and political. Government institutions are organised sectorially and resist co-ordination. Political power in most Latin American countries is highly centralised. While lip service is paid to decentralisation and planning at a sub-national level is encouraged, when it comes to financing the implementation of development, central government usually maintains tight control over the purse strings. That frequently results in huge gaps between the plan and reality and a tendency for integrated plans to unravel along sectoral lines in response to the actions of individual government ministries and agencies. As a result of unravelling of carefully conceived packages of investment projects, environmental problems which had been dealt with in the original plan may suddenly re-emerge.

A particularly dramatic illustration was the case of the integrated plan for the development of the Darien Region of Panama (OAS, 1978b). A five-year integrated development plan for this humid tropical region was completed with OAS help in 1978. It contained a package of investment projects to focus development on the most promising areas of the Darien region where sustainable agriculture, and forestry development projects, with associated investment in agro-industry and infrastructure, had been designed to benefit local populations and migrants to the region who where expected to arrive as soon as the Darien Highway was completed. The whole plan and investment package was designed to draw migrants away from areas of poor soils and steep topography along the major penetration road. The investments in productive projects of agriculture, agro-industry and forestry were to be made simultaneously with completion of the road construction efforts.

Unfortunately the signing of the Panama Canal Treaty with the United States diverted government attention and financial resources away from the Darien Region. The investments in infrastructure, particularly road construction, however, went ahead without the associated investments in either the productive or conservation projects which had been formulated. The result was lamentable. As soon as the Darien Highway was completed and additional local roads were constructed by the Ministry of Public Works, the migrants arriving in the region occupied the areas along the highways, cut down the tropical rainforest and planted traditional crops irrespective of the quality of the land or government regulations to the contrary. The burning and destruction of vast areas stand in testimony to the failure of implementation of the plan and investment strategy. The key problem was that the public works sector investment went ahead, but the agriculture, forestry, and other sector investments did not. Even today in the early dry season it is difficult to operate aircraft in the Darien Region because of the smoke from the burning of tropical forests and brushland.

But not all integrated development plans come to such a sad conclusion. For example, nearly twenty-five years of integrated regional development planning in the Dominican Republic and Ecuador has had a profound effect on the national approaches to planning and on the way in which government agencies at the federal level cooperate with each other in either country. Geographic regions have been formally defined and used at the national level to assess natural resource potential, formulate development strategies and identify major investment projects. In the Dominican Republic, sectoral agencies are now routinely asked to help prepare and assign priority to those projects. Multi-sectoral investment budgets are drawn up for regions and sub-regions. Moreover, sectoral agencies are required to participate in a national dialogue on the use of the country's natural resources. In Ecuador, regional development authorities of various types have been granted significant authority over local development and environmental consideration carry increasing weight in their decisions.

In a recent study of the United Nations Center for Human Settlements (HABITAT) (United States Centre for Human Settlements, 1989), it was pointed out that while regional development agencies in the Americas have not acquired great power over central governments' financial decisions and allocations they are increasingly given greater authority over decisions affecting environmental management.

5. Institutional Considerations in Planning and Managing Natural Resources

5.1 Institutional arrangements for integrated development planning

A wealth of experience has been accumulated in Latin America on the subject of integrated development planning focused on natural resources. Some of it is analyzed in the OAS publication on integrated regional development planning mentioned previously (OAS, 1984). Essentially, what is required in most countries is an institutional framework which combines various government agencies. Some of the arrangements that have worked in a variety of settings are described below with comments on their strengths and weaknesses. The options which have been attempted include:

-- Setting up a task force of national agencies to prepare the plan and disbanding the mechanism when the plan is complete. This works well for planning, but obviously does not serve for implementation. Such a system was utilised in the plan for the Panama-Darien Region described previously.

-- Assigning the responsibility for preparing the plan to a major sectoral ministry or agency which, however, will work under the aegis of the national planning agency. This system assures better follow-up while the planning recommendations are being implemented, but its effectiveness is frequently constrained by the limits of the sectoral agency's mandate. In Ecuador, a major regional development plan was put together by the national water resource agency under the guidance of the national planning board. The water resource development proposals moved ahead but the agricultural projects floundered. The failure to establish a viable regional development authority further limited the implementation of those aspects of the plan, other than in the water resource sector.

-- Placing the responsibility to prepare the plan in the hands of an agency specialised in renewable natural resources or environment. Most such agencies in Latin America have a broad mandate and sometimes a spatial orientation comparable to a regional development organisation. However, few have financial or political power and some have legal mandates that put them at odds with other sectoral agencies. For example, Peru's Office for Evaluation of Natural Resources has a broad multi-sectoral focus but has no significant control over government investments that pertain to natural resources development. Peru's Ministry of Agriculture manages the country's national parks as well as its forests and wildlife reserves, but this broad mandate brings it in conflict with the Ministry of Mines and Energy which has a mandate to explore and exploit mineral and petroleum resources *throughout* Peruvian territory.

-- Designating a regional development corporation or a similar institution as the agency responsible for the integrated plan. When adequately funded this can prove to be one of the best of all institutional arrangements. There are few such agencies, however. In Venezuela the powerful Zulia Regional Development Corporation (CORPOZULIA), which is responsible for Venezuela's principal oil producing region, commissioned the preparation of a natural resources development plan in 1972-75 and saw to it that most of the resulting recommendations and projects were implemented. Even when the regional development agency is relatively weak it can still be a good choice as an institution to supervise integrated natural resource development plans. The Colombian Corporation for Development of the Uraba Region (CORFOURABA) was a newly created agency with a small budget and limited operating experience when it undertook a major programme. But in-service training of its staff, acquired by working with international personnel, and the infusion of public and private funds resulting from the approval of project proposals galvanised the agency, which was then able to implement much of planned action.

-- Establishing a national or regional independently funded study team that can evolve into a regional development or resource management institution when the study is completed. This option usually involves an initiative of the national planning agency, a substantial budget commitment by government and the tentative decision to establish a new institution. This arrangement has proven successful in a few cases; however, mounting a large institution-building effort during a planning study is difficult. In the study of the Naino-Putumayo region of Colombia the study teams later became staff members of a regional development corporation. The training provided to them was well utilised.

5.2 Institutional arrangements for environmental management

Environmental management by definition requires an integrated, multi-sectoral approach. The two basic methods to achieve this are: (a) developing co-ordinating mechanisms at the national level, and (b) decentralising management responsibility to local levels where co-ordination occurs more readily because there are fewer actors and horizontal communication and interaction is easier. The tendencies in Latin American public institutions are centrist and hierarchical, and most institutions are organised sectorially so both of these approaches have to work uphill.

At the national level

The previous section on regional planning arrangements gives a flavour of the problem and some of the solutions attempted are just as applicable to environmental management as to planning. One major lesson learned from the experience of the OAS with integrated planning is that teamwork and multi-agency co-ordination can be brought about if there is political will to do so and if the work is funded and supported in subtle ways. Integrated task forces of agencies can work well as long as there are funds to pay for the extra costs to the agencies or if some outside agency is supporting the effort. Agencies cooperate with each other when it is financially attractive to do so. The traditional systems of reward and punishment in most Latin American bureaucracies do not automatically favour inter-agency cooperation and co-ordination. Even under strong leadership, co-ordinated efforts which begin well tend to weaken with the passage of time. Busy government officials stop coming to inter-agency meetings and working groups when demands of their sectoral agency take precedence. Agency "homework" that was supposed to be done between meetings does not get done and the process slows down.

A recent experience in Costa Rica, however, has proved very eye opening. The challenge is the management of the La Amistad national park and biosphere reserve which includes 12 per cent of the national territory (Government of Costa Rica *et al.*, 1990). This area of 612 570 hectares constitutes the most extensive area of natural forest in Costa Rica. It is the country's principal zone of biodiversity, and contains 65 per cent of its indigenous population. The reserve is administered by a Co-ordinating Commission that was created in 1988 and includes the National Park Service, The Forest Service and the Wildlife Administration of the Ministry of Natural Resources, Energy and Mines as well as the National Commission of Indigenous Affairs of the Ministry of Culture and the Organization of Tropical Studies -- a non governmental organisation.

Other agencies which have authority over resources in the area include: two regional offices of the Ministry of Planning (MIDEPLAN), the Costa Rican Petroleum Refinery which has a mandate to search for, exploit and distribute the hydrocarbon, coal and peat reserves of the country and the Costa Rican Electrical Agency which can exploit the hydro-energy potential of the La Amistad region as well as use its authority to obtain rights of way for energy distribution; and finally the Ministry of Public Works and Transportation which can programme and construct large infrastructure projects in the region.

The presence of a co-ordinating commission to deal with such a wide spectrum of agencies and overlapping authority is not unique, but its current basis for operation in Costa Rica is noteworthy. In 1988 Conservation International (CI), a North American non-governmental organisation on the environment, cooperated with the Government of Costa Rica in a debt-for-nature swap to which CI donated $46 000 for the purchase of monetary stabilization bonds. These funds, over a period of five years and nine months, are expected to generate $320 000 which will pay operating costs for the Co-ordinating Commission until the latter can become self supporting. Every indication so far is that this has been a highly successful debt-for-nature swap operation created to address the central issues of environmental management, namely inter-agency cooperation. It is also a successful example of international technical assistance since, apparently, a key element in building up the technical capacity of the Co-ordinating Commission for the La Amistad Reserve was the outside technical help in planning development in the Biosphere Reserve -- in managing the core area and in creating a strategy to help the Co-ordinating Commission identify potential conflicts in resource use before they caused damage. It should also be added here that the technical staff of the Co-ordinating Commission now constitute a permanent trained core group of professionals which continues to provide planning and management expertise to the other national agencies which have responsibilities within the biosphere reserve. They also formulate an evolving but still well-co-ordinated set of management objectives for the biosphere reserve and the area surrounding it.

While mechanisms can be created at the national level to provide for inter-agency co-ordination and there is a significant role for international assistance in strengthening such mechanisms, the challenge in Latin America is complicated by the manner in which the environmental dimension is incorporated into the organisation of government agencies. Table 1 shows the scale of variation in the location of environmental agencies within the central governments of Latin American countries. Some of the resulting problems for co-ordinated action are self-evident.

Table 1

THE LOCATION OF PUBLIC SECTOR ENVIRONMENTAL AGENCIES WITHIN THE GOVERNMENTS LATIN AMERICA AND THE CARIBBEAN

	Separate unit Environment Ministry	In productive Ministries: Agriculture, Tourism, etc.	In Urban Development or Housing	In Social Sector: Health	Ministry of Interior or Planning	Inter-sectoral executive commissions
Argentina			X	X		X
Bahamas				X		
Barbados			X			
Bolivia					X	
Brazil	X					X
Chile						X
Colombia		X				
Costa Rica						X
Dominican Republic		X				
Ecuador					X	
El Salvador					X	
Guatemala						X
Guyana	X					
Haiti					X	
Honduras					X	
Jamaica		X				
Mexico			X	X		
Nicaragua		X				
Panama						X
Paraguay		X				
Peru					X	
Surinam						X
Trinidad & Tobago						X
Uruguay			X			
Venezuela	X					

Source: Barcena Ibarra, 1987.

At the regional and local level

It is becoming gradually accepted that local governments are able to be more sensitive to the wide range of problems that we call environmental, that their approach can be more integrated because of the scale of their operations, and that they can avoid some of the costly mistakes of the sectoral agencies of central governments. The problem in Latin America is that local government is traditionally weak, underfinanced and poorly staffed. At the sub-national level the operational planning system in most countries differs considerably from the one that is described in official documents and legal texts.

Since inadequate financing of government action at the local level seems to be one of the main obstacles to strengthening environmental management, many different solutions to this problem are currently being sought, including by international organisations. The traditional problem is to identify a potential source of funding to pay for local services of resource management when central government is reluctant to commit funds from the federal budget.

In addition to the imaginative use of funding from debt-for-nature swaps, as described previously, and external assistance from both public and private institutions, an effective mechanism is the formulation of development projects which generate funds for use in local areas. Eco-tourism projects which benefit rural areas are a good example of this. The key to success is to ensure that the funds generated by tourism benefit the local community and are utilised to pay for the management of the park or protected area which is the focus of the investment. Some very interesting examples of this process have been recently developed in the Caribbean.

Decentralisation brings continuing and large benefits when local institutions are granted authority over the management of natural resources or are financed with part of the revenue generated by those resources. Some of the strongest regional development agencies in the Americas are those that derive their budgets from such arrangements. Some of the best examples of this include CORPOZULIA which is responsible for the major oil producing region of Venezuela, the Corporacion de Santa Cruz de la Sierra which manages the area of natural gas production in Bolivia, the Corporacion Guyana which is in charge of the huge Venezuelan industrial complex in the Guyana Region, and the Cauca Valley Authority which controls development in the Cauca River Basin of Colombia.

6. Conclusion

In conclusion, it can be seen that strengthening of environmental management capacity in Latin America necessitates appropriate national environmental policies, adequate environmental legislation, a strong data base on natural resources and the environment, institutional mechanisms for co-ordinating actions of many governmental agencies at the national level, strengthened regional and local institutions with greater responsibilities for environmental management and adequate training of government personnel at all levels. To accomplish the strengthening of government institutions three principal mechanisms have been discussed:

1. Obtaining additional financing for government environmental institutions by designing development projects which mobilise external resources and have institution building effects, or debt-for-nature swaps which convert national debt into funds to provide direct support for institutions involved in environmental management.

2. Using proven mechanisms for multi-sectoral co-ordination of government actions at all levels.

3. Increasing international technical assistance and training efforts to directly strengthen relevant institutions.

The Latin American experience is rich with practical examples of all of the above types of institutional strengthening but deserves further analysis.

BIBLIOGRAPHICAL REFERENCES

BARCENA IBARRA, Alicia, *Reflections on the Incorporation of an Environmental Dimension into the Institutional Framework and Operations of the Public Sector in Latin America and the Caribbean*, Harvard University, 1987.

GOVERNMENT OF COSTA RICA/CONSERVATION INTERNATIONAL/OAS, *Estrategia para el Desarrollo Institutional de la Reserva de la Biosfera "La Amistad"*, Costa Rica, 1990.

GOVERNMENT OF URUGUAY and INTER-AMERICAN DEVELOPMENT BANK (IDB) *Technical Cooperation Agreement for a National Environmental Study*, December 1988.

ORGANIZATION OF AMERICAN STATES (OAS), *Physical Resource Investigation for Economic Development. A Casebook of OAS Field Experience in Latin America*, Washington, D.C., 1969.

Environmental Quality and River Basin Development: A Model for Integrated Analysis and Planning, Washington, D.C., 1978a.

Proyecto de Desarrollo Integrado de la Région Oriental de Panama-Darien, Washington, D.C., 1978b.

Minimum Conflicts: Guidelines for Planning the Use of American Humid Tropic Environments, Washington, D.C., 1987.

Inventory of Caribbean Marine and Coastal Protected Areas, Washington, D.C., 1988.

OAS in cooperation with NATIONAL PARK SERVICE (U.S.) and USAID, *Integrated Regional Development Planning: Guidelines and Cases Studies from OAS Experience*, Washington, D.C., January 1984.

ONERN/OAS, *Lineamienos de Politica de Conservacion de Los Recursos Renovables del Peru*, Lima, May 1974.

UNITED NATIONS CENTRE FOR HUMAN SETTLEMENTS (HABITAT), *Institutional Arrangements for Regional (Subnational) Development Planning*, Nairobi, 1989.

L'EXPÉRIENCE DU RWANDA EN MATIÈRE D'ENVIRONNEMENT

par

Augustin NGIRABATWARE *

* Augustin Ngirabatware est le Ministre du Plan de la République Rwandaise.

SUMMARY

The major environmental problem facing Rwanda is the imbalance between available resources and population. Population pressure affects the area available for agricultural production and for housing, as well as the protected zones. Therefore, Rwanda has prepared a National Environmental Strategy and an Environmental Action Plan based on the concept of sustainable development. The aim is to achieve a balance between population, resources and environment which would meet the criteria of sustainability, equity and efficiency. From the early stages of the design of the strategy, both public and private institutions were involved. To fully involve the entire population, environmental education and awareness raising activities will be introduced.

RÉSUMÉ

Le problème majeur auquel le Rwanda fait face en matière d'environnement est le déséquilibre entre les ressources et la population. La pression démographique affecte l'espace productif agricole aussi bien que l'espace habité et les zones protégées. En conséquence, le pays a élaboré une Stratégie Nationale de l'Environnement et un Plan d'Action Environnemental qui s'inscrivent dans le cadre du développement durable que vise le Rwanda, consistant en l'équilibre durable, équitable et productif entre la population, les ressources et l'environnement. Dès les travaux préparatoires, un effort a été fait afin d'associer les institutions publiques et privées à cette entreprise, pour laquelle la population entière sera mobilisée par l'éducation et par des activités de sensibilisation.

1. *Problématique de l'environnement au Rwanda*

Encore épargné de la pollution industrielle telle qu'on la connaît dans les pays industrialisés, le problème majeur auquel le Rwanda fait face en matière d'environnement demeure, sans nul conteste, le déséquilibre entre les ressources et la population. Déjà, avec une population d'environ 7.5 millions d'habitants augmentant à un rythme annuel de 3.7 pour cent alors que la production n'augmente qu'à un taux estimé à 2.2 pour cent, la dégradation de l'environnement ne peut être qu'évidente.

Au Rwanda nous assistons à des phénomènes de dégradation de l'environnement multiples, liés à :

-- la pression démographique sur l'espace habité caractérisée par l'habitat dispersé en milieu rural ;

-- la pression démographique sur l'espace productif à prédominance agricole ;

-- la pression démographique sur l'espace des réserves et des zones protégées telles que les forêts naturelles et les parc nationaux ;

-- la pression démographique sur l'espace urbain qu'il faut lotir et assainir en vue de garantir la santé et le bien-être humain.

Cette pression démographique a des incidences également sur l'énergie, les transports, l'eau et sur les industries ; car il faut nourrir, habiller, déplacer et assurer une vie relationnelle à toute cette population.

Afin de parvenir à un développement harmonieux dans le respect des écosystèmes, le Rwanda a voulu que l'exploitation et la transformation de ses ressources en vue de satisfaire les besoins matériels et immatériels des Rwandais ne se fasse pas au détriment de ces ressources naturelles.

En conséquence, le pays a tout mis en oeuvre pour se doter d'une Stratégie Nationale de l'Environnement et d'un Plan d'Action Environnemental dans le but de parvenir à la difficile, mais pas impossible, équation entre "exploiter et conserver" ; laquelle équation constitue une condition de possibilité du développement durable, à savoir : un développement qui doit être économiquement viable, écologiquement rationnel et socialement acceptable.

2. *La stratégie nationale de l'environnement au Rwanda et le plan d'action environnemental*

2.1 Historique

La dégradation de l'environnement au Rwanda a été perçue depuis longtemps. Celle-ci s'est d'ailleurs progressivement aggravée au fur et à mesure que la croissance annuelle de la population exerçait une pression de plus en plus intense sur les ressources dont dispose le pays.

A cet égard, de nombreux signes ont montré que la persistance de certains phénomènes risquait d'entraîner une forte détérioration de l'environnement et de graves problèmes socio-économiques si des mesures urgentes n'étaient pas mises en oeuvre pour y faire face. Les cas ainsi observés concernent principalement l'érosion, la baisse des rendements des exploitations agricoles, la réduction des superficies réservées aux forêts naturelles, la raréfaction du bois de chauffe, la pollution de l'eau et, en certains endroits, les rejets industriels.

Naturellement, l'ampleur de ces problèmes ne pouvait laisser indifférentes les autorités du pays qui, pour y faire face, ont initié des actions incluant une forte composante environnementale et auxquelles les bailleurs de fonds ont apporté des appuis appréciables par leur soutien technique et financier. Il y a lieu de citer à ce propos l'institutionnalisation de la journée de l'arbre, la réalisation d'un vaste programme de lutte anti-érosive, le renforcement de l'hydraulique rurale, la protection des forêts naturelles et des Parcs Nationaux, etc...

L'ensemble de ces opérations a certes permis d'enregistrer des résultats largement positifs et d'accumuler une solide expérience dans les divers domaines touchés, mais il s'est vite avéré nécessaire de concevoir et de mettre sur pied une politique cohérente visant une meilleure gestion à court, moyen et long terme des ressources de l'environnement.

Aussi, dans l'optique d'une plus grande sensibilisation et d'une large concertation, deux séminaires ont-ils été organisés respectivement en 1985 et 1987 et ont constitué une occasion de rassembler des fonctionnaires de l'Administration Centrale, des représentants des organisations non gouvernementales (ONG) ainsi que des opérateurs économiques. Les débats qui ont eu lieu au cours de ces deux rencontres ont abouti notamment à la conclusion selon laquelle les politiques destinées à réaliser les objectifs socio-économiques devaient aller de pair avec une gestion écologiquement saine des ressources et de l'environnement.

L'élaboration d'une stratégie nationale de l'environnement au Rwanda fut donc l'une des principales recommandations issues de ces deux séminaires.

Il était d'abord prévu que l'étude sur la stratégie serait réalisée par un bureau d'études étranger. Etant donnée la grande expertise dans les questions environnementales disponibles au Rwanda, ainsi que les travaux impressionnants déjà réalisés au cours des dernières années, il a été décidé que cette étude serait réalisée par une équipe rwandaise avec seulement un support extérieur complémentaire dans les domaines spécifiques où une insuffisance dans l'expertise ou l'expérience nationale était prévisible.

Conçue comme un tout cohérent, cette étude sur la stratégie nationale de l'environnement au Rwanda et le plan d'action environnemental avait pour but d'identifier les problèmes environnementaux inhérents à chaque secteur d'activités socio-économiques, de responsabiliser chaque opérateur, tant public que privé, au sujet des problèmes environnementaux générés par ses activités, de planifier les actions à mener pour concilier les exigences du développement du pays (sous ses multiples aspects) avec la nécessité de protéger et de sauvegarder les écosystèmes de l'environnement du pays.

2.2 Contenu de la Stratégie Nationale de l'Environnement au Rwanda

Compte tenu de la situation spécifique du Rwanda, à savoir : un petit pays, classé parmi les moins avancés, surpeuplé, enclavé et aux ressources très limitées, la Stratégie Nationale de l'Environnement au Rwanda s'articule sur huit thèmes principaux, à savoir :

1) L'impact négatif de la pression démographique sur l'espace destiné à la production, sur les établissements humains caractérisés par l'habitat dispersé et les agglomérations, sur les zones protégées telles que le Parc National des Volcans qui abrite les gorilles de montagne, le Parc National de l'Akagera et les forêts de montagnes (Nyungwe, Mukura et Gishwati) ;

2) L'impact de la production agricole sur l'environnement : l'analyse du problème met en exergue le danger qui peut exister lorsqu'on vise l'augmentation de la production agricole par l'utilisation des intrants (les engrais minéraux, les pesticides, etc...) sans le souci de la protection de l'environnement ;

3) La valorisation du tourisme et l'aménagement des milieux naturels dans le respect de l'équilibre des écosystèmes ;

4) La formation de la population en matière d'environnement ainsi que la recherche en vue de dégager l'impact sur l'environnement des activités socio-économiques ;

5) L'interaction difficile à maîtriser entre l'énergie, l'eau, les industries, l'urbanisme, la santé et l'environnement ;

6) La coopération internationale dans le domaine de l'environnement ;

7) La mise sur pied d'un cadre juridique et d'une structure chargée de la bonne gestion de l'environnement ;

8) Le rôle de la femme rwandaise dans l'établissement d'un équilibre durable, équitable et productif entre la population, les ressources, l'environnement et le développement.

Tous ces thèmes ont été abordés sous trois aspects. L'aspect DIAGNOSTIC qui présente la photographie des problèmes environnementaux tels qu'ils sont vécus au Rwanda. L'aspect STRATÉGIE qui constitue une prescription de programmes à mettre sur pied pour faire face aux problèmes environnementaux déjà diagnostiqués. Et enfin, l'aspect PLAN D'ACTION qui est un inventaire des actions prioritaires à mener dans le court, moyen et long terme pour remédier à cette situation. Le Plan d'Action indique également qui doit faire quoi et comment. A ce propos, il précise les actions qui nécessitent un appui extérieur.

2.3 Orientations de la Stratégie Nationale de l'Environnement au Rwanda

La Stratégie Nationale de l'Environnement au Rwanda s'appuie sur la nécessaire inter-relation entre les activités socio-économiques des hommes, le respect de l'équilibre de l'environnement et une exploitation rationnelle des ressources, et considère que la recherche d'intégration et de complémentarité de ces éléments constitue une condition de survie de la société.

Cette stratégie environnementale insiste sur le fait que la solution ne saurait valablement être trouvée dans l'addition des mesures ponctuelles prises par à-coup quand survient telle ou telle catastrophe, elle préconise au contraire d'opérer à travers une vision d'ensemble cohérente recherchant un équilibre durable des écosystèmes et une gestion efficace des ressources, équilibre indispensable pour atteindre l'autosuffisance alimentaire.

S'agissant des orientations particulières et spécifiques à l'environnement, elles sont essentiellement axées sur les points suivants :

-- Assurer une utilisation des ressources de l'environnement qui concilie les exigences du développement actuel et les intérêts des générations futures ;

-- Réaliser les études d'impact de tous les projets comportant des volets susceptibles d'altérer l'environnement ;

-- Faire supporter les frais de restauration des dégâts d'ordre environnemental par leurs acteurs ;

-- Mettre sur pied des programmes de sensibilisation, de formation et d'information de toutes les couches de la population sur la nécessité de sauvegarder l'environnement ;

-- Organiser un cadre juridique et institutionnel apte à assurer la cohérence des actions menées dans le cadre de la protection de l'environnement et le suivi des politiques édictées dans ce domaine.

Au niveau des thèmes énoncés ci-dessus et des secteurs, les stratégies environnementales préconisées peuvent être synthétisées de la manière suivante :

Population et aménagement du territoire

L'objectif général visé concerne la promotion d'une occupation rationnelle et d'une utilisation efficace de l'espace national afin de relever la productivité tant dans les zones rurales que dans des centres urbains et de faciliter la diffusion des politiques relatives à la planification familiale.

L'environnement et le secteur agricole

Il est préconisé d'accroître la productivité des terres arables par des méthodes de conservation qui ne nuisent pas à l'environnement, notamment par l'amélioration du programme national de lutte anti-érosive, la rationalisation des techniques de l'élevage, une gestion efficace des ressources forestières et une exploitation équilibrée des marais.

L'aménagement des milieux naturels, les catastrophes, le climat et le tourisme

Le but poursuivi dans le cadre de ces domaines est le maintien de l'équilibre des différents écosystèmes et la valorisation des ressources naturelles rencontrées dans ces différents milieux.

L'énergie, l'eau, l'industrie, l'urbanisme et les transports

Un accent particulier est mis sur la nécessité de mettre sur pied des mécanismes de contrôle de la qualité des eaux, de l'air et de la fumée qui proviennent des usines, de renforcer les services d'inspection et d'assurer le traitement des rejets. La sécurité des travailleurs et la reconstitution des milieux détruits constituent également un centre de préoccupation.

L'éducation, la recherche et l'information

Ces programmes d'accompagnement ont comme objectif d'accroître les capacités scientifiques de toutes les structures appelées à jouer un rôle de sensibilisation de tous les opérateurs sur la question environnementale.

Le cadre juridique et institutionnel

Pour assurer efficacement le suivi et la coordination de la mise en oeuvre des politiques environnementales, il est recommandé de revoir la réglementation en la matière pour l'adapter aux exigences actuelles et de renforcer les structures institutionnelles à tous les échelons.

La coopération internationale

L'objectif visé à ce niveau est d'amener nos partenaires, tant régionaux qu'internationaux, à prendre en compte, dans leur coopération, la nécessité de ne pas porter atteinte au milieu lors de la mise en oeuvre de projets de développement et de prendre en commun des initiatives destinées à la protection de l'environnement.

La femme rwandaise et l'environnement

La stratégie préconisée à ce sujet est de promouvoir la femme rwandaise pour en faire une partenaire active dans le domaine de la protection, la conservation et la promotion de l'environnement.

Plusieurs voies sont envisageables à ce niveau dont notamment la formation et l'augmentation de ses sources de revenus ; mais avant tout et surtout la sensibilisation accrue de la femme rwandaise à la planification familiale pour l'amener à jouer un rôle déterminant dans l'établissement de l'équilibre durable, équitable et productif entre la population, les ressources, l'environnement et le développement.

3. *La Stratégie Nationale de l'Environnement au Rwanda : valeur et efficacité de l'outil*

3.1 Articulation entre la Stratégie Nationale de l'Environnement au Rwanda et les plans quinquennaux de développement

La Stratégie Nationale de l'Environnement au Rwanda s'inscrit dans le cadre du développement durable que vise le Rwanda et qui résultera de l'équilibre durable, équitable et productif entre la population, les ressources et l'environnement.

Ce triple équilibre commande donc que nous procédions à une intégration des préoccupations environnementales dans notre système de programmation des investissements et de planification du développement.

Aussi, la Stratégie Nationale de l'Environnement au Rwanda se donne t-elle comme option fondamentale :

1. Amener le pays à parvenir à un équilibre entre la population et les ressources, et même à inverser la tendance en vue de rendre davantage disponibles les ressources en faveur des populations dans le respect de l'équilibre des écosystèmes ;

2. Contribuer au développement socio-économique soutenu, durable et harmonieux, tant en milieu rural qu'en milieu urbain où les Rwandais pourront s'épanouir dans un environnement sain et agréable pour leur bien-être ;

3. Protéger, conserver et valoriser les milieux naturels parce que ceux-ci constituent des ressources indispensables pour la population sur le plan socio-économique, scientifique, culturel et touristique.

La Stratégie Nationale de l'Environnement au Rwanda a également pour mission d'orienter les actions de développement vers l'objectif majeur de l'auto-suffisance et la sécurité alimentaires durables et ce, en tenant compte d'abord des réalités locales.

Une telle mission constitue en soi un défi voire une gageure ! Quels sont les moyens que la Stratégie Nationale de l'Environnement au Rwanda prévoit pour relever ce défi?

3.2 Les outils de gestion et les mesures d'accompagnement de la Stratégie Nationale de l'Environnement

Une Stratégie environnementale n'est rien d'autre qu'un outil dont l'efficience demeure conditionnée par la façon dont on s'en sert. Pour le cas du Rwanda, nous sommes déjà d'avis que notre Stratégie environnementale ne servirait à rien si elle ne reposait pas sur l'adhésion et la participation massive de tous les Rwandais. C'est dans ce cadre que nous n'avons pas voulu, même dès sa conception et tout au long de son élaboration, en faire une affaire du Ministère du Plan et des experts chargés de sa confection.

Ainsi, départements ministériels, institutions publiques et privées, organisations non gouvernementales locales et internationales ainsi que tous nos partenaires de développement ont été régulièrement associés aux travaux préparatoires de cette Stratégie environnementale et ce, à travers les séminaires qui ont été organisés en vue de recueillir les avis des principaux acteurs socio-économico-politiques qui seront les premiers à la traduire en actes.

La Stratégie Nationale de l'Environnement au Rwanda est, et doit être, l'affaire de tous les Rwandais. Elle ne peut donc réussir que si toute la population, sans distinction d'âge, de sexe et de catégorie socio-professionnelle est imprégnée de cette dynamique individuelle et collective de protection, de conservation et de promotion de l'environnement, seule garantie du bien-être durable.

Aussi, le Gouvernement rwandais attache-t-il une importance capitale à la sensibilisation, à l'information et à la formation du public en matière d'environnement comme mesures d'accompagnement indispensables à la réussite de cette Stratégie environnementale.

Autant donc dire que, dès leur tendre enfance, Rwandais et Rwandaises doivent être formés à travers l'éducation formelle et informelle, pour leur faire acquérir et développer des attitudes, des réflexes et un mode de pensée et d'action qui intègrent la dimension environnementale dans tous les faits et gestes du quotidien.

En plus de cette mobilisation sociale autour du thème environnement et développement, la mise en place et la réussite de la Stratégie Nationale de l'Environnement au Rwanda, qui sera bientôt traduite en action, demandent que la structure chargée de sa gestion soit redynamisée et consolidée. Le rôle de cette structure sera de coordonner, d'orienter, et d'assurer le suivi et l'évaluation régulière de la politique définie en matière d'environnement. Elle ne devra donc pas se substituer à d'autres institutions pour ce qui est de la responsabilité qui incombe à tout un chacun dans le domaine de la conservation et la défense de l'environnement.

Dotée d'un personnel compétent, cette structure devra également disposer des outils de gestion de l'environnement, nous entendons par là une législation claire, nette et distincte en matière d'environnement qui envisagerait le volet de la fiscalité pour asseoir le principe du "pollueur-payeur". Cette législation devra également statuer sur les études d'impact environnemental qui doivent précéder tout projet, entreprise ou autre activité de grande envergure à entreprendre au Rwanda.

En bref, sensibilisation de la population pour l'amener à participer massivement et en toute responsabilité à la défense de son environnement ; mise en place d'une structure solide pour jouer le rôle d'inspecteur de l'environnement, tels sont les outils qui nous permettront d'asseoir la Stratégie Nationale de l'Environnement au Rwanda et le Plan d'Action Environnemental.

Les travaux en rapport avec cette stratégie environnementale sont presque terminés. Elle sera bientôt soumise aux hautes instances de décision de notre pays pour approbation, après quoi elle sera mise en application.

Toutefois, la mobilisation des efforts de la population rwandaise, à travers notamment les travaux communautaires de développement -- UMUGANDA -- et à travers les institutions gouvernementales et non gouvernementales, bien que préalable indispensable pour la mise en oeuvre de la Stratégie Nationale de l'Environnement au Rwanda et le Plan d'Action Environnemental, ne suffira pas à elle seule, eu égard à l'acuité des problèmes environnementaux déjà identifiés et à la conjoncture particulièrement difficile que traverse le pays. Un apport de ressources externes par le biais des organismes internationaux s'avère donc très nécessaire.

C'est dans ce sens que le Rwanda compte organiser au cours du premier trimestre 1991, à Kigali, une table ronde des bailleurs de fonds pour le Plan d'Action Environnemental afin de susciter la participation des organisations internationales.

ENVIRONMENTAL MANAGEMENT IN POLAND

by

Piotr Wilczyński *

* Piotr Wilczyński is Adviser to the Minister of Environment Protection, Natural Resources and Forestry, Poland. He is based at the Oskar Lange Academy (Akademia Ekonomiczna im. Oskara Langego we Wrocławiu, Instytut Ekonomii Politycznej) in Wrocław, Poland.

RÉSUMÉ

La Pologne souffre de l'un des niveaux de pollution industrielle les plus élevés du monde. Plusieurs de ses voisins immédiats partagent cette caractéristique comme ils partageaient, jusqu'à une époque récente, une économie planifiée dans laquelle les objectifs de production, et non l'efficacité et la réduction des coûts, constituaient la principale motivation des entreprises. La gestion de l'environnement en Pologne (2ème et 3ème parties) a commencé à se développer dans les années 70, avec des institutions qui existaient surtout sur le papier, et la mise en oeuvre laissait fort à désirer. Lorsqu'à la fin des années 80, le pays a commencé à s'orienter vers un système politique représentative, des ONG ont commencé à faire part de préoccupations touchant l'environnement, amenant ensuite le gouvernement à reconnaître l'urgence de la situation et à réorganiser les services chargés de la gestion de l'environnement (4ème partie). L'application des instruments économiques a eu jusqu'à présent peu d'effet sur le comportement des pollueurs en Pologne et tant les entreprises que les décideurs, opérant dans un système où ne jouent pas les mécanismes du marché, se sentent plus sûrs avec la réglementation et négligent les incitations à une plus grande efficacité. Dans les cas où les incitations et la réglementation ont apporté quelque amélioration, la gestion de l'environnement s'est généralement concentrée sur les solutions "en aval", en partie parce que les conditions macro-économiques générales (subventions) favorisent la surexploitation des ressources naturelles et de l'énergie. En conclusion, l'auteur insiste surtout sur la nécessité d'une aide extérieure accrue, tant financière que technico-administratif. Cette conclusion est en partie justifiée par l'argument que les avantages marginaux de l'investissement dans la protection de l'environnement en Pologne pourraient être les plus élevés d'Europe.

SUMMARY

Poland suffers from one of the highest levels of industrial pollution in the world. Several countries immediately neighbouring her share this characteristic and until recently a centrally planned economy where output targets, not efficiency and cost minimisation constituted the primary motivation of firms. The development of environmental management in Poland (Parts 2 and 3) began in the 1970s with institutions that largely existed on paper and was poorly implemented. As the country began to move in the direction of a representative political system in the late 1980s environmental concerns began to be expressed by NGOs and later on led to a government's recognition of an urgency and the reorganisation of agencies responsible for environmental management (Part 4). The use of economic instruments has so far had little effect on the behaviour of polluters in Poland and both firms and policy makers operating in a non-market system appear to feel more secure with regulation and disregard incentives for efficiency. Where incentives and regulation have led to limited improvement environmental management tended to concentrate on "end-of-the-pipe" solutions in part because the general macroeconomic conditions (subsidies) encourage the overuse of natural resources and energy. The author's conclusion places the heaviest emphasis on the need for increased financial and technical/managerial assistance from abroad. This is in part justified with the argument that in Poland marginal benefits from environmental investment might be the highest in Europe.

1. Introduction

The quality of environment in a given country reflects how the economic and political system uses its natural and environmental resources plus the country's so-called environmental assimilative capacity.

Available data indicate that, in general, countries basing their development on the principles of a market economy are better off environmentally than those following the so-called centrally planned, non-market approach.

The non-market model of economic growth has lead to an excessive usage of natural resources per unit of output (see Table 1). When accompanied by very weak, or in some cases the absence of environment management efforts, it results in great pressure on the environment, leading to degradation and pollution, which affects the health conditions of the people in those countries.

Poland is one of the main polluters of Europe and faces serious problems due to that pollution. The economic losses are estimated at 8 per cent of annual GNP. This is mainly due to air and water pollution, plus solid waste generation and storage. About 11 per cent of the country's territory, inhabited by 30 per cent of the whole population, is described as seriously polluted with ambient levels exceeding national standards for SO_2, CO_2, NO_x. Heavy metal and toxic pollution, especially that of lead and PCBs, have reached alarming levels in those areas. The most critical is the situation of Upper Silesia where life expectancy is lower compared to other parts of the country and genetic malformations are found. Only 4 per cent of Polish rivers are of first class purity, and as much as 40 per cent of the rivers are unfit for any use.

Countries of central and eastern Europe, not to mention the Soviet Union, all face environmental problems. The scale of these problems varies depending on the role that industry, especially heavy industry, and the energy sector based on fossil fuels, play in the economy. Additionally it must be said, no matter how paradoxical it may sound, that as a general tendency, the bigger the stock of natural resources in a country, the greater the environmental problems observed there. This is so because in such countries natural resources are not treated as scarce goods in the economic sense of the word. The policy of centrally determined low prices of natural resources has resulted in a high intensity of use per unit of output, compared with highly developed countries. It must be underlined that the soft budget policy of central planners totally subverted prices for all factors of production. Economic scarcity in such a system was suppressed and the main focus of attention was how to increase the supply of natural resources, energy, water, etc.

Table 1

ENERGY AND MATERIAL INTENSIVENESS OF THE EUROPEAN CMEA COUNTRIES AND SELECTED DEVELOPED COUNTRIES, 1980

Country	Gross energy consumption Kca/cap.	Raw steel consump-tion Kg/cap.	National income $/cap.	Energy use Kgoe/$	Steel use Kg/$
Bulgaria	5 678	320	4 150	1.37	0.08
Czechoslovakia	6 482	706	5 320	1.11	0.12
Hungary	3 850	340	4 180	0.92	0.08
GDR	4 708	566	7 180	1.03	0.08
Poland	5 690	513	3 900	1.43	0.13
Rumania	4 593	562	2 340	1.96	0.24
Austria	4 160	355	10 230	0.41	0.03
Denmark	5 225	356	12 950	0.40	0.03
France	4 351	422	11 730	0.37	0.04
FRG	5 727	609	13 590	0.42	0.04
Italy	3 318	412	6 480	0.51	0.06
Japan	3 690	512	9 890	0.37	0.05
Spain	5 727	244	5 400	1.06	0.05
United Kingdom	4 835	237	7 920	0.61	0.03
United States	10 410	490	11 360	0.92	0.04

Sources: P. Wilczyński, *Environmental Management in Centrally-Planned Non-Market Economies of Eastern Europe*, Environment Department, Working Paper No. 35, Washington D.C., World Bank, July 1990, Table 3, p. 5. A. Budnikowski, M. J. Welfens, and S. Sitnicki, *Rozwoj gospodarczy, a ochrona srodowisksa w krajach RWPG,* (Economic Development and Environment Protection in the Countries of the CMEA) Warsaw, National Economic Publishers (PWE), 1987.

At the same time, pollution control and environmental management did not receive adequate political attention and support. The official policy was that the country must first reach a high level of development and afterwards it will be able to afford pollution control and carry out the clean-up programme. Environment protection was viewed as a burden, slowing down economic growth -- understood as a process of increases in the volume of production.

2. Stages of Development

The development of environmental management in Poland began in 1949 and has passed through several stages since.

The first stage can be distinguished as the period of nature conservation. In 1949 the Polish parliament passed a bill on the conservation of nature. The bill created necessary conditions to protect flora and fauna, national parks and natural monuments. In the years 1949-70 nature conservation was the responsibility of the Ministry of Forestry which was assisted by the State Commission for Nature Conservation and a nationwide organisation called the League for Nature Conservation. The activities of these bodies in regard to the natural environment were rather passive but the League did play an important role in education and public awareness for nature conservation.

Initial steps were taken for pollution prevention and control in the mid-1960s. The concept at that time was to concentrate on media protection i.e. water and air, with some ideas for ecosystems protection being included, e.g. more stringent standards for areas of special interest (recreation areas, areas in the vicinity of national parks, etc.). Effluent standards for air and water were introduced.

The 1970s can be described as the second stage in the development of environmental management. However, despite growing problems, environmental management was still very weak and environment protection was neglected. This was despite the creation in 1970 of a State Commission for Environment Protection followed by the Ministry for Environment Protection in 1972. State censor did not allow any significant publications on the state of the environment and the data were confidential. At the same time the Ministry of Environment was given a very low profile. Thus, although effluent standards for air and water were reviewed and a monitoring system was created, in reality the environmental regulation and laws were neglected both at the central and provincial levels of administration.

Thus, the environmental management system was a paper tiger, which had little influence on decision making. Environmental planning was introduced during the 1970s. The plans however were not fulfilled by sectoral ministries and provincial administrations. At the end of the 1970s, as the social and economic costs of ignoring environmental management began to grow rapidly, intellectuals grouped in academic circles started lobbying for change.

In 1980 the parliament passed a comprehensive bill on environment protection and development. With that bill the third stage of development of environmental management began. Without going into details it can be said that with later amendments the bill laid the foundations for the current environmental management system in Poland.

3. Main Features of the System in the 1980s

The environmental management system established in Poland during the 1980s can be briefly described as follows. There was a system of institutions covering all the elements of the environment, with the Ministry of Environment Protection and Natural Resources and Forestry (henceforth, Ministry of Environment) at the apex. Monitoring was conducted by two separate institutions: one working for the Minister of Environment, and the second at the local level, for the Governors of *voivodships* (provinces). A wide range of emission norms, permits and ambient standards was introduced. This was accompanied by a broad variety of economic instruments that fulfil the "polluter pays" and "user pays" criteria as well as tax allowances and preferential interest rates for investment in environmental improvement. The main problem, however, was that the existing system, far from being able to achieve environmental goals in a cost-effective way, was first of all, under the existing political conditions, incapable of enforcing environmental norms and standards. In addition, the system did not allow for sufficient financing of environment protection. The system was also highly centralised, leaving very little room for local initiatives. Local representatives of the Minister of Environment were members of the local state administration which, first of all, was responsible for fulfilling the goals of centrally determined production plans. The political system made it difficult for localities to put pressure on the administration to enforce the environmental laws. The Minister of the Environment could grant exemptions of payment of fines for violation of environmental norms and standards. In general, there was no (or very little) political will to enforce environmental protection.

If central authority undermined and weakened local authority, the local authority approach had its own problems. The organisational structure was adapted to the administrative division of the country. Therefore the system did not allow seeking least-cost solutions on a regional or ecosystem level. There was no (or very little) linkage between data collection by the provincial environmental inspectorates and local (or central) economic policy making. Co-ordination of activities of different bodies responsible for environment protection within the government was very weak which resulted in the lack of integration of environmental policies within economic sectors.

4. Economic Instruments in Environment Protection

As mentioned earlier, the Polish environmental management system includes an array of economic instruments which have been in use for at least ten years. They can be divided into three groups:

a. pollution fees and fines,

b. user charges, and

c. taxes and subsidies.

The first group of instruments played a very marginal role in promoting environmentally benign behaviour by enterprises. As studies done by different research groups show, in most cases, the rate of the fees was below the average or marginal abatement costs. Thus, managers of plants treated them as a very unimportant tax which had to be paid. In addition, it must be mentioned that for several years there was no mechanism for inflation adjustment.

The only function that effluent charges had was revenue raising, and in no way did their level reflect economic efficiency.

Fines for non-compliance with emission norms (when these were applied by authorities) had a more severe effect because they reduced profits directly and hence the staff bonuses. Thus, whenever fines were imposed efforts were made to obtain an exemption from payment. Moreover, if the provincial department of environment protection knew that a relatively high fine would cause bankruptcy, then it would refrain from using the instrument. This was especially true in cases of enterprises heavily subsidised by the state.

A charge on dumping and storage of industrial wastes has been levied on enterprises. Its rate is very low and revenues are ear-marked to ecological funds. Recycled materials are exempted from payment. Again, the impact of the exemption as an encouragement for the recycling of industrial wastes was negligible because of the extremely low rate of the charge avoided (typically below the costs of storage and maintenance).

User charges are commonly used for the collection and treatment of municipal solid waste and wastewater discharged into sewerage systems. The charges have been very low and below levels adequate for cost recovery. That is one of the reasons why this part of the public sector has been heavily subsidised by the central government. Moreover, underfunding has resulted in a serious underdevelopment of the infrastructure of municipalities -- over 50 per cent of them are lacking wastewater treatment plants. Some major towns are reporting water supply shortages and have drinking water of low quality. All towns in Poland are facing problems with solid waste disposal.

In the 1980s tax allowances, that were aimed at stimulating polluters to undertake pollution abatement activities, were also added to the system. Tax reductions were granted to any enterprise that invested in environment protection. Tax relief amounted to 30 per cent of the total cost of investment, provided the project was completed in less than five years. Turnover tax relief was granted to enterprises which sold products made from wastes instead of high quality raw materials. Another tax based incentive gave enterprises a waiver of amortization payments for investments in pollution abatement.

These tax allowance have been in use for several years, but it seems from the available data that they had no or marginal impact on investment decisions of enterprises. This was partly because the sum of all tax rebates could not exceed 30 per cent of the tax due. In general, enterprises were still more interested in increasing the volume of production and paying low effluent fees and other environmental charges than in pollution abatement.

Soft loans were also available for enterprises ready to invest in pollution abatement with an interest rate 50 per cent below the prevailing rate, the difference being paid to the banks from the central budget. Also, grants were provided from the central budget and the central and local environmental funds. The resources of the local (*voivodship*) environmental funds were used to induce the heavy polluters to undertake anti-pollution measures. This local policy, first applied in the main environmental "black-spot" of Poland, Katowice, and later on in other places, proved to be more successful. In many cases firms were offered more than 50 per cent of the required financial resources. Of course the danger with using subsidies to encourage pollution abatement lies in the fact that end of the pipe solutions receive preference. But in some cases this may be the only way of dealing with the problem, once the firm is established.

Polish experience in using economic instruments to change the behaviour of polluters and promote efficient solutions is generally negative thus far. But it must also be said that policy makers in Poland have been and still are reluctant to change the primary function of those instruments from revenue raising to the incentive function. One could say that proper tools have been applied in a wrong economic environment (i.e. the centrally planned, non-market economy). One might also say that such tools are inconsistent with the general logic of such a system.

There is probably little doubt as to the efficiency of mixed policies in environmental protection because of the specific nature of the problems and in the present state of knowledge. But one conclusion seems obvious, that when economic instruments fulfil an additional function, i.e. revenue generation, then environmental goals can be achieve more efficiently. But in order to make this happen environmental economists must keep on repeating textbook knowledge to policy makers, that command and control policies are less cost-effective than policies which rely on properly designed fees, charges, etc. "Properly designed" often means higher charges, but those higher charges will lead to lower pollution abatement costs. Experience shows however that economic instruments might be assigned smaller value and importance because politicians and policy makers feel more secure with a command and control system. In addition, trade unions might oppose any economic instruments which might increase prices and further lower the standard of living. Thus at this stage it is still unclear what policy measures will the government take in solving pollution abatement and environment protection problems.

5. Subsidies and Environmental Degradation

As it was mentioned at the beginning of the paper, the quality of environment is heavily influenced by the general efficiency of the economic system. In practice this means that the efficiency of natural resource and energy utilisation has an important impact on the state of environment. In other words if an economy is characterised by high energy, resource and material intensity, this by itself is a factor that leads to environmental pollution and degradation. Polish experience is a good illustration of this process. One of the main economic reasons for this is that subsidies and tax preferences were granted to the extracting and heavy industries as a result of centrally determined prices. The soft budget policy worked against the environment in the sense that it promoted inefficient use of energy, natural resources and materials.

It can be said that if the general framework of taxes and subsidies distorts the whole price structure, whereby prices do not reflect scarcity and opportunity costs of natural resources, energy, etc. then both the producers and the consumers will tend to overuse those resources. The misallocation of resources in the economy will work against the environment, understood here as both a supplier of resources and a natural receiver of pollution.

If inputs are undervalued then there is little impetus for resource substitution and conservation by introducing more efficient technologies. At the same time there is no demand for clean technologies since there is no real economic pressure to protect the environmental assimilative capacity. All of this has been proven in Poland as well as in other centrally planned non-market economies.

6. Present Concern about the Environment

By the mid-1980s non-governmental organisations (NGOs), led by the Polish Ecological Club, began to publish a number of reports on the state of the environment which led to a growing concern among the public. This made it possible to include the environmental issues in the Round Table Talks. Following the election of a new government headed by Prime Minister T. Mazowiecki, the necessity to improve the state of environment in Poland has become one of the important issues that the government has to deal with.

Under the new government and with a new Minister of Environment, B. Kaminski, in office for the last year, intensive work is being done to reform the environmental management with the help of international institutions (World Bank, the EC) and through bilateral agreements. The efforts are being concentrated on short and medium term objectives. The short term goal is to strengthen and add to the institutions forming the environmental management system, adjust the legal system to EC standards, prepare a new set of economic instruments, and arrange for sources of financing for environment protection, all in accordance with the general economic reform which is taking place now. A medium term investment programme is being prepared, concentrated on energy conservation as well as on reducing emission of particulates, SO_2 and NO_x, especially in areas suffering from a highly adverse health impact, e.g. Upper Silesia. An investment programme for solving the problem of municipal solid wastes and hazardous industrial wastes is also being prepared. Although within the new institutional structure, water will be managed by Water Basin Agencies, the government is working on an investment programme for the public sector which will include a list of priority investments in this sector. By the end of this year, several new acts will create the conditions for institutional changes and new policy instruments.

This brief outline of the activities of the Ministry of Environment serves to indicate the considerable efforts which are being made to increase the effectiveness of environmental management in Poland. At the same time it should be noted that the main political parties as well as the trade unions and some members of the parliament are putting a lot of pressure on the Ministry of Environment to increase its efforts for improving the quality of the environment and the efficiency of natural resource utilisation.

Under these conditions and against a background of very limited finance (Poland's debt is over $40 billion), severe budget constraints and increasing unemployment the Ministry of Environment has prepared the *National Environment Policy* to be approved by the government. This document presents the corrective actions that will be taken to address the short-, medium- and long-term priorities. The short-term priorities concentrate on institutional upgrading and development that will increase the efficacy and economic efficiency of the environmental management system. In addition, the monitoring system will be improved, and environmental regulations and laws reviewed and new ones introduced. Energy and water conservation measures will be adopted involving pricing policy and auditing. In the short run, investment projects will address the most crucial pollution problems and sources with the most negative health impacts -- toxic wastes. Investments will be carried out only for economically viable enterprises that under market conditions will remain on the market. In the water sector, finance will be directed towards the completion of waste water and sewerage systems and to protect water intake reservoirs. Increased afforestation and nature conservation is also a short-term priority. What is expected by decentralising environmental management, strengthening NGOs and introducing environmental education on a wide scale, is that social participation in solving environmental problems by localities themselves will develop.

This policy document addresses the environmental problems in all the sectors of the economy within the framework of the general economic reform. It assumes that the market economy will bring down high energy, material and natural resources intensity, and force the restructuring of the industry which by itself will reduce pollution levels and improve resource utilisation. In other words, this document introduces the guidelines for sustainable economic development, the only development option that the country can and must adopt to overcome its critical situation in the long run.

7. Macroeconomic Limits of Environmental Improvement

The efforts presented above are severely constrained by the present economic conditions, which limit the restructuring programme of industry, including the fuel and energy sector and environmental protection.

The Ministry of Environment is finding it difficult to put more pressure on polluters to change their behaviour when it is obvious that they lack the necessary financial resources for importing new clean technologies. At the same time the market in Poland for anti-pollution devices (end of pipe treatment) is underdeveloped. In the immediate future, what can be accomplished in Poland in terms of improving the quality of natural environment will also be directly determined by the burden of foreign debt repayments.

The pace of the clean-up programme largely depends upon the overall activity of the economy and the availability of financial resources. Under the existing economic conditions it is impossible to increase government spending on environment protection.

8. The Need for International Aid and Assistance

The current state of environment in Poland has received a relatively broad publicity in the world. There is no doubt that the problem is serious and has its domestic and international dimensions, the latter due to trans-boundary pollution. The new government fully recognises the urgent need to reduce the burden of pollution and environment degradation for the Polish people. At the same time it is fully aware of the necessity to reduce Poland's high contribution to the world's total amount of pollution.

The efforts of the government to upgrade the environmental management system and to overcome the technological barriers, especially those connected with human health protection in the black-spot areas, have been properly recognised by the international community. The international aid and assistance which Poland has received for this purpose is of great importance but it covers only 0.5 per cent of priority needs. That is why Poland is asking that aid be increased to at least 1 per cent. International aid and assistance is also badly needed to quicken the pace of institutional upgrading and building. A well organised institutional system allows for achieving environmental goals in a least cost way and provides an adequate basis for defining medium and long term policy goals. International assistance is also needed to help train specialists for different levels of operation in the new institutional design of the environmental management system. Technologies for dealing with industrial and municipal solid wastes, especially hazardous and toxic wastes, are of particular importance in the black-spot areas. The experience gained there can be spread on other regions of the country.

The approach outlined above is important and necessary but we must bear in mind that overcoming environmental degradation and pollution requires carrying out a comprehensive restructuring programme. The present structure of the economy, and especially that of industry, is one of the main factors causing the whole problem. Restructuring of industry is a key task in reducing pollution and changing the trend. But this programme is on hold because of the extremely high foreign debt which sets a financial limit for investment and badly needed new loans. Unfortunately that debt is growing and therefore the solution of environmental problems is being pushed away. This is a side effect of the debt problem.

In order to fulfil its international commitments regarding trans-boundary pollution Poland needs to increase investments in environment protection, but without external financial aid it is simply impossible. Therefore it would be very helpful if the governments of highly developed countries consider and approve writing off a part of the debt as well as agree with the Polish government that the equivalent in Polish currency be spent on environment protection. It would allow financing technology transfer and tackle pollution problems at source. Foreign investment, together with technology transfer, accompanied by market management schemes, will allow for energy, material, and natural resource savings, which in the end will reduce the generation and flow of all kinds of pollutants and wastes. Marginal benefits of environmental investments in Poland might be the highest in Europe.

NEW CO-OPERATION MODELS FOR STRENGTHENING ENVIRONMENTAL MANAGEMENT CAPACITIES IN DEVELOPING COUNTRIES: A CASE STUDY OF BRAZIL

by

Hans-Jürgen Karpe *

and

Hans-Peter Winkelmann *

---

* Institute for Environmental Protection (INFU) -- University of Dortmund

RÉSUMÉ

Il y a besoin de main-d'oeuvre qualifiée pour faire face aux exigences à court terme des décisions quotidiennes et aux aspects à long terme des principes et des méthodes de gestion efficace de l'environnement industriel. La coopération pour le développement peut aider à couvrir ce besoin, donnant ainsi aux pays la capacité de discerner eux-mêmes les choix qui s'offrent à eux en matière d'orientation. Pour pouvoir développer les capacités de gestion de l'environnement, il faut d'abord savoir quelles sont les structures institutionnelles dont on a besoin, quelles sont les compétences nécessaires et quel est le type d'approche méthodologique et conceptuelle qui convient le mieux au pays considéré.

L'exposé décrit un modèle de coopération bilatérale entre une université brésilienne et une université allemande (sous les auspices du GTZ, l'agence allemande de coopération technique) visant à promouvoir des activités de recherche et de formation axées sur les problèmes dans le domaine de l'environnement. A cet effet, un centre interdisciplinaire pour la protection de l'environnement a été créé à l'université de Salvador, Bahia, qui travaillera en consultation avec le secteur privé et avec le gouvernement.

SUMMARY

There is a need for qualified manpower to cope with both the short-term requirements of day-to-day decisions and the long-term aspects of the principles and procedures for effective management of the industrial environment. Development co-operation can help to meet that need and thus give countries the ability to discern for themselves the policy choices available to them. The development of capabilities in environmental management has to be based on an understanding of what institutional structures are required, what skills are needed and what kind of conceptual and methodological approach is best suited for the country in question.

The paper describes a bilateral co-operation model between a Brazilian and a German university (under the auspices of GTZ, the German technical co-operation agency) to promote problem-oriented training and research activities in the environmental field. For this purpose, an interdisciplinary centre for environmental protection has been set up at the university in Salvador, Bahia, to work in consultation with industry and government.

1. The Need to Enhance the Endogenous Capacity

The increase in the extent of environmental deterioration during the past decades from regional problems to the global level has led to serious devastating impacts on the innate prerequisites of life on earth. The irony of this situation is that it springs from causes located at separate ends of a spectrum: wealth and poverty. Thereby, the environment is not any longer an issue which concerns only industrialized countries. The dumping of solid and liquid waste and gaseous emissions into rivers, lakes and oceans, into the atmosphere and the underground, seepage into potable water systems which sometimes causes outbreaks of epidemics, the wholesale deforestation which is underway throughout the developing world, all these are, along with the excessive exploitation and consumption of natural resources, the major causes destroying the livelihood for mankind.

But the environmental crisis is not simply limited to problems relating to the quality of the air, water and the preservation of the atmosphere. It has now become a set of deeply intertwined socio-economic problems of vastly significant political and security implications. While exploring the possible options to reverse the ill-effects on the environment, special attention must be paid to the developmental perspectives of the third world countries which are not the same as those of the industrialised countries.

In many industrialised countries there is a growing public awareness of the environmental issues, which is not yet the case among the majority of developing countries. Consequently the industrialised countries are engaged in a serious examination of environmental pollution and related problems, in part, because they possess the capacity to reduce or to eliminate them. On the other hand, the developing countries faced with the pressures of meeting the basic economic and social demands of vast populations, are very often not in a position to respond likewise properly to ecological demands. They are again, this time in terms of the environmental capacity, the "have nots". For the developing countries it is meaningful in the first place to overcome the seemingly intractable problems of how to accelerate economic growth and social development while protecting and preserving the local and global environment.

Obviously, many obstacles are preventing developing countries from using environmentally sound management practices. Some of these obstacles are: insufficient awareness of the environmental effects of production processes, lack of understanding of practices to safeguard the environment, no access to technical advice, insufficient knowledge to implement new technologies, lack of financial resources, or simply management inertia and resistance to change. Many attempts have been made to overcome these obstacles, but, unfortunately, progress has been too slow, and there is a clear need to strengthen the efforts much more.

It is the task of governments to set the comprehensive regulating framework which will lead to the solution of the environmental crisis. Stricter environmental regulations on emissions and disposal, and tight enforcement procedures are necessary. But these must be combined with supplementary measures: research and development, training activities and education programmes, collection and transfer of information etc. Environmental protection is not only a matter of legislation or technology: it involves planning and organisation, common sense, an innovative attitude, good housekeeping -- in other words, environmentally sound management practices. In order to analyze, plan, programme and then control the environmentally sound industrial management in Third World countries, there is a need for qualified manpower which will be able to cope with both the short-term requirements of day-to-day decisions and the long-term aspects of the principles and procedures for effective management of the industrial environment.

It is also obvious that there is an overriding need to create a positive synthesis between environmental and developmental imperatives. The issues cannot be divided into two separate categories with environment on the one hand and development on the other. Each issue has an environmental as well as a developmental dimension. Climate change, for example, can be dealt with effectively only through measures which integrate environmental and developmental considerations. The issue of climate change is global in nature and any attempt to resolve it would require the co-operation in the development of all countries. It is now evident that common efforts have to be undertaken by all countries for remedial action without further delay. But would every country be ready and prepared for such concerted action? There are some doubts allowed because it became more and more evident in the ongoing deliberations on global environmental issues at the diplomatic front, that, in particular developing countries which are faced with the pressures of growing socio-economic demands, are not in a position to act in the global interest, even while agreeing on the harmful consequences of global warming and climate change.

It must be therefore recognized that effective co-operation in all kinds of environmental issues will be possible only if the proposed remedial measures take into account the vastly differing socio-economic situations between industrialised and developing countries. Therefore there is an urgent need to strengthen the endogenous capacities of the developing countries to enable them to respond and participate in the global efforts as well as adopt policies that consistent with global environmental needs.

We now face the challenge of making the environment - development relationship work in practical terms at the levels of micro-development and economic policy, in sectoral policies in key areas such as energy, industry, transportation and resource operations. In this, the role of development co-operation, bilateral and multilateral, is crucial. The growing commitment to integrate the environmental dimension into development activities and contributions will be essential. Most important, however, is the ability of nations to be able to discern for themselves the policy choices that are available to them in the common battle to preserve the global environment for their own benefits and environmental protection.

The leading edge of development is founded on knowledge, policies, skills and infrastructure which the majority of developing countries lack. The questions for developing countries as they embark on new patterns of development and environment therefore are complex and many. They must decide which options are essential to satisfy the needs to protect the environment and to conserve natural resources. They must be able to carry out the diagnosis of an environmental problem and to assess practical solutions.

Even before they can approach those decisions, they need institutions, policies and a core of human resources to analyze possibilities of all open options. Above all else, they need an endogenous decision-making framework in their national development process to enhance knowledge of the principles and procedures for effective management of the industrial environment.

Such a framework leading to the strengthening of their endogenous capacities should include:

-- Collecting data to promote the transfer of information;

-- Informing to respond to specific requests for technical information on the industrial environment;

-- Catalyzing to stimulate the exchange of information and experience by promoting technical co-operation;

-- Training to enhance knowledge and experience.

There is a key role in all this for the various constituencies as important elements in development from all walks of life: science and technology, education and training, the financial community, industry, labour unions, youth, women, special interest groups. It is necessary to ensure that these important constituencies can participate and contribute fully to the process of endogenous environmental capacity building itself.

By strengthening its local knowledge-base, a society has the capacity to add more value to its resources and to achieve a sense of autonomous directions. The ability to add value to physical and intellectual resources is a key to generating local wealth and a prerequisite to a more equitable development. Thus, the benefits of a more knowledge-based development strategy begin to emerge along with the recognition that such a strategy presents possibilities for renewing development planning approaches.

The development of capabilities in environmental management and related fields essentially consists of understanding what institutional structures are required, what skills are needed and have to be developed and what kind of conceptual and methodological approach is best suited for the country or region in question. Different countries face different constraints and opportunities, but in a basic sense, certain features can be said to be common. Take endogenous capability, for example, which contains within it the sense that a country should endeavour to develop a capacity that enhances its ability to guide its own dynamics and decisions with respect to environmental change. The relevance of these capabilities in the social, economic and cultural as well as political contexts of the society is also a common feature. At the conceptual level, an interdisciplinary approach is essential if the full spectrum of implications of environmental change is to be assessed. Finally, the involvement of the different groups within society that are affected by environmental change as producers, users or those involved in its assessments and management is an essential component of a successful environmental management capability.

2. Capacity Building to Respond to Local Demands in Bahia (Brazil)

Brazil, with its rapidly growing economy, is not necessarily a typical case study for a developing country because it suffers not only from environmental conditions which are specific for developing countries, but also, due to its fast industrialisation in the past, from problems which are more typical for a heavily industrialised country. The combination of environmental problems embraces industrial plants emitting large quantities of pollutants; contamination of air, water and soil; noise; waste of natural resources; bad housing conditions; poor medical care etc.

Without adopting the remedial measures it will become inescapable that this situation will form a serious obstacle for the long-term socio-economic development process in Brazil. It is in everyone's interest to take the necessary action and the sooner this is done, the less it will cost, environmentally and economically. The dissemination and appropriate application of knowledge and experience on environmental matters is an indispensable prerequisite to stop the further deterioration of the environment.

In spite of the rather progressive environmental legislation in Brazil the overwhelming environmental problems could not be solved yet. One main reason for this situation can be found in the lack of both appropriate experts and know-how concerning the protection of the environment and the natural resources. Although universities play traditionally an important role in the transfer of know how and experience, there is an evident gap in training and education at Brazilian universities. There are neither study courses for experts with an additional knowledge on environmental issues nor for environmental experts to carry out environmental impact assessment. Further education for industry and administration in this field or diagnostic studies in collaboration with local specialists which would put industry managers and government officials in step with the future virtually don't exist.

In order to meet these demands and to fill the evident gap in adequate training in the field of environmental management, the Federal University in Salvador, Bahia (UFBa), was selected for a bilateral co-operation model to promote problem-oriented training and research activities related to environmental matters. This project is funded by the German Agency for Technical Co-operation (GTZ) and carried out in general accordance with the policy priorities of the federal government in Brazil and the regional government in Bahia as well as with the focus on training and education of the German guidelines for bilateral co-operation. The German contributions to the project consists of:

-- Consulting with short-time and long-time experts.

-- Further academic training of Brazilian experts.

-- Financing of training activities.

-- Joint research and training projects.

-- Supply of technical equipment.

On the basis that prevention is better than cure, the intention of this pilot project is to create an appropriate instrument to institutionalise an interdisciplinary and problem-oriented approach for training, R&D, and information. It should also contribute to the long-term success of other environmental projects in Brazil which would be simply impossible without considerably enhancing the number and skills of local experts. The training and further education of local experts will be a particular obligation for Brazil in the next future due to its commitment to host the important United Nations World Conference on Environment and Development in 1992. Therefore, an overall time range of 15 years is estimated for the entire project, with the first start-up phase now underway projected to last five years.

The University of Salvador (UFBa) was selected in connection with a supra-regional survey in Africa, Asia and Latin America which was done for the BMZ/GTZ project "Environmental Training in Developing Countries". It fulfils the requirements to carry out such a project properly because it is quite advanced in environmental research and training and has already conducted in recent years several interdisciplinary research projects focusing on industrial pollution out of which some contacts with governmental agencies for environmental protection and industry inevitably emerged.

Some years ago, the department of chemistry launched a specialised study course in analytical chemistry to meet the demand for experts in this area. Since 1980 a postgraduate course on ecology of aquatic ecosystems at the department of biology exists. Research projects on the impacts of pollution in such systems are also carried out by that department. The institute of architecture and planning is undertaking studies on a small-scale base for plans on noise abatement, waste disposal and the damage of materials through pollution. The damage to public health through pollution forms a particular field of medical research in a Master's Degree Programme at the department of medicine. This department is involved since many years in conducting research projects on public health and industrial pollution. Additionally, UFBa offers a joint programme together with the regional authority for environmental protection (CRA) in environmental planning and management. This course enjoys a high reputation for the qualifications of participants from industry and administration.

The existence of an environmental capacity was a basic condition for two central features of the project in Salvador: firstly, at the conceptual level, the promotion of the already existing activities in research and training activities related to environmental issues at the departments of biology, medicine (preventive health care), chemistry, and architecture and town planning. Secondly, at the institutional level, enhancing the interdisciplinarity of environmental research and training.

To ensure the interdisciplinarity at the institutional level, there is a need to strengthen the institutional capacity through the establishment of a comprehensive centre for environmental protection (**N**úcleo **I**nterdisciplinar do **M**eio **A**mbiente - **NIMA**), mainly for the curriculum design and the management of the collaboration between the departments. The objective for the centre in the start-up phase is therefore to carry out coordinating activities among the various departments mentioned.

To facilitate the transfer of information and the sharing of knowledge and experience, the following complementary initiatives are projected:

-- Implementation of interdisciplinary R&D projects in consultation with industry and governmental agencies as well as other administrative bodies to provide a basis for training activities.

-- Organisation of additional academic courses on environmental training and further education in co-operation with other UFBa departments.

-- Creation of new "combined" courses with the participation of other UFBa departments and other relevant institutions outside the university.

-- Launching a course in environmental planning and management.

-- Integration of educational objectives and priorities in graduate level business and executive education into the overall institutional programme.

-- Creation of a library and a data base for a query-response service on environmental problems and the development of information tools.

-- Establishment of a mobile monitoring service with test equipment to measure various environmental indicators.

-- Organisation of workshops, seminars, conferences and other meetings on selected topics related to environmental matters to stimulate the exchange of information and experience.

The goals for the UFBa are to encourage the incorporation of environmental criteria in industrial development, facilitate the implementation of procedures and principles for the protection of the environment and stimulate the exchange of information and experience in industry, government and administration. The measures concerning education, training and further education to be introduced should enable the local manpower in practical terms to carry out diagnostic studies or planning schemes for measuring emissions and the grade of pollution in water, air and contaminated soils, for waste management, industrial siting, open space planning, legislation setting environmental standards, through data processing, and disseminating information (video equipment, literature etc.)

Consequently, the above measures are aimed first of all at scientists, engineers and students of the participating university departments, but furthermore also at local decision-makers and experts from administration, industry and other agencies, and the local people in the field area. The entire project is directed very strongly towards extending and facilitating the transfer of knowledge and experience. Hence, additional target groups should come in the future not only from other UFBa departments but also from other Brazilian universities. Even the co-operation with other Latin American institutions could be feasible in the long run.

In order to implement this multi-layer project, for which no other example exists so far in Latin America, it is necessary to coordinate and harmonize the various activities at the university in the field of environmental protection at large. To accomplish the overall project target of offering problem-oriented and interdisciplinary training, research and information activities, the joint research projects related to environmental issues should be coordinated by NIMA.

For that reason NIMA will function in the first place as a coordinating body under the direct responsibility of the rectorship of the university provided with its own staff. The organisational structure of NIMA should be flexible to allow the involvement of other departments and institutions at any time oriented towards the two central features of the centre, interdisciplinarity and management. It is planned to involve NIMA with various international organisations and their ongoing programmes within or outside the UN family which would fit into the general objectives and initiatives.

The function as a "nucleus" will be demonstrated in the accommodation of the centre in a specially erected building on the premises of the university. In order to facilitate the complex project management a German institution will be involved as counterpart for each participating department as well as for the centre NIMA itself.

Equivalent to the function of NIMA, the German partner institution should take over likewise a coordinating responsibility for the project management on the German side of this bilateral project. The coordinating function will be carried out by the Institute for Environmental Protection (INFU) at the University of Dortmund which has a broad experience in the general areas of planning, economic and mathematical methods for decision-making, and applied engineering. INFU has the task to carry out, initiate and enhance interdisciplinary research in the environmental field. Policy development, environmental planning along with environmental impact assessment, environmental technologies, and capacity building in developing countries are among the most important concerns of INFU's work. Research, teaching, and consultancy are the main activities in these areas NIMA will benefit from.

INFU plays an important key role for the project management as a whole. As a catalyst it will conceptualise the research projects and will monitor them. In detail, INFU will help to identify areas for joint research projects according to the basic needs identified together with the local experts and then involve appropriate German institutions as counterparts for the implementation. The counterparts will come, first of all, from different departments at the University of Dortmund. The departments of chemistry, statistics and spatial planning are already involved in the project as sister departments. The partnership in the field of biology and ecology will be fulfilled by INFU with its own capacities in this area.

Furthermore, other German institutions specialised in certain areas related to environmental protection will be involved by INFU on a case by case basis. These institutions will be involved for the environmental diagnosis of a particular problem. In collaboration with local specialists from Brazil, diagnostic studies will be carried out and practical solutions will then be assessed. The co-operation of these institutions with INFU is therefore also an important tool in the efforts to promote the transfer of experience and the sharing of knowledge according to the principle of "learning by doing". INFU is also in-charge of further education and academic training of Brazilian experts in Germany. For this purpose the exchange of students and academic staff will be organised.

The co-operation of INFU with NIMA is based on three main pillars which underline the problem-oriented approach of the project:

- Research projects
- Workshops and seminars
- Publications

Areas for possible joint research are currently assessed by INFU and the participating departments and will soon be formulated as proposals. A first scientific workshop organised by NIMA is planned for the end of March 1991. The objective of this event is to bring together local experts from UFBa, industry and government with experts in international co-operation and from German counterparts to discuss strategies on endogenous environmental management capacity building. The publications should describe as technical reviews and guidelines appropriate solutions for the prevention and treatment of pollution. The guidelines are addressed to government officials, industry managers and members of environmental protection associations and could also serve as teaching material. It is important to mention that all three activities are interconnected. Publications could emerge from research projects or from workshops, workshops can deal with topics of research projects and so on. This is to ensure the problem-oriented approach of the co-operation model.

NON-GOVERNMENTAL ORGANISATIONS AND ENVIRONMENTAL MANAGEMENT: LESSONS FROM THE COSTA RICAN EXPERIENCE

by

Alvaro Umaña *

* Alvaro Umaña, formerly Minister of Natural Resources, Energy and Mines, Costa Rica, is now the head of the Central American Business Administration Institute (Instituto Centroamericano de Administracion de Empresas -- INCAE).

RÉSUMÉ

En dépit d'une succession de revers sur bien des fronts de la gestion de l'environnement, un facteur a incontestablement progressé dans la dernière décennie, à savoir l'ampleur et l'efficacité des organisations non gouvernementales (ONG) et de leurs initiatives. Au Costa Rica, elles ont joué un rôle important dans l'organisation de la conversion de créances pour promouvoir la conservation des ressources naturelles dans les zones de forêt tropicale. L'article relate en détail l'expérience de conversion des créances au Costa Rica, les sommes modestes sur lesquelles ont porté les premières opérations, la participation des acteurs extérieurs, gouvernementaux et non gouvernementaux, et le rôle de coordonnateur joué par le gouvernement national. Les mécanismes d'acheminement de l'aide vont de l'habilitation du gouvernement national à superviser l'exécution des programmes, à l'exécution directe par des ONG internationales (étrangères). Malgré quelques controverses sur la souveraineté et sur le niveau de participation étrangère qui est acceptable, le rachat de créances à des fins écologiques est entré en usage dans près d'une douzaine d'autres pays. Le succès relatif jusqu'à présent remporté par les ONG montre qu'il faut renforcer les capacités administratives et techniques de ces organisations pour éviter qu'elles ne perdent de leur efficacité et de leur crédibilité devant la tâche gigantesque qui les attend.

SUMMARY

Despite continued setbacks on many fronts of environmental management, one factor that has clearly been improving in the last decade is the size and effectiveness of non-governmental organisations (NGOs) and their initiatives. In Costa Rica their role has been significant in the organisation of debt swaps to promote conservation of natural resources in tropical forest areas. The article gives a detailed account of Costa Rica's experience with debt swaps, the modest sums that initiated the process, the involvement of external governmental and non-governmental actors, and the coordinating role of the national government. Mechanisms for channelling assistance range from giving the national government the authority to supervise the execution of programmes through direct execution by international (foreign) NGOs. Despite some controversies on the question of sovereignty and the level of acceptable foreign involvement, debt-for-nature swaps have come to be used in nearly a dozen other countries. The relative success that the NGOs have so far met point to the need to strengthen their managerial and technical capabilities, and to prevent their loss of efficiency and credibility in the face of the enormous task that remains ahead.

1. *Introduction*

During the last few decades we have become increasingly aware of the growing intervention that global societies impose on the biosphere. Population and economic growth, industrialisation and urban development, existing and emerging technologies, have all contributed to environmental deterioration worldwide.

Alteration of global biogeochemical cycles has become acute and truly represents a threat to the Earth's metabolism and life support systems. Among these threats, global carbon emissions stemming from fossil fuel combustion and deforestation are critical and becoming increasingly so. Energy utilisation patterns in industrialised nations are presently responsible for the largest share (nearly three-quarters) of carbon dioxide emissions, but tropical deforestation has shown a rapidly growing contribution and presently accounts for nearly one quarter of total emissions. This example shows the global nature of environmental problems, the complexity of the situation and the basic environmental interrelationship between the industrial and developing worlds.

In addition to carbon emissions from burning and the destruction of future carbon-assimilative capacity, the disappearance of the tropical forests has much wider implications for the future of life on the planet. Perhaps the most serious and imminent of all environmental threats is the direct assault against species inhabiting the tropical forests, which are located almost exclusively in developing countries.

Within these forests live nearly two thirds of the plants and animals that share the planet with us. Nevertheless, with each second that passes, more than an entire football field of tropical forest disappears, and with it, all the organisms that live in these ecosystems. We are extinguishing life on Earth at a rate thousands of times greater than in any previous period in the evolution of life. This process is similar to burning an entire library without even cataloguing the volumes, let alone reading the books.

The fate of the overwhelming majority of these forests will be decided during the present decade, and only very few will survive into the XXIst century. The remaining tropical forests are likely to become the cathedrals of the XXIst century, vestiges of the diversity of life that was once abundant on Earth. This tragic situation is generating a global response in which non-governmental organisations are playing an increasingly important and effective role.

Although many problems have not changed or have deteriorated during the last two decades, one factor that has changed dramatically is the role of non-governmental organisations (NGOs). They have grown enormously in numbers, membership power and influence. At the same time, they have played a fundamental role in raising grass-roots awareness, focusing public attention on new problems, sponsoring studies and projects, as well as influencing the media, the private sector and the educational process, both formal and informal. The NGOs of several developed countries have also been quite effective in influencing the bilateral aid programmes and have exerted pressure on multilateral development banks to introduce environmental policies and evaluation processes in their operations.

Finally, they have been able to establish a positive feedback relation with the media that has resulted in a more widespread concern about the environmental crisis.

As a result of these critical global environmental problems, awareness and perceptions regarding the environment have risen considerably during the last decade. Today, both in the industrialised and in the developing world, public opinion has shifted considerably towards including ecological values and concerns. In the United States, for example, 53 per cent of the population considered in 1979 that "protecting the environment is so important that requirements and standards can not be too high, and continuing improvements must be made regardless of cost". Today, nearly 80 per cent of those polled agreed with the same question. Similar statistics can be cited from other developed nations, and although priorities are different in the developing world and awareness has not reached the same level, there is now little doubt that environmental issues, from global warming to acid rain, from tropical deforestation to soil erosion, will be at the forefront of any developing nation's international agenda.

As it was mentioned earlier, considerable growth has taken place both in the number of non-governmental organisations in the environmental field, and in their membership. The National Wildlife Federation of the United States, for example, has reached a membership of over six million affiliates and an annual budget of over $100 million per year. It is the largest non-governmental organisation in the world working in the conservation and environmental fields.

To give an example at the international level, the World Wildlife Fund (WWF) has experienced impressive growth and its programmes now reach every continent and over one hundred nations. Many existing non-governmental organisations from developing countries are starting to become active in international environmental issues. Some have started their involvement in traditional conservation but later on shifted their emphasis to sustainable development. Others have evolved from related fields of health and rural development. New ones have been born and grown tremendously over a short period of time.

One of the unique examples is the Children of the Rainforest (Barnens Regnskog) of Sweden. This organisation was started by a teacher and her schoolchildren in 1987, and they chose to try to save a forest near the Monteverde Biological Reserve in Costa Rica. So far they have donated over $1 million to a Costa Rican NGO to purchase over 7 000 hectares of rainforest and their organisation has grown to include the membership of over 10 000 Swedish children. Similar examples are starting to sprout in other developed nations.

In the developing world, awareness is also rising, and in Central America and Panama alone there are close to six hundred non-governmental organisations active in the environmental field.

These examples clearly show the increasing relevance and power of non-governmental organisations worldwide, and in particular with relation to environmental management. The following sections of the paper consider their relations to governments, key areas for their participation and lessons learned.

Three specific thorny issues illustrate with the fact that environmental NGOs have traditionally stressed conservation more than development (the so-called species vs. children issue), the difficulties posed by "green conditionality", and the need for additional resources to finance sustainable development. Examples will be drawn primarily from the experience of Costa Rica, where NGOs have a very significant role, but common principles of general applicability will be sought.

2. *Governments, NGOs and Environmental Management*

The question of relations between governments and non-governmental organisations, even when restricted to the environmental field, is extremely complex and allows few generalisations. At the outset, it is critical to recognise that both governments and NGOs have specific objectives and agendas that sometimes put them in adversarial roles, although the ultimate objective may be common. In other cases the objectives of an environmental NGO may be more restrictive than those of the government, or they may be narrowly focused on a region or a particular end-use for a resource. For example, a young and powerful NGO emerged in Costa Rica to attempt to save the Pacuare River from a large hydroelectric development proposed by the national electric utility (ICE). This organisation received initial funding and support from companies working white-water rafting trips in the river, but rapidly sought to widen its support base with other environmental groups and local populations. These groups have a clear agenda of attempting to stop the hydroelectric projects to maintain the white-water option, while the government must consider wider issues dealing with national energy planning and strategy. Tourist revenues, intrinsic values and natural rivers must be weighed against the country's need for electricity (with a 90 per cent electrification rate, the issue affects almost every corner of the land), alternative options including geothermal, fossil-fuel generation and energy conservation.

There are a variety of options and strategies through which NGOs and governments interact. Many NGOs prefer to play an adversarial role, denouncing specific problems or governmental policies and many governments, correspondingly, would like to sweep them under the rug. Others, while maintaining their advocacy role, seek dialogue and influence in government decisions. There are others that survive with government funding and fill specific needs. Finally a new kind of NGOs are those set up specifically by governments to support conservation objectives and carry out tasks that may be difficult or cumbersome to tackle within the traditional apparatus of government.

In general, environmental NGOs have played an important advocacy role in raising awareness about dangerous projects and also by starting and supporting specific conservation efforts. They have been extremely effective in addressing local environmental problems and in mobilising public support for their specific causes. As such they are frequently in opposition to governmental decisions the latter of which is more likely to take a broader perspective taking account of not only local issues, but also national priorities.

The Pacuare River case exemplifies some of the traditional conflicts between governments and environmental NGOs. However, there are many cases in which the goals and strategies of both governments and environmental NGOs can be reconciled to reach working agreements. Commercial debt-for-nature swaps utilising environmental NGOs constitute an illustrative example of this category. These debt swaps have proven to be one of the most successful methods of empowering and providing long term stability to environmental NGOs.

3. *NGOs and Debt Swaps to Promote Sustainability*

Debt obligations from the developing world have come to be recognised as a major impediment to economic growth in those areas, an additional burden to the already precarious quality of life in poor countries, a menace to socio-political stability and a threat to international economic relations. As a response to these problems, several options related to debt condonation or relief are being discussed by the international community. The Brady Plan and the "Enterprise for the Americas" initiative by President Bush, have been two of the most important initiatives now under implementation to solve the problem. The United States, as well as most industrialised countries are actively searching for new approaches to lead the way out of the debt crisis. Debt for nature swaps, by themselves, are not the mechanism to solve the entire debt problem. Yet, they constitute a unique opportunity to convert a pressing burden into local resources for conservation and environmental protection.

The so-called debt-for-nature swaps have proven to be one of the most innovative and effective alternatives to create value in the form of local currency bonds which yield resources that can be utilised to transform the debt problem into a new opportunity to support conservation, resource management and reforestation. It is worth analyzing the Costa Rican experience in detail, since over 6 per cent of the country's commercial debt has already been purchased and exchanged for local currency bonds for conservation and related programmes. Although Costa Rica is a very small country of only three million people, it has undertaken the most ambitious debt for nature programme in the world, having traded nearly $100 million of debt for conservation.

Through this programme, Costa Rica has been able to strengthen tremendously several local non-governmental organisations, foremost among which is the National Park Foundation, an environmental NGO created by the Government in 1978, but operating as a private foundation under Costa Rican law. Other recipients included the Neotropical Foundation, Tropical Science Center and the Monteverde Conservation League.

In general, commercial swaps require the participation of local NGOs and debt swaps have become the primary mechanism in strengthening environmental NGOs.

4. Debt-for-nature Comes of Age in Costa Rica

The idea of linking debt to conservation was first set forth in 1984 by Dr. Thomas Lovejoy, then a Vice-President of the World Wildlife Fund. In *The New York Times*, he said that "under the best circumstances, debtor nations find it hard to address critical conservation problems because of multiple social needs... Stimulating conservation while ameliorating debt would encourage progress on both fronts".

In 1986, when the Arias Administration took office in Costa Rica, informal negotiations between the Ministry of Natural Resources, Energy and Mines (henceforth the Ministry of Natural Resources) and the Central Bank had produced positive results and one initial debt-for-equity swap was approved by the Central Bank in January 1987. On February 2, 1987 the Ministry of Natural Resources proposed to the Central Bank a debt-for-nature programme of $5.4 million, which was approved in August of that year, as the first allocation of a longer-term programme. During that year, in addition to Costa Rica, Bolivia and Ecuador also approved individual swaps or programmes.

Since then, the mechanism of converting commercial debt into local currency instruments for conservation projects has gained widespread recognition and hundreds of articles have been written on the subject. Despite the publicity, only about ten countries have approved projects of this nature, but many developed countries as well as developing ones have expressed their reservations.

In the case of Costa Rica, in less than three years, over $95 million in debt-titles have been purchased for conservation and sustainable development projects. This is the equivalent of 6.5 per cent of a commercial debt of $1.5 billion. Although this entire commercial debt has recently been restructured, the debt for nature programme carried out was the largest in the world and preceded the overall negotiation.

To understand how this process came about, it might be helpful to consider the evolution and characteristics of the programme from its humble $5.4 million beginning.

One of the most important features of the Costa Rican programme was the fact that the idea originally came from the Ministry of Natural Resources and support from the Central Bank for it had slowly grown over time. The Bank eventually approved a programme to be administered by the Ministry and carried out through the National Park Foundation. The existence and respectability of this foundation was critical to the success of the programme. Funds from a variety of donors, primarily U.S. environmental groups and foundations were donated to the National Park Foundation, to be converted into local currency bonds for a variety of projects. Another unique feature of the programme, is that it included environmental education, ecological and scientific tourism, and sustainable forestry as well as additional funds to purchase land for absolute preservation and management of those new areas.

Costa Rica had also pursued the possibility of obtaining donations from friendly governments, and through the active participation of the Ministries of Natural Resources and Planning, as well as the personal support of President Arias, the idea was well received in Europe. In early 1988 Costa Rica proposed to the Netherlands a specific debt-for-sustainable development swap. The idea was quickly endorsed by both governments and on June 22, 1988 it was agreed that 10 million guilders ($5 million) would be devoted to purchasing debt titles to be converted by the Central Bank at 33 per cent of face value, but with a maturation of four years maximum and interest rates at 15 per cent per annum. It must be pointed out that, in addition to conservation, the Dutch Government always intended to support the Central Bank's policies and Costa Rica's overall debt renegotiation efforts.

In this transaction, the Dutch Government bought the debt-titles through a designated financial intermediary and nearly $33 million were purchased with the donated funds. The main objective of the programme was reforestation and sustainable development with social interest groups like co-operatives and peasant organisations. In 1989 nearly four thousand hectares were planted by these groups through funds from interest payments on the local currency bonds. Just like in the case discussed above, the bonds are held in an escrow account and the utilisation of interest payment is determined jointly by the Ministries of Natural Resources and Planning, in consultation with the Dutch Government. These local resources have also been utilised to strengthen a variety of local NGOs such as Anai, local co-operatives, agricultural centres promoting reforestation, etc. Again it must be stressed that the executing agencies for these resources have been almost exclusively NGOs.

Shortly after this negotiation had been started with the Dutch Government, a parallel effort was undertaken with the Swedish Government for the completion and endowment of Guanacaste National Park, a major conservation project in northern Costa Rica. Swedish students and private conservation groups had been quite active in supporting the project and a total of $3.5 million were allocated to be used in debt conversion for Guanacaste National Park, out of a donated total of nearly $15 million.

A third quota of $5.6 million was approved by mid 1988, but the Central Bank had lowered the conversion to 30 per cent of face value, partly due to the fact that some Costa Rican debt could be purchased for as low as 12 cents on the dollar.

A final quota of $10.8 million was approved in December of 1989 for additional Swedish funds. These have been the debt-for-nature transactions carried out thus far, and one may believe that the mechanism could be used indefinitely. However, limits exist in terms of their inflationary impact.

Ultimately, debt-for-nature swaps are a mechanism through which developing country governments create value by multiplying the impact of donations for conservation by providing local currency bonds in amounts several times larger than the original grant. If we assess the overall Costa Rican programme, nearly $14 million of grants and donations were used to purchase over $90 million of debt titles and obtain close to $45 million in local currency bonds. The net result is that the Central Bank has provided three colones in bonds per each colon donated to Costa Rica. It is critical to bear this fact in mind in order to understand the alchemy of debt-for-nature swaps, because in the last count the colones injected into the economy by local currency bonds can have a significant inflationary effect. In order to minimise the inflationary impact, the bonds are non-negotiable and only interest and principal payments are monetised.

Viewed from a different perspective, the overall result has been for the Central Bank to purchase $90 million worth of face-value titles for $45 million in local currency bonds, or less than 50 per cent of face value. From this perspective, the Central Bank and the original donor have shared the discount obtained in the purchase of debt titles in secondary markets. If titles are purchased close to 15 cents on the dollar, the Central Bank can match the grant on a three to one basis and still pay less than 50 per cent of the face value of the title, thereby reducing future interest payments on this amount.

5. NGOs and Debt for Nature Swaps

The debt-for-nature mechanism has received widespread attention in the media during the last three years, and has slowly spread to nearly a dozen countries including Argentina, Bolivia, Ecuador, Dominican Republic, Madagascar and the Philippines. Other countries like Panama and Nicaragua are in the process of establishing similar programmes.

The unique relation of commercial debt-for-nature swaps to strengthening of environmental NGOs is based on the fact that governments themselves are barred from purchasing discounted commercial debt directly, and NGOs can therefore act as intermediaries either purchasing debt directly, or receiving donations of debt titles purchased by a donor.

In Costa Rica, the National Park Foundation played this critical role. From a budget of a few million colones per year before the debt swaps, today it handles endowment funds of over two billion colones, including the funds for Guanacaste National Park donated by the Swedish Government. In Ecuador, Fundación Natura was the recipient of a $10 million debt swap. In each of the countries that have carried out swaps, a local or an international NGO has been utilised, and at the same time benefited from the opportunity to become stronger and work more closely with the government.

Debt for nature swaps have also been criticised on the grounds that recipient countries are losing sovereignty over their resources to international groups or NGOs. This also brings up the broader question of the role of international environmental NGOs in developing countries, their relationship to governments and to local NGOs.

In this respect it is interesting to note that, in 1987, the Costa Rican government was in the process of starting a debt-for-nature programme (initially $5.4 million) that was independent of any particular NGO and instead attempted to include a variety of funding sources orchestrated by the government (Ministry of Natural Resources) and under the National Park Foundation. At the same time, several U.S. based NGOs were attempting to structure debt swaps in different countries. One of them was able to persuade the Bolivian government to accept a donation of $100 000 (which purchased $650 000 of debt titles) in exchange for setting up the Beni Reserve and some local currency resources. The deal attracted enormous media attention for the NGO, but created problems for both Bolivia and the mechanism itself. First of all, it was signed and announced in Washington. Second, through an incredible diplomatic *faux-pas*, the Bolivian Ambassador is said to have announced that there were a lot more forests in his country, if additional donations were forthcoming. This initiated a wave of reaction and created a sense of loss of sovereignty that was embraced by the President Sarney of Brazil, among others. The proposal of a U.S. Senator that Brazil turn over the management of the Amazon to an international NGO also added considerable heat to this debate.

The question of whether or not international environmental NGOs should own land in recipient countries is a very important and controversial one. It is clear that all developing countries need assistance in their conservation efforts, and environmental NGOs from the developed world have effectively raised resources from their membership and donors to this end. Yet it is also important to decide on the way in which aid is delivered and managed.

NGOs from developed countries are taking an increasingly forceful role in promoting conservation in the tropical developing countries. Traditionally, they had focused primarily on conservation of parks and reserves with little attention to development of local populations. However, recently concern for sustainable development alternatives began to be recognised as a priority of both international and local NGOs.

6. *Mechanisms of Co-operation*

International conservation organisations are increasingly becoming interested in providing assistance to developing countries in the environmental area.

There are a variety of mechanisms that can be utilised to channel the assistance and supervise the execution of programmes. The first option is direct assistance to recipient country governments, either as general support or for specific projects. A second approach is to channel the assistance and delegate the project's implementation to a local NGO by means of collaborative agreements. A third option is the direct execution of programmes of projects by an international NGO in a recipient country. There are also many possible combinations of the basic approaches, and most projects include elements from each of them.

Each option has its own advantages and drawbacks. For example, assistance to recipient country governments is easy to deliver but may become entangled in bureaucratic red tape. On the other hand, it may be difficult to identify a local NGO capable of executing the programme or project. The costs of direct execution of projects are high and require set-up and start-up costs that may be considerable. In each particular case it is important to weigh the positive and negative aspects of the options. However, it is always critical that the host government be informed and allowed to participate in the decision making process, even if the project may not be executed directly by a government agency. It is equally critical that the projects undertaken have been designated as important and have priority with the host government. Sometimes it is necessary to increase the awareness of local officials, NGOs and others. These steps are crucial to the success of any project because they lead to the creation of a partnership of the international and local NGOs with the host country government. All successful efforts share this common characteristic that a partnership or understanding has been reached by all parties.

Given the enormous limitations that developing country governments face in terms of basic personnel, budgets and rising financial constraints, both international and local NGOs can become an important partner with governments to execute or implement projects and programmes. Therefore, the host government may work to strengthen the NGOs if sufficient trust and credibility exist between them.

In Costa Rica, for example, the government has financed the National Park Foundation through direct budgetary allocations, through debt-swaps and also by allowing the Foundation to receive foreign aid. In turn, the Foundation has purchased inholdings in national parks and new areas of particular value or interest to the government. Eventually, all the lands purchased by the Foundation are donated to the Costa Rican Government. Although the country promotes private conservation efforts -- and in the case of Monteverde, a private reserve was the seed for Arenal National Park -- Costa Rica encourages the donation of all lands to the state.

Through a reform of its conservation and development strategy during the Arias Administration, higher priority was given to decentralised management of conservation areas with the participation of international and local NGOs, taking into account the needs of rural groups and population, as well as scientific and tourism interests.

Environmental NGOs must be encouraged to widen their traditional focus on species or ecosystem preservation to include as a priority the needs and aspirations of local populations. They should provide full support to the creation of development options through education, technical assistance and financing. If sustainable development options can be provided for populations living in reserves or buffer zones, their influence on the parks is likely to be beneficial and the effective conservation areas can be enlarged and enriched. Eventually, these populations can become frontline defenders of the parks if they learn to survive and prosper without destroying the forests.

Newly established parks and reserves in several Latin American countries rival those of many developed countries in ecological representation and percentage of land area protected. Yet many of these recent reserves have only legal protection and their management systems are understaffed, underfunded and sometimes non-existent. It is estimated that nearly three quarters of the declared parks and reserves in Latin America lack effective protection, and that an even larger percentage lacks long term management plans and financial resources to guarantee their preservation in the long run.

Environmental NGOs, both local and international, are playing an increasingly effective role in helping country governments manage protected areas and opening new development options for their inhabitants. Examples of these new partnerships are still rare but are growing fast in all regions of the world.

The growth of NGOs in the environmental area is one of the most significant trends of the past decade, and it is likely to become even more important in the future. Direct citizen participation in environmental management is becoming more critical.

7. *Conclusions*

It is clear that much can be gained from the collaboration of NGOs, both international and local, with governments in the field of environmental management. The objective should be the creation of a stable partnership, where differences in objectives and agendas are clearly recognised, and specific areas of common interest are identified. Under these circumstances, the government and NGOs can strengthen each other and accomplish a great deal, by empowering organised participation to help solve environmental problems.

The ways to arrive at this partnership are complex and dependent on socio-cultural factors and traditions. Yet it is difficult to find substitutes to open discussion, written agreements and commonly agreed strategies.

Preservation of biodiversity in tropical regions appears to be one of the highest priorities for collaboration, both in terms of management of conservation areas that have already been established, as well as the creation of new ones. As mentioned earlier, decentralised and regionally-based conservation approaches can be established to include the active participation of NGOs, local interests, scientists, etc.; under the leadership and orchestration of governments.

Experiences up to date have been positive, although many negative examples can be found. In the Costa Rican case, the decentralisation of the system of management of protected areas has opened up considerable new options as well as attracting additional resources, for joint projects between a large number of NGOs and the government. Dozens of regional and international environmental organisations have programmes and field offices in Costa Rica, and hundreds of natural scientists carry out research programmes in the country every year. This positive experience can be adapted by other developing countries, although many characteristics make the Costa Rican experience unique.

It is very likely that NGOs will continue to play a valuable role in environmental management and in promoting sustainable development. Yet, this role is dependent on the capabilities of local NGOs to grow and mature, both in terms of membership, financing and administration. Debt swaps funds, for example, have provided unique opportunities to several NGOs. Bilateral debt swaps through the "Enterprise for the Americas Initiative" of President Bush of the United States, will rely primarily on NGOs as beneficiaries of the country environmental funds that will be created. If NGOs can prove that they are efficient managers, able to carry out projects and programmes effectively, their future role could grow considerably. On the other hand, if they become mired by inefficiency, lack of transparency in financial management or are unable to meet objectives, they could quickly lose their credibility.

Therefore, one of the critical areas to catalyse this process is the strengthening of NGOs through training, establishing strategies and plans, and generating a managerial capability commensurate with the enormous tasks at hand. Bilateral aid agencies, foundations and other international agencies could play a very useful role by establishing programmes to strengthen the capabilities and organisational effectiveness of NGOs.

INTERNATIONAL NGO EXPERIENCE *

by

Richard Sandbrook **

* Transcription of oral presentation.

** Executive Director, International Institute for Environment and Development (IIED).

RÉSUMÉ

Bien que l'on ait mis en garde contre la grande diversité des ONG, celles-ci ont suffisamment de choses en commun dans leur parcours pour que l'on puisse tracer une esquisse des résultats obtenus à travers les objectifs qu'elles poursuivent (ou devraient poursuivre). Ainsi, elles ont très bien réussi à mobiliser l'opinion comme en témoigne la rapide coloration en "vert" de l'aide et le ralliement d'autres mouvements à la bannière de l'écologie. Elles ont aussi diffusé beaucoup d'informations qui sont la matière d'une sensibilisation du plus grand nombre aux problèmes de l'environnement. S'agissant de la mobilisation des ressources, elles ont bien réussi sur des questions d'environnement clairement délimitées, mais non lorsqu'il s'est agi des questions étroitement liées impliquant les grands thèmes du dialogue Nord-Sud, c'est-à-dire la pauvreté, l'habilitation, etc. Jusqu'à présent, les ONG n'ont donc guère dépassé le stade de la description des problèmes d'environnement, sans en éclairer beaucoup les causes ni proposer des instruments appropriés pour résoudre ces problèmes. Ceci s'explique, pour une part, parce que les ONG sont parties de l'environnement pour aller vers le développement, et, pour une autre part, parce que la masse de recherches véritables sur des questions telles que les liens entre pauvreté et environnement, développement et destruction de l'environnement etc., est étonnament maigre. Une dernière gageure sera de former une véritable coalition avec les institutions qui ont leur base dans le Sud ; la vision propre au Nord est un grand obstacle pour plaider ces causes avec efficacité.

SUMMARY

Despite caveats about the large diversity of the NGOs, there is enough commonality in their track record to sketch their performance across the objectives they pursue (or should be pursuing). Thus, they have performed very well in mobilising opinion as witnessed by the rapid greening of aid and the attraction of other movements to the environmental banner. They have also served up a great deal of information that is the stuff of broad-based environmental education. In mobilising resources they have done well on environmental issues narrowly defined, but not well in the closely related issues involving the major subjects of the North-South dialogue, i.e. poverty, empowerment etc. Thus far, the NGOs have not moved far beyond the stage of describing environmental difficulties, with little on causes or appropriate tools to fix the problems. This is partly because they have started from environment and are moving towards development. And it is partly that the quantum of effective research on issues such as poverty-environment links, development and environmental destruction etc., is appallingly limited. A final challenge is to undertake effective coalition building with the South-based institutions; northern bias greatly hampers effective advocacy on these issues.

I am faced with some difficulty because anybody who is familiar with the NGO (Non-Governmental Organisation) community knows that it is a very dangerous thing indeed to stand up and represent or speak on its behalf in a collective sense. The NGOs, I assure you, are as diverse as governments -- more so -- and it is very difficult in a sense to speak of a unified front. Also I have first to address the question of definition of what is an international NGO. I will not bore everybody with the ECOSOC (Economic and Social Council of the United Nations) rules for list A, B, C and D, etc., but I would just like to point out that there are some very distinct kinds of international NGOs who are now involved in the environment development arena.

Obviously, there are the confederate-type NGOs such as Greenpeace or Friends of the Earth International which are made up of lots of national organisations, North and South. Then there are coalition NGOs at international level: classic amongst them is the Environment Liaison Centre International in Nairobi which tends to represent community and campaigning organisations. Then there is the International Union for the Conservation of Nature and Natural Resources which tends to represent the ecological scientific community and the traditional conservation movement. There is ICSU (International Council of Scientific Unions) for the scientific unions, there are the social science equivalents and so on. And then there are a group of international NGOs who call themselves "international", such as my own, (the International Institute for Environment and Development (IIED) we include the word "international" in our title on the basis of two claims to internationalism. First is because we work across a very great range of countries and topics. Secondly, because some of us have bases in more than one country. Included in this group is the World Resources Institute, the Stockholm Institute, IIED as I say, and so on.

Now, I do not want to talk today about the experience of all of the other NGOs who are international. They collectively come under the term of CONGO (I have never quite understood what it stands for) at the UN, but basically include trade unions, businesses, church groups, humanitarian concern groups, peace groups, etc. I am just going to confine my remarks to those groups that I have just listed. These basically started out with environment as their focus and have moved towards development. I want to give a report card on them and explain where we are now in the run up to 1992. I do this because I think our role is going to be quite pivotal and important.

The first thing I have to say is that all of us who work in the environment and development business realise that we are as much a part of the entertainment business as serious providers of opinion. The allegation to this effect made earlier in this meeting is true. We know that. And one of the reasons why we are in the entertainment business is because environment organisations are quite good at is mobilising political opinion; and political opinion, if I may be so bold, is mobilised in the entertainment way -- on television, in the press, etc. I would be greatly encouraged if some of those in the academic community, or the development community, actually got in on the act as well and started to draw on some of the lessons which we think have been very beneficial in the environment community. So I have no elitism about this at all. I am proud to be part of the entertainment business.

The second point I would like to make is that a lot of NGOs outside of the environment business have realised that we are quite effective and are jumping in with us. We are rapidly forming what I would call a "rainbow coalition of concern".

Now, contrary to opinions which are often expressed, I would be very hard pressed to find people in the international environment business who do not welcome this with open arms. There has been a very long-run understanding in the environment community that we are concerned with poverty -- also that we are concerned with development, with gender issues -- all of these are facets of the sustainable development agenda and we are much better off standing as a coalition than standing as something separate. And those who represent us as being only concerned with furry animals and pollution control really are being mischievous, because our concerns are much wider than that, and have been for some considerable time.

Now, equally as the NGOs are coming together, so governments too are beginning to develop an "environmental reflex" right across their own activities. The recent policy statements of the Netherlands, the United Kingdom, Sweden etc. illustrate this well. This trend includes the foreign policy of the OECD countries. We are seeing the rapid greening of foreign policy. I personally have a theory about this and it is based on a classic British view of things; namely, that foreign policy -- good foreign policy -- is always based on a stable three-cornered stool. If it only has two legs it tends to fall over -- if it has only one leg it has to spin or gyrate to stay up -- the three rationales for aid are changing: As the moral imperative, and the mutual trading and the Brandtian-type arguments (of well perceived self-interest for development assistance are maintained, one element has gone down very rapidly. That is the strategic reason for investing in developing countries. The East/West conflict, the old ideological position has melted away. That is being very rapidly replaced by the green imperative on the environmental imperative.

So, it is little wonder that we have just been through two days of fascinating meetings here in the working group on environment of the DAC (OECD's Development Assistance Committee), where aid agencies rush to "green" every part of the aid agenda as fast as they can. Parliamentary and political pressure is on them to show their green bonafides!

This is a great opportunity rather than a cynical conversion. It is a great opportunity because environmental issues are just not dealt with unless you get right down there to the lowest levels of society and start addressing poverty, basic needs and empowerment issues. Therefore, I think that this "greening" (although you can be cynical and say it is still all about biological diversity) is a serious and a great opportunity for us all.

The score card of international NGOs in responding to this opportunity, I must confess, is not so good. When it comes to doing something about information, I think the international NGOs have done a very reasonable job. We have done a lot to make the available information on environment a common property resource. We have put information into multiple packages, we have made books, film shows, and so on. On the information-sharing line we would score six out of ten on the scorecard. Also, we have not done badly in terms of case material, case studies -- actually how the environment is cared for in practice. I think we could do a lot more but we would get six out of ten on the case material as well.

When it comes to another function of an international NGO namely to try to facilitate international consensus on issues we have done well and not so well. First, in building an international consensus on the environment (the *strictu sensu* environment), the record is very good. The *World Conservation Strategy* (Gland, Switzerland, IUCN, 1980) which was published some ten years ago is an example. Another would be the coalitions of concern around strictly environmental issues such as pesticides, forestry and endangered species trade. But we would only get five out of ten in building international consensuses around the wider clutch of issues.

The Brundtland report was very much an output of the international NGO community. We had a lot to do with its preparation and I think it was useful (if not a little wordy) but I am not sure that it was altogether as useful as some people would hold. I think 1992 is going to be an extraordinarily important point for finding out and maybe for building a deeper international consensus on its thesis. So far the international NGOs are building up to that event well, with the Secretariat, and so prospects for the future are better.

The next thing which I would score is the ability of the international NGOs to mobilise resources and here I would split the analysis into two.

First, technical assistance resources. In fact, the international NGOs have become rather like public interest consultancy firms. They are now delivering a vast range of technical assistance packages. As we have heard from Kirk Rodgers and others, IUCN has done much in the planning arena, and there are other areas. And in the technical assistance arena we have mobilised new government aid money and we have mobilised new money from publics as well. In short, we have done reasonably well to date and we are still growing rapidly. But the international environmental NGOs have done virtually nothing about mobilising additional financial resources for the North-South equity issues with which we are faced. Part of the reason for this is because the lobby which is environmental domestically is essentially a "not in my back-yard lobby". It is not yet an international lobby in that sense. In other words, we have to do far more to link the international environmental issues to equity amongst those who support environmental organisations in Europe and North America before the pressure will be on to mobilise new and additional resources for the international issues. We are going in the right direction and I am reasonably optimistic. But this far the score is only four out of ten.

On the question of how the international NGOs have related to empowering communities and working at a local level, carrying into practice all the rhetoric about participation in development, I would have to give three out of ten. But that is changing rapidly. Basically, the international NGOs have been through phases of development. We have had to raise the issues, we have had to learn a lot about development and we have learnt it quite fast. But now we have to get out there and become pro-active -- much more active within the community and in building up partnerships.

The great challenge in this direction is to get the development organisations such as OXFAM, with 700 field workers, to make partnership and common cause with us so that these issues are addressed. We have far to go on that.

I am going to give two out of ten to policy leadership. Basically the international environmental NGOs so far have not moved much beyond the stage of describing the symptoms of environmental difficulties. They have not got to the causes and they have not really done too much to actually bring together tools for addressing the causes. We heard of examples in earlier presentations but really the research content of the international environment agenda is appalling. The linkages between environment and economy are very poorly understood. For example, there is not much work to show the relationship between poverty and environmental destruction. Yet, we often assume it. Certainly, in the relationship of debt to environmental destruction there is much too much assumption rather than research. Thus, the international environment NGOs have far more to do in stimulating policy research and bringing the academic community into the arena in a way that is useful to the international process.

Finally, just to finish this controversial report card, I would like to conclude on the performance on advocacy (which is the one thing which everybody knows us for). The difficulty that the international environment NGOs face in the advocacy arena, is that they are far too biased towards the North or the industrialised world. They are made up essentially of Northern organisations or coalitions and Northern expertise. There is just not a sufficient coordinated voice as yet in the NGO community of the South. There is a very strong and growing national group of NGOs but coalition building in an international way is still sadly lacking. Joining up with the South is still the top priority. So on that, I will stop.

THE ROLE OF ENVIRONMENTAL EDUCATION IN DEVELOPING COUNTRIES: ISSUES FOR RESEARCH

by

Hartmut Schneider *

* Development Centre of the Organisation for Economic Co-operation and Development, Paris.

RÉSUMÉ

Le rôle de l'éducation dans le domaine de l'environnement (EE) en tant que transmission de connaissances et de valeurs pour encourager un comportement plus respectueux de l'environnement semble facilement accepté sur une base intuitive. Il est moins courant d'y voir un instrument de gestion de l'environnement, complétant les instruments économiques et la réglementation. En théorie, l'EE peut être justifiée au plan de l'écologie et de l'économie. Toutefois il n'existe pas, semble-t-il, la moindre analyse empirique pour plaider la cause de l'EE sur le terrain de l'économie. En outre, il est proposé de tenter de définir les conditions dans lesquelles l'EE peut être la plus efficace, sans toutefois imposer une trop lourde charge financière qui limiterait *de facto* sa viabilité. Une approche participative, des communications fonctionnant dans les deux sens, l'intégration des connaissances traditionnelles et des connaissances scientifiques modernes au message dispensé par l'EE et la formation d'un électorat de sensibilité écologiste sont, suppose l'auteur, au nombre des conditions du succès de l'EE.

SUMMARY

The role of environmental education (EE) as the transmission of knowledge and values stimulating more environment-friendly behaviour seems to be easily accepted on an intuitive basis. It is less common to see it as an instrument of environmental management, complementing economic and regulatory instruments. EE can in theory be justified on both ecological and economic grounds. However, hardly any empirical analysis seems to exist to support the economic case in favour of EE. Furthermore, research is proposed to define the conditions under which EE can be most effective, without however imposing too heavy a financial burden which in itself would limit its sustainability. It is hypothesized that a participatory approach, two-way communication, the integration of traditional and modern scientific knowledge in the EE message, and the building up of an environmental constituency are among the conditions for successful EE.

The Development Centre's research programme 1990-1992 on "Coping with Environmental Threats" singles out environmental education (EE) and public attitudes among the factors to be considered in improved environmental management. This note presents further ideas on how EE in a wide sense, i.e. including public awareness raising, could be studied within this programme.

1. Rationale and Objective

Considerable work has been done on EE but mainly from a pedagogic perspective, for example defining curricula and requirements for teacher training and teaching materials. The UNESCO/UNEP International Environmental Education Programme (IEEP) has been most prominent in this approach. But hardly any work seems to have been undertaken from a management perspective, where EE is seen as an instrument among others (economic and regulatory instruments) to cope with environmental problems.

We may, however, adopt the definition of EE given by UNESCO/UNEP in the *International Strategy for Action in the Field of Environmental Education and Training for the 1990s* (Paris, UNESCO/UNEP, 1987) since it is very comprehensive: "A permanent process in which individuals gain awareness of their environment and acquire the knowledge, values, skills, experiences, and also the determination which will enable them to act -- individually and collectively -- to solve present and future environmental problems".

Our general hypothesis is that EE is potentially a powerful and cost-effective tool in environmental management. It is necessary at all levels of society, from national decision-makers to the public at large. It can, for example, provide the knowledge and attitudes necessary for the formulation of national and sectoral environmental policies and measures on the one hand, and motivate the public to support these policies on the other hand. In the extreme case, one could see EE to change values and behaviour patterns to such an extent that regulatory or incentive measures are made redundant. More realistically, one may expect from EE to reduce the cost of other measures, by reducing the level of expenditures necessary for the enforcement of regulations, and for incentives.

Furthermore, EE can have an effect where other measures cannot be applied in practice or are limited in their reach. For example, the administrative burden of introducing and policing regulatory and incentive measures in all environmentally relevant spheres would be beyond the capacity of the most efficient of public administrations, let alone of the usually weak and overstrained administrations in developing countries. While one can justify EE as a useful activity in its own right, much like other education, one would expect it to be most effective in contributing to better environmental management if it is part of a coherent set of mutually supportive measures. The general objective pursued with this research is therefore to define the conditions under which EE can be most effective, without however imposing too heavy a financial burden which in itself would limit its sustainability. Cost-effectiveness of EE is thus an important concern which seems to have attracted little attention in the literature reviewed for the preparation of this note. Finally, the objective is also to define ways and means to strengthen EE, both through external assistance and through gradually increasing national and local self-reliance.

2. Some Theoretical Points of Reference

It may be useful to search in various fields of theory and experience for concepts and ideas on which to base this rather innovative approach to EE from a management perspective. Turning to economic theory, one finds education treated as an investment within the theory of human capital. The underlying reasoning is that time and expenditures spent on education will repay for the individuals engaging in education. This theory is established empirically with a number of qualifications which do not have to be considered here. EE, however, is largely different from general or advanced education, in the sense that it does not confer marketable qualifications (except where it includes training of certain skills). EE can nevertheless be useful at two levels, that of the individual and of the community, depending on its focus and message. In some instances, an individual may benefit directly from EE, for example if he/she learns how to obtain safe drinking water or how to handle toxic substances.

More often, however, EE goes beyond the realm of the individual and concerns issues which are described in economic theory as externalities, public goods and collective action. In these cases, according to neoclassic economic theory, it cannot be assumed that individuals will act in environmentally desirable ways, since their action would either benefit others (externalities), or on its own would not make a perceptible difference in the outcome for the individual, while, on the other hand, the individual could still benefit, as a free rider, from the action of others. Thus the paradigm of individual utilitarianism underlying neoclassic economic theory is confronted with situations which imply inequitable burden sharing or which are inferior for the collectivity as a whole since no individual on his/her own perceives an incentive for action.

This state of affairs provides a rationale for EE even if one reasons within this limited framework of economic theory. EE can provide information which the market does not provide in the case of public goods which are therefore not appreciated to their full economic value. Furthermore, by introducing new ethical values, EE can provide some selective incentive (e.g. social pressure) necessary for the individuals to overcome the collective action problem. In this way, the ecological paradigm, which is originally based on moral values that are different from those underlying the neoclassical paradigm, can be seen to function within the latter. While there is an ongoing theoretical debate about the compatibility between these two paradigms, it should be clear from the above that they are not necessarily mutually exclusive.

EE can, however, stand on its own within an ecological paradigm as an instrument used to change values of individuals in such a way that they behave more environment-friendly out of ecological civic spirit even if they are not compelled by regulation or induced by economic incentives. An example for the existence of such ecological civic spirit is provided by those who sort household waste and carry part of it (e.g. bottles and paper) to separate collection points for recycling although this is not obligatory and not rewarded economically for the individual (e.g. no reduction of the fee paid for garbage collection).

Research into EE within a management perspective can thus refer to both the economic and the ecological paradigm, depending on the specific issue concerned. In principle, EE could be analyzed in terms of its costs and benefits and thus be compared to other measures. No such analysis has been found in the literature reviewed. The reason for this may be that it would in practice be very difficult to get a full quantification and a satisfactory valuation of all the components of the relevant costs and benefits. Therefore, it may be more realistic to consider the possibility of undertaking some research into the cost-effectiveness of EE in a situation where different instruments can be compared.

In trying to define conditions for successful EE from a management perspective one has to go beyond the requirements concerning syllabi, teaching materials and teachers' training. While these requirements are of course very important elements in any strategy of EE which have been dealt with in the so far dominating pedagogic perspective of EE, they are not sufficient when dealing with aspects lying outside the educational system, be it formal or informal.

EE as an activity introducing new knowledge and attempting to change attitudes and behaviour may draw on the experience of similarly structured activities such as extension services in rural development and public health. This would seem to apply where EE addresses large numbers of producers or consumers. In this context, one has to recall the failures or very limited success of extension efforts which took insufficient account of the local situation, i.e. the motivation and constraints determining individuals' behaviour. Top-down one-way channels of communication are therefore suspicious. EE has to make sure that those to whom its message is addressed indeed understand it fully and have the possibility and a subjective reason to act in the desired way.

Understanding may be enhanced if traditional knowledge is combined with modern scientific knowledge and if EE makes an effort of explaining and convincing rather than of preaching. Credibility of those engaged in EE is also essential for the environmental message to be accepted. Ideally, this would imply that the information on which EE is based is collected, stored, analyzed and disseminated by an independent centre rather than by an authority who may be suspected to pursue its own interests.

Public participation is a concept often decried as a slogan rather than a reality. Nevertheless, it seems to be a condition for successful EE on several grounds, such as credibility, acceptance of the message and widespread sustainability of the activity. Appropriate ways of involving the public have therefore to be found for each specific situation. If the public is involved in data collection, monitoring, campaigning and conservation activities, savings may be possible at several levels while at the same time enhancing credibility and commitment.

To be truly effective in a pervasive and lasting manner, EE requires a *constituency* which may be built up in the process of the educational activities in a wide sense. Political science may have to offer insights and advice on how best to create and use such a constituency.

3. EE and Management Issues in Practice

While the above paragraphs offer some conceptual and normative statements about EE which may well deserve to be developed further, it seems desirable to define possibilities for future work by the Development Centre which adopts an empirical perspective. The reason for this is that it appears that not very much is known in an easily accessible and reasonably comprehensive way about how EE functions in practice in developing countries. There is a potential for learning from those developing countries which are most advanced in this field. This might help to distinguish reality from theory in this area. Furthermore, those interested in supporting environmental activities in developing countries may gain a more realistic view of what can be achieved with EE and under what conditions.

The purpose of the list of proposals for research developed below is to stimulate further discussion and to offer a range of projects from which one could choose those which are most promising and feasible given data and resource constraints for empirically based work.

First it should be restated that we use a broad definition of EE, including the formal and non-formal educational system as well as a variety of other activities designed to inform the public about environmental problems, to change attitudes and behaviour patterns. Such activities may address the public at large at the national level (e.g. through regular national media or ad hoc campaigns), or be more limited in scope. They can be regrouped as indicated below and could be the object of research either individually or in some combination.

1) EE addressed at the *general public*, calling for civic action, e.g. to protect animal or plant species, or to pollute less etc. These calls may take different forms, such as the celebration of an Environment Day or more frequent and specific activities, encouraging debate rather than ceremony.

2) EE addressing *consumers* to adopt environment-friendly behaviour, for example with regard to energy or water consumption, use of polluting products, etc. This may be accompanied by voluntary or obligatory labelling to help the consumer to choose "green" products. Nevertheless, one should be reminded of the complexity of the issues involved in certain cases which may give rise to manipulation and litigation as experienced recently in certain OECD countries.

3) EE addressing *producers*, especially where they are numerous, to use less polluting or depleting production methods, for example in agriculture.

4) EE addressing *public decision-makers/authorities*, e.g. information and lobbying campaigns by NGOs with a view to promoting specific legislation or government action concerning acute environmental problems.

5) EE addressing *opinion leaders* such as journalists, youth leaders and teachers may precede or accompany other activities of EE whose effect can be greatly reinforced by this kind of activity.

Rather than taking the audience of EE as the focal point of the analysis as in the preceding typology, one might also (or alternatively) take different *actors* of EE as the starting point:

* *GOVERNMENT*, which plays a role through the formal and perhaps informal education system, but possibly also outside it, e.g. through general public information. One might also ask whether and how official declarations on EE such as those contained in National Conservation Strategies and similar documents are acted upon subsequently.

* *Environmental NGOs*, both national and international, can be important actors in EE. In fact most of their activities are likely to be in this field. The role they play in specific countries, on their own or in co-operation (respectively confrontation) with others may be worth analyzing and documenting for a wider audience.

* *The MEDIA* (radio, television, press) are generally considered a powerful actor in building up public opinion. To what extent is this potential used for environmental concerns in developing countries?

The activities of these actors might be analyzed at the national or any sub-national (local) level. Relations between these levels may be of particular interest since they may reveal discrepancies between theory and practice. Relations between these actors are also worth attention since they may greatly enhance or reduce the impact of certain activities, depending on whether these relations are mutually supportive or conflictual.

Finally, instead of choosing specific actors or audiences of EE as the entry point for research one could also select one or several issues as the focal point. Inevitably, however, one will also touch upon the categories of actors and audiences. The entry point chosen will therefore be more a question of particular emphasis and perhaps of access to data than of exclusive focus. From our earlier discussion we recall some major issues which might be analyzed separately or in some combination:

* *The relationship between EE and environmental management*
This is a potentially very comprehensive issue. It includes questions such as whether there is co-ordination and mutual support, sub-ordination or independence, conflict or stimulation between the two. One might look at different aspects such as the messages of EE and how they relate to environmental policies, the institutions and people involved on both sides, financial relations etc. Furthermore, the relationship could be analyzed with regard to one sector of environmental concern, e.g.forestry, or it could cover several sectors and concerns. The perception of the relationship by different actors, at the conceptual and at the practical level, may also be worth looking into. This could also include questions of sequencing between educational and management activities.

* *Public participation in EE*
Starting from the hypothesis that participation would be a desirable feature, the question is whether it is actually happening, in which ways and with what benefits. Where public participation is very limited or non-existent one may ask for the reasons for this state of affairs and its implications for effectiveness and costs.

* *EE and the building of environmental constituencies*
This issue clearly overlaps with the preceding one but its emphasis is more political and it concerns perhaps more, though not exclusively, the national level. The hypothesis would be that EE and environmental constituencies are mutually supportive. What is the evidence for this and what sequences of activities and processes can be observed, which are most helpful?

* *Cost-effectiveness and impact of EE*
While there is some evidence in the literature that EE has increased knowledge and changed attitudes (at least at the level of statements) it would be useful for purposes of resource allocation to seek evidence for the verification of our initial hypothesis that EE is very cost-effective. Various avenues may be pursued in this respect. For example to the extent that resources can be mobilised for EE without financial outlay and at low

opportunity costs, there is a good chance for high cost-effectiveness. Another avenue might be to compare in a given setting the cost of different activities of EE which have comparable results.

Research along the lines presented above would try to document and analyze what is effectively done in the field of EE within a country, or part of it, or even in a few communities. While this work would include certain evaluative elements it would be different from ordinary evaluation studies by taking a broader look from an "outside" perspective, and not the perspective of the sponsors of a project or programme.

However, this is not to say that ordinary evaluation studies would be without interest. In fact, if we could find co-operating agencies, governmental or non-governmental, one could envisage doing some work in this framework. In this case, one of two approaches, or a combination of the two, might be followed. One approach would consist of "secondary" analysis of evaluation reports, with a view of preparing an overview and drawing more general conclusions. The other approach would be to engage ourselves in evaluations (or join evaluation teams). If feasible, such an approach would have immediate operational relevance for those involved in the EE activities concerned.

Another kind of quasi-evaluative approach would consist of the analysis of EE in a few "model" countries, which are known to be relatively advanced in this field. While some information is available, for example on India, Kenya, Malaysia and Venezuela, in a comparative survey published by IEEP no full-fledged country studies could be found in the literature search undertaken for the preparation of this note.

Annex 1

LIST OF CONFERENCE PARTICIPANTS

Dr. Torsten AMELUNG
The Kiel Institute of World Economics
PO Box 4309, D-2300 Kiel 1, Germany

Professor Dennis ANDERSON
University College London, and
Institute of Economics and Statistics, University of Oxford
St. Cross Building, Manor Road, Oxford OX1 3UL, United Kingdom

Mr. Walter ARENSBERG
Deputy Director, Environmental Planning and Management
Center for International Development and Environment
World Resources Institute
1709 New York Avenue, NW, Washington, DC 20006, United States

Mr. Jacques BUGNICOURT
Executive Secretary
ENDA (Environemental Developement Action in the Third World)
B.P. 3370, Dakar, Senegal

Mr. Michael COCKERELL
Director, Administration and Management
International Union for the Conservation of Nature and Natural Resources (IUCN)
Avenue du Mont-Blanc, CH-1196 Gland, Switzerland

Dr. Nitin DESAI
Deputy Secretary-General
United Nations Conference on Environment and Development
160 Route de Florissant, P.O. Box 80, CH-1231 Conches, Switzerland

Ir. Carel DRIJVER
Coordinator, Centre for Environmental Studies (CML)
Leiden University
PO Box 9518, 2300 RA Leiden, The Netherlands

Mr. Paul DRIVER
International Union for the Conservation of Nature and Natural Resources (IUCN)
Avenue du Mont-Blanc, CH-1196 Gland, Switzerland

Dr. Delfin J. GANAPIN, JR.
Director, Environmental Management Bureau
Department of Environment and Natural Resources, The Philippines
6th Floor, Philippine Heart Centre Building, East Avenue
Diliman, Quezon City, Metro Manila, The Philippines

Ms. Faith HALTER
44 Prospect Park West, # D-8, Brooklyn, New York 11215, United States

Dr. Faisal KASRYNO
Director, Bureau of Planning
Ministry of Agriculture, Indonesia
Jalan Hersono RM No. 3, Pasar Minggu, Jakarta Selatan, Indonesia

Dr. W. KREISEL
Director, Division of Environmental Health
World Health Organisation (WHO)
20 Avenue Appia, 1211 Geneva 27, Switzerland

Professor Deepak LAL
Department of Economics, University College London
Gower Street, London WC1E 6BT, United Kingdom

Mr. Kevin LYONETTE
Director, Sustainable Resource Use Programme
World Wide Fund for Nature International (WWF)
CH-1196 Gland, Switzerland

Dr. Michael NELSON
Casilla 209-12, Santiago, Chile

Mr. Auguste NGIRABATWARE
Le Ministre du Plan, Rwanda
Ministère du Plan
B.P. 46, Kigali, Rwanda

Dr. Theodore PANAYOTOU
Harvard Institute for International Development
Cambridge, Massachusetts 02138, United States

Professor David PEARCE
Department of Economics, University College London
Gower Street, London WC1E 6BT, United Kingdom

Dr. Dhira PHANTUMVANIT
Director, Natural Resources and Environment Program
Thailand Development Research Institute Foundation
Rajapark Building, 163 Asoke Road, Bangkok, 10110 Thailand

Mr. Börje PAULSSON
Swedish National Environmental Protection Agency
Box 1302
17125 Solna, Sweden

Dr. Diana POMBO HOLGUIN
Perfil Ambiental de Colombia
Cra.14, No.87-91, Of.102, Bogota, Colombia

Dr. Atiq RAHMAN
Director, Bangladesh Centre for Advanced Studies
626 Road 10A, Dhannondi, GPO Box 3971, Dhaka 1205, Bangladesh

Dr. Kirk RODGERS
Director, Department of Regional Development
Organization of American States
17th & Constitution Ave NW, Washington, DC 20006, United States

Dr. David RUNNALLS
Director, Sustainable Development Program
Institute for Research on Public Policy
275 Slater Street, Ottawa K1P 5HP, Canada

Dr. Ivan RUZICKA
Natural Resource Economist, Office of the Environment
Asian Development Bank
PO Box 789, 1099 Manila, The Philippines

Mr. Richard SANDBROOK
Executive Director,
International Institute for Environment and Development (IIED)
3 Endsleigh Street, London WC1H 0DD, United Kingdom

Dr. Ronaldo SERÔA DA MOTTA
Instituto de Planejamento Econômico e Social (IPEA)
Av. Res. Antonio Carlos 51/17° andar
20020 Rio de Janeiro, RJ Brazil

Mr. M. M. L. SHONGWE
Chief, Social and Environmental Policy Division
Central Projects Department
African Development Bank
01 BP 1387, Abidjan 01, Côte d'Ivoire

Mr. Andrew STEER
Senior Advisor to the Vice President, Development Economics
and Chief Economist,
The World Bank
1818 H Street, N.W., Washington, D.C. 20433, United States

Dr. Alvaro UMAÑA QUESADA
Director, INCAE
(Instituto Centroamericano de Administracion de Empresas)
Apartado 960, 4050 Alajuela, Costa Rica

Dr. Piotr WILCZYŃSKI
Advisor to the Minister of Environment Protection, Natural Resources and Forestry, Poland
Oskar Lange Academy
ul. Komandorska 118, 53 345 Wrocław, Poland

Mr. Hans-Peter WINKELMANN
Institute for Environmental Protection
University of Dortmund
PO Box 50 05 00, 4600 Dortmund 50, Germany

Dr. XU Qinghua
Chief, Division of Environmental Standards
National Environmental Protection Agency (NEPA)
115 Xizhimennei Nanxiaojie, Beijing, 100 035 China

Mr. A. ZUIDERWIJK
Centre for Environmental Studies (CML)
Leiden University
PO Box 9518, 2300 RA Leiden, The Netherlands

Development Centre

Mr. David TURNHAM

Mr. Hartmut SCHNEIDER

Ms. Winifred WEEKES-VAGLIANI

Mr. David O'CONNOR

Mr. C. Denizhan ERÖCAL

Annex 2

CONFERENCE ON ENVIRONMENTAL MANAGEMENT IN DEVELOPING COUNTRIES PARIS, 3RD-5TH OCTOBER 1990

CONFERENCE OUTLINE

First Day (Wednesday, October 3)
Morning Session

PART 1. Introductory statements and presentations on the status of environmental management in the developing countries

* Welcome Address
  by the President of the Development Centre
* Keynote Speeches
  by *Nitin Desai* and *David Runnalls*
* Conference Themes and Approaches
  by Development Centre Staff

PART 2. Priorities, Planning and Institutions

a) Country Environmental Studies

* Theme Paper by *Walter Arensberg*
* Country Case Study on **Thailand** by *Dhira Phantumvanit*
* Country Case Study on **Colombia** by *Diana Pombo Holguin*
* FLOOR DISCUSSION

Afternoon Session

b) Strengthening the Capacity of Government

* Theme Paper by *Kirk Rodgers*
* Country Case Study on **Rwanda** presented
  by *Auguste Ngirabatware* and *Tharcisse Urayeneza*
* The Approach in **Poland** by *Piotr Wilczynski*
* A **Brazilian** Project by *Hans-Peter Winkelmann*
* FLOOR DISCUSSION

c) Non-Governmental Institutions and Priorities

* Theme Paper by *Alvaro Umaña Quesada*
* Grassroots Action Programmes by *Jacques Bugnicourt*
* The Role of Environmental Education by *Hartmut Schneider*
* International NGO Experience by *Richard Sandbrook*
* FLOOR DISCUSSION

Second Day (Thursday, October 4)
Morning Session

PART 3. Policies, Incentives and Regulation

a) Recent Thinking in OECD Countries

* Theme Paper by *David Pearce*
* FLOOR DISCUSSION

b) The Use of Fiscal Incentives

* Theme Paper by *Theodore Panayotou*
* A **Zambian** Case Study by *Carel Drijver* and *A. Zuiderwijk*
* Environment and Agriculture in **Indonesia** by *Faisal Kasryno*
* **Latin American** Experience by *Michael Nelson*
* FLOOR DISCUSSION

Afternoon Session

c) An Economic Perspective on Management in the Public Sector

* Theme Paper by *Dennis Anderson*
* Country Case Study on **Brazil** by *Ronaldo Serôa Da Motta*
* FLOOR DISCUSSION

d) Towards more Effective Regulation

* Theme Paper by *Faith Halter*
* Country Case Study on **the Philippines** by *Delfin Ganapin*
* Country Case Study on **Bangladesh** by *Atiq Rahman*
* FLOOR DISCUSSION

Third Day (Friday, October 5)
Half-Day Session

PART 4. Conclusions and Future Directions

a) Affordability of Environmental Improvement
FLOOR DISCUSSION

b) Coherence of Policies and Programmes
FLOOR DISCUSSION

Concluding Remarks

WHERE TO OBTAIN OECD PUBLICATIONS – OÙ OBTENIR LES PUBLICATIONS DE L'OCDE

Argentina – Argentine
CARLOS HIRSCH S.R.L.
Galería Güemes, Florida 165, 4° Piso
1333 Buenos Aires Tel. 30.7122, 331.1787 y 331.2391
Telegram: Hirsch-Baires
Telex: 21112 UAPE-AR. Ref. s/2901
Telefax:(1)331-1787

Australia – Australie
D.A. Book (Aust.) Pty. Ltd.
648 Whitehorse Road, P.O.B 163
Mitcham, Victoria 3132 Tel. (03)873.4411
Telefax: (03)873.5679

Austria – Autriche
OECD Publications and Information Centre
Schedestrasse 7
D-W 5300 Bonn 1 (Germany) Tel. (49.228)21.60.45
Telefax: (49.228)26.11.04

Gerold & Co.
Graben 31
Wien I Tel. (0222)533.50.14

Belgium – Belgique
Jean De Lannoy
Avenue du Roi 202
B-1060 Bruxelles Tel. (02)538.51.69/538.08.41
Telex: 63220 Telefax: (02) 538.08.41

Canada
Renouf Publishing Company Ltd.
1294 Algoma Road
Ottawa, ON K1B 3W8 Tel. (613)741.4333
Telex: 053-4783 Telefax: (613)741.5439
Stores:
61 Sparks Street
Ottawa, ON K1P 5R1 Tel. (613)238.8985
211 Yonge Street
Toronto, ON M5B 1M4 Tel. (416)363.3171

Federal Publications
165 University Avenue
Toronto, ON M5H 3B8 Tel. (416)581.1552
Telefax: (416)581.1743
Les Publications Fédérales
1185 rue de l'Université
Montréal, PQ H3B 3A7 Tel.(514)954-1633

Les Éditions La Liberté Inc.
3020 Chemin Sainte-Foy
Sainte-Foy, PQ G1X 3V6 Tel. (418)658.3763
Telefax: (418)658.3763

Denmark – Danemark
Munksgaard Export and Subscription Service
35, Nørre Søgade, P.O. Box 2148
DK-1016 København K Tel. (45 33)12.85.70
Telex: 19431 MUNKS DK Telefax: (45 33)12.93.87

Finland – Finlande
Akateeminen Kirjakauppa
Keskuskatu 1, P.O. Box 128
00100 Helsinki Tel. (358 0)12141
Telex: 125080 Telefax: (358 0)121.4441

France
OECD/OCDE
Mail Orders/Commandes par correspondance:
2, rue André-Pascal
75775 Paris Cédex 16 Tel. (33-1)45.24.82.00
Bookshop/Librairie:
33, rue Octave-Feuillet
75016 Paris Tel. (33-1)45.24.81.67
(33-1)45.24.81.81
Telex: 620 160 OCDE
Telefax: (33-1)45.24.85.00 (33-1)45.24.81.76

Librairie de l'Université
12a, rue Nazareth
13100 Aix-en-Provence Tel. 42.26.18.08
Telefax : 42.26.63.26

Germany – Allemagne
OECD Publications and Information Centre
Schedestrasse 7
D-W 5300 Bonn 1 Tel. (0228)21.60.45
Telefax: (0228)26.11.04

Greece – Grèce
Librairie Kauffmann
28 rue du Stade
105 64 Athens Tel. 322.21.60
Telex: 218187 LIKA Gr

Hong Kong
Swindon Book Co. Ltd.
13 - 15 Lock Road
Kowloon, Hong Kong Tel. 366.80.31
Telex: 50 441 SWIN HX Telefax: 739.49.75

Iceland – Islande
Mál Mog Menning
Laugavegi 18, Pósthólf 392
121 Reykjavik Tel. 15199/24240

India – Inde
Oxford Book and Stationery Co.
Scindia House
New Delhi 110001 Tel. 331.5896/5308
Telex: 31 61990 AM IN
Telefax: (11)332.5993
17 Park Street
Calcutta 700016 Tel. 240832

Indonesia – Indonésie
Pdii-Lipi
P.O. Box 269/JKSMG/88
Jakarta 12790 Tel. 583467
Telex: 62 875

Ireland – Irlande
TDC Publishers – Library Suppliers
12 North Frederick Street
Dublin 1 Tel. 744835/749677
Telex: 33530 TDCP EI Telefax: 748416

Italy – Italie
Libreria Commissionaria Sansoni
Via Benedetto Fortini, 120/10
Casella Post. 552
50125 Firenze Tel. (055)64.54.15
Telex: 570466 Telefax: (055)64.12.57
Via Bartolini 29
20155 Milano Tel. 36.50.83
La diffusione delle pubblicazioni OCSE viene assicurata dalle principali librerie ed anche da:

Editrice e Libreria Herder
Piazza Montecitorio 120
00186 Roma Tel. 679.46.28
Telex: NATEL I 621427

Libreria Hoepli
Via Hoepli 5
20121 Milano Tel. 86.54.46
Telex: 31.33.95 Telefax: (02)805.28.86

Libreria Scientifica
Dott. Lucio de Biasio 'Aeiou'
Via Meravigli 16
20123 Milano Tel. 805.68.98
Telefax: 800175

Japan – Japon
OECD Publications and Information Centre
Landic Akasaka Building
2-3-4 Akasaka, Minato-ku
Tokyo 107 Tel. (81.3)3586.2016
Telefax: (81.3)3584.7929

Korea – Corée
Kyobo Book Centre Co. Ltd.
P.O. Box 1658, Kwang Hwa Moon
Seoul Tel. (REP)730.78.91
Telefax: 735.0030

Malaysia/Singapore – Malaisie/Singapour
Co-operative Bookshop Ltd.
University of Malaya
P.O. Box 1127, Jalan Pantai Baru
59700 Kuala Lumpur
Malaysia Tel. 756.5000/756.5425
Telefax: 757.3661

Information Publications Pte. Ltd.
Pei-Fu Industrial Building
24 New Industrial Road No. 02-06
Singapore 1953 Tel. 283.1786/283.1798
Telefax: 284.8875

Netherlands – Pays-Bas
SDU Uitgeverij
Christoffel Plantijnstraat 2
Postbus 20014
2500 EA's-Gravenhage Tel. (070 3)78.99.11
Voor bestellingen: Tel. (070 3)78.98.80
Telex: 32486 stdru Telefax: (070 3)47.63.51

New Zealand – Nouvelle-Zélande
GP Publications Ltd.
Customer Services
33 The Esplanade - P.O. Box 38-900
Petone, Wellington
Tel. (04)685-555 Telefax: (04)685-333

Norway – Norvège
Narvesen Info Center - NIC
Bertrand Narvesens vei 2
P.O. Box 6125 Etterstad
0602 Oslo 6 Tel. (02)57.33.00
Telex: 79668 NIC N Telefax: (02)68.19.01

Pakistan
Mirza Book Agency
65 Shahrah Quaid-E-Azam
Lahore 3 Tel. 66839
Telex: 44886 UBL PK. Attn: MIRZA BK

Portugal
Livraria Portugal
Rua do Carmo 70-74
Apart. 2681
1117 Lisboa Codex Tel.: 347.49.82/3/4/5
Telefax: (01) 347.02.64

Singapore/Malaysia – Singapour/Malaisie
See "Malaysia/Singapore" – Voir «Malaisie/Singapour»

Spain – Espagne
Mundi-Prensa Libros S.A.
Castelló 37, Apartado 1223
Madrid 28001 Tel. (91) 431.33.99
Telex: 49370 MPLI Telefax: 575.39.98

Libreria Internacional AEDOS
Consejo de Ciento 391
08009-Barcelona Tel. (93) 301.86.15
Telefax: (93) 317.01.41

Sri Lanka
Centre for Policy Research
c/o Mercantile Credit Ltd.
55, Janadhipathi Mawatha
Colombo 1 Tel. 438471-9, 440346
Telex: 21138 VAVALEX CE Telefax: 94.1.448900

Sweden – Suède
Fritzes Fackboksföretaget
Box 16356
Regeringsgatan 12
103 27 Stockholm Tel. (08)23.89.00
Telex: 12387 Telefax: (08)20.50.21

Subscription Agency/Abonnements:
Wennergren-Williams AB
Nordenflychtsvägen 74
Box 30004
104 25 Stockholm Tel. (08)13.67.00
Telex: 19937 Telefax: (08)618.62.32

Switzerland – Suisse
OECD Publications and Information Centre
Schedestrasse 7
D-W 5300 Bonn 1 (Germany) Tel. (49.228)21.60.45
Telefax: (49.228)26.11.04

Librairie Payot
6 rue Grenus
1211 Genève 11 Tel. (022)731.89.50
Telex: 28356
Subscription Agency – Service des Abonnements
Naville S.A.
7, rue Lévrier
1201 Genève Tél.: (022) 732.24.00
Telefax: (022) 738.48.03

Maditec S.A.
Chemin des Palettes 4
1020 Renens/Lausanne Tel. (021)635.08.65
Telefax: (021)635.07.80

United Nations Bookshop/Librairie des Nations-Unies
Palais des Nations
1211 Genève 10 Tel. (022)734.14.73
Telex: 412962 Telefax: (022)740.09.31

Taiwan – Formose
Good Faith Worldwide Int'l. Co. Ltd.
9th Floor, No. 118, Sec. 2
Chung Hsiao E. Road
Taipei Tel. 391.7396/391.7397
Telefax: (02) 394.9176

Thailand – Thaïlande
Suksit Siam Co. Ltd.
1715 Rama IV Road, Samyan
Bangkok 5 Tel. 251.1630

Turkey – Turquie
Kültur Yayinlari Is-Türk Ltd. Sti.
Atatürk Bulvari No. 191/Kat. 21
Kavaklidere/Ankara Tel. 25.07.60
Dolmabahce Cad. No. 29
Besiktas/Istanbul Tel. 160.71.88
Telex: 43482B

United Kingdom – Royaume-Uni
HMSO
Gen. enquiries Tel. (071) 873 0011
Postal orders only:
P.O. Box 276, London SW8 5DT
Personal Callers HMSO Bookshop
49 High Holborn, London WC1V 6HB
Telex: 297138 Telefax: 071 873 2000
Branches at: Belfast, Birmingham, Bristol, Edinburgh, Manchester

United States – États-Unis
OECD Publications and Information Centre
2001 L Street N.W., Suite 700
Washington, D.C. 20036-4910 Tel. (202)785.6323
Telefax: (202)785.0350

Venezuela
Libreria del Este
Avda F. Miranda 52, Aptdo. 60337
Edificio Galipán
Caracas 106 Tel. 951.1705/951.2307/951.1297
Telegram: Libreste Caracas

Yugoslavia – Yougoslavie
Jugoslovenska Knjiga
Knez Mihajlova 2, P.O. Box 36
Beograd Tel.: (011)621.992
Telex: 12466 jk bgd Telefax: (011)625.970

Orders and inquiries from countries where Distributors have not yet been appointed should be sent to: OECD Publications Service, 2 rue André-Pascal, 75775 Paris Cedex 16, France.

Les commandes provenant de pays où l'OCDE n'a pas encore désigné de distributeur devraient être adressées à : OCDE, Service des Publications, 2, rue André-Pascal, 75775 Paris Cédex 16, France.

75810–6/91

OECD PUBLICATIONS, 2 rue André-Pascal, 75775 PARIS CEDEX 16
PRINTED IN FRANCE
(41 91 10 3) ISBN 92-64-03503-6 - No. 45666 1991